Sport History
in the Digital Era

Sport History in the Digital Era

Edited by
GARY OSMOND AND
MURRAY G. PHILLIPS

UNIVERSITY OF ILLINOIS PRESS
Urbana, Chicago, and Springfield

© 2015 by the Board of Trustees
of the University of Illinois
All rights reserved
Manufactured in the United States of America
C 5 4 3 2 1
♾ This book is printed on acid-free paper.

Library of Congress Cataloging-in-Publication Data
Sport history in the digital era / edited by Gary Osmond and
Murray G. Phillips.
pages   cm
Includes bibliographical references and index.
ISBN 978-0-252-03893-8 (hard cover : acid-free paper) —
ISBN 978-0-252-09689-1 (e-book)
1. Sports—History—Sources. 2. Sports—Archival resources—
Digitization. I. Osmond, Gary. II. Phillips, Murray G.
(Murray George).
GV571.S573   2015
796—dc23   2014029018

We dedicate this book to
Anthony (Gary) and to Kath and Alex,
Drew, Elliot, Elyse, and Wesley (Murray).

Contents

Foreword   ix
Stephen Robertson

Acknowledgments   xiii

Introduction: The Bones of Digital History   1
Gary Osmond and Murray G. Phillips

PART I: DIGITAL HISTORY AND THE ARCHIVE   33

1. The Library's Role in Developing Web-Based Sport History Resources   35
Wayne Wilson

2. Sport History and Digital Archives in Practice   53
Martin Johnes and Bob Nicholson

PART II: DIGITAL HISTORY AS ARCHIVE   75

3. @www.olympic.org.nz: Organizational Websites, E-Spaces, and Sport History   77
Geoffery Z. Kohe

4. "Dear Collective Brain . . .": Social Media as a Research Tool in Sport History   97
Mike Cronin

5. Into the Digital Era: Sport History, Teaching and Learning, and Web 2.0   113
Tara Magdalinski

6. "Get excited, people!": Online Fansites and the Circulation of the Past in the Preseason Hopes of Sports Followers   132
Matthew Klugman

7. Interactivity, Blogs, and the Ethics of Doing Sport History   157
Rebecca Olive

8. Death, Mourning, and Cultural Memory on the Internet: The Virtual Memorialization of Fallen Sports Heroes   180
Holly Thorpe

PART III: DIGITAL HISTORY IS HISTORY   201

9. On the Nature of Sport: A Treatise in Light of Universality and Digital Culture   203
Synthia Sydnor

10. Who's Afraid of the Internet? Swimming in an Infinite Archive   227
Fiona McLachlan and Douglas Booth

Conclusion: Digital History Flexes its Muscle   251
Murray G. Phillips and Gary Osmond

Contributors   271

Index   275

Foreword

STEPHEN ROBERTSON

The 2014 Annual Meeting of the American Historical Association featured fifteen sessions devoted to digital history. That range of presentations is in stark contrast to the absence bemoaned by Dan Cohen in 2009. Growth came slowly, as Cohen charted on his blog: nine digital history sessions in 2010, two in 2011, twenty-two in 2012, and the same number again in 2013. The picture is similar at the meetings of the other major American historical organization, the Organization of American Historians: two digital history sessions in 2009, six in 2010, three in 2011, eleven in 2012, two in 2013, and seven in 2014. However, in both conferences digital history still appears almost only in sessions devoted to that work; few papers from digital historians are found in sessions discussing other fields and topics. At this moment, then, digital history is still trying to make the journey from the margins to the mainstream of the discipline.

That situation is why this collection is important. Broad discussions of digital history—and even more so, digital humanities—require historians to step outside their fields of expertise, making it more difficult for them to see what digital history might offer for their research and teaching. Framing the discussion in terms of a specific field, grounding digital history in the sources and questions of scholars in that field of study, makes it easier for them to see its possibilities.

The time is ripe to bridge the gap between digital history and other fields thanks to the availability and widespread use of digital resources and to the wave of open access tool development in recent years. To take the example of my own project, *Digital Harlem*, conceived almost ten years ago, most of what then could only be done in the context of the kind of funded, collaborative project that has defined digital humanities can now be achieved with a fraction of those resources. While the legal records that were a core source for that project can still only be accessed in Municipal Archives in New York City, they can now be readily digitized using a camera, while Harlem's two newspapers, which we read on microfilm, are now fully searchable online—although available only to subscribers. It is now commonplace for historians to use digital research tools, with cameras ubiquitous in archives, and online full-text databases of secondary sources and digitized records consulted in place of print and microfilm. Although few of those employing such practices would consider themselves digital historians, the digitization of their research eases their path to using digital tools to analyze that material.

When *Digital Harlem* was conceived, we planned to use ArcGIS software to map events, locations, and individual lives in the neighborhood in the 1920s gleaned from our sources. Before we embarked on that project, the appearance of Google Maps gave us another option, a light, browser-based approach to GIS better suited to our qualitative data and questions. Now someone seeking to create such a geospatial visualization of their sources has many more options: Neatline, GeoCommons, Leaflet, DHPress, Maphub, WorldMap, QGIS, and Viewshare, to name just a few. Using such tools is not without challenges for scholars without programming skills; the limited and often quite technical nature of the documentation provided for many open access tools is a barrier to their use. In some cases, online tutorials such as those offered on Geospatial Historian (http://geospatialhistorian.wordpress.com) and the Programming Historian (http://programminghistorian.org) mitigate those barriers. Detailed accounts of how digital historians work with sources and tools would help equip other scholars to negotiate those hurdles, but few exist.

The editors of this collection, as they note in the Introduction, are looking beyond digital methodology to a vision of digital history as transformative "comprehensive, hyperlinked, interactive digital history projects." They point to my own project, *Digital Harlem*, as an example of such work, but I am acutely aware that the site does not entirely warrant that praise. Digital Harlem does present information in a way that allows users to interact with it, and in that sense is a "dynamic site of history making, enquiry, and discussion." And it has played a central role in the arguments that my collaborators and I have made in a variety of print publications about life in the neighborhood in the 1920s. But it does not invite people "to experience, read, and follow an argument" online about highly complex historical topics and to contribute in various ways. That vision of digital history has yet to be realized, as one of its early proponents, Edward Ayers, pointed out in an article published in *Educause Review* in 2013. The literature on hypertext central to that concept is no longer on digital history and digital humanities syllabi. In its place are discussions of the range of computational tools now available: the focus has shifted from presenting arguments to analyzing data, from what Ayers calls digital scholarship to digital methodology.

In hindsight, the transformative potential of hypertext appears to have been swamped by the wave of digital data that has poured forth in recent years. As much as hypertext theorists anticipated and highlighted the scale of the Internet, the realization of that potential attracted the attention of scholars in more positivist fields and gave traction to quantitative and computational approaches. What we need to guard against, as Tim Hitchcock warned in his talk to the 2013 CVCE conference on "Reading Historical Sources in the Digital Age," is allowing the technology to define the questions we ask. Bridging the gap between digital history and the mainstream of the discipline, as this collection seeks to do, plays a crucial role in that effort by ensuring that questions grounded in qualitative approaches are provocations to innovations in digital history.

Attention does seem poised to return to the challenge of presenting an argument or narrative in the digital medium. There are increasing experiments with digital storytelling and transmedia narrative that are moving online writing from an exclusive focus on text (the editors' own Australian Paralympic history project is an example of historical work influenced by that approach). More examples are appearing of historical projects that, in terms of Trevor Owens' helpful formulation, use visualization not for discovery, as *Digital Harlem* does, but for communication (of something we already understand). Two exemplary examples are Vincent Brown's "Slave Revolt in Jamaica: A Cartographic Narrative" (http://revolt.axismaps.com/) and Emily Thompson and Scott Mahoy's "The Roaring Twenties," exploring the soundscape of New York City (http://vectorsdev.usc.edu/NYCsound/777b.html), but neither of those compelling visualizations in themselves conveys an argument, which instead continues to reside largely in the associated text. Nor are they derived from analysis conducted using digital tools.

To pursue a transformative digital history we need to go further: to bring together digital methodologies and digital scholarship, computational and qualitative approaches; to move between distant and close readings, individuals and big data, using and making history. We need more historians, from a wider range of fields, willing to experiment. One of the most effective ways to achieve that end would be for more digital historians to follow the lead of the contributors to this collection and open a conversation with their mainstream colleagues about how they do digital history.

Acknowledgments

Early ideas for this book were presented at conferences held by the North American Society for Sport History (NASSH) in 2011, 2012, and 2013, and we would like to thank all those attendees who offered commentary, encouragement, and insight. In particular, we are grateful for the input provided to these sessions by Linda Borish, Russell Field, Rita Liberti, Jaime Schultz, Holly Thorpe, Stephen Townsend, and Travis Vogan.

An enormous team effort goes into a book of this kind, and we wish to acknowledge the dedication, enthusiasm, and patience of the anonymous reviewers, the editorial and administrative staff at UIP, and especially the contributing authors. Our colleague, Deb Noon in the School of Human Movement Studies at The University of Queensland, provided much-appreciated technical support. And finally, a special thanks to Bill Regier at UIP for supporting this project from the outset and for his professional guidance along the way.

INTRODUCTION

The Bones of Digital History

GARY OSMOND AND MURRAY G. PHILLIPS

In early 2011, the Australian Paralympic Committee (APC), the national body responsible for the participation of Australian athletes with a disability at the Paralympic Games, published a tender to write their history. The tender proposal was placed online and targeted both national and international historians. As the tender indicated, the APC has an extensive archive of annual reports, summaries of the Summer and Winter Paralympic Games, minute books, newspaper clippings, 45,000 photographs, 1,100 video items, and considerable alumnae with their own personal records and scrapbooks. All of this archival material was being catalogued by the premier sports library in Australia, the National Sports Information Centre in Canberra, for the successful tenderer. This archival material was complemented with twenty oral histories from prominent people involved in disability sport in Australia organized through the National Library of Australia. Furthermore, the organization had a 40,000-word history already written from the inception of disability sport in Australia until the late 1980s. Finally, the APC would pay for accommodation, travel, and living expenses for research in Australia's capital cities, and requested that tenders provide an additional budget for writing of the history. In many ways, this was the ideal commissioned history project: it was well resourced from an archival perspective; the archival material was very organized; there was a number of professionally conducted oral histories and a historical manuscript to work with; the organizing body was committed and motivated to produce their history; and the APC was prepared to pay for the appropriate expertise to provide a substantial history of their movement. Ideal project, yes; popular with sport historians, no. Not one sport historian from around the world submitted a tender to write the history.

This begs the obvious question: why were sport historians unwilling to tender for this project? The answer was related to additional requirements by the APC. As was made clear: "Priority will be given to tenderers who can communicate a vision of how they will create an effective multi-media project and can demonstrate an understanding of the use of web-based techniques and a capacity to identify and engage stakeholders."[1] More specifically, the APC envisaged "a well-researched and referenced multi-media document which can be published online—and linked to video, audio and photographic content—or adapted for print publication." They wanted a history of their movement, and it would probably take the form of a book, but they wanted the project to have a digital dimension. They were not clear what that dimension should be. The successful tenderer not only had to be a competent traditional historian but also had to come to grips with how to present that history in a digital form that would engage the Paralympic community. The Australian Paralympic history project required the successful tenderer to confront the digital era. Sport historians, including ourselves, were not up for it.[2]

The Australian Paralympic history project is not an isolated example of the reluctance of sport historians to engage with digital history. Increasingly, sport historians incorporate digital research techniques, some innovatively, but to our knowledge there are no major digital sport history projects and certainly none along the lines of those comprehensive online histories that have won the American Historical Association's Roy Rosenzweig Prize for Innovation in Digital History, or the ABC-CLIO Online History Award.[3] This situation raises important questions about sport history in the digital era and highlights the opportunities and challenges for sport historians.

The aim of this book is to explore these issues, opportunities, and challenges for sport history in the digital era. The topic is important for a number of reasons. First, the range of digital tools and their implications for history making raises important philosophical, epistemological, ontological, methodological, and ethical questions. Second, digital media is increasing engagement with the recent past, something that sport historians cannot ignore. This is especially important given that the public relates to sport through digital media such as fansites, chat rooms, and online gambling sites, creating a symbiosis between sport and the Internet.[4] Additionally, sport historians are already engaging and experimenting with history in various online forms but often in isolation from one another. Through this book we hope to open a wider conversation about this existing relationship. We do not argue that digital history is superior to traditional historical methods, or that sport historians are dinosaurs, or even that sport historians should necessarily do more digital history. Instead, we aim to distinguish between sport historians' use of digital tools and engagement with digital history, consider how philosophical and theoretical understandings of the meaning of history influence the willingness to engage with digital history, conceptualize the relationship between history making and the digital era, and share the thoughts and experiences of sport historians from five countries.

The digital era provides extensive options for sharing the thoughts and experiences of sport historians on any topic. In addition to publication and circulation as a traditional paper book, the Internet facilitates exclusive electronic publication and enables hybrid publishing options involving combinations of paper and electronic access. The digital era also opens new avenues for pre-publication review, including open-access feedback channels for either the general public or for specific communities of readers. In line with the approach adopted in *Writing History in the Digital Age,* we availed ourselves of electronic opportunities for review by circulating the full text of this book to all contributing authors through an electronic, shared-access platform for feedback that was integrated with the standard refereeing process through the University of Illinois Press.[5] There was multidirectional dialogue between editors and contributors as the Introduction, chapters, and Conclusion were read, assessed, and revisited before the final submission was completed. In terms of publishing format, we opted for initial publication as a traditional, paper book with the option for the production of an electronic version. This decision recognizes both the increasing demand for electronic copies and the enduring appeal of printed books among our intended readership.

This book has several intended audiences. Primarily, it is written for sport historians who, like the contributors to this book, may be aware of some of the broad issues, opportunities, and challenges presented by the digital era; have limited experience with digital history; and are interested in exploring the topic more deeply. Our conceptual contribution to the broader field of digital history is the three-fold analytical device—*Digital History and the Archive, Digital History as Archive,* and *Digital History is History*—which transcends the sporting past and attempts to encapsulate dimensions, directions, and features of contemporary history making. Many of the issues raised in this book will also be relevant for scholars in the fields of sport studies and the sociology of sport. And finally, the book engages digital humanities scholars who are interested in how history—as a specific discipline of the humanities with its own discursive traditions—is responding to the concepts and possibilities of digital era.

Digital History vs. Digital Tools

What do we mean by digital history? At its most basic, digital history is a method for "gathering, preserving and presenting the past on the web."[6] Historian William G. Thomas III posed a useful working definition in 2008 that acknowledges the broad remit of those activities and extends our understanding of the concept of digital history:

> Digital history is an approach to examining and representing the past that works with the new communication technologies of the computer, the Internet network, and software systems. On the one level, digital history is an open area of scholarly production and communication, encompassing the development of new course materials and scholarly data collections. On another, it is a methodological approach framed by the hypertextual power of these technologies to make, define, query, and annotate associations in the human record of the past. To do digital history, then, is to create a framework, an ontology, through the technology for people to experience, read, and follow an argument about a historical problem.[7]

Implicit in Thomas's definition is a distinction between digital tools and digital history. As sport historians, we make widespread use of digital tools in our research, teaching, and communication. Few sport historians are digitally born, but we are increasingly digitally engaged. As Toni Weller argues, "most historians are not digital Luddites."[8] At the very least we use e-mail, listserves, and search engines. Most also use online research aids like journal databases and digitized archives, and some employ tools like Zotero to organize our online findings. In our teaching we use PowerPoint, lecture-recording technologies, and online course platforms. And at least on a personal if not a professional level, many of us have Facebook, Instagram, Skype, and Twitter accounts, and others create or contribute to blogs, fansites, and Wikipedia pages. As some of these uses suggest, digital tools are "*embedded in our everyday lives*,"[9] epitomizing what Steven Jones has referred to as the process of eversion: "If cyberspace once seemed a transcendent elsewhere, someplace other than the world we normally inhabit, that relationship has inverted as the network has everted."[10]

Whereas digital tools can be adapted for a variety of purposes in historical research, teaching, and communication, digital history uses the digital tool box to create or analyze particular forms of online historical representations. These can range from relatively straightforward narratives like Wikipedia entries; to accounts of past events that unfold through a series of tweets (like the Titanic voyage @TitanicRealTime Twitter feed project[11]); to Facebook sites for historical objects, figures, or events that merge multimedia postings of photographs, videos, written memories, and commentary (like the *Quilt Index*[12]); to more comprehensive, hyperlinked, interactive, digital history projects. A broad range of comprehensive, hyperlinked, interactive, digital history projects exists that vary in type, purpose, and interactivity. These include well-known examples such as *Who Built America* and *The Valley of the Shadow* in the USA, *Digital Harlem: Everyday Life, 1915–1930* and the Paralympic history project in Australia, and *Europe, Interrupted*.[13] What all of these diverse examples have in common is that they invite people, as Thomas suggests, "to experience, read, and follow an argument" online about highly complex historical topics and to contribute in various ways.[14]

Digital histories, at their most expansive, are not facsimiles of static, hard-copy, published histories, but are intended to be dynamic sites of history making, enquiry, and discussion. Despite the diversity of digital history projects, one commonality stands out. As Sherman Dorn argues, none present a "polished argument about the past" as is typical in non-digital histories, but instead deliberately reveal the complex range of possible arguments and/or invite audiences to engage with the evidence provided.[15]

Indeed, active engagement with audiences is a defining feature of digital histories. As Shawn Graham and colleagues assert, "Digital history is public history: when we put materials online, we enter into a conversation with individuals from all walks of life, with various voices and degrees of professionalism."[16] This conversation via feedback mechanisms and direct public engagement with evidence and argument is not accidental, is "more than accessorizing," but is instead a deliberate feature.[17] The award-winning *Digital Harlem: Everyday Life, 1915–1930* project, established by Shane White, Stephen Garton, Graham White, and Stephen Robertson at the University of Sydney to explore daily life in New York City's Harlem district through online documents and interactive maps, demonstrates one advantage of engagement with social media platforms.[18] Digital Harlem was predicated on the assumption that "going online immediately delivers an audience." It didn't. Although it was well conceptualized, meticulously researched, and extremely comprehensive, it found few visitors via search engines. To attract more visitors, Robertson began to write Wikipedia articles on topics linked back to the *Digital Harlem* site. While Wikipedia's rules on primary sources and self-referencing posed challenges, it enabled him to connect the site with other aspects of the web.[19]

Digital histories also engage with Wikipedia and social media in other meaningful ways beyond outreach and publicity. Some projects encourage readers to contribute wikis that detail their own stories, memories, and experiences. Other projects use social media sites like Twitter and Facebook for feedback, engagement, and active contribution to crowdsource public history and co-create knowledge.[20]

While many sport historians are familiar with some of the better-known examples of comprehensive, interactive, digital history projects, few of us consider ourselves to be digital historians. Even the most digitally savvy sport historian among us would more likely identify with historian Michael Frisch, who described himself as a "working historian with a 'tool' orientation" rather than a digital historian.[21] As noted above, few sport historians are doing digital histories in Thomas's sense of creating digital frameworks or ontologies for public online engagement and interaction.

Shying Away: Resisting Digital History

Why have sport historians yet to comprehensively engage with digital history, especially by producing online sport histories? The answer is complex. It is not because sport historians are academic ostriches with their heads in the sand. Sport historians are more typical of humanities scholars and historians more broadly, who have been slow to adapt to the possibilities of digital history despite the existence of several admired exemplars, the initiatives of the Roy Rosenzweig Center for History and New Media (CHNM) at George Mason University, and the encouragement and interest shown by professional bodies such as the American Historical Association.[22] Robert B. Townsend's 2010 survey of over 4,000 American historians found that while many had publications on journal websites, very few published in blogs, Wikipedia, and other open websites or considered using new media to "to do something new or different" with their scholarship.[23] In his micro-analysis of Townsend's data, Sean Takats, professor of history and director of research projects at the CHNM, detailed the limits of historians' engagement with digital media: while 99 percent used word processors and 94 percent regularly consulted library-supported databases, fewer than 6 percent of historians used social media and only 1% employed text-mining software.[24]

A combination of factors contributes to the dearth of digital history projects, with much discussion focusing on three issues: the nature of historical scholarship, quality, and technical roadblocks. Each of these concerns is multifaceted and complex, but a brief overview is worthwhile. To begin, the nature of traditional historical scholarship resists many of the opportunities and challenges of the digital era. As much as historical study might stand to benefit from digital innovations, the Internet destabilizes established historical philosophical approaches and methodological practices. Whereas the culture and approach of traditional historians has been characterized broadly by individualism, even by "*possessive* individualism," digital history emphasizes collaboration, sharing, and openness.[25] And whereas academic historians have held a privileged place as history-makers and as interpreters of the past, the Internet democratizes history, granting greater public access than ever before to the archive and to history making. For good or for bad, it has created a situation in which "everyone becomes his or her own historian," or has the potential to do so.[26] For many historians, this openness can be threatening. Digital historians have also noted that large, interactive, and dynamic online histories can involve more curating than detective work.[27] Some of this curatorial work involves large data sets and a shift toward greater quantitative analysis, which further challenges historians' accepted philosophies and practices. The broad issues around destabilization of historical practice, and the specific issue of repugnance to quantitative history, are hugely significant in terms of understanding historians' responses to the digital era, and we will return to them in the Conclusion of this book.

Quality is another of the perceived "dangers or hazards on the information superhighway," in particular a wariness of the suspected or known vacuity, triviality, and reliability of some Internet sources.[28] David Greenberg, who argues that television is an under-examined source for historians, lists some perceived shortcomings of broadcast news that could equally be applied to many digital sources—"brief and superficial, obsessed with images and aesthetics, inclined to cover events and crises more than persistent conditions."[29] Criticisms leveled at specific Internet sources amplify these concerns with superficiality, depth, and emphasis on the present. For example, one commentator decried Wikipedia as "the Internet-based reference work of choice for the generation that calls celebrities by their first names (you know: 'Brad,' 'Jessica,' 'Paris,' 'Tom' etc)."[30] And social media like Facebook and Twitter have been characterized as "frivolous spaces."[31] Even where criticisms are less cutting, concerns remain about the accuracy, depth, scope, and partisanship of many online sources.

Technical, literacy, and financial concerns further restrict engagement with digital history. Few historians are trained or skilled in Internet technologies, and the speed of change in cyberspace and obsolescence of both hardware and software can act as deterrents to full practical engagement. Others feel constrained by time, or by the costs of training, infrastructure, technical support, and ongoing website maintenance.

While general issues around the nature of historical scholarship, quality concerns, and technical roadblocks have been well canvassed in discussions of digital history, we argue that a deeper philosophical issue underpins the reluctance of historians (sport historians included) to engage in digital history projects. This philosophical objection revolves around the relationship between the past and the present and what constitutes legitimate historical study. Historians conceptualize and reconcile the complex relationship between the past and present in various ways from denial, to resigned acceptance, to reflexive embrace. For those historians who see a clear distinction between the past and the present, digital history lacks appeal because it is too present-focused in terms of content, tools, and public engagement.

Still Living: Digital History and the Recent Past

History, no doubt, concerns the past. Less evident is where the past ends and the present begins, yet history is "premised on the belief that there is a break between the present and the past, and that the past is a realm distinct from the present."[32] This tacit break between past and present defines which topics, areas, and periods constitute legitimate areas for history. Recent historical events—those that occurred in the last few decades and those that are still unfolding—are widely seen by historians as too recent for historical scholarship.[33] Indeed, as Renee C. Romano and Claire Bond Potter argue in their 2012 edited book on the topic, the phrase *recent history* "seems like an oxymoron."[34]

Of course, there have always been histories written about events in the recent past. And as historical scholarship cross-fertilizes with other disciplines, as historical questions expand, and as historians embrace material, visual, and digital sources, recent histories are increasing apace. Romano and Potter cite several political and social histories of very recent events in the USA—perhaps most pointedly a special 2002 edition of the *Journal of American History* on the September 11, 2001, terrorist attacks in the USA—to underscore their point that not only is recent history thriving but it is "making aggressive claims for the relevance of history to understanding ongoing events."[35] In sport history, particularly in journals, articles that address recent history are increasingly common.

Yet despite the growth of recent history scholarship, the broad field remains suspect because it transgresses the divide between the past and the present. Romano identifies and challenges four major criticisms of recent history faced by its practitioners: sources, historiography, narrative finality, and perspective.[36] A brief summary of each criticism is useful. The first concerns sources. In traditional history, written primary sources, particularly official archival sources and newspaper articles, are the most highly valued remnants of the past.[37] While not devalued by historians of recent events, official written records are often nonexistent or unavailable due to archival sequestering. Instead, recent history requires engagement with a different range of sources—including oral histories, material artifacts, visual records, and online materials—sources that to varying degrees lack the perceived legitimacy of written documents. The second criticism revolves around the dearth of an established historiography on recent history topics with which historians can engage and situate their arguments. Third, recent history concerns ongoing matters that resist the creation of neat and necessary narrative arcs and endings. Finally, Romano discusses issues of perspective, especially the lack of critical distance, that are raised in objection to recent histories. How can historians write about recent and still-unfolding events or topics without the adequate passage of time to allow for proper reflection?

Our purpose in raising the four criticisms deftly rebutted by Romano is to argue that these objections to recent history also explain the resistance of historians to some forms of digital history. After all, digital history and digital media can capture the *very* recent past—five minutes, five hours, five months, let alone five years or five decades. While digital history projects can, and often do, address topics and engage with sources from the distant past, they intersect philosophically and methodologically with recent histories both in the sense of their emphasis on public collaboration and interactivity and in terms of the present-focused nature of many digital topics and tools (especially social media). Indeed, digital history magnifies many of the criticisms leveled against recent history, as we will now discuss.

If arguments about sources taint the legitimacy of recent histories, they plague digital history. For one, digital tools have vastly expanded the range of sources available. Not only has digitization opened the historic archive, but blogging and social media like Facebook and Twitter have effectively created new digital archives. Given previously mentioned quality concerns, especially surrounding social media, these new sources are highly suspect to many historians. But can historians engage in digital history while ignoring these sources because they are perceived to be dubious? The answer is no.

While many digital history projects incorporate or even rely on digitized documents from the distant past, including newspapers, official records, correspondence, and maps, it is rare today for an effective digital history project simply to place curated documents online for passive public consumption. And, as the creators of the *Digital Harlem* project discovered, more than a static presence is needed if visitors are to be attracted to use the online history. Digital historians reach out by interconnecting with Wikipedia and social media, but they also encourage public involvement, for example through tagging or commentating via blogs and social media. Thus, social media and other digital tools that are considered by many historians to be misleading, flippant, or irrelevant are increasingly integral to the creation, development, and viability of many digital history projects.

Digital history also intensifies the other issues that premise the recent history debate—historiography, narrative finality, and perspective. If the lack of sufficient historiographic scaffolding might call into question the legitimacy of a recent history project, it could condemn some digital history projects. While comprehensive online histories can engage with historical debates just as easily as a written history on the same topic, much online discussion of, or around, historical topics is not framed by written historiography (and can be ahistorical or ill-informed). Some Wikipedia pages or Facebook sites devoted to a historical theme or YouTube videos and comments are cases in point.

Concerns about narrative integrity and finality raised about recent history can also be exacerbated in digital history. Again, this is less the case when a narrative history is the aim of the digital exercise, such as in an extensive Wikipedia entry on a finished topic or a deceased person. Yet two aspects of digital history complicate narrative. One is the expanded range of sources and voices available. These can resist narrative closure, and instead open the possibility for multiple perspectives or questions enabling online audiences or participants to develop multifaceted arguments or narrative threads. The second complication is the range of possible forms of representation that online platforms facilitate. Digital history can include traditional narrative forms, but can extend to include various non-linear, non-narrative, or multinarrative representations in words, images, and sound.

Finally, digital history amplifies concerns about the inadequate perspective available to historians who study the recent past. If historical treatment of events that occurred within a couple of decades are "just over our shoulder" histories,[38] what are tweeted comments that address yesterday's sporting scandal or a fansite that celebrates, dissects, and historicizes last week's athletic triumph? Such utterings might look and sound to some like insignificant ephemera, but in reality they are instantly archived for posterity through digital capture. How do we work with such dynamic material, and how do we assess online histories that elicit and/or incorporate public commentary? And if creation of new sources and instant archiving poses issues about historical perspective, the digital era also creates perspective issues for historians who themselves engage in online, interactive discussion (for example, blogs) on topics about which they research and write.

Wikipedia

In many ways, Wikipedia brings the issues of sources, historiography, narrative, and perspective into stark relief and highlights how digital history practices confront traditional approaches to written histories. The Australian Paralympic history project that opened this chapter decided to engage Wikipedia as one of the digital platforms for its multimedia document. Wikipedia, which Anne Burdick and colleagues described as "the most comprehensive, representative, and pervasive participatory platform for knowledge production ever created by humankind," was chosen because of its global popularity and accessibility, and the potential for building a Paralympic community through volunteer contributors.[39] On this basis, Wikipedia is proving to be an ideal multimedia platform for the history project of the Australian Paralympic Movement.

Wikipedia, however, demonstrates the nuances of digital history that, in some cases, challenges established historical practices in relation to sources, historiography, narrative, and perspective and, in the process, can dissuade historians from engagement. In terms of sources, Wikipedia is very specific: "**Do not** analyze, synthesize, interpret, or evaluate material found in a primary source yourself; instead, refer to reliable secondary sources that do so. **Do not** base articles and materials entirely on primary sources. **Do not** add unsourced material from your personal experience, because that would make Wikipedia a primary source of that material."[40] At this point, historians of all persuasions—reconstructionists, constructionists, and deconstructionists[41]—are challenged by the philosophical disparities between Wikipedia and the ways historians work with the past. The reliance on secondary sources, and the marginal and problematic status of primary sources in Wikipedia, confronts the ontological, epistemological, and methodological premises of many historians. In relation to historiography, Wikipedians can be hamstrung by limited access to literature. While Wikipedians are encouraged to use a wide body of literature, the nature of online research can restrict access to digitally available resources. Substantial amounts of material still remain in hard copy and are much more demanding, in terms of financial resources and time, for a digital community to access. In contrast, historians with technical and financial support from their libraries and universities are able to engage more comprehensively with the historiography associated with a topic. Historians may legitimately ask: how valid is a narrative that has been written without consideration of the appropriate body of knowledge?

The process of constructing narratives in Wikipedia also presents a dilemma. Narrative making is collaborative, as opposed to traditional history, which, as Rosenzweig contends, "is a deeply individualistic craft."[42] Wikipedia is collaborative, written and edited by interested parties (some novice, some expert) and the content is fluid, only momentarily fixed in time. The online encyclopedia has created an environment with very low barriers to engagement and which provides support for creation and sharing, encourages forms of mentorship and socialization, and acknowledges those who make contributions.[43] The titles of two recent books on Wikipedia, *A New Community of Practice* (2010) and *Wikipedia: Good Faith Collaboration* (2009), capture the collaborative dimensions of this community.[44] For historians, this requires a shift from an individualistic work culture to a collaborative community of practice that creates, and recreates, narratives through the editing process.[45] In regard to perspective, Wikipedia requires contributors to write from a neutral point of view (NPOV). NPOV is recognized as "the epistemic foundation of the project and intentional stance of contributors," which implores editors to act as disinterested judges: impartial, dispassionate, and objective.[46] For some historians, this does not present a philosophical dilemma, but for others, who believe that neutrality is not achievable and have either reconceptualized a new version of objectivity or rejected objectivity altogether, writing for Wikipedia is difficult. The philosophical dilemma posed by trying to achieve neutrality helps explain a dominant feature of Wikipedia, specifically the debates and extended discussions on the "Talk" pages about alleged breaches of NPOV. In summary, Wikipedia has a clearly articulated, explicit, and unique "story space"[47] with different parameters and requirements to traditional history that might deter historians from engaging with this online phenomenon as a representation of the past in the present. Wikipedia therefore raises specific issues that are particular to its own protocols and user policies and, in doing so, also represents some of the broader concerns held by historians about digital history.

Conceptualizing Digital History

Given the range of digital tools and philosophical issues surrounding their usefulness for historians, how can we conceptualize sport history in the digital era? Developing typologies for the array and uses of digital media is tempting but also problematic. Distinctions between Web 1.0 (as essentially read-only) and Web 2.0 (as facilitating audience production as well as simply consumption of web-based materials) are no longer meaningful because Web 2.0 has now effectively supplanted its predecessor. Thinking about digital history in terms of research, teaching, and communication possibilities can be helpful, but these distinctions ignore the crossover potential and realities of historical scholarship in the digital era. Levels of interactivity can be a useful conceptual tool for distinguishing between various websites and platforms, but interactivity between digital creator and consumer is now possible, and encouraged, on even the most traditional websites: most prominent museums and archives encourage visitor interaction through social media. Given these various limitations, new conceptual categories are required. We propose a tripartite conceptualization of the relationship between history making and the digital era: *Digital History and the Archive*, *Digital History as Archive*, and *Digital History is History*. Defined in the following pages, these categories help conceptualize digital history according to their defining features and traits, but they are not definitive and, in reality, there is a porous membrane between the categories that allows for an understanding of the fluidity of history making in the digital world.

DIGITAL HISTORY AND THE ARCHIVE

Digital History and the Archive involves at least two major conceptual components. The first addresses the consequences of replicating paper records in the archive with digital documents on the web. In some ways, digitization offers a utopian dream: the ability to copy, store, and access virtually every form of record from official sources, to correspondence, to media, to websites, to blogs—the list is endless, and theoretically open to all. Scarcity has been replaced by the abundance of the "new infinite archive."[48] In reality, however, there are significant issues with copying, storing, and accessing material. Who decides what records are copied: archivists, academics, government bureaucrats, commercial operators? Is it possible, or even desirable, to copy and store everything? If not, what records will be stored, which will be lost and forgotten? How are these records stored, and by whom? Will it be public institutions—government, libraries, and museums—and/or commercial companies? Equally importantly, will records be accessible as digital technology dates, and who will have access? Will the records be publicly available, or only accessible for a fee? If access is fee-based, will this entrench the distinction between institutionally funded scholars and amateur historians? Finally, will those records that require a fee, and those that are not digitally available at all, take on a different status based on their scarcity?[49] In this sense, the digital archive—not unlike the historical development of the analogue archive—is shaped by ideological, institutional, political, and financial factors.[50]

In his chapter titled "The Library's Role in Developing Web-Based Sport History Resources," Wayne Wilson addresses these questions in the context of the future of sport libraries in the digital era. He acknowledges the end-of-libraries debate, but argues that libraries will not cease to exist; rather, they have modified and will continue to change their structure and function to meet the digital world. In the contemporary economy of networked information, libraries have become hybrid or gateway institutions that provide access to a mix of digital and paper-based sources. Rather than continuing the traditional function of building book and journal collections, libraries in the digital era increasingly collect and store both hard-copy and born-digital documents in conjunction with disseminating this information and facilitating scholarly communication.[51] In many ways, sport libraries and major sport collections—such as the Australian National Sports Information Centre, the LA84 Foundation, and the International Olympic Committee's Olympic Studies Centre in Lausanne—have mirrored the functions of digitizing material, disseminating information, and promoting scholarly communications that characterize contemporary libraries. Not surprisingly, however, the digitization and dissemination of special sport collections is enmeshed with issues about ownership, public profile, and access. Sport collections, like libraries more generally, have to make decisions about whether they take control of the digitization and dissemination process or collaborate with much larger institutions. Collaboration reduces costs and increases accessibility, but institutional identity is blurred, and institutional recognition is important for sport libraries. As Wilson argues: "A digital collection provides a way to raise the public profile of a school, sport, team, club, governing body or museum." Digital sport collections also help to brand institutions and to differentiate them from their rivals in the competition for students, staff, private donors, and public funds. In this context, sport libraries have ethical, political, and social decisions to make: what do they digitize in terms of existing archival material and born-digital sources? Who has access to this information and in what forms? And is access free or for a fee? How sport libraries address these issues, Wilson contends, will shape their role in the digital era.

The second component of *Digital History and the Archive* is the explosion of available digital historical records. This process has involved the creation of effective search engines, discovery systems, and large databases. While these dimensions are the most obvious features of the digital era for historians, what is contested is the effects of what has been termed the "information turn" on the history-making process.[52] Are we witnessing "a revolution that has transformed records, record keeping and the research that is based on them,"[53] often understood as a fundamental paradigm shift in history,[54] or a continuation of traditional historical practices that have always been changing ontologically, epistemologically, methodologically, and ethically?

How you answer this last question depends on your philosophical position on the discipline of history.[55] Nevertheless, the increased availability of digital records and the associated search engines designed to conduct large-scale research is a new phenomenon. The days of research visits to libraries and archives; the anticipation of requesting items never seen before; of touching, feeling, and smelling archival material; of reading microfilm and microfiche records with strained eyes; and scribbling down personal and professional reactions to discoveries in the archives are not always mandatory anymore. It is now possible, and productive, for historians to sit at their desks requesting searches of archival material from national and international institutions and within hours, possibly even minutes, having a plethora of primary documents examined and sorted according to the search criteria, ready to be analyzed. The archive, the web, and the office are blending: they can be one and the same.

While the advantages of digital access to the archive might seem incredible—an unprecedented glut of documents and materials that enables the boundaries of research to be extended with new research questions asked and answered—there are many unresolved issues. Historians recognize that only a small quantity of the total analogue archive has been digitized and, as a consequence, available online sources will not be sufficient for many historical projects. In this way archival materials, only available to be viewed in person, remain very important for historians, even in the digital era. Furthermore, how much credence do we place on the (deliberately romanticized version of) archival experience described previously? How much does the embodied experience of archival research, what Robert Darnton refers to as "a kind of marinating," relate to the history-making process?[56] This not only includes the aesthetic and sensorial dimensions of archival work but also the importance of original primary sources that is beautifully captured in Arlette Farge's *The Allure of the Archives*.[57] Finally, what effect does the change in medium create when material shifts from a hard-copy newspaper in a library, for instance, to the digital page on a screen? Communication theorists have contended for a long while that "media do not simply convey messages, they affect our very relationship within the world."[58] Digitized newspaper articles are a prime example. The content of the newspaper article does not change, but it may be stripped of context. And as Weller argues, "context is everything—where a particular article is situated on a page or within an issue gives us clues about the value and importance placed upon it by the editor, helps us understand how a contemporary reader would have first seen the item, and can give us intangible but very significant contextual information which may be lost in a digitized collection."[59] This argument, of course, can be extended to all forms of digitized archival material.[60] The advantages of digital historical research have to be assessed with the same kind of rigorous analysis about provenance that has characterized analogue records.[61]

These issues are explored in Martin Johnes and Bob Nicholson's chapter, "Sport History and Digital Archives in Practice." Their focus is primarily on newspapers—one of the most popular resources for sport historians—more specifically, what is lost and gained in research based on quantitative cultural history. Frustrated by the debates on digitization that have centered on the content providers, including archivists, libraries, and digital publishers, Johnes and Nicholson investigate the agency of researchers. They acknowledge the limitations of the process of digitization.

First, copyright restricts the scope of digitization of some twentieth-century newspapers and periodicals. As Christian Vandendorpe argues, we have digital access to the majority of print material from ancient Greece and Rome, as well as a good part of the published sources from the eighteenth and nineteenth centuries, "while texts that are closer to us and more likely to enlighten and enrich our thinking on today's world are kept in their paper prison."[62] Copyright is an issue recognized by a range of professionals—from archivists, to scholars, and to lawyers—as one of the largest impediments to large-scale digitization.[63] Second, digitization is compromised when the quality of newspaper print affects the ability to scan accurately and when scanning software confuses letters in texts using old fonts. Finally, searching by scanning software relies on an exact match between the keyword selected by the researcher and the description used by the journalist. At first glance, keyword selection seems simple and logical. But when you consider the multiple meanings associated with a word like *football*, which in early-twentieth-century English newspapers could refer to rugby union, rugby league, and soccer, difficulties associated with scanning software become evident.

Even though digital scanning has these limitations, Johnes and Nicholson appreciate and advocate its innovation: "thousands of pages can be searched for the name of a place, person, or sport in an instant." Digital archives enable sport historians to access and examine large databases in relation to individuals, sports, teams, events, and sporting metaphors as these topics arise in newspapers and in other sources such as Google Books and court records. The specific approach for digital research advocated by Johnes and Nicholson is a new form of quantitative cultural history, culturomics, which records both statistically and graphically the number of hits for keywords in digitized sources. As Johnes and Nicholson caution, however, culturomics without a qualitative dimension is inadequate. Culturomics does not provide any material about context, nor does it offer any idea about what the readers or audiences thought, and they conclude that "one of the biggest challenges facing historians will be to ensure that the historical agency and complexity of print culture is not forgotten in a rush to mine the contents of digital archives." Ultimately Johnes and Nicholson recognize, and this is something we stress in the Conclusion to this book, that the real potential for sport historians is to combine the strengths of quantitative analysis with more traditional qualitative approaches to historical research to produce, as Matthew L. Jockers argues, a "blended approach" that combines both "macro and micro scales."[64]

DIGITAL HISTORY AS ARCHIVE

For many sport historians, digital history is most comfortably conceptualized in terms of access to official archives and other documentary records, notwithstanding the questions raised above. But the Internet delivers much more in terms of history and historical resources. In their 2006 book *Digital History*, Daniel J. Cohen and Roy Rosenzweig discuss the contents of what they called the "History Web"—the "aggregate of history-related websites."[65] This history web extends beyond official archives to include online museum exhibits, film, various forms of scholarship, blogs, primary and secondary sources, fansites, teaching and learning materials, discussion lists, e-mail, and organizational sites.[66] To this we can add various social media platforms, like Facebook, Instagram, Twitter, and YouTube. In addition, there are various hybrid forms, including "invented archives" or thematic collections of original documents from "real" archives,[67] and websites that bring together various elements of all of the above—material from official archives presented along with, and making use of, these other tools and media.

The availability of these various resources, sites, and media enables us to conceptualize *Digital History as Archive*. In thinking about *Digital History as Archive*, it might be helpful to think of the digital archive as encompassing all of the above types of online sources, vs. the digitized official archive or printed sources that have been digitized by official archives. While there is some overlap between the two, the digital archive has unique features, prospective uses, and potential limitations that require consideration.

Unlike the digitized official archive, in which documents have been assessed, organized, and presented according to professional, agreed-upon protocols, the digital archive is outside the control of any one professional body or practice and is amorphous, unregulated, and dynamic. The digital archive contains widely disparate content, many of which are born-digital, that is, documents that were created digitally and may exist only in digital form. Like the digitized archive, however, efforts are made to preserve for posterity contents of the Internet. Some of these are private, particular to the institutions that create documents, whereas others are public. In 2013, for example, the British Library announced plans to preserve for the historical record the contents of one billion web pages from five million UK websites, plus public tweets and Facebook entries, and other national libraries have similar web-preservation programs.[68]

Thinking about *Digital History as Archive* requires a broad awareness of the potential uses of digital tools, platforms, and content for research, communication, teaching, and the creation of new, online representations. The Internet provides opportunities for richly layered, unique, online histories, from semi-interactive narratives on Wikipedia, for example, to comprehensive, interactive, and hyperlinked sites like that of the International Olympic Committee (IOC). Geoffery Z. Kohe provides an example of the possibility for creative digital representations in his chapter titled "@www.olympic.org.nz: Organizational Websites, E-Spaces, and Sport History" that examines the website of the New Zealand Olympic Committee (NZOC), the country's premier sport authority. NZOC has responded to museological e-trends to ensure its prominence, position, and relevance by appealing to the widest possible audience via a website that is an archive/history in its own right while also drawing partially on other, traditional records. It includes mixed media—historical entries and blog postings, announcements, and links—and is ever-changing. It contains both fact and affect, allowing visitors to "furrow in its histories, understand its present administration, interact with elite athletes, and network our private online existence(s) with an increasingly popular and populated social sporting space." The extensive nature of the NZOC site, and its merging of historical and contemporary elements, raises issues about how sport historians might best use such spaces, and, what work might result.

Critically, Kohe contextualizes the NZOC site within broader historiographical discussion. In many ways it represents the realization of David J. Staley's belief that "future historians will value digital visualizations as tools of scholarly inquiry and narrative" and not only simply as means of storing and accessing textual culture.[69] Digital visualizations and creations like the NZOC website provide opportunities to examine "how sport cultures are created, reproduced, dissolved, and reassembled" through links to fan sites, e-zines, blogs and video blogs (vlogs), Facebook, Twitter, YouTube, club web pages, and sport organization websites. Kohe acknowledges and assesses pitfalls and limitations, canvassing issues such as the fragility of records and e-spaces, technical obsolescence, training challenges, and the susceptibility to overt politicization of memories stemming from the democratizing of history making through community involvement.

In addition to its potential for new, amalgamated, forms of digital representations, the Internet can be useful as a research tool. Many websites and digital tools, including social media, have strong research potential, both for gathering data and for recruiting research participants. Mike Cronin's chapter, "'Dear Collective Brain . . .': Social Media as a Research Tool in Sport History," explores the potential of social media as a research tool. Cronin draws on his own experiences using Facebook and Twitter to engage research participants and collect data for Irish sport history projects on which he was the lead researcher between 2008 and 2012: an oral history of the Gaelic Athletic Association (GAA) and an investigation into Ireland's built sporting heritage. Drawing parallels with the excitement generated around oral history in the 1970s, he argues that social media is "an exciting new frontier, full of (and fraught with) exciting possibilities." In particular, he identifies three key uses of social media: gaining assistance from fellow sport historians and researchers, collecting data, and accessing already-collected data via the social media archive of posts.

Based on his experiences, Cronin explores some of the practical issues that he faced in using social media for these projects. The biggest problem, he reflects, is "simply getting the message out there." This was a particular issue with Facebook, where the reluctance of individuals to extend their usage beyond their own social relationships and networks of friends frustrated attempts to engage the public in participating in the research projects.

The problem may be surmountable, but Cronin argues it would require a reconfiguration of traditional research methodologies for the particular purpose. Twitter, he proposes, has the greater potential as a research tool because of its more open access and focussed style of engagement. For all forms of social media, he concludes that accessing previously collected data is simpler than generating or "harvesting" new data.

Cronin also explores the complex raft of legal, ethical, and methodological issues around social media, raising a number of practical questions, caveats, and scenarios. Who will own the material archived and available via social media sites? How will the policing of information, and legal and scholarly controls over social media archives, affect researchers? What ethical responsibilities will researchers have to their social media friends, the people who supply data and engage with research projects? While such questions have been asked in other research contexts, Cronin's reflections in the context of his own two research projects around the GAA and built sporting heritage in his chapter offer a particularly useful lens for sport historians contemplating how to use the research tools offered by social media.

The history web also contains many pedagogical platforms and opportunities for new or revised approaches to teaching and learning. Tara Magdalinski's chapter, "Into the Digital Era: Sport History, Teaching and Learning, and Web 2.0," explores the numerous opportunities for incorporating interactive, Internet-based technologies for collaborative learning into sport history pedagogy. These include blogs, wikis, Wikipedia, Twitter, and Facebook, and extend to lesser-known platforms and tools such as Curatr and TED-Ed "Flip this Lesson." Indeed, as new platforms continue to be developed, and as students—who are already largely digital natives—engage with these, and as pedagogical practice continues to move away from passive receipt of static knowledge toward active engagement in knowledge creation, Magdalinski argues that sport historians themselves need to be "competent and critical users." The interactive and collaborative potential of many web-based platforms offers possibilities for engagement both within the classroom and with external communities of interest.

Importantly, Magdalinski acknowledges constraints and obstacles, including resource and skill acquisition for ensuring appropriate, customized activities, outcomes, and assessment; pedagogic anxiety over learning processes and content creation; authenticity of sources; students' own comfort and skill levels; and the potential impact on academic language discourse of informal communication methods used in social networking sites. These are all valid concerns, addressed here realistically and sympathetically. Yet at the same time, the large and expanding online archive of pedagogical platforms and tools offers unprecedented opportunities for teaching sport history. Magdalinski's chapter surveys several of these and offers practical suggestions for experimenting. These include using online platforms to develop students' appreciation of the historical method by creating customized digital museums, employing video-editing tools to aid students' ability to locate their enquiry within broader theoretical paradigms, engaging with blog sites of existing historical institutions and bodies, creating digitized primary sources based on students' own experiences, linking students across institutions of learning both nationally and internationally, developing social media sites for historical figures and events, and producing multimedia online histories.

Thinking about *Digital History as Archive* also requires awareness of new forms of archive. Discussion of Internet sources often distinguishes between born-digital materials and traditional printed documents that have been, are being, or could be digitized.[70] The proliferation of born-digital documents raises questions about their importance to future historians, and poses further questions about their abundance and their fragility. As important as these questions are, however, they bypass discussion of how these born-digital documents might also be important and useful to historians *now*. Prime among these documents is the huge cache of material generated by social media. Tweets on specific topics, for example, or Facebook and fansite postings or blog comments, constitute online archives for new forms of data collection.

Matthew Klugman's chapter, "'Get excited, people!': Online Fansites and the Circulation of the Past in the Preseason Hopes of Sports Followers," explores how sport fansites can be mined by sport historians as "a wonderfully rich resource." Each week, he argues, "thousands, if not millions" of sport fans congregate online to "read, chat, and blog" about their favorite teams. Importantly, he argues that these sites exist as free-standing histories produced and consumed voraciously by contributors in collaboration with one another and subject to their own internal rules, protocols, and modes of expression and meaning. Engaging with this massive digital archive of fan postings and discussion can offer insight into new communities surrounding sports teams, fantasy engagement, and humor, as well as gendered, racial, and sexualized aspects of spectator sports culture. More broadly, sport fansites provide opportunities to consider questions of sporting memory and popular history.

Specifically, Klugman considers fan blogs and discussion forums in the Australian Football League (Australian Rules football) and the American National Football League to investigate how the past circulates in the present in the often-obsessive seasonal hopes and fears of sports fans. Many fans of these sports, he argues, take an obsessive interest in one particular aspect of the past—players' playing history—that influences fans during preseason recruitment. Through extensive citation of sport fans' online postings, he explores how this obsession invokes both unrealistic hope and the specter of past suffering. This chapter draws on the works of Mircea Eliade and insights from religious studies and psychoanalysis to theorize on the "attempted annihilation of past mistakes" as integral to hope. Klugman's aim in exploring these sites is to "create space for further exchange between studies of religion, passions, memory, and the history of sport." In so doing, he offers a compelling argument for the merits of exploring fansites to better understand how the sporting past circulates in the present.

Blogs offer other possibilities. In "Interactivity, Blogs, and the Ethics of Doing Sport History," Rebecca Olive explores the potential of blogs and blogging for sport historians. Blog posts, using a variety of media but largely focused on written text, are produced by single authors or collectives for a variety of purposes, including to "provide information, as self-representation, to tell a story, to work toward a political goal, or to represent a culture, experience, idea or issue, outside of mainstream media." Their global reach is linked to the rapid expansion of social networking sites and social media, with platforms like Twitter representing a form of micro-blogging. While blogs invite feedback and direct communication, they are semi-interactive spaces where the producer ultimately retains control over site content.

Olive considers blogs from two perspectives. Drawing on work by various historians, she argues that blogs can be a research source for understanding the processes of collectively constructing cultural and social memories. Like other social media archives, blog posts contain a wealth of commentary and information that is potentially valuable to historians as they grapple with understanding meanings of particular pasts in the present. In addition, Olive argues that blogs offer the potential for reflexive historical practice. Using a cultural studies lens, she considers how sport historians might use blogs to engage with contemporary research issues and approaches.

The "qualities of blogs—accessible, instantaneous, community-based, archival, multimedia, moderated, dialogic—make them a potentially productive resource in terms of the ethics and politics of doing sport history, and as an addition to established research methods." Sport historians, she suggests, with "their training, experience, and capacity for critical thinking about the past," are well placed to use blogs effectively to become both producers and curators of these virtual sources. Through a reflection on her own blogging practice on a collective website about surfing, Olive argues that amateur and professional historians can learn from each other how to produce and consume rigorous, accessible forms of history online.

In her chapter "Death, Mourning, and Cultural Memory on the Internet: The Virtual Memorialization of Fallen Sports Heroes," Holly Thorpe addresses Facebook and other websites as historical sources. Specifically, she examines the cultural production of memory in the digital era via Facebook memorial pages and virtual memorial websites dedicated to deceased sporting heroes. Increasingly, she argues, fans, family, friends, and journalists are turning to the Internet to express their condolences, communicate with other mourners, and memorialize the deceased in "highly creative, interactive, and dynamic ways." Often, communications are addressed directly to the deceased individual. Thorpe's focus is on surfer Andy Irons and skier Sarah Burke, who died in 2010 and 2012, respectively, and who have been memorialized extensively online. Constituting a "record of the multiple, contested, and changing emotional responses," these websites become "valuable archives of the public affective responses to cultural trauma." Through an examination of online reactions to the deaths of Irons and Burke, Thorpe identifies five key arguments regarding Facebook memorialization pages.

More broadly, Thorpe argues that these new social media are not just new means for expression of memory, a step on from letters and videos in their time, but they operate in new ways with different impacts. Besides offering greater accessibility, "they also create space for a wider array of voices and the coproduction of cultural memory." She nonetheless cautions against seeing the Internet as more open and democratic; despite the wide range of memorial expressions, voices, and opinions captured via social media, certain individuals and groups are more powerful, and particular dominant narratives emerge. And while social media may be transforming some mourning practices, the web "is not free from the politics of cultural memory construction and memorialization."

Of course, fansites, blogs, Facebook, and other forms of digital archive are not without their limitations. Their sheer abundance poses a challenge for researchers, for example, as can the superficiality of content or the repetition of ideas. For researchers who hope to harness social media for research purposes, there are other challenges, as discussed in these chapters and in the Conclusion of the book.

DIGITAL HISTORY IS HISTORY

It is also possible to conceptualize digital history as inseparable from history—*Digital History is History*—in at least two fundamental ways. The first is to dissolve the tag digital as something that sets digital history apart from history in any fundamental way. In this approach, digital tools are simply that, tools used and adapted by humans in the age-old quest for storytelling to understand the past. In her chapter "On the Nature of Sport: A Treatise in Light of Universality and Digital Culture," Synthia Sydnor questions the assumption that digital culture is "new, even futuristic" and argues that digital culture is a recent addition to myriad forms of expression and expressiveness that have occurred since time immemorial. Digital media then, "are tools that enable humans to continue doing what has always been at the core of the human condition: living in community, communicating, consuming, gathering, playing." In other words, they are new but not new. Certainly, to date at least, the digital era has not revolutionized traditional professional history as some early commentators predicted it would. As Alun Munslow has argued, historical websites still contain constructed narratives and are still "narratively managed" by their creators.[71] It "is certainly too strong a claim," Munslow continues, "to say that the new media requires the re-invention of the discipline [history]."[72]

Sydnor adapts perspectives from classic anthropology to develop a treatise on the nature of sport that takes into account both the digital era and theories of play, ritual, and culture. She argues that there is a "universal nature to play, sport, and the Internet" that is rarely acknowledged in scholarship. Sport lends itself to the digital era because it is ritualistic. Cyber activities around sport, including "fantasy league play; social and individual memories of sports performance; video/computer games; the seemingly infinite growth of sport performances/stunts showcased on YouTube, tweets, and the colossal transglobal economy associated with sport," replicate the "fun, thrills, danger, gravity play" and other affective sensations surrounding participation in sport itself. Ultimately, she argues, the digital revolution confirms the formal, symbolic ritualistic nature of sport more than it transforms.

In contrast, the second dimension of *Digital History is History* accepts that the digital era is changing history as it has been understood and practiced. Viewing digital history in this way requires shifting ontological, epistemological, and methodological focus from traditional history thinking and practice that privileges the academic historian over public historians and academic histories over public histories. With a similar objective as attempts to involve the public in creating history, such as the People's History movement in Britain in the 1980s,[73] technology has created a "participatory culture" marked by the increased contribution of individuals in and to cultural discourse, including historical discourse.[74] Digital technologies and platforms, from genealogical websites, to Wikipedia, to social media, have ushered the public into the history game, both as researchers and as creators of histories who can and do make their own meanings about the past without the mediation of professional historians. As Luke Tredinnick argues, "the role of the historian in creating the historical narrative out of the detritus of documentary culture is supplemented" in the digital era "by the role of individuals in making their own sense of the past."[75] This increased popularization of history as practice and pursuit challenges the traditional separation between the distant and recent past. It also requires seeing history as something living, ongoing, and dynamic rather than quarantined to the past—a "living and mutable, political and personal part of the wider social matrix."[76]

For the sport historian, seeing history through this lens can broaden and change methodological practice. As seen in the chapters by Matthew Klugman, Rebecca Olive, and Holly Thorpe, social media such as blogs, Facebook, fansites, and Twitter, can be more than simply sources of data for research but also as (or providing) rich, stand-alone histories. In "Who's Afraid of the Internet? Swimming in an Infinite Archive," Fiona McLachlan and Douglas Booth argue that the Internet and its broad array of social media effectively constitute an endless historical archive that immerses historians "in an expanded, and expanding, collection of fragments." This immersion coincides time-wise with changing historical approaches that embrace cultural forms and new ontologies, epistemologies, and methodologies. Using three historical genres—reconstructionism, constructionism, and deconstructionism—they analyze the ways that sport historians do, and could, engage with the Internet, using swimming as an example. The Internet is awash with sources linked to the broad theme of swimming, as with other physical activities and sports.

Reconstructionist historians typically view many Internet sources with skepticism, accepting digitized documents from official sources only and using them in an attempt to recreate the past. For reconstructionists, the Internet facilitates research by providing access to sites, artifacts, news, and official documents, but does not fundamentally alter practice. Constructionists use social theory to investigate not only the documents and other remnants of the past but also the repositories of those items, such as libraries, archives, museums, and the Internet itself. While the Internet and its component sites expand the scope for theorization of sports and their representation, McLachlan and Booth argue that the Internet remains contested terrain for constructionists. For deconstructionists, who focus on the production and form of historical narratives, the Internet changes the way narratives are represented and understood and enables new ways of arranging and presenting subject matter. McLachlan and Booth see this promise as "highly liberating," and propose the fragment as the "appropriate unit of analysis" for historians and the arrangement of fragments as constituting a history. In an applied example of this potential, they arrange a series of Internet-derived fragments using a deconstructionist, reconfigurationist lens to create a brief narrative history of "wild swimming" as a cultural and social practice. The result indicates the possibility offered by the Internet for "rearranging the remnants of the past in new ways" and for changing the way history is conceptualized and practiced.

* * *

Many historians see digital history as an interesting aside to the main game of history, or as a contemporary fad that inflates its own importance, like other perspectives that have claimed or threatened to revolutionize history. For some, this is reason enough to avoid or minimize engagement. Other historians, like many of the contributors to this anthology, are more willing to engage either because it constructively contributes to their own research, teaching, and scholarly communication, or because they are convinced digital history is a game-changer. We are genuinely unsure of how the digital world will shape history in the long term, but we have tried to understand the contemporary features of the relationship between the digital world and history. In essence, in this Introduction we have provided the bones of digital history through our three-fold hermeneutic device. In the Conclusion, we will extend this discussion, and our anatomical analogy, and critically appraise how digital history might flex its muscle by examining the strengths, limitations, and potential of *Digital History and the Archive*, *Digital History as Archive*, and *Digital History is History*.

Notes

1. Wikiversity, "The History of the Paralympic Movement in Australia/Tender."

2. The APC later contracted Murray Phillips to be the historian managing this project. The structure of the project includes a traditional paper book, an e-history, and, in partnership with Wikimedia Australia, an unlimited number of Wikipedia articles about the Australian Paralympic Movement. See Wikiversity, "The History of the Paralympic Movement in Australia/Tender."

3. American Historical Association, "AHA Award Recipients—Roy Rosenzweig Prize for Innovation in Digital History"; Reference and User Services Association, American Library Association, "ABC-CLIO Online History Award." For an example of online histories that provides information on sport history, see http://www.rte.ie/centuryireland/. One of the contributors to this book, Mike Cronin, has been heavily involved in this project.

4. Leonard, "New Media and Global Sporting Cultures."

5. Dougherty and Nawrotzki, *Writing History in the Digital Age*.

6. Cohen and Rosenzweig, *Digital History*, subtitle.

7. Cohen et al., "Interchange," 454.

8. Weller, "Introduction," 3.

9. Evans and Rees, "An Interpretation of Digital Humanities," 37 (emphasis in the original).

10. Jones, *The Emergence of Digital Humanities*, 19.

11. The History Press, "TitanicVoyage."

12. Sikarskie, "Citizen Scholars."

13. For a list of digital humanities projects, see http://anterotesis.com/wordpress/dh-gis-projects/; for an overview of American examples, see Dorn, "Is (Digital) History More than an Argument about the Past?"

14. Cohen et al., "Interchange," 454.

15. Dorn, "Is (Digital) History More Than an Argument about the Past?"

16. Graham, Massie, and Feuerherm, "The HeritageCrowd Project."

17. Dorn, "Is (Digital) History More than an Argument about the Past?"

18. University of Sydney, "Digital Harlem: Everyday Life, 1915–1930."

19. Robertson, "Putting Harlem on the Map."

20. Graham, Massie, and Feuerherm, "The HeritageCrowd Project"; Sikarskie, "Citizen Scholars."

21. Cohen et al., "Interchange," 458.

22. Nawrotzki and Dougherty, "Introduction."

23. Townsend, "How Is New Media Reshaping the Work of Historians?" 34–35.

24. Takats, "The Quintessence of Ham."

25. Rosenzweig, "Can History Be Open Source?" 117 (emphasis in the original); Brown "Commentary," 334.

26. Rosenzweig, "Scarcity or Abundance?" 757.

27. Nawrotzki and Dougherty, "Introduction," note 15 (citing Takats, "The Quintessence of Ham").

28. Cohen and Rosenzweig, *Digital History*, 3.

29. Greenberg, "Do Historians Watch Enough TV?" 188.

30. Board, "The False Promise of the 'Peoples' Encyclopedia," 11–12.

31. Sikarskie, "Citizen Scholars."

32. Romano, "Not Dead Yet," 25.

33. In their edited collection, Renee C. Romano and Claire Bond Potter define recent history as events that occurred within the past forty years: Romano and Potter, "Introduction," 3.

34. Romano and Potter, "Introduction," 1.

35. Ibid., 2.

36. Romano, "Not Dead Yet," 28–42.

37. Elton, G.R., *Return to Essentials*; Marwick, *The New Nature of History*.

38. Arthur M. Schlesinger, cited in Romano and Potter, "Introduction," 2.

39. Burdick et al., *Digital_Humanities*, 85.
40. Wikipedia, "Wikipedia: No original research" (emphasis in the original).
41. Munslow, *Deconstructing History*.
42. Rosenzweig, "Can History Be Open Source?" 117.
43. Reagle, *Good Faith Collaboration*, 46–47.
44. O'Sullivan, *Wikipedia: A New Community of Practice?*; Reagle, *Good Faith Collaboration*.
45. Munslow, *The New History*, 93.
46. Reagle, *Good Faith Collaboration*, 58.
47. Munslow, *Narrative and History*, 16–28.
48. Berry, "Introduction," 2.
49. Thomas and Johnson, "New Universes or Black Holes?"
50. Hamilton et al., *Refiguring the Archive*.
51. The term "born-digital" is regularly used in the literature to refer to documents that were created online: see, for example, Cohen and Rosenzweig, *Digital History*, 15; Nawrotzki and Dougherty, "Introduction."
52. Weller, "Conclusion," 199.
53. Thomas and Johnson, "New Universes or Black Holes?" 178.
54. Rosenzweig, "Scarcity or Abundance?"
55. For example, Dougherty et al. See digital history in terms of continuity rather than discontinuity: "Conclusions."
56. Darnton, "The Good Way to Do History," 52.
57. Farge, *The Allure of the Archives*.
58. Evans and Rees, "An Interpretation of Digital Humanities," 22.
59. Weller, "Introduction," 7.
60. See Maidment, "Writing History with the Digital Image," for the influence of digitization on photographs.
61. Weller, "Introduction."
62. Vandendorpe, *From Papyrus to Hypertext*, 164.
63. Jockers, *Macroanalysis*, 173–175.
64. Ibid., 26.
65. Cohen and Rosenzweig, *Digital History*, 18.
66. Ibid., chap. 1.
67. O'Malley and Rosenzweig, "Brave New World or Blind Alley?" 135.
68. Meikle, "British Library Adds Billions of Webpages and Tweets to Archive."
69. Staley, *Computers, Visualization, and History*, 5.
70. Weller, "Introduction," 11.
71. Munslow, *Narrative and History*, 77.
72. Ibid., 78.
73. Davison, "Paradigms of Public History," 4–15.
74. Jenkins, *Convergence Culture*, 3.
75. Tredinnick, "The Making of History," 48.

76. Ibid., 56.

References

American Historical Association. "AHA Award Recipients—Roy Rosenzweig Prize for Innovation in Digital History." Accessed August 15, 2013. http://www.historians.org/prizes/awarded/RosenzweigWinner.cfm.

Berry, David M. 2012. "Introduction: Understanding the Digital Humanities." In *Understanding Digital Humanities*, edited by David M. Berry, 1–20. Houndmills: Palgrave Macmillan.

Board, Graham. 2007. "The False Promise of the 'Peoples' Encyclopedia." *CHA Bulletin* 33, no. 1: 11–12.

Brown, Joshua. 2004. "Commentary: Rambling Thoughts while on a Virtual Stroll." *Rethinking History* 8, no. 2 (June): 333–35.

Burdick, Anne, Johanna Drucker, Peter Lunenfeld, Todd Presner, and Jeffrey Schnapp. 2012. *Digital_Humanities*. Cambridge, MA: The MIT Press.

Cohen, Daniel J., Michael Frisch, Patrick Gallagher, Steven Mintz, Kirsten Sword, Amy Murrell Taylor, William G. Thomas, III, and William J. Turkel. 2008. "Interchange: The Promise of Digital History." *The Journal of American History* 95, no. 2: 452–91.

Cohen, Daniel J., and Roy Rosenzweig. 2006. *Digital History: A Guide to Gathering, Preserving, and Presenting the Past on the Web*. Philadelphia: University of Pennsylvania Press.

Darnton, Robert. 2014. "The Good Way to Do History." *The New York Review of Books*, January 9, 52, 54–55.

Davison, Graeme. 1991. "Paradigms of Public History." In *Packaging the Past: Public Histories*, edited by John Rickard and Peter Spearritt, 4–15. Melbourne: Melbourne University of Press .

Dorn, Sherman. 2013. "Is (Digital) History More than an Argument about the Past? (Spring 2012 version)." In *Writing History in the Digital Age*, edited by Jack Dougherty and Kristen Nawrotzki. Ann Arbor: University of Michigan Press. Trinity College (CT) web-book edition, Spring 2012. Accessed July 20, 2013. http://WritingHistory.trincoll.edu.

Dougherty, Jack, and Kristen Nawrotzki (eds). 2013. *Writing History in the Digital Age*. Ann Arbor: University of Michigan Press. Trinity College (CT) web-book edition, Spring 2012. http://WritingHistory.trincoll.edu.

Dougherty, Jack, Kristen Nawrotzki, Charlotte Rochez, and Timothy Burke. 2013. "Conclusions: What We Learned from *Writing History in the Digital Age* (Spring 2012)." In *Writing History in the Digital Age*, edited by Jack Dougherty and Kristen Nawrotzki. Ann Arbor: University of Michigan Press. Trinity College (CT) web-book edition, Spring 2012. Accessed July 20, 2013. http://WritingHistory.trincoll.edu.

Elton, G. R. 1991. *Return to Essentials: Some Reflections on the Present State of Historical Study*. Cambridge: Cambridge University Press.

Evans, Leighton, and Sian Rees. 2012. "An Interpretation of Digital Humanities." In *Understanding Digital Humanities*, edited by David M Berry, 21–41. Houndmills: Palgrave Macmillan.

Farge, Arlette. 2013. *The Allure of the Archives*. Translated by Thomas Scott-Railton. New Haven, CT: Yale University Press. Originally published as *Le Goût de l'archive* (Paris: Le Seuil, 1989).

Graham, Shawn, Guy Massie, and Nadine Feuerherm. 2013. "The HeritageCrowd Project: A Case Study in Crowdsourcing Public History (Spring 2012 version)." In *Writing History in the Digital Age*, edited by Jack Dougherty and Kristen Nawrotzki. Ann Arbor: University of Michigan Press. Trinity College (CT) web-book edition, Spring 2012. Accessed July 16, 2013. http://WritingHistory.trincoll.edu.

Greenberg, David. 2012. "Do Historians Watch Enough TV? Broadcast News as a Primary Source." In *Doing Recent History: On Privacy, Copyright, Video Games, Institutional Review Boards, Activist Scholarship, and History That Talks Back*, edited by Claire Bond Potter and Renee C. Romano, 185–99. Athens: The University of Georgia Press.

Hamilton, Carolyn, Verne Harris, Jane Taylor, Michele Pickover, Graeme Reid, and Razia Saleh, eds., 2002. *Refiguring the Archive*. Cape Town: David Philip.

Jenkins, Henry. 2008. *Convergence Culture: Where Old and New Media Collide*. New York: New York University Press.

Jockers, Matthew L. 2013. *Macroanalysis: Digital Methods and Literary Theory*. Urbana: University of Illinois Press.

Jones, Steven E. 2014. *The Emergence of Digital Humanities*. New York: Routledge.

Leonard, David J. (ed.). 2009. "New Media and Global Sporting Cultures." Special Issue, *Sociology of Sport Journal* 26, no. 1 (March).

Maidment, Brian. 2013. "Writing History with the Digital Image: A Cautious Celebration." In *History in the Digital Age*, edited by Toni Weller, 111–26. London: Routledge.

Marwick, Arthur. 2001. *The New Nature of History: Knowledge, Evidence, Language*. 4th ed. Basingstoke, UK: Palgrave.

Meikle, James. 2013. "British Library Adds Billions of Webpages and Tweets to Archive," *The Guardian*, April 5. Accessed May 1, 2013. http://www.guardian.co.uk/technology/2013/apr/05/british-library-archive-webpages-tweets.

Munslow, Alun. 1997. *Deconstructing History*. London: Routledge.

———. 2003. *The New History*. Harlow, UK: Longman.

———. 2007. *Narrative and History*. Basingstoke, Hampshire: Palgrave Macmillan.

Nawrotzki, Kristen, and Jack Dougherty. 2013. "Introduction (Spring 2012 version)." In *Writing History in the Digital Age*, edited by Jack Dougherty and Kristen Nawrotzki. Ann Arbor: University of Michigan Press. Trinity College (CT) web-book edition, Spring 2012. Accessed July 20, 2013. http://WritingHistory.trincoll.edu.

O'Malley, Michael, and Roy Rosenzweig. 1997. "Brave New World or Blind Alley? American History on the World Wide Web." *Journal of American History* 84, no. 1 (June): 132–55.

O'Sullivan, Dan. 2009. *Wikipedia: A New Community of Practice?* Burlington, VT: Ashgate.

Reagle Jr., Joseph Michael. 2010. *Good Faith Collaboration: The Culture of Wikipedia.* Cambridge, MA: MIT Press.

Reference and User Services Association, American Library Association, "ABC-CLIO Online History Award." Accessed August 15, 2013. http://www.ala.org/rusa/awards/abcclio.

Robertson, Stephen. 2013. "Putting Harlem on the Map (Spring 2012 version)." In *Writing History in the Digital Age*, edited by Jack Dougherty and Kristen Nawrotzki. Ann Arbor: University of Michigan Press. Trinity College (CT) web-book edition, Spring 2012. Accessed July 20, 2013. http://WritingHistory.trincoll.edu.

Romano, Renee C. 2012. "Not Dead Yet: My Identity Crisis as a Historian of the Recent Past." In *Doing Recent History: On Privacy, Copyright, Video Games, Institutional Review Boards, Activist Scholarship, and History That Talks Back*, edited by Claire Bond Potter and Renee C. Romano, 23–44. Athens: The University of Georgia Press.

Romano, Renee C., and Claire Bond Potter. 2012. "Introduction." In *Doing Recent History: On Privacy, Copyright, Video Games, Institutional Review Boards, Activist Scholarship, and History That Talks Back*, edited by Claire Bond Potter and Renee C. Romano, 1–19. Athens: The University of Georgia Press.

Rosenzweig, Roy. 2003. "Scarcity or Abundance? Preserving the Past in a Digital Era." *The American Historical Review* 108, no. 3 (June): 735–62.

———. 2006. "Can History Be Open Source? *Wikipedia* and the Future of the Past." *Journal of American History* (June6): 117–46.

Sikarskie, Amanda Grace. 2013. "Citizen Scholars: Facebook and the Co-Creation of Knowledge (Spring 2012 version)." In *Writing History in the Digital Age*, edited by Jack Dougherty and Kristen Nawrotzki. Ann Arbor: University of Michigan Press. Trinity College (CT) web-book edition, Spring 2012. Accessed June 30, 2013. http://WritingHistory.trincoll.edu.

Staley, David J. 2002. *Computers, Visualization, and History: How New Technology Will Transform Our Understanding of the Past.* Armonk, NY: M.E. Sharpe.

Takats, Sean. "The Quintessence of Ham." Accessed October 26, 2012. http://quintessenceofham.org/2010/10/28/adoption-of-new-media-by-historians/#identifier_1_279.

The History Press. "TitanicVoyage." Accessed July 20, 2013. https://twitter.com/TitanicRealTime.

Thomas, David, and Valerie Johnson. 2013. "New Universes or Black Holes? Does Digital Change Anything?" In *History in the Digital Age*, edited by Toni Weller, 173–93. London: Routledge.

Townsend, Robert B. 2010. "How Is New Media Reshaping the Work of Historians?" *Perspectives on History* (November): 31–36.

Tredinnick, Luke. 2013. "The Making of History: Remediating Historicized Experience." In *History in the Digital Age*, edited by Toni Weller, 39–60. London: Routledge.

University of Sydney. "Digital Harlem: Everyday Life, 1915–1930." Accessed July 20, 2013. http://www.acl.arts.usyd.edu.au/harlem/.

Vandendorpe, Christian. 2009. *From Papyrus to Hypertext: Toward the Universal Digital Library*. Urbana: University of Illinois Press.

Weller, Toni. 2013. "Introduction: History in the Digital Age." In *History in the Digital Age*, edited by Toni Weller, 1–19. London: Routledge.

———. 2013. "Conclusion: A Changing Field." In *History in the Digital Age*, edited by Toni Weller, 196–205. London: Routledge.

Wikipedia. "Wikipedia: No original research." Accessed May 5, 2013. http://en.wikipedia.org/wiki/Wikipedia:No_original_research.

Wikiversity. "The History of the Paralympic Movement in Australia/Tender." Accessed May 5, 2013. http://en.wikiversity.org/wiki/The_History_of_the_Paralympic_Movement_in_Australia/Tender.

PART I

Digital History and the Archive

The first dimension of our tripartite conception of history in the digital era is *Digital History and the Archive*. As historians, we face a growing abundance of readily accessible digitized newspaper and archival documents as well as new search engines and technologies designed to access and evaluate what has been termed the new infinite archive. This situation raises a host of political, ideological, and financial issues for archivists, historians, citizen scholars, and cultural institutions. In his chapter, Wayne Wilson addresses the ways in which issues about digitization, storage, preservation, and access are being negotiated by libraries. At the same time, the infinite archive presents significant challenges for history practices that have traditionally included close reading. One of the key issues is the sheer size of the archive, and how to manage, use, and represent the ballooning quantity of information and research data. This unprecedented volume of data requires historians to engage with new research methodologies, primarily quantitative methodologies, which allow for distant reading to explore anomalies, patterns, and trends in digitized texts. While data aggregation, data mining, visualizations, and quantitative text analysis may generate some philosophical angst for historians, Martin Johnes and Bob Nicholson explore the opportunities offered and argue that data-driven scholarship should not supplant the practice of close reading, but rather should work in combination with traditional methodologies by adding to the history-making process.

1

The Library's Role in Developing Web-Based Sport History Resources

WAYNE WILSON

In his 2005 essay "The Bookless Future: What the Internet is Doing to Scholarship," historian David A. Bell extolled the virtues of online research and predicted that libraries likely would become "virtual information retrieval centers, possibly located thousands of miles from the readers they serve." The advent of "bookless or largely bookless libraries," wrote Bell, is "too large and powerful a change to be held back."[1] Bell's essay was a clear articulation of one widely held vision of the future of libraries, but it was old news to librarians, whose own professional literature since the 1990s had featured a steady stream of research articles and think pieces about the impact of the Internet and related information innovations on their field.

The organization of sport history as an academic subfield took place at a time when researchers used card catalogs, printed indexes, and abstracting services. They read information printed on paper or microform. Most students lived on campuses and attended lectures in classrooms. The International Committee for the History of Physical Education and Sport was founded in 1967. The North American Society for Sport History (NASSH) was founded in 1972 and launched its journal in 1974. The International Association for the History of Physical Education and Sport began in Zurich in 1973. Yet, even in these early years of sport studies, technological advances and innovative products were laying the groundwork for profound changes in the way that sport historians, their students, and the librarians who supported their work would produce, store, and retrieve information.

The digital revolution's disruption of the world of libraries is far from complete. The future remains as unknown for librarians who develop and manage sport collections as it does for other librarians. The overriding question, of course, is whether libraries and librarians will become obsolete. If not, what form will libraries take and what exactly will librarians do? For librarians working in sport history, a related question is whether sport possesses characteristics that will differentiate the development of sport history resources from resources supporting other kinds of research.

The answer to the last question is a nuanced one. The singular nature of sport as a social institution may enable or inspire sport librarians to follow a path that diverges subtly from the mainstream. Nevertheless, the sheer force of institutional change in libraries will shape and constrain everything that librarians who curate sport collections do in the future. Therefore, to consider in an informed way the manner in which libraries will develop sport history resources in the digital era, it is necessary to understand the current, unsettled state of libraries generally.

The Debate About the Future of Libraries

The debate about the future and survival of libraries predates the Internet. The rise of the Internet as a public information utility is only the most recent example of technology prompting a discussion about libraries' future.

The discourse about the impact of information technology on modern libraries is more than a century old. In 1907, for instance, John Cotton Dana envisioned an "automated question and answer machine" called the "Automatic Who, What and Why Machine." The imagined device was an early version of FAQ. A user would stand in front of a machine, scan a list of frequently asked questions, push the relevant button and a card would appear providing the answer.[2] A more sophisticated vision of information storage and retrieval appeared in 1945 when Vannevar Bush proposed his "memex" system, a machine-based research system that looked very much like today's hypertext.[3] Bush and others who believed that libraries were unable to properly manage the explosion of information in the sciences continued to propose automated solutions for the next several decades. In 1976, at a conference in Finland, F. W. Lancaster predicted a paperless research environment. Lancaster expanded on this theme in his much-cited 1978 book, *Toward Paperless Information Systems*. Among Lancaster's predictions was the assertion that libraries as institutions storing physical collections would become obsolete. In his 1985 essay, "The Paperless Society Revisited," Lancaster held to his earlier predictions, adding, "we are so far along the road to a paperless society that it is difficult to see what might occur that would permanently reverse the trend."[4]

In a similar vein, about a decade later, as the Internet gained in popularity, Gordon Bell and Jim Gray of Microsoft predicted that in fifty years "almost all information will be in cyberspace . . . including all knowledge and creative works. All information about physical objects including humans, buildings, processes, and organizations will be online. This trend is both desirable and inevitable."[5]

The growing popularity of the Internet in the mid- and late-1990s simply added urgency to the existing debate about the future of libraries. Librarians, on balance, responded positively to the Internet, but the embrace was not without reservations. This ambivalence did not derive from computer phobia. Librarians had used computer-based information systems for more than thirty years. However, online database systems that appeared in the 1960s and 1970s such as LexisNexis, DIALOG, and BRS, as well as various local, regional, and national online catalogs were created with librarians in mind. They were expert systems that put librarians in control, or at least gave them a central role in guiding other people's usage.

By contrast, the browsers and search engines that made the Internet, and more specifically the World Wide Web, broad-based public information tools in the 1990s were not developed for librarians, but rather for the general public. And the newly empowered public embraced the new technology enthusiastically. That fact, combined with advances in electronic publishing and the increased ease with which paper documents could be converted to digital format and become full-text searchable, represented a heightened threat not only to the authority and expertise of librarians but to the very concept of libraries.

The discussion that has ensued since the 1990s represents a continuum of opinions in which the center point of the continuum has shifted over time. Gregg Sapp in his *A Brief History of the Future of Libraries* recalls how he and his fellow students reacted to Lancaster's book on the paperless society in the early 1980s at the University of Washington Graduate School of Library and Information Sciences. "At the poles of the debate were two opposing schools of thought" regarding Lancaster's predictions. Traditionalists believed that "print-on-paper would assuredly prevail." Technologists foresaw a day when "every citizen owned a computer that could instantly search and retrieve anything." Most students, however, were somewhere in the middle.[6]

Three decades and hundreds of articles and books later, writes Sapp, "the profession as a whole *has* changed successfully and significantly because the middle ground, where consensus can be reached around core values, has shifted progressively forward."[7] This, of course, is a fancy way of acknowledging that the technologists were more correct than the traditionalists. Indeed, it is impossible today to find any serious observer who does not recognize that digital documents will displace at least to some extent paper-based publications. The only question is the extent to which that will occur and what structural implications it has.

The end-of-libraries position continues to represent one pole of the continuum. Proponents maintain that the Internet and related digital resources will make libraries irrelevant. Young people, particularly in affluent nations, have grown up in an electronic information environment. The only finding aids and research tools they use are electronic ones. These "New Millennials" or "digital natives" are technologically savvy and simply will not settle for anything less than the efficiency and user-friendliness of online documents, full-text search engines, and hypertext. Public projects and private companies such as Google will create resources and products that provide anything a researcher needs. Futurist Seth Godin, while not an advocate of the end-of-libraries argument, vividly depicts the threat that private information providers pose to libraries: "Want to watch a movie? Netflix is a better librarian, with a better library, than any library in the country. The Netflix librarian knows about every movie, knows what you've seen and what you're likely to want to see. If the goal is to connect viewers with movies, Netflix wins."[8]

The extreme end-of-libraries position provides a useful foil for most writers, who predict that while content, services, and space usage may change radically, the library as a "place" will endure. This argument rests on several points that can be summarized as follows. The wholesale switch from paper to digital format is neither desirable nor feasible. Books and periodicals represent a flexible, functional, and user-friendly technology. The retrospective digitization of paper collections is prohibitively expensive for many institutions. Even if individual libraries sit back and wait for various private and publicly funded paper-to-digital conversion projects to create massive online book collections, libraries in aggregate will continue to hold billions of pages of unique or rare documents that will escape capture by cooperative conversion projects and not be scanned anytime soon. Finally, and perhaps most importantly, people are social animals. They seek places to congregate, and interact socially and intellectually. The library as a "place" built of bricks and mortar therefore will continue to have value as it evolves into a cultural center that does more than house books.

The examples of several libraries and archives with valuable sport history holdings underscore the unlikeliness of moving rapidly to an all-digital environment. The University of Massachusetts, Amherst, in 2010, acquired the Mark H. McCormack Collection. The collection documents the life of sports marketing pioneer Mark McCormack and his company IMG. It consists of 8 million pages in 4,000 archival boxes occupying 6,000 linear feet of shelf space and an entire library floor. The staff has no plan at this time to undertake a comprehensive scanning project. Rather, they anticipate the strategic digitization of selected documents that meet specific needs.[9] The H. J. Lutcher Stark Center for Physical Culture and Sports at the University of Texas, Austin, has aisles of unique, primary materials about physical culture and strength sports. The center has digitized only about 1 percent of its archival materials.[10] The Olympic Studies Centre in Lausanne, Switzerland, owns a comprehensive archive of the Olympic Movement. The center has developed a number of useful digital resources for researchers, but relatively few of them are documents converted from paper. The great bulk of the archive remains exclusively in paper format.

Those who believe that libraries will not disappear as physical spaces maintain that most traditional libraries already have become hybrid libraries—or gateway libraries—that provide a mix of electronic and paper-based sources. Hybrid libraries hold paper documents in varying amounts, but more importantly provide the hardware and software needed to use online information. They aggregate electronic sources and are staffed by librarians who are experts in the use of those sources. Chris Rusbridge, a proponent of the hybrid library concept, contends that hybrid libraries represent more than "an uneasy transitional phase between the conventional library and digital library." Rather, the hybrid library is "a worthwhile model in its own right which can be usefully developed and improved."[11]

Even writers who believe that digital resources will completely replace paper foresee the continued existence of the physical library. Godin describes it as follows:

> Just in time for the information economy, the library ought to be the local nerve center for information . . . I'm not saying I *want* paper to go away, I'm merely describing what's inevitably occurring . . .
>
> The next library is a place, still. A place where people come together to do co-working and coordinate and invent projects worth working on together. Aided by a librarian . . . who can bring domain knowledge and people knowledge and access to information to bear.
>
> The next library is filled with so many web terminals there's always at least one empty. And the people who run this library don't view the combination of access to data and connections to peers as a sidelight—it's the entire point.

. . . There are one thousand things that could be done in a place like this, all built around one mission: *take the world of data, combine it with the people in this community and create value.*[12]

It remains to be seen if hybrid libraries really are something more than a transitional phase on the way to an all-digital library, or to a future with no libraries. It seems unlikely, though, that during the next decade any significant number of libraries will completely discontinue the use of books, or that the library as a place will disappear.

Symbiosis Between Sport and the Internet

If the Internet has affected libraries, it has had an equally significant impact on sport. Yet while the Internet disrupts and even threatens libraries, it has a symbiotic relationship to sport. The intersection of the Internet's inherent characteristics and the inherent nature of sport will influence libraries' development of sport history resources.

The Internet is almost ideally suited to delivering and consuming sport information. Sport is visual and aural. The movement of human bodies and objects is intrinsic to sport. Crowd noises and a wide range of other sounds are important ingredients of sport. Sport is quantifiable, giving birth to a multitude of statistics. And, sport attracts and engages public attention in a way that few other phenomena do.

A website is a multimedia delivery system. A sophisticated website combines the power of print media, radio, and television by providing, in one place, text, graphics, moving images, and sound. The Internet can provide live coverage of sports events, and it can archive these events as audio and visual files. Updating information on a website can happen instantaneously and be achieved manually or automatically. Finally, the Internet offers to sport consumers a number of interactive capabilities that other media forms cannot provide. It is no coincidence, then, that major sports events regularly set records for usage levels of web-based media.

In addition to the inherent characteristics of sport and the Internet, the historical development of sport also has contributed to the symbiosis. The Internet is a global technology whose growth has been greatly influenced by commercial media companies. Sport is a highly globalized enterprise that historically has exploited technological innovations while consciously nurturing a close and mutually beneficial relationship with media companies. The historical nexus of sport, globalization, technology, and mass media has shaped the present-day sport information environment, which in turn offers resource-building opportunities to librarians.

It is significant and revealing that sport organizations, sport media companies, and sport libraries were relatively early adopters of web-based technology. The International Olympic Committee (IOC), the United States Olympic Committee, International Association of Athletic Federations (IAAF), Fédération Internationale de Football Association (FIFA), ESPN, and the Australian Sports Commission were among the many sport organizations that launched websites in 1995. The media company Allsport Photography (now Getty Images) launched its website for the delivery of digital photographs even earlier, in 1994.

In 1995, or earlier, an organization with a website was the exception rather than the rule. As late as November of 1995, a *New York Times* reporter observed that the Internet "appears to be on the verge of becoming a mass medium."[13] Efforts to quantify the growth of the Internet are imprecise, but by standard estimates a website launched in mid-1995 would have been among the first 30,000 and well within the first 1 percent of the first 1 percent of all website produced to date.[14]

The decision by influential organizations in sport to establish an early presence in cyberspace reflected longstanding attitudes within the culture of sport regarding technology, mass media, and the geographic scope of sport. The example of the IOC and various Olympic host-city organizing committees is a case in point.

The Olympic Games have long been a locus of technological innovation. Miquel de Moragas has noted that historically "the Olympic Games have been a privileged space" for the introduction of information technologies.[15] Television, timing equipment, specialized cameras, and computer-based information systems had an Olympic connection at early stages of their development.

The Olympic penchant for technological adventurousness did not develop in a vacuum. Much of the impetus came from the desire of Olympic leaders, inspired by a variety of motives, to tell their stories to national and worldwide audiences. They looked to mass media, employing innovative technology, as natural allies in this effort.

The emerging relationship between the Olympic Movement and mass media was evident from the beginning. The official report of the 1896 Athens Games thanked the "foreign press" for having "contributed to the success of the games." At the 1908 London Games, the Olympic Stadium included space for a pressroom. The organizers of the 1912 Stockholm Games established a press task force that met twenty-five times in the year before the Games. The 1932 Games in Los Angeles were backed by a sophisticated marketing campaign using several media. The organizing committee sent bi-weekly bulletins to 6,000 overseas news outlets in five languages. It formed partnerships with 1,500 ham radio operators, feeding them news items to be shared with their counterparts throughout the world. The committee provided photographs to major stock photography agencies, and worked closely with Pathé, Fox-Hearst, Paramount, and Universal to produce newsreels promoting the Games. Before and during the Games, the organizers employed an integrated multiplatform system of telephones, teletypewriters, and telegraphs throughout the competition venues, Olympic Village, press stand, and committee headquarters. The organizers later bragged that the telephone system "was designed with such care and function and with such automatic smoothness that members of the Organizing Committee were hardly conscious of its existence as a mechanical device."[16]

So, by the 1990s, the IOC and other international sports organizations were the products of a decades-old sport culture that was global in outlook, accepting of technological innovation, and eager to exploit mass media. Sport administrators as well as sport journalists and sport information managers were quick to grasp the possibilities of the Internet as it emerged as a mass information medium. As a result, the Internet and sport have become inextricably linked. That linkage not only provides opportunities to develop sport history resources, it obligates sport libraries aspiring to high levels of service and collection development to have a sustained and systematic interaction with the Internet.

Sport History and the Internet

The opportunities offered by the Internet did not go unnoticed by librarians working with sport collections. The North American Sport Library Network, a working group of sport librarians, featured a session on the Internet at its 1994 annual conference.

The first wave of web-based sport history resource development involved paper-to-digital conversion projects and was very much driven by a globalist perspective. The library of LA84 Foundation (formerly the Amateur Athletic Foundation of Los Angeles) was an early adopter of the virtual library concept as applied to sport history. The first documents that the library respectively converted from paper to digital format were official post-Games Olympic organizing committee reports and the house organ of the IOC, *Olympic Review/Revue Olympique*.

The foundation's decision to invest in creating digital resources was motivated by the staff's realization, based on years of experience working in a traditional environment, that the library held resources of interest to a global audience of researchers who wanted to use but had no access to the library's paper-based Olympic collection. For its part, the IOC granted the foundation permission to digitize and web-publish *Olympic Review/Revue Olympique* precisely because it wanted an international audience to have access to its official magazine.

Having undertaken the conversion of Olympic documents, the foundation's next objective was to create a virtual collection of secondary sport history source materials, the journals of the societies such as North American Society for Sport History (NASSH), Australian Society for Sports History, International Society of Olympic Historians, and International Society for Comparative Physical Education and Sport. All of these organizations had international memberships, and all were motivated by a desire for their members' work to be more widely read.

The LA84 collection now includes more than 100,000 documents stored as PDFs. These documents have been created from approximately 500,000 paper pages. In 2010, website visitors downloaded the PDFs 12 million times. It is important to note, though, that the collection is nothing more than an electronic version of traditional books, reports, and periodicals.

Several other online sport history collections that developed in the past fifteen years followed a similar pattern. Their historically valuable resources resulted from paper-to-digital conversion projects. Examples include the Library of Congress' collection of annual Spalding athletic guides, the United States Golf Association's (USGA) Seagle Electronic Golf Library, and the IOC Olympic Studies Centre's online collection of historical Olympic charters. In every case, these projects offered the sponsoring libraries a way to ensure that their resources could be used by a worldwide audience of professional and amateur researchers.

FUTURE DEVELOPMENT OF SPORT HISTORY RESOURCES

As libraries continue to develop sport history resources, advances in technology, researchers' heightened expectations, and an increasingly complex array of information sources will require a willingness and ability to do more than web-publish what used to be paper publications. Yet, even as the development of sport history resources enters a new phase, the future will resemble the past in one important way. Retrospective conversions of paper collections to digital format will remain a central function.

RETROSPECTIVE CONVERSION PROJECTS

In the digital era, libraries are placing an increased emphasis on the development of specialized or distinctive collections. As Clifford Lynch puts it, "special collections are a nexus where technology and content are meeting to advance scholarship in extraordinary new ways."[17]

Sport provides unusually rich opportunities for the retrospective conversion of special collections. The historical development of sport has created thousands of distinctive (albeit often unorganized) collections. The reasons are not hard to discern. First, sport is an organization-based enterprise consisting of teams, clubs, associations, and governing bodies. Second, modern sport by its nature involves record keeping and narratives. For most of modern sport's history these records were kept on paper. Third, sport organizations tend to be memory-driven and self-celebratory. Gary Alan Fine's assertion that the "essence of sport is not exercise, but memory" may be an overstatement, but it is not far from the truth.[18] Witness the proliferation of sports museums and halls of fame throughout the world, and particularly in North America. The International Sports Heritage Association has 130 members ranging from such well-known groups as the USGA to the lesser-known Rural Sports Museum and Hall of Fame in Indian Head, Saskatchewan. The point is that all of these organizations possess ready-made content treasure troves.

Libraries involved in retrospective conversions will face a decision about whether to maintain sole control of the process and its end product, or to collaborate with other libraries and information producers to create a common pool of resources. The Association of College and Research Libraries (ACRL) noted in 2010, "New scholarly communication and publishing models are developing at an ever-faster pace, requiring libraries to be actively involved or be left behind."[19] Among the models cited by ACRL were the HathiTrust and the Digital Public Library of America, collaborative projects that draw on contributions from many libraries to create large centralized aggregations of full-text documents. These collaborative arrangements create immense collections that benefit researchers. They reduce conversion costs significantly and take much of the managerial onus off of individual libraries. At the same time, they submerge the identity of the contributing library.

Libraries holding sport collections must navigate between the attraction of joint ventures such as the HathiTrust and the desire of parent institutions to differentiate themselves from other colleges, universities, sports organizations, museums, and halls of fame. Special collections serve a dual function. First and foremost, they are sources of rare or unique information to researchers. In addition, special collections also have marketing and branding value. That value becomes more pronounced when the collection is available on the Internet. A digital collection provides a way to raise the public profile of a school, sport, team, club, governing body, or museum.

In the academic context, special collections provide a way for universities to differentiate themselves from their competitors—and make no mistake, institutions of higher learning most definitely are competing against each other for students, faculty, private donors, and public funds. The recent acquisition of the Mark H. McCormack Collection by the University of Massachusetts Libraries was directly a result of the university's Sports Management Department's desire to maintain its credibility as a leader in the field.[20] The University competed against twelve other schools to acquire the collection. The H. J. Lutcher Stark Center for Physical Culture and Sports at the University of Texas, which includes the archive of the school's athletic department sports information office and the papers of venerable football coach Darrell Royal, is viewed by the university's development office as a valuable asset that raises the prestige of the university while connecting emotionally with alumni interested in University of Texas athletics.[21] At this stage in their development, both the McCormack and Stark collections are overwhelmingly paper-based, but the potential for digital conversion is enormous. The branding benefits that will result will be significant for both the collections and the universities.

Commercial sports enterprises, governing bodies, and museums and halls of fame are at least as brand conscious as universities. Among sports museums, the United States Golf Museum has been a leader in digitizing old books and magazines. The USGA believes in the value of heritage promotion. It has invested in a new museum building, a first-rate traditional library collection, and a digital collection. The golf museum's mission states: "The USGA Museum is an educational institution dedicated to fostering an appreciation of the game of golf, its participants, and the Association. It serves as a caretaker and steward for the game's history, supporting the association's role in ensuring the game's future."[22] In plain language, the museum and its library serve both as educational and marketing arms of the USGA. It seems unlikely that the USGA would want to invest in cooperative arrangements in which the branding or marketing impact of its resources would be diluted in a huge virtual collection originating from thousands of other sources.

CHANGING ROLE OF LIBRARIANS

The ability of librarians to manage retrospective conversion projects and also branch into new areas of resource development will be made possible in part by the diminished need to perform some traditional tasks. It is very likely, for example, that building general book collections and comprehensive journal collections will cease to be the central function of sport bibliographers and subject specialists in libraries supporting work in sport history. This will be especially true in academic and public libraries. Many researchers already have figured out that an intelligently crafted search of Google Books will provide full-text access to the relevant portions of many in-print and out-of-print books. Google Books combined with the availability of free- and fee-based resources like the HathiTrust, Internet Archive, and JSTOR that aggregate content from many sources are disincentives to the development of local sport history book and journal collections. Similarly, the ability to purchase or license the use of individual scholarly journal articles from publishers will provide a reasonable justification for not buying annual subscriptions to expensive journals. Why build an expensive comprehensive journal collection when the individual articles researchers want can be cherry-picked as needed at a lesser cost? To cite one example of a sport history resource, if the *International Journal of the History of Sport* costs a library over $1,900 (US) a year and is used by clients only twenty times a year, a librarian can easily calculate that it is less expensive to purchase the individual articles than an annual subscription to the entire journal. As part of a trend called patron-driven acquisitions (PDA), many libraries have instituted buying plans that allow their users to purchase or license, without librarian involvement, a pre-determined number of titles of their own choosing. In short, collection development is rapidly moving from a "'just-in-case' to a 'just-in-time' philosophy."[23] PDA is a recent development, the implications of which will reveal themselves over time, but the expectation is that it will reduce personnel needs and acquisitions costs.

Being relieved of traditional collection development responsibilities and possibly having fewer funds dedicated to acquisitions will enable librarians to concentrate on other tasks. The most obvious of these will be providing access to current and recent sports publications that were born digital and may never have existed in paper form. Providing access will entail collecting and storing such documents, or creating portals to them.

Major sports organizations and media companies since the mid-1990s have produced an untold volume of digital documents. Unfortunately, in many cases the creators of these digital publications have not done a good job of saving or organizing them. One role for librarians will be the attempt to recover, store, and organize digital documents created during the first ten or fifteen years of website development and widespread Internet use.

Simultaneously, sport librarians need to begin collecting documents that may not have historical significance for many years. This may involve the capture of individual reports, press releases, and the like, or the archiving of entire websites. The National Library of Australia's website archiving project in conjunction with the 2000 Sydney Olympic Games is a prime example of a library preserving targeted websites. More than a decade after the Sydney Games, the online archive is a valuable historical resource.

National libraries that collect individual digital publications or whole websites may be free to put those resources on their own websites where they will be accessible to the public at no cost. Other libraries—academic, local, public, and private special—will be more restricted by copyright laws. That is, without seeking and obtaining the needed permissions, most libraries will be unable to web-publish documents originally published and currently owned by other entities.

Fair use protections, however, will allow sport librarians to amass considerable collections of digital documents and websites for use on local networks, or intranets. Because sports organizations and media companies are so intent on propagandizing, branding, and marketing, a vast array of information will be available at no cost. Thus, one irony of future sport collections is that while the Internet will provide a bonanza of information resources that can be used to build wonderful collections at little cost, the Internet, because of legal considerations, will not provide an avenue for broad public dissemination. Rather, these digital collections will be accessible only to local users.

The distinguishing characteristics of sport will play a role in determining what types of documents and websites are collected. For example, one of the most salient characteristics of sport is the phenomenon of spectators and fandom. On the Internet, fandom has found new forms of participation and expression through discussion boards, as well as blogs, opinion pieces, and straightforward news stories that invite comments. All of these are information-rich resources for historians and other scholars who wish to analyze fan behavior. It is not hard to imagine the preservation of these websites, or specific threads, being carried out by librarians building a digital sport history collection.

LIBRARIAN AS FACILITATOR

Because no single library can build a completely comprehensive collection, librarians traditionally have served as guides to outside collections and resources. As librarians seek to define their role in a changing information landscape, many observers inside and outside the profession have suggested that librarians can be valuable as guides to the digital wilderness. Some have gone a step further, calling on librarians to use emerging community-building tools to take the lead in bringing together online communities with shared intellectual interests. This scenario will require collaboration between librarians and academics in various subject areas. The ACRL Research Planning and Review Committee predicts, "Increased collaboration will expand the role of the library within the institution and beyond . . . Libraries will continue to lead efforts to develop scholarly communication and intellectual property services."[24] Godin expresses the same idea more colorfully, calling on librarians to act as "producer, concierge, connector, teacher and impresario."[25]

This activist model already is in place in many libraries, and chances are it will become more prevalent. Librarians have an interest in and aptitude for information systems. They have a higher level of knowledge of such systems than most others in the academic community simply by virtue of their daily work experience. The model is consistent with librarians' service orientation and their mostly unspoken, but ardently held belief that they know more about where information is buried than other people do. Frankly, they relish their potential role as expert guides.

It is telling that in the process of successfully bidding for and subsequently organizing the new Mark H. McCormack Collection, the Special Collections Department at the University of Massachusetts has articulated a vision of the collection as a dynamic teaching and research tool. The staff will proactively interpret and highlight the archive. Through liaison with academic departments and the judicious digitization of materials, the Special Collections staff will actively seek to integrate materials from the collection into the curriculums of several departments across campus including sport management, communications, economics, sociology, and women's studies.[26]

FROM VISION TO REALITY

The ACRL Research Planning and Review Committee, in 2010 and 2012, published reports on the most important trends in academic libraries. The reports were based on e-mail surveys completed by thousands of librarians, discussions with library leaders, and a literature review. The responses and resulting analyses reveal a profession scrambling to keep pace with the disruption of not only libraries but higher education generally. Yet, despite the discomfort caused by rapid change, what emerges from the ACRL reports and works of other analysts is a coherent vision of the present and near-future state of libraries.

This vision holds that digital information will displace paper-based publications. Acquisitions practices will place greater authority in the hands of users. Private companies will continue to erode what was once a library monopoly on information aggregation, storage, and access. Information sources will increase in number and complexity. Libraries will collect and organize digital resources. The retrospective digitization of specialized collections will grow in importance. Libraries will continue as physical places, but their space will be used less for book storage and more for cultural activities. And, librarians will assume a role as facilitators of scholarly communication, collaborating with scholars and connecting researchers with each other and information sources.

Much of this vision is reflected in current work of librarians working with sport collections. The British Library website, for example, in conjunction with the London 2012 Olympic Games, launched a project providing information on the London Olympic and Paralympics "through the lens of social science." Its purpose was to support "researchers by opening up and enabling access to our content and resources." As the British Library explained it, "Our aim is to inspire research, promote collaboration and knowledge exchange, and support capacity building among the current and next generation of researchers. This site takes the Olympic and Paralympic Games as a platform upon which to introduce the wide range of materials held at the British Library which can support research into the social aspects of sport."[27]

The site provides access to articles written by British Library staff, full-text works on Olympic topics licensed to the library by commercial publishers, and links to full-text documents off-site. It includes a blog and Twitter feed, as well as an appeal to publishers to contribute to the British Library: "Calling all publishers! We need your London 2012 publications—printed and electronic—for the researchers of the future."[28]

Several established sport libraries and information centers also have created online portals designed to facilitate scholarly communication and connect users to sport history resources. Examples include the Australian National Sport Information Centre, the Stark Center's Scholarly Sports Sites, the IOC's Olympic Studies Centre's web pages, and Olympic Studies Centre at the Autonomous University of Barcelona. Similarly, a close collaboration between librarians, archivists, and sport historians exists at the Stark Center in Texas, and will grow at the University of Massachusetts as the McCormack Collection becomes better known.

The Olympic Studies Centre in Lausanne, the Australian Institute of Sport, and the Barcelona center provide access to growing collections of born-digital documents. The German-based SPONET provides free full-text access to articles on sport training science, which one day will be valuable to students of sport science history. The USGA and LA84 Foundation are carrying forward their paper-to-digital conversion projects.

Sport libraries continue to exist as physical places. Most of them combine their bibliographic activities with cultural events such as lectures and exhibitions either in their libraries or in immediately adjacent spaces.

Clearly then, librarians working in sport history are following a path that is well within the mainstream of library transformation in the digital era. For sport librarians this transition has been expedited by the public's intense interest in sport, the ready availability of specialized paper-based collections with the potential for digital conversion, the sport's industry own early and enthusiastic adoption of technology, and a wealth of free digital sport information. The development of digital sport history resources and ancillary services in libraries is so well underway that, to paraphrase Lancaster, it is difficult to see what might occur that would permanently reverse the trends.

Notes

Portions of this essay have been updated and expanded from my presentation, "The Next Decade: Will the Internet Kill Sport Libraries?" Keynote Address, 12th International Association for Sport Information World Congress, Beijing. May 2005.

1. Bell, "The Bookless Future."
2. Dana, *Libraries, Addresses and Essays*, 150.
3. Bush, "As We May Think."
4. Lancaster, "The Paperless Society Revisited," 554.
5. Bell and Gray, *The Revolution Yet to Happen*, 2.
6. Sapp, A *Brief History of the Future of Libraries*, v.
7. Ibid., vi.
8. Godin, "Future of the Library."
9. Wilson, "A Preview of the Mark H. McCormack Collection," 603.
10. Jan Todd, Co-Director of Stark Center, telephone conversation with author, September 7, 2012.
11. Rusbridge, "Towards the Hybrid Library."
12. Godin, "Future of the Library" (emphasis in the original).

13. Markoff, "If Medium is the Message."
14. Zakon, "Hobbes' Internet."
15. Moragas, *Internet and the Olympic Movement*.
16. Coubertin et al., *Olympic Games*, 104; Cook, *The Fourth Olympiad*, 12; Bergvall, ed., *The Fifth Olympiad*, 242; Xth Olympiade Committee of the Games of Los Angeles, *Games*, 156.
17. Lynch, "Special Collections," 4.
18. Fine, "Team Sports," 299.
19. ACRL Research Planning and Review Committee, "2012 Top Ten."
20. Wilson, "A Preview of the Mark H. McCormack Collection," 601.
21. Jan Todd, Co-Director of Stark Center, telephone conversation with author, September 7, 2012.
22. USGA, "Mission."
23. ACRL Research Planning and Review Committee, "2010 Top Ten."
24. Ibid.
25. Godin, "Future of the Library."
26. Wilson, "A Preview of the Mark H. McCormack Collection," 602.
27. British Library, "Sport & Society."
28. Ibid.

References

Association of College and Research Libraries Research Planning and Review Committee. "2010 Top Ten Trends in Academic Libraries: A Review of the Current Literature." Accessed August 18, 2012. http://crln.acrl.org/content/71/6/286.short.

———. "2012 Top Ten Trends in Academic Libraries: A Review of the Trends and Issues Affecting Academic Libraries in Higher Education." Accessed August 18, 2012. http://crln.acrl.org/content/73/6/311.full.

Bell, David A. 2005. "The Bookless Future: What the Internet is Doing to Scholarship." *New Republic*, May 2 & 9. Accessed August 12, 2011. http://www.tnr.com/article/books-and-arts/the-bookless-future#.

Bell, Gordon, and Jim Gray. 1997. *The Revolution Yet to Happen, Technical Report MSR-TR-98–44*. Redmond: Microsoft, March. Accessed September 1, 2012. http://research.microsoft.com/~gray/Revolution.doc.

Bergvall, Erik, ed. 1913. *The Fifth Olympiad: The Official Report of the Olympic Games of Stockholm, 1912*. Translated by Edward Adams-Ray. Stockholm: Wahlström & Widstrand.

British Library. "Sport & Society: The Summer Olympics and Paralympics through the Lens of Social Science." Accessed August 1, 2012. http://www.bl.uk/sportandsociety/index.html.

Bush, Vannevar. 1945. "As We May Think." *Atlantic Monthly*, July. Accessed August 12, 2012. http://www.theatlantic.com/doc/194507/bush.

Cook, Theodore Andrea. 1909. *The Fourth Olympiad: Being the Official Report of the Olympic Games of 1908 Celebrated in London under the Patronage of His Most Gracious Majesty King Edward VII and by the Sanction of the International Olympic Committee.* London: British Olympic Association.

Coubertin, Pierre de, et al. 1897. *The Olympic Games, Second Part B. C. 776. - A. D. 1896. Second Part, The Olympic Games in 1896.* Athens: Charles Beck.

Dana, John Cotton. 1916. *Libraries, Addresses and Essays.* White Plains, NY: H.W. Wilson. Accessed August 18, 2012. http://archive.org/stream/librariesaddress005731mbp#page/n7/mode/2up.

Fine, Gary Alan. 1985. "Team Sports, Seasonal Histories, Significant Events: Little League Baseball and the Creation of Collective Meaning." *Sociology of Sport Journal* 2, no. 4: 299–313.

Frey, Thomas. "The Future of Libraries Beginning the Great Transformation." DaVinci Institute. Accessed August 18, 2012. http://www.davinciinstitute.com/papers/the-future-of-libraries/.

Godin, Seth. "The Future of the Library." Accessed August 18, 2012. http://sethgodin.typepad.com/seths_blog/2011/05/the-future-of-the-library.html.

Lancaster, F. W. 1978. *Toward Paperless Information Systems.* London: Academic Press.

———. 1985. "The Paperless Society Revisited." *American Libraries* 16 (September): 553–55.

Lynch, Clifford A. 2009. "Special Collections at the Cusp of the Digital Age: A Credo." *Research Library Issues* 267 (December): 3–8. Accessed September 1, 2012. http://publications.arl.org/prvp3/4.

Markoff, John. 1995. "If Medium is the Message, the Message is the Web." *New York Times,* November 20.

Moragas, Miquel de. 2001. *Internet and the Olympic Movement.* Barcelona: Centre d'Estudis Olimpics I de l'Esport. Accessed September 3, 2012. http://olympicstudies.uab.es/pdf/OD012_eng.pdf.

Rusbridge, Chris. 1998. "Towards the Hybrid Library." *D-Lib Magazine,* July/August. Accessed August 18, 2012. http://www.dlib.org/dlib/july98/rusbridge/07rusbridge.html.

Sapp, Gary. 2002. *A Brief History of the Future of Libraries: An Annotated Bibliography.* Lanham: Scarecrow.

Xth Olympiade Committee of the Games of Los Angeles. 1933. *The Games of the Xth Olympiade, Los Angeles, 1932 Official Report.* Los Angeles: Xth Olympiade Committee.

United States Golf Association. "Mission of the USGA Museum." Accessed August 31, 2012. http://www.usgamuseum.com/about_museum/mission_statement/.

Wilson, Wayne. 2012. "A Preview of the Mark H. McCormack Collection." *Journal of Historical Research in Marketing* 4, no. 4: 599–603.

Zakon, Robert. "Hobbes' Internet Timeline 10.2." Accessed September 8, 2012. http://www.zakon.org/robert/internet/timeline/.

2

Sport History and Digital Archives in Practice

MARTIN JOHNES AND BOB NICHOLSON

The nature of historical research is changing and changing fast.[1] Sources as varied as government minutes and medieval manuscripts are being digitized and made available online at a rate that makes it difficult for scholars to keep up with what is happening, even within their own specialized fields. Slowly, but steadily, it is becoming possible to conduct primary historical research from the comfort of one's own desk. Expensive and hurried trips to archives and libraries are no longer quite so necessary. Keyword searches make it possible to locate information instantly. The archival experience, of long hours far from home trawling through dusty papers, is becoming less common.[2] Digitization has thus been recognized as a practical revolution: it has made research faster, easier, and more convenient. Traditional research still takes place, of course, but some younger (and not so young) scholars are now choosing research projects specifically because they are possible through digital research.[3]

Not all are quite so welcoming of this revolution and there are acknowledged pitfalls and drawbacks. Much digitization has been undertaken by private companies, and subscriptions are often very expensive and beyond the means of smaller universities, let alone scholars not affiliated with a university. Some researchers have thus expressed concerns about access to commercial archives and the ownership and selection of their contents.[4] There are intellectual problems, too. Leary has warned of an overreliance on online archives and the dangers of an "offline penumbra"; an "increasingly remote and unvisited shadowland into which even quite important texts fall if they cannot yet be explored [or identified] by . . . electronic means."[5] Moreover, researchers can be not just tempted into relying on those newspapers that have been digitized but into conflating their content with the press as a whole. The accuracy of optical character recognition (OCR) has also attracted much criticism, a significant problem given that the keyword searching that is at the heart of digital research relies on this software. Commentators have further warned of the dangers of what might be termed "keyword blinkers"—arriving directly at a source and bypassing its wider context.[6] Finally, a growing number of historians have raised concerns about the relationships between digitization and the materiality of sources.[7] Digital archives are incapable of capturing the weight and texture of a newspaper page, while covers and other ephemera associated with the original text are often jettisoned. Digital newspaper archives have typically been created from microfilmed copies of bound volumes rather than original single issues.[8] By the time we access them, many digital newspapers have been remediated three times (single issue > bound volume > microfilm > digitization); each step serves to distance us from the original text. Thus, when a newspaper is digitized, it is fundamentally changed. It is sensible, therefore, to ask what is lost in the process. But it is equally essential, and potentially far more rewarding, to ask the opposite question—to unpack the new, methodological opportunities created by the digitization process and to explore what they mean for academic research.

Discussions of digitization have tended to downplay the agency of researchers. They often end up considering what digitization is *doing to* historical research, as if it were an uncontrollable force. To borrow from the nomenclature of digital publishing, this perspective has placed agency almost entirely with content providers rather than end users. For much of the last ten years, debates on digitization have primarily been driven by librarians, digital publishers, and a small community of digital humanists whose pioneering work has only recently begun to substantively engage the mainstream profession. As a result, the methodological implications of digital archives—their ability to extend the boundaries of research and answer questions that were previously unanswerable—have remained frustratingly absent from the debate.

Digital archives have the potential to fundamentally alter the kind of research that we are able to do. Used creatively, they allow us to access and explore past cultures and societies in powerful new ways; to ask new questions, make new connections, construct new arguments, explore new topics, and re-examine old ones from new perspectives. They allow us to imagine new kinds of research. This chapter explores both the more conventional and more innovative possibilities of digital research within the field of British sport history. It acknowledges the practical and intellectual problems that accompany the possibilities, but it argues that, if designed and employed well, digital archives have the potential to transform the practice of history.

Locating Information

Newspapers are the staple source in the methodology of sport history. Yet searching them has always been a long and painstaking process. Once sport was well established in the late nineteenth century, historians could at least rely on the knowledge that there would be some sports coverage in almost any issue of a local paper. However, using the press to track any specific theme or to study the emergence of organized sport was far more difficult because references were usually limited and scattered. In the absence of indexes, it was a matter of searching for the proverbial needle in a haystack. For those willing and able to put in the time and effort, it was a rewarding experience. Yet few, beyond doctoral students, had that luxury.[9]

The mechanics of historical newspaper research have now changed. Thousands of English-language newspapers, magazines, and periodicals are now available online and the number is growing. Major titles, such as the *Illustrated London News,* the *Scotsman,* the *Financial Times,* and the *Economist,* are all available in individual databases. However, these projects have been dwarfed by the emergence of multi-title databases such as Gale's *19th Century British Library Newspapers* (71 titles), *19th Century UK Periodicals* (180), *19th Century U.S. Newspapers* (500), and *17th and 18th Century Burney Collection* (1,271); ProQuest's *Historical Newspapers* (36) and *British Periodicals* (460); and noncommercial projects such as *Chronicling America* (686), *Nineteenth-Century Serials Edition* (6), New Zealand's *Papers Past* (70), and Australia's *Trove* (255). This extraordinary growth shows little sign of slowing down. At the time of this writing, the *British Newspaper Archive* holds more than 180 titles and is expanding at a rate of 8,000 pages per day, while Gale's recently launched *Nineteenth-Century Collections Online* will play host to a growing number of more focused collections. When combined with other online archives such as *Project Gutenberg, Eighteenth-Century Collections Online,* the *John Johnson Collection,* the *Database of Mid-Victorian Illustration, Google Books,* and the *Internet Archive,* this adds up to a significant amount of print culture—all available online, all searchable by keyword. Historians have never had such a wealth of information at their fingertips.

Yet, employing these resources is not straightforward and the revolution is not as complete as it might first seem. Copyright concerns have limited the digitization of twentieth-century newspapers and periodicals. Major UK papers such as *The Times,* the *Illustrated London News,* the *Daily Mirror,* and the *Daily Express* are all available post-1900, as are most of the titles included in ProQuest's *Historical Newspapers* database. However, these publications add up to a mere fraction of the total available to historians of earlier periods.

Whereas the *British Newspaper Archive* now provides access to a small number of provincial newspapers that span the late nineteenth and early twentieth centuries, the majority of multi-title databases end their coverage in 1900. Digital archives of seventeenth- and eighteenth-century print culture, meanwhile, have been marred by problems of quality rather than quantity. As James E. Tierney has argued, the inconsistency of the period's typography reduces the accuracy of scanning and OCR software, while an over reliance on materials accumulated by contemporary collectors has left large gaps in the archive.[10] The British Library's *Burney Collection*, for example, draws upon newspapers and pamphlets collected by the Reverend Charles Burney (1757–1817); while it appears to contain an impressive 1,271 titles, most of these are not available in complete runs.[11]

Limitations in OCR recognition are not just restricted to texts from the eighteenth century and earlier. Some nineteenth-century publications also suffer from poor quality print and typefaces that OCR software struggles with. Confusion between "s" and "f" is particularly common with publications from the early part of the century, but the problems extend far wider. A study of *19th Century British Library Newspapers* reported the following results:

- Character accuracy 83.6%
- Word accuracy 78%
- Significant word accuracy 68.4%
- Words with capital letter start accuracy 63.4%.[12]

Thus, keyword searches can easily miss the words being sought. These problems are compounded by the fact that some major archives are not as complete as they appear to be. *19th Century British Library Newspapers* initially appears to offer full, uninterrupted coverage for most of its seventy-one titles, but a closer examination of the archive reveals many hidden gaps. The *Wrexham Advertiser*, for example, appears to cover the period 1855–1900, but has year-long gaps in 1862, 1865, 1872, 1879, 1886, and 1889. These interruptions distort search results and, when not taken into account, can lead even the most careful of historians into making errors. For example, search results appear to suggest that the *Daily News* failed to report the death of Charles Dickens (its founding editor) in 1870, and that the sport-loving readers of *Lloyds's Weekly News* were not informed about the formation of the International Olympic Committee in 1894. In truth, these apparent oversights were not the result of peculiar editorial decisions but have been caused instead by small gaps in the database's holdings. The sheer volume of material presented to us by digital archives should not, in other words, be mistaken for completeness.

Even with archives that are complete and not blighted by OCR problems, a researcher is still at the mercy of the design of the search interface. In most newspaper archives, the search interface is only designed for one, very basic form of digital research: keyword searches that lead to close reading of the content of articles found. Yet even that process can be undermined by software that does not highlight keywords, something that leaves the reader scanning pages for the word in question. This is very frustrating when searching a large number of articles, let alone when the investigation is quantitative and very large sets of results are being examined.[13] With the exception of the recently launched *Nineteenth-Century Collections Online*, few of the interfaces of commercial archives have been designed with any kind of quantitative research in mind. The total number of hits that result from a search is normally given, but most digital newspaper archives still leave researchers manually counting how these are distributed across publications or decades.

Caveats aside, digitization still means that hundreds of thousands of pages can be searched for the name of a place, person, or sport in an instant. Suddenly it is possible to search for passing mentions that would otherwise be lost in the forest of newspaper pages, and the results can challenge orthodoxies. One such example is research conducted by fans of Wrexham FC on the date of their club's formation. The club had dated this to 1873, but searching for the word "football" in the now digitized local press has provided evidence that some form of club of the same name was in existence in 1864. That does not necessarily indicate a straightforward continuity, but the new press sources certainly show some of the people traditionally credited as forming the club in 1873 as being involved before this. The exact date of formation of the town's club might depend on how a club is defined, but it seems reasonable to suggest that the new digital research means that Wrexham can now claim to be Wales' oldest football club and the third oldest professional club in the world.[14] Of course, these press sources could have been found without digitization, but the fact remains that they were not. Nonetheless, establishing exactly what happened in Wrexham is complicated by the fact that the *Wrexham Advertiser* for 1865 is missing from the digital archive. There is nothing in the archive's guide to actually indicate this and the example also acts as a reminder of the hidden problems in relying too heavily on the digitized press.

Effective digital research depends on having effective keywords to search for. In the Wrexham example, the searching was relatively straightforward because "football" is an easy keyword to search for and the volume of hits could be limited by restricting the search to the local newspaper. Searching across the national picture is more difficult, especially when the actual name of the sport might also refer to other things. Searches for cricket and rugby, for example, produce places as well as the games. Locating the game of rugby is further complicated by the fact that it was often referred to as football. Even more distinctive names, such as hockey or snooker, can still bring many returns relating to people of that name. Of course, a manual search could be done of all the hits to distinguish between the relevant and the irrelevant, but when the sheer scale of some searches is considered, then it becomes clear why it is desirable to minimize the return of nonrelevant hits. For example, a search for billiards in the *19th Century British Library Newspapers* archive returns 84,920 articles containing that word, and this is with a distinctive keyword for a relatively unusual game. Searching for cricket gives 397,398 hits, a number that would take a doctorate to go through. Searching for people can be particularly problematic. Take the example of the Victorian archery champion extraordinaire, Horace Alfred Ford. Sometimes the press called him by his full name, and sometimes by one or both of his initials. Moreover, the *19th Century British Library Newspapers* database also returns hits for place names that end in "ford." The most common way of referring to him was H. A. Ford, but searching for that in the text of articles returns 695,938 hits because the search interface struggles when looking for initials. Combining keywords is another solution. Searching for "Ford AND archery" returns 8,793 hits. Searching for articles with archery in the title and Ford somewhere in the text narrows the results even further to 173 hits, nearly all of which are about the man in question. This might give the most relevant articles, but it also means passing mentions of him are missed, a shame because these are often the most useful because they might shed light on his non-sporting life and on his impact and profile outside sports tournaments.

The digital researcher thus has to accept that a full range of results will not arrive instantly and there is still a trawling of articles to undertake if the research is to step beyond the most directly relevant material. But, if he or she is willing to do that, then new avenues open up. For example, one clear advantage of using digital libraries to study the development of sport is that it takes us back beyond the conventional chronologies and thus focuses attention on the roots of games rather than just on their codification. The advantages of this can be seen by looking at hockey. The roots of the modern sport are normally attributed to the Blackheath club, which dates its formation to sometime in the 1840s before being reconstituted in 1861, while rules were drawn up at Eton College in 1868.[15] Yet a search of the press locates articles that demonstrate the breadth and roots of the game before the 1860s. A study of the scattered 735 pre-1860 hockey references from the *19th Century British Library Newspapers* collection indicates that, as well as being a surname, the term referred both to hitting a ball with sticks and hitting some form of disc while skating. Indeed, the first reference to hockey as a game appears to be in 1829 when the *Morning Post* reported that hundreds of mostly lower-class men and boys had been playing hockey on the frozen river Serpentine (in Hyde Park, London). Notably, however, it felt it had to point out what hockey was: "striking a bung with a knobbed stick."[16] In 1843, the *Jackson's Oxford Journal* noted the death of a student at Sandhurst military school after being accidentally hit by a stick during a game of hockey. An inquest noted that the game was "often played with much spirit at the college."[17] By 1863, five years before the Eton rules, the game was common enough for the first located advertisement for hockey sticks.[18] Such scattered and fragmented pieces of information, derived from a range of publications, would probably have been near-impossible to find without digitization. Their significance may not be revolutionary, but they clearly illustrate that the codification of rules was not the beginning of sport as either an organized, commercial, or popular pastime.

Searching thousands of articles is not just about taking known chronologies backwards; it can also be about understanding sport's development after codification. It can help avoid the impression that sports immediately cemented themselves after their formal establishment. Searching for terms allows us to plot the emergence and establishment of sports, teams, and events in popular culture. For example, the Football Association (FA), formed in 1863, is only mentioned twice in the seventy-one newspapers in the *19th Century British Library Newspapers* collection before 1866. It is not mentioned in *The Times* until 1869 and then only in the context of a letter complaining about the lack of standardized rules, the precise thing the FA was supposed to have brought about.[19] Coverage in *The Times* is a particularly important marker because the newspaper was central to the interests of the British establishment. What it thought worthy of mention meant something. Similarly, despite its first matches being held in 1871, it appears to be 1874 before the FA Cup is mentioned in *The Times*.[20] That article cannot be located through searching for "FA Cup" (that phrase does not appear in the newspaper until 1920). Instead, it turns up through a search for articles that contain both the words "cup" and "football." The article itself calls the competition the Association Challenge Cup and thus illustrates the importance of experimenting with keywords by trying different alternatives and combinations.

Not being restrictive in the use of keywords and the reading of the returns also allows scholars to see how individual sports, people, and events sat within a wider cultural discourse. It means the development and discussion of ideas can be traced and that the press can be used as a living dictionary, accessing the minutiae of everyday cultural discourse and tracking the complex way in which words and phrases circulated, looking at how their meanings evolved and how their usage changed. In particular, the digitized press can be used to see how sport became so engrained in British culture that its terminology became accepted as metaphors in other contexts.

One example of this can be seen by searching *The Times* for the phrase "hit for six," a term originating in cricket but which spread into daily usage as a metaphor for vanquishing or demolishing an idea or opponent. The phrase is first used in *The Times* in 1856, but it was 1943 before it was used in a context different from cricket—as a description of a demonstration of tank firepower in 1943, raising the possibility that war might have encouraged the use of sporting analogies in different contexts. A year later saw the phrase used within a crossword clue, another sign that cricket needed little explanation.[21] By 1953, the newspaper was even discussing how the phrase had extended beyond sport, and in 1957 it was first used in describing play in a different sport.[22] The growing postwar diffusion of the term in wider language is confirmed through seven of its 27 occurrences in *The Times* in the 1960s not being related to cricket. The suggestion that the diffusion of the term into everyday language only happened long after its use in cricket is confirmed by a search of nineteenth-century newspapers and periodicals, which reveals more than 200 hits for the phrase but none from a non-cricket context. Further evidence of a mid-twentieth-century adoption of the term in non-sporting contexts comes from a search of the online version of Hansard (the record of what is said in the British Parliament). This reveals that the phrase "hit for six" was first used in Parliament in 1948, although in an explicit cricket analogy.[23] However, the limitations of keywords again restrict the utility of this avenue of research. Uses of the analogy might not use the exact phrase, meaning it does not show up by keyword searching. Indeed, the earliest use of the phrase noted by the *Oxford English Dictionary* is in 1937 when the *Times Literary Supplement* referred to someone "chiefly concerned to hit swots and cads and foreigners for six." Yet no historical record is ever complete, and the problems here are no different than dealing with the fragmented traces that any historical phenomenon leaves behind. Digitized sources give no more complete picture of the past than conventional archives, but they do make locating and interrogating that past easier.

That is also clear when it is considered how digitization can make expanding the range of sources that sport historians employ more practical. Sport historians have relied heavily on newspaper sources because they know they will find something there to make the hours of trawling worthwhile. There are plenty of other historical archives that also contain sporting information, but locating their very occasional relevance is always difficult when there is no means of electronically searching their content (rather than titles and descriptions).

One illustration of this is court records. Few legal records directly center on sport, but sport is there in the background, mentioned in passing by witnesses and other participants. Searching for these passing mentions in the few legal records that are fully digitized allows the historian to get a glimpse of the place of sport in popular culture.[24] The first nineteenth-century mention of football in the *Proceedings of the Old Bailey* (London's central criminal court) comes in 1878 in an account of a drunken clerk talking about football to another clerk who he did not know. This might be a trivial incident, but there is very little other evidence to show that in the late 1870s football had become a topic of conversation between strangers.[25] By 1887, the game was well known enough that a witness could even compare the shoving of a crowd to a game of football to illustrate his point about the nature of physical contact.[26] The court cases throw up other interesting illustrations of the place of sport in people's lives. One clerk in 1901 did not investigate the gunshot he heard because he was too interested in an account of a football match he was reading.[27] Other details emerge about people going to games after work and the pub after games, kicking balls about in the street, placing bets, or just talking with other people about sport. No digital source is required to locate these incidental details, but court records, where sport arises only rarely, were not used by British sport historians prior to digitization. The results may not change our understanding of sport, but diversifying the type of sources used can offer a vivid glimpse of how ingrained sport became in ordinary life, and one that would probably not be noticed if it were not for the ease of digital sources.

Perhaps most exciting is how digital resources can open up new possibilities in transnational and global history. It is now possible for researchers around the world to consult major archives in Britain, the United States, Canada, Australia, South Africa, New Zealand, and India without so much as leaving their desk. As Adrian Bingham has noted, access to these archives "makes it much easier to compare the journalism of different countries, and to trace flows of ideas and information across national boundaries."[28] Bob Nicholson, for example, has recently combined a range of national archives to trace the circulation of an individual joke around the English-speaking world, while Patrick Leary has drawn upon similar databases to explore the transatlantic exchange of gossip.[29] There is much research still to be done on the transnational development of particular sports, and comparative studies of national sporting cultures will bring valuable new perspectives to a field that still operates primarily within the boundaries of the nation-state. In particular, tracking the transnational movements of individual people, texts, practices, and ideas reveals just how interconnected different national sporting cultures had become by the late nineteenth century.

Take the case of John L. Sullivan, an American fighter who became the first heavyweight champion of gloved boxing. By combining British and American newspaper databases, it is possible to track his movements, first as he undertook a coast-to-coast fighting tour of the United States in 1883 and 1884, and second as he embarked upon a high-profile trip across the Atlantic. By the time he visited Britain in 1887, coverage of his exploits clipped by British papers from the American press had already made him a celebrity and huge crowds gathered at the country's railway stations to catch a glimpse of the famous Boston Strong Boy.[30] Although Sullivan's European trip is a well-known episode in boxing history, keyword searches of British and American archives reveal new insights into how the transnational dimensions of his reputation were shaped by the forces of international journalism.

Culturomics

The examples above have centered on finding specific pieces of information within digital archives, but the biggest and more innovative possibilities are not what can come from a close reading of specific sources but from taking a much wider, bigger, and more quantitative approach, from what a team of Harvard scientists has recently dubbed "'culturomics."[31] This is a development of what social scientists call content analysis and, at its simplest, involves counting the number of hits for certain keywords. While it is important to recognize the limitations of such an approach—it does not, after all, reveal the meaning of the texts it counts—it provides a useful way to visualize broad cultural trends and identify areas for closer exploration. In their study, the Harvard team text-mined a corpus of 5 million digitized books and quantified the evolution of grammar, the speed at which society forgets its past, the adoption of new technologies, the effects of censorship, and the changing nature of fame.[32] In a similar study, Dan Cohen and Fred Gibbs text-mined millions of titles of nineteenth-century books to explore changes in the Victorian frame of mind, plotting the numbers of books with certain words in their titles to demonstrate shifts in attitudes toward religion and the like.[33]

Within sport history, the potential of this might be as simple of counting the number of times a sport is mentioned within a specific newspaper. Thus, the technique discussed above, of measuring the diffusion and establishment of sport by the first mentions of its primary competition and governing body in a major newspaper, can be supplemented by plotting the mentions of a sport over time to produce a visualization of that sport's growth. Unfortunately, because most digital newspapers' search facilities have not been designed with culturomics in mind, Figure 2.1 had to be constructed by manually counting the number of hits for each year.

Apart from the laborious process of assembling it, such quantitative information is limited by two key factors. The first is that it depends on the quality of the OCR process (and thus the original print). If the numbers of hits being plotted are low, then particular caution needs to be exercised in their interpretation because just a few incorrect articles will skew the results. This is especially likely with short keywords that could easily resemble another word on the printed page. A vivid illustration of this is that just three of the forty hits for a search of the word "golf" in *The Times* during 1860 are actually correct. The OCR mostly returns hits for "gulf" but it also confuses "golf" with "off", "self", and even "solicitor". Such errors matter less when the hits are in the thousands, but even with larger numbers it is important to remember that what is being produced is a trend rather than a precise measurement.

The second limitation is, of course, the reliability of the keyword used in the first place. During the nineteenth century, football referred to both association football and rugby, and thus Figure 2.1 actually plots the growth of

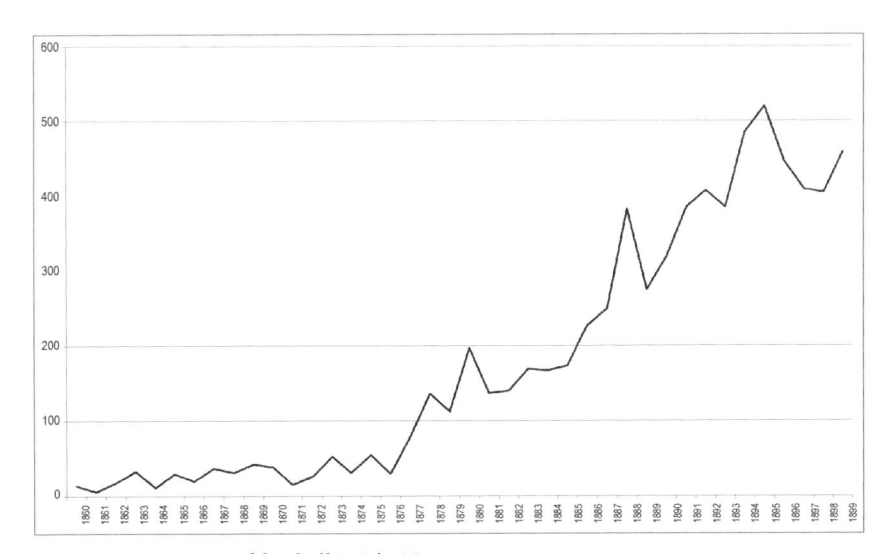

Figure 2.1: Mentions of football in *The Times*, 1860–1899.

two different sports (or three from 1895 after rugby itself divided). The graph might also be missing results if the topic was discussed by a journalist without using the keyword. It is, after all, quite possible to write a match report without using the word football once, especially once the sport was established enough that readers would know what the report referred to. Some words can also appear in slightly different ways. Early nineteenth-century newspapers, for example, sometimes spoke of "foot-ball" rather than "football." In this case, some search interfaces locate the articles but others do not. The key issue again is to make not too grand a claim, nor to read too uncritically the quantitative results; they are trends, not absolutes. As with fragmented qualitative sources, their analysis needs to be discussed in cautious, careful terms.

The utility of the above example is also limited by the fact that it relies on one newspaper. Its suggestion of when football became established could be different from the impression given by a local newspaper. The task could be replicated for a local newspaper to give a more bottom-up view, but the real potential of culturomics lies in using the scale of digitized sources and in plotting sports across a multitude of different newspapers. Achieving this is complicated by the fact that, as the nineteenth century progressed, there were more newspapers published. This means there are more digitized titles for the later end of the period. Inevitably, the result is that if the number of hits is plotted for nearly any search of a multi-title digital newspaper archive it will show an upward trend. This problem can be avoided by identifying the total number of articles published in a particular period and using this data to normalize results by calculating the percentage of articles from a period containing the keyword.[34]

For example, rather than claim that eighty-seven articles in a sample of thirty-eight newspapers from 1860 featured the word "football," we might argue that 0.06643 percent of articles published in the sample newspapers that year contain the word. This percentage can then be tracked over time without worrying about the changing size of the archive. Using an effective normalized study of hits from a multitude of newspapers, however, can also mean not using every newspaper available. Large gaps in the run of a particular title can throw off the overall result, especially if that newspaper produced more than average hits for the years in which it *is* available.[35]

The different results that can be derived from looking at a single newspaper and a collection of titles is evident in the following two graphs (Figures 2.2 and 2.3), which show normalized results for a sample of thirty-eight local

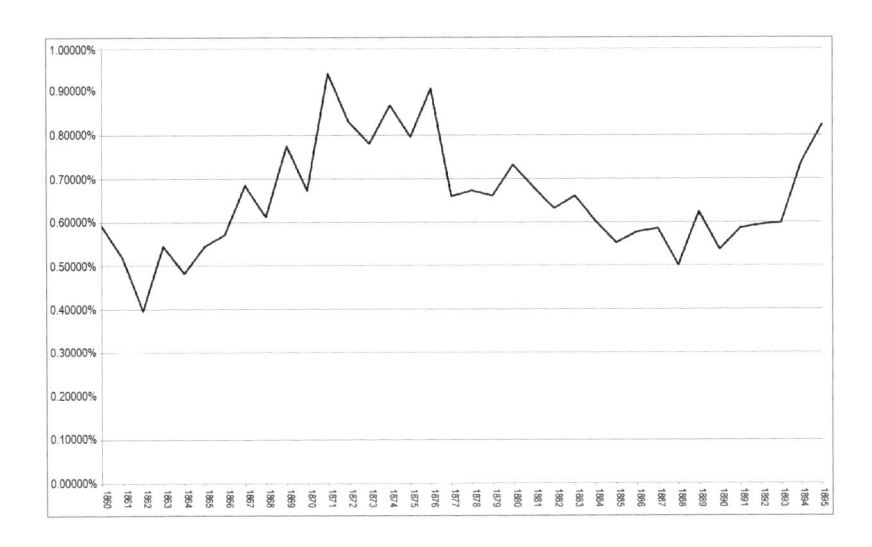

Figure 2.2: Percentage of articles in a sample of thirty-eight local newspapers mentioning *regatta*, 1860–1895.

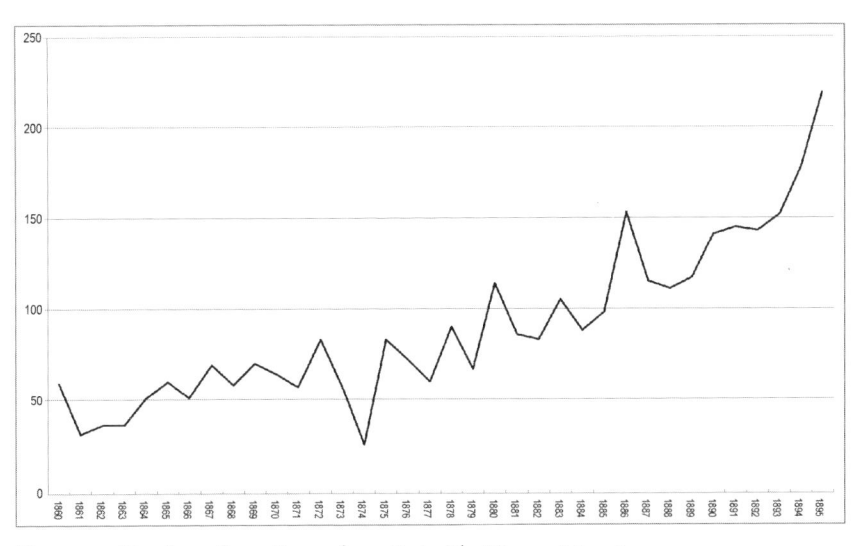

Figure 2.3: Number of mentions of *regatta* in *The Times*, 1860–1895.

newspapers (chosen for the fact that they contain few gaps in the period in question) and a simple count of the number of hits from *The Times*. The trends are clearly quite different. The first graph (Figure 2.2) reminds us of the danger of assuming that the sporting revolution of the late nineteenth century represented a straightforward growth in sport. Sailing regattas may have been getting more coverage from the establishment's newspaper (*The Times*), but localized newspapers appear to be more continuous in their coverage, suggesting a rather different picture. What these graphs again illustrate is how culturomics alone cannot explain anything.

Such techniques can also be applied to the content of Google Books using a piece of software known as Ngram Viewer. This measures the frequency with which words appear in the Google Books archive and plots the normalized frequency against the dates of publication.[36] Whereas the tool does not search the entire archive, it does cover over 5.2 million books. Although the ability to manipulate the parameters of searching is limited, Ngram Viewer offers a quick and easy way of looking for patterns in publishing. What takes hours on digital newspaper archives can take seconds with Ngrams. Moreover, the tool has been specifically designed for plotting trends. Thus, whereas newspaper archive searches can struggle to take into account capitalizations and punctuation, Ngram Viewer searches for the exact phrase or word entered. The results may not be definitive, but they can help confirm and visualize existing arguments through quantitative means. They can also be used to set out and test hypotheses.

Ngrams can thus be used to illustrate trends in the changing popularities of sport. For example, the fashion for archery at the turn of the nineteenth century, and then subsequently in the late 1830s and 1840s, is clearly evident in the results (Figure 2.4). So, too, is the growing popularity of first croquet, which undermined archery, and then tennis, which in turn undermined croquet. The Ngram does not, however, neatly illustrate the idea, which contemporaries noted, that croquet replaced archery as the sport of fashion around 1870, presumably because archery's military use meant it was still

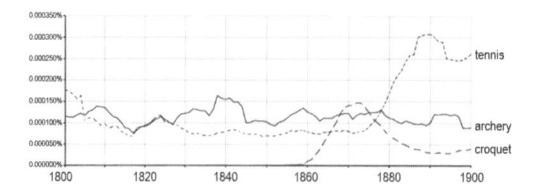

Figure 2.4: Ngram of mentions of archery, tennis, and croquet in nineteenth-century British books digitized in the Google Books collection.

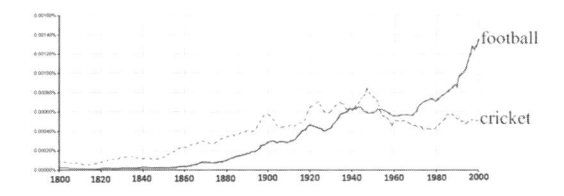

Figure 2.5: Ngram of mentions of football and cricket in nineteenth- and twentieth-century British books digitized in the Google Books collection.

being discussed in print culture. But the results do suggest that croquet itself suffered from the rise of tennis, another point noted by contemporaries.

The power and limitations of Ngrams to illustrate trends is further evident when football and cricket are plotted against each other. Figure 2.5 by itself does not explain what is happening and cannot be interpreted literally. Cricket was not more popular than football in the late nineteenth and early twentieth centuries, but rather its more middle-class base gave it a stronger place in book culture. This is evident by comparing the Ngram with the normalized results of thirty-eight local newspapers. Figure 2.6 has football catching up with cricket's place in print culture in the 1880s, the decade that historians have always seen as the key period when football's popularity really took off.

Such problems do not mean the Ngram is useless. It is still a powerful visualization of the place of the two sports in book culture. Indeed, its trend

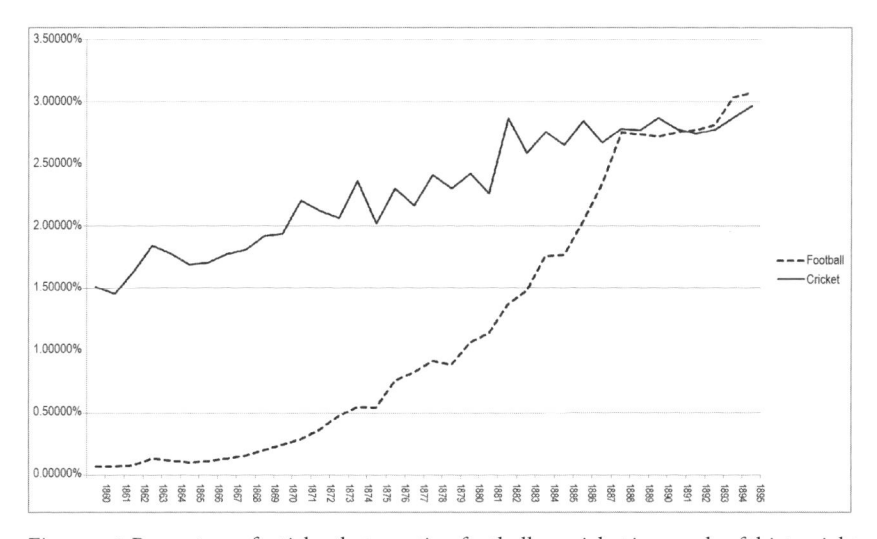

Figure 2.6: Percentage of articles that mention football or cricket in sample of thirty-eight local newspapers.

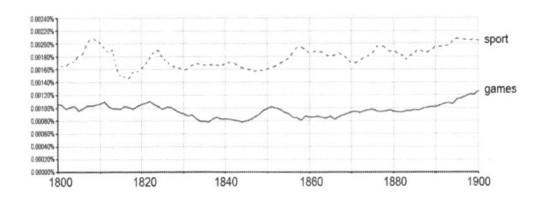

Figure 2.7: Ngram of mentions of sport and games in nineteenth-century British books digitized in the Google Books collection.

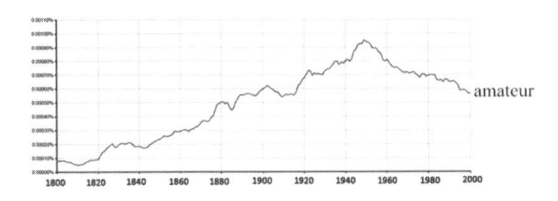

Figure 2.8: Ngram of mentions of amateur in nineteenth- and twentieth-century British books digitized in the Google Books collection.

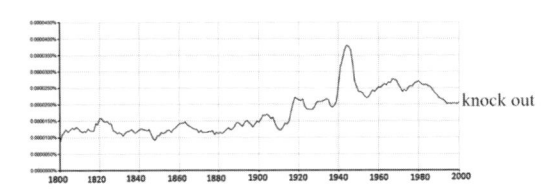

Figure 2.9: Ngram of mentions of knock out in nineteenth- and twentieth-century British books digitized in the Google Books collection.

can also be explained. In the 1950s, football gained in respectability with the middle classes, and contemporaries noted it was overtaking cricket in the middle-class's affection. The Ngram might not pinpoint the exact date, but it does confirm that broad trend at that approximate time.

The real potential of Ngrams lies not in searching for individual sports but ideas. Here they can be used to play around with hypotheses and to remind us of the danger of relying on assumptions. For example, although the late nineteenth century is thought of as a time of sporting revolution, the concept of sport and games is actually far more continuous (Figure 2.7). The late nineteenth century saw not a revolution in sport, per se, but in how sport was organized. The concept of amateurism also looks rather different to our assumptions when plotted over time (Figure 2.8). Rather than being a late nineteenth-century sport obsession, it actually appears to have become more discussed in the 1950s, a decade when the modernization of the UK and the legacy of old ways of doing things became significant public concerns. In contrast, the hypothesis discussed earlier that it was war that saw sport-

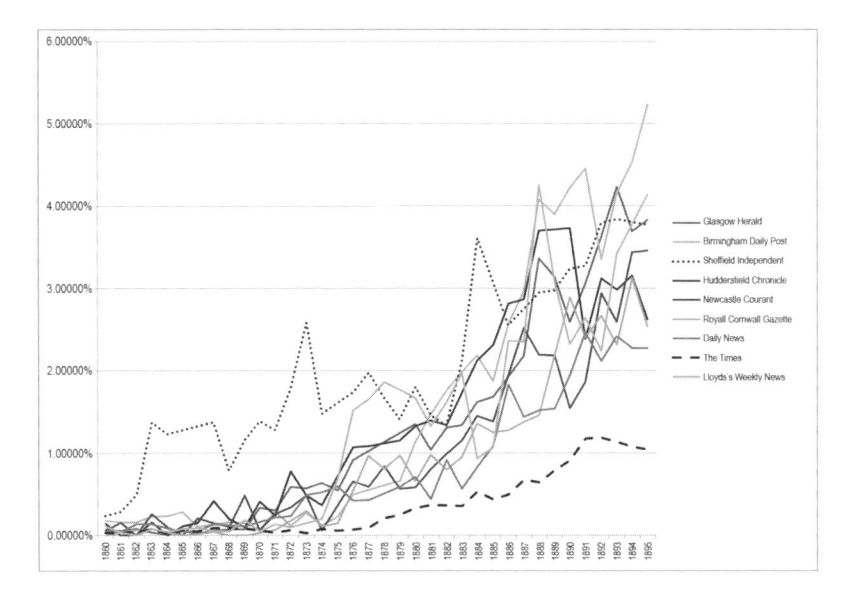

Figure 2.10: Percentage of articles that mention football in different newspapers, 1860–1895.

ing analogies enter the English language is vividly supported by a search for "knock out" in the twentieth century (Figure 2.9).

Culturomics also offers new opportunities for transnational and regional comparisons. The majority of titles available in the *British Library Newspaper Archive* are drawn from the provincial press, and these texts can be used to explore the similarities and differences between regional sporting cultures. Figure 2.10 shows the percentage of articles mentioning football in nine British newspapers. Several features of the graph are worth noting. First, it appears that the *Sheffield Independent* began to devote serious coverage to the sport some fifteen years before the other papers in the sample, which is significant because of debates about the role of that city in the development of a national football culture. Second, coverage of the sport in the majority of the other papers increased in similar patterns. Finally, while *The Times* devoted some coverage to football from the late 1870s onward, its cautious enthusiasm for the sport contrasts with the stratospheric trajectories exhibited by the graphs of populist and provincial papers. These results represent a crude early foray into a new form of quantitative cultural history, and a greater range of papers needs to be consulted to establish clear regional patterns. However, the potential of culturomics to map the social and cultural geography of nineteenth-century sport is clear.

Conclusion

In parts of rural England there is a sport known as shin-kicking. It dates back to at least the seventeenth century, but if it was still around in the late nineteenth century then it is not easy to locate. There is seemingly just one mention of it as a deliberate pursuit in all seventy-one newspapers in the *19th Century British Library Newspapers*. An article in the *Preston Guardian* spoke of a "new scientific and interesting pastime," which involved groups of young men finding a spot near but out of sight of an approaching policeman and then kicking a chosen one of their group until they all had to beat a retreat from the patrolling officer of the law. When he had passed by, the kicking resumed with another victim taking his turn. The "hazard and real spirit of the game" was avoiding being caught by the police. Anyone caught was considered a duffer and had to withstand the jeers of his friends. The reporter concluded that if fox hunters risked breaking their necks in their sport, then "why shouldn't hobbledehoys have their shins broken in innocent recreation?"[37]

This one source sums up many of the problems of digitized archives, problems sometimes forgotten as researchers rush to plunder what they can find from their desks. Understanding why men played this game is impossible without an understanding of the importance of physical toughness in working-class masculinity, of the ambivalence that could exist toward the police, and of the relatively slight punishment likely to be imposed on anyone caught. Further sustained research can give that context, but it is probably entirely impossible to know how common this game was, how the reporter knew about it at all, and quite how ironic or serious he was being in his comments on it.

Perhaps most importantly, the article tells us nothing of what readers thought. Were they bemused, shocked, indignant, or indifferent? Did they recognize or even understand the scene? Newspapers have agency in themselves, helping to influence readers and interacting with their pre-existing ideas and beliefs.[38] Did this one article feed into the readers' sense of the stupidity of young ruffians or even create that sense where it did not exist before? Did the readers even notice the article?

What this example reinforces is the importance of understanding the context of any piece of evidence and the dangers and challenges of using fragmented and isolated examples. In the coming years, one of the biggest challenges facing historians will be to ensure that the historical agency and complexity of print culture is not forgotten in a rush to mine the contents of digital archives. No newspaper or book can be treated as a mere bucket of words to be plundered for examples and evidence.

But there is a very rich vein of ideas and information within digital sources and not only can this be found more easily than ever, it also can be counted, plotted, and even followed around the world. The value of digital sources will be measured by the research that they produce and the potential is huge. It might even be on the scale of shifts in intellectual paradigms that encourage scholars to ask new questions and to envisage and write new kinds of history, a kind of digital turn.

That has yet to happen, and its realization will require digital archives with search interfaces that allow researchers to step beyond cherry-picking evidence. It will also require historians not to be seduced by the idea that either numbers or fragmented articles alone can explain the past. The triangulation and comparison of sources perhaps is more important than ever when dealing with digital research. It may have many practical benefits but it is not a straightforward or simple shortcut. To be done properly, digital research still requires considerable digging, sifting, and patience, especially while so many search interfaces are so poor. Above it all, it requires a proper understanding of how distorting keywords can be because they discourage researchers from looking at the wider content of newspapers. That content should help with an understanding of context, and context is crucial to trying to understand what is found. But that understanding is never simple. Indeed, for all the potential of the digital revolution in archives, it may raise as many new questions as it answers old ones.

Notes

1. For an illustration of how fast, see Cox and Salter, "The IT Revolution and the Practice of Sport History," which discusses the IT revolution in terms as basic as e-mail and Internet shopping.

2. For an insightful meditation on the experience of archival work, see Steedman, *Dust*.

3. A word of caution here. Recent research on UK doctoral students born between 1983 and 1992 suggests far less comfort with digital tools than might be supposed. See JISC, *Researchers of Tomorrow*.

4. Mussell, "Ownership, Institutions, and Methodology."

5. Leary, "Googling the Victorians."

6. Bingham, "The Digitization of Newspaper Archives."

7. Ironically, these concerns have stimulated far more conversations about the materiality of the press than occurred in the pre-digital age. See Plunkett, "From Optical to Digital (and Back Again)," and Brake, "The Longevity of 'Ephemera.'"

8. Brake, "The Longevity of 'Ephemera.'"

9. Adrian Harvey, for example, used a trawl of the press to demonstrate the existence of a commercial and vibrant sporting culture before the late Victorian period. Harvey, *The Beginnings of a Commercial Sporting Culture in Britain*.

10. Tierney, "The State of Electronic Resources for the Study of Eighteenth-Century British Periodicals."

11. For an extensive review of the *Burney Collection*, see Marshall and Hume, "The Joys, Possibilities, and Perils of the British Library's Digital Burney Newspapers Collection."

12. Tanner, Muñoz, and Ros, "Measuring Mass Text Digitization Quality and Usefulness."

13. *UK Press Online*, which holds the *Daily Mirror* and *Daily Express*, is, for example, a near-unusable mess that fails to implement even basic features such as hit-term highlighting.

14. For discussion of this and an example of digital newspaper research being carried out, see Stead, "Wrexham FC—Founded in 1866?"

15. See Blackheath and Old Elthamians Hockey Club, *"Blackheath HC—First 100 Years."*

16. *Morning Post*, December 31, 1829.

17. *Jackson's Oxford Journal*, October 28, 1843.

18. *The Era*, October 25, 1863.

19. *The Times*, September 25, 1869. There is only one earlier mention—in 1863 an advertisement for a *Boy's Journal* made reference to an article written on football by a member of the FA.

20. *The Times*, March 16, 1874.

21. *The Times*, June 29, 1943; May 2, 1944.

22. *The Times*, December 24, 1953; September 23, 1957.

23. Hansard, HL Deb, July 13, 1948, vol. 157, cc761–4. Accessed August 1, 2012. http://hansard.millbanksystems.com/lords/1948/jul/13/lords-amendment.

24. For similar arguments about court records and disability history, see Turner, "Disability and Crime in Eighteenth Century England."

25. *Old Bailey Proceedings*, December 9, 1878, Howard Pembroke (t18781209-86). Accessed March 2, 2013. http://www.oldbaileyonline.org/browse.jsp?ref=t18781209-86.

26. *Old Bailey Proceedings*, October 24, 1887, Charles Keys (t18871024-1083). Accessed March 2, 2013. http://www.oldbaileyonline.org/browse.jsp?ref=t18871024-1083.

27. *Old Bailey Proceedings*, May 13, 1901, Frederick Sully (t19010513-371). Accessed March 2, 2013. http://www.oldbaileyonline.org/browse.jsp?ref=t19010513-371.

28. Bingham, "Reading Newspapers."
29. Nicholson, "You Kick the Bucket; We Do the Rest!"; Leary, "How the Dickens Scandal Went Viral."
30. For a sample of Sullivan's British press coverage, see: *Reynolds's Newspaper,* November 13, 1887; *York Herald,* November 8, 1887; and *Leicester Chronicle*, November 26, 1887.
31. Michel et al., "Quantitative Analysis."
32. Ibid.
33. See Cohen, "Searching for the Victorians."
34. A blank search should give the total number of articles published in a year.
35. For a recent discussion of newspaper culturomics and some tips on how to construct methodologically sound searches, see Nicholson, "Counting Culture," and Liddle, "Reflections on 20,000 Victorian Newspapers."
36. For more on Ngrams, see Michel et al., "Quantitative Analysis."
37. *Preston Guardian*, February 22, 1873.
38. For a discussion of this and the difficulties of interpreting the anecdotal evidence found in the press, see Hill, "Anecdotal Evidence."

References

Bingham, Adrian. 2010. "The Digitization of Newspaper Archives: Opportunities and Challenges for Historians." *Twentieth Century British History* 21, no. 2: 225–31.
———. 2012. "Reading Newspapers: Cultural Histories of the Popular Press in Modern Britain." *History Compass* 10, no. 2: 140–50.
Blackheath and Old Elthamians Hockey Club. 1961. *"Blackheath HC—First 100 Years."* Accessed August 1, 2012. http://blackheath.co.uk/hockey/?page_id=465.
Brake, Laurel. 2012. "'The Longevity of 'Ephemera': Library Editions of Nineteenth-Century Periodicals and Newspapers." *Media History* 18, no. 1: 7–20.
Cohen, Dan. 2010. "Searching for the Victorians." October 4. Accessed August 1, 2012. http://www.dancohen.org/2010/10/04/searching-for-the-victorians/.
Cox, Richard W., and Michael A. Salter. 1998. "The IT Revolution and the Practice of Sport History." *Journal of Sport History* 25: 283–302.
Harvey, Adrian. 2004. *The Beginnings of a Commercial Sporting Culture in Britain, 1793–1850*. London: Ashgate.
Hill, Jeffrey. 2006. "Anecdotal Evidence: Sport, The Newspaper Press, and History." In *Deconstructing Sport History: A Postmodern Analysis*, edited by Murray G. Phillips, 117–29. Albany: State University of New York Press.
JISC. 2012. *Researchers of Tomorrow: The Research Behaviour of Generation Y Doctoral Students*. London: British Library. Accessed August 1, 2012. http://www.jisc.ac.uk/media/documents/publications/reports/2012/Researchers-of-Tomorrow.pdf.
Leary, Patrick. 2005. "Googling the Victorians." *Journal of Victorian Culture* 10, no. 1: 72–86.

———. 2013. "How the Dickens Scandal Went Viral." In *Charles Dickens and the Mid-Victorian Press*, edited by Hazel Mackenzie and Ben Winyard, 305–25. Buckingham: University of Buckingham Press.

Liddle, Dallas. 2012. "Reflections on 20,000 Victorian Newspapers: 'Distant Reading' *The Times* using *The Times Digital Archive*." *Journal of Victorian Culture* 17, no. 2: 230–37.

Marshall, Ashley, and Robert D. Hume. 2010. "The Joys, Possibilities, and Perils of the British Library's Digital Burney Newspapers Collection." *The Papers of the Bibliographical Society of America* 104, no. 1: 5–52.

Michel, Jean-Baptiste, Yuan Kui Shen, Aviva Presser Aiden, Adrian Veres, Matthew K. Gray, The Google Books Team, Joseph P. Pickett, Dale Hoiberg, Dan Clancy, Peter Norvig, Jon Orwant, Steven Pinker, Martin A. Nowak, and Erez Lieberman Aiden. 2011. "Quantitative Analysis of Culture Using Millions of Digitized Books," *Science* 331 (6014) (January 14): 176–82.

Mussell, James. 2008. "Ownership, Institutions, and Methodology." *Journal of Victorian Culture* 13, no. 1: 94–100.

Nicholson, Bob. 2012. "Counting Culture; or, How to Read Victorian Newspapers From a Distance." *Journal of Victorian Culture* 17, no. 2: 238–46.

———. 2012. "'You Kick the Bucket; We Do the Rest!' Jokes and the Culture of Reprinting in the Transatlantic Press." *Journal of Victorian Culture* 17, no. 3: 273–86.

Plunkett, John. 2008. "From Optical to Digital (and Back Again)." *19: Interdisciplinary Studies in the Long Nineteenth Century*, 6. Accessed August 3, 2012. www.19.bbk.ac.uk.

Stead, Phil. "Wrexham FC—Founded in 1866?" Accessed August 1, 2012. http://ffwtbol.co.uk/2012/02/17/wrexham-fc-founded-in-1866/.

Steedman, Carolyn. 2001. *Dust: The Archive and Cultural History*. Manchester: Manchester University Press.

Tanner, Simon, Trevor Muñoz, and Pich Hemy Ros. 2009. "Measuring Mass Text Digitization Quality and Usefulness: Lessons Learned from Assessing the OCR Accuracy of the British Library's 19th Century Online Newspaper Archive." *D-Lib Magazine* 15, no. 7/8 (July/August). Accessed August 1, 2012. http://www.dlib.org/dlib/july09/munoz/07munoz.html.

Tierney, James E. 2012. "The State of Electronic Resources for the Study of Eighteenth-Century British Periodicals: The Role of Scholars, Librarians, and Commercial Vendors." *Age of Johnson* 21: 309–35.

Turner, David M. 2012. "Disability and Crime in Eighteenth Century England." *Cultural and Social History* 9, no. 1: 47–64.

PART II

Digital History as Archive

The second dimension of our tripartite conception of history in the digital era is *Digital History as Archive*. The rise of social media since the turn of the twenty-first century has created dynamic new sites for public conversation, communication, and interaction, including blogs, Facebook, fansites, Instagram, Twitter, Wikipedia, YouTube, and specialist online forums. Because many of these social media are surrounded by issues of usefulness, validity, and trustworthiness, we understand that *Digital History as Archive* can be a challenging dimension of the digital humanities. Despite the reluctance of many historians to engage professionally with social media beyond exploring its capacities for communication, opportunities abound for extending historical practice. Because much social media content is created digitally and only exists in digital form, social media also constitute archives in and of themselves that can be used for research, as explored by Geoffery Z. Kohe, Matthew Klugman, Rebecca Olive, and Holly Thorpe in the context of organization websites, fansites, blogs, Facebook, and other interactive, online forums. Social media can also present opportunities for researchers to solicit contributions from particular communities, although various methodological, ethical, and legal issues can complicate this, as Mike Cronin illustrates in his chapter. And, as Tara Magdalinski highlights, the vast range of social media and online technologies and their capacity for public engagement pose rich opportunities for teaching and pedagogic practice.

3

@www.olympic.org.nz
Organizational Websites, E-Spaces, and Sport History

GEOFFERY Z. KOHE

Being a sport historian can be frustrating. The occupation can often involve travelling vast distances to historic sites and/or sport organizations, long hours ferreting away in archival repositories, analyzing dusty documents in darkened rooms, tiresome genealogical searches on athletic ancestry, and pursuits of elusive characters and artifacts. Indeed, this is how many historians in the discipline come to learn their craft. More recently, however, the discipline has undergone significant shifts that have altered sport historians' attitudes and practices.[1] Within these perpetual debates, challenging theoretical and methodological questions have been raised around the nature of archives, the modes of representation, the possibilities for new forms of narrative making, and the ethics of reflexivity and historical subjectivity. One response to some of these historiographical redirections and concerns has been for some sport historians to seek new spaces for examination.[2] This is all novel, insightful, exciting, and indeed welcome scholarship. Yet, there are new trends afoot, found in the enticing avenues of digital culture.

That sport historians have developed a predilection for the personal computer (PC) (or Mac) and its contents is, perhaps, unsurprising. Having e-(electronic), or i-(Internet) based interests makes considerable sense given the amount of time contemporary academics spend at their computers, the ongoing digitization of archival material, the steady influx of younger technology-savvy graduates, the increasing demands placed upon university staff to better acquaint themselves with the many forms of digital media, and the academy's incessant pressure for research innovation. As this very book attests, sport historians wanting to dabble with the digital turn have not had to look very far for new research spaces. Sport variously, routinely, and simultaneously produces spectacles of physical prowess, offers a site for consumer practices, enables social interactions, manufactures statistics, evokes individual and collective affectations, and engenders frequent nostalgia. These characteristics have found a home in the electronic age where they have been promoted by sports fans, journalists, media producers, sponsors, athletes, stakeholders, and administrators, all of whom are complicit agents in proliferating sport culture(s) on the web.

The digital realm is, consequently, a veritable treasure trove for sport historians. The proliferation of e-zines, fansites, blogs, Facebook, Twitter, club webpages, and sport organization websites, for example, has opened novel locales for analysis and representation. Digital sources, sites, and spaces may excite sport historians; however, they also raise questions about narrative making, collective memory, and the archival record. This chapter addresses some of the issues sport historians face in this electronic epoch. First, it discusses some of the connections between historiography, sport organizations, and the web. Second, it examines the website of the New Zealand Olympic Committee (NZOC), the country's premier sport authority.

NZOC was established in 1911, under the auspices of the International Olympic Committee (IOC), to facilitate the participation of New Zealand athletes at the Olympic Games and to promote the principles of the Olympic movement abroad. Today, these aims remain central to the organization's work. Like other National Olympic Committees (NOCs), NZOC is an independent, nonprofit, agency that receives funding from sponsorship, donations, the IOC, subscriptions, and the national government's sport and recreation body. NZOC comprises a small executive board of just ten members who maintain authority over the country's various Olympic engagements and work to secure New Zealand's continuous presence and performance at the highest level of international sport. Continually promoting the organization online and off, therefore, remains a necessary strategy for enabling NZOC to go about its work. Their specific website, quite unlike conventional archives, is an unusual source for historians. NZOC's site is novel with regard to the non-linear ways it merges historical and contemporary sporting vignettes with real-time sport announcements and social networking efforts. Consequently, the third section of this chapter argues that such sites provide scholars with valuable material for understanding aspects of sport culture and history. In addition, the blurred lines between archival source and historical narrative on the site, and the site in totality, demonstrate the possibilities for creative digital reconfigurations in the field.

Sport Organizations and E-Spaces

Sport historians are fortunate to have a variety of spaces to use and examine in their work. While conventional archival repositories continually attract many scholars, an increasing number of researchers are turning to alternative sites for narrative making. The researchers cited for their innovation here, for instance, are all also contributors to this book. Fiona McLachlan, for example, has examined the ephemeral nature of poolside graffiti imagery to comment on sexuality discourses within pool spaces and the treatment of evidence within postmodern histories.[3] Holly Thorpe has used the vibrant physical culture and sites of snowboarding to demonstrate the fluidities of personal and collective memory making.[4] Gary Osmond and Murray Phillips have also made historiographical forays by using cricket stamps to unify philately and visual culture and illustrate the utility of, and promises within, atypical sources.[5] Carrying forward the pursuit of new historiographical terrain, Douglas Booth has used Sydney's iconic Bondi Beach to explain how the cultural, political, and social topographies of sport spaces may hold fresh possibilities for sport historians.[6] In finding novel ways to ply their craft, sport scholars are also demonstrating a warmer appreciation for the historical potential of the digital realm and its contents.

Of course, many researchers within the discipline are already familiar with conventional electronic archives. For some time, for instance, many national libraries, governments, museums, private institutions, and some sport bodies have made extensive archival collections available online. Digitized material is either provided free, or for a nominal fee, or via paid subscription. The microfiche and microfilm are not yet dead, and trips to far-flung repositories are not yet a feature of the past, but the digital era has made it increasingly easier for sport historians to access sources and collate information from a wider array of locales more quickly than previously imagined.

In addition to facilitating access to archival material, the onset of the digital era, and the proliferation of technological innovation therein, also offers sport historians a new means and medium upon, and within, which to work. Digital technologies present many opportunities to examine facets of sport cultures. Fansites, e-zines (electronic magazines), blogs/vlogs (video blogs), Facebook, Twitter, YouTube, club webpages, and sport organization websites, for example, all provide ways to understand how sport cultures are created, reproduced, dissolved, and reassembled. Historians may also be drawn to the plethora of sport-related websites, plenty of which emphasize past performances (the sociocultural antecedents of their existence), link past and present global communities of supporters, promote recollection and the establishment of collective memory and, on occasion, blur the lines of reality with nostalgia and amnesia.

NZOC's website (www.olympic.org.nz), the exemplar used in this chapter, is a perfect example in this regard. The site, not unlike those of other sport organizations, serves several purposes: public interface, marketing and communication tool, news outlet, promoter of national identity, history maker, global social networker, mouthpiece for the Olympic movement, political platform, and educator. Sport organization websites, particularly those created by the most innovative of the international and national sport bodies, moreover, can further offer means for historians to evaluate ideological and political change and continuity, assess reactions to broader forces, and analyze key disciplinary concepts such as memory, reflexivity, and criticality. Sport historians may find these sites appealing for such reasons.

As tantalizing as the Internet may be, the rapid progress of digital technology, and more specifically the coalescence of the digital with the historiographical, has been cause for some trepidation within the field. Scholars have warned us to be wary of the temporality of the Internet and to temper our attractions to its historical promises.[7] Reiterating the basic practicalities of digital technology, Belinda Barnet reminds us that "we discard six-month old PCs. We upgrade digital networks as regularly as our finances will allow it. Archives are often lost to technological obsolescence."[8] Echoing general concerns about accessing our work in the future, Barnet continues, "unless you refresh it, you will need an antique machine in twenty years."[9]

We might pause to consider, at this point, what tools, experience, and digital ability future sport historians might need to go about their work. Practical concerns notwithstanding, David Staley suggests the primary issue may be to shift the discipline's underlying pretensions.[10] Historians' predilection for consuming and producing the written word, he believes, is evidently changing as scholars seek out and become competent with using digital technology in its various forms. While recognizing that "most historians use computers conservatively: to laterally transfer textual culture from paper to screen," Staley acknowledges that the discipline is largely unable to escape the e-revolution and the allure of the alternative modes of visual representation that the Internet offers.[11] The acceptance of digital-based/generated/inspired/derived work by the field is, nevertheless, not a foregone conclusion. Traditionally, the discipline has been reluctant to change and relatively slow to embrace methodological innovation or approaches that confound conventional epistemes. As such, Staley forewarns, the legitimacy and success of history in the digital era may be dependent on how willing scholars are to reconsider their allegiances to traditional modes of inquiry and narrative making.

Beyond these concerns, there are other conceptual issues for historians to consider, foremost of which is the relationship between the digital era and the establishment and/or reconfiguration of cultural memories. Alison Landsberg's valuable work on the constraints of collective memory and its relationship to a technology-driven mass culture is useful in this regard.[12] Drawing on the work of Arjun Appadurai, Jacques Derrida, and Walter Benjamin, Landsberg posits that the global permeation of media forms, in tandem with cultural commodification practices, has effectively altered the ways in which individuals and groups engage in collective memory-making processes. "A commodified mass culture," Landsberg asserts, "opens up the possibility that people who share little in the way of cultural or ethnic background might come to share certain memories."[13] As an example we might look to the ways that NZOC's website distorts the ethnic, class, and political tensions of the country's sporting history to promote a unifying, and unified, projection of collective sporting harmony.[14] "In response to the urgency of twentieth-century memory projects," Landsberg continues, "technologies of mass culture have been called on to play a new and important role in circulating images and narratives about the past."[15] As a well-promoted, professional, public interface, dedicated to manufacturing sporting memories, iconic imagery, and national identity discourse, NZOC's website is part, albeit a small one, of the process of cultural circulation and production.

The essential premise of Landsberg's work, and one that warrants foregrounding here, is that the exponential advancements of the digital era have enabled new means of cultural production and collective memory making. However, these processes are not value free, but rather are ideologically laden, subjective, and innately political. Invariably, "popular historical texts," of which websites are a key part, "often tend to express national historical moments and events. In many ways, this is because they seemingly serve a national interest.... They reflect the domestic histories of nationhood, contribute to the imagined community of the nation, and develop a narrative and trajectory of national history."[16] In addition to this, we need to be mindful that the openness of the Internet has disrupted the conventional boundaries, legitimacy, and ownership of collective memories. This is certainly the case with NZOC's website, how it remembers the country's sport history, and the ways visitors get to participate in the remembering.

Although for the most part the discipline, and subdisciplines, of history/historiography have been relatively slow to connect with or embrace virtual space, one group with particular foresight in this regard is the constituents of museums and cultural heritage. The propensity that museums, and similar institutions, have shown to ride the digital wave by creating public-interface websites appears commonsensical. In many cases, such sites rely on public patronage for much of their economic support. Related to this, at times the continued existence of the museum depends on, or at least is heavily aided by, maximizing the promotional activities to the general public. The extensive global exposure offered by the Internet is thus an all-too-alluring mechanism to procure a larger fan/supporter/visitor/audience base. Establishing an online presence also helps to leverage the investments of sponsors, benefactors, and stakeholders.

Although essentially a nonprofit organization, NZOC, too, is driven by marketing imperatives and, as such, the development of its website is important for the promotion of its work and public outreach activities, including its museum and history projects. "The use of the internet," Ross Wilson concurs, "to provide greater access, support exhibitions or engage with communities and research has developed quickly, to a point where nearly all major institutions and the majority of local or specific interest museums have their own existence online."[17] Expressing similar sentiments, Yehuda Kalay argues that at a time of cultural crisis—in which historical sites have been put under pressure from a variety of sociocultural, political, and economic forces—developing a firm foothold in the digital marketplace is invariably a necessity.[18]

The process of conceiving, developing, producing, and maintaining innovative online spaces is, nonetheless, fraught with obstacles. At the outset, Amitai Etzioni and Oren Etzioni have cautioned that establishing, and indeed understanding, the needs and dynamics of computer-mediated communities is complex.[19] The communities of users that museums seek to attract online should be, first and foremost, understood as organic entities whose demographic characteristics cannot be easily defined. Thus, website developers and administrators need to employ creative strategies to cater to visitors' potentially omnivorous consumer needs. David Peacock adds that the World Wide Web has exposed members of the broad church of museum practice to a host of technological innovations and promises.[20] "Yet," Peacock contests, "while change and its synonyms—*adaptation, evolution, revolution* and *transformation*—are now ubiquitous in museum work and talk, change processes are still not well understood, particularly in relation to the effects of digital ICTS [Information Computer Technologies]."[21] One issue that Andrea Bandelli feels has become a key concern with regard to virtual spaces is the necessity for institutions to provide online experiences that are more clearly integrated with their physical spaces, and in which visitors are afforded as much freedom in the interaction and navigation as possible.[22] Bandelli's assertions are reflected in NZOC's website, a space that provides visitors the privilege of negotiating historical elements (for example, stories, facts, statistics, images, icons, and ephemera) in ways that differ from those available at the institution's physical site.

The ways in which historically minded institutions attend to the multifarious engagement of website visitors is an ongoing concern. "A proper understanding of how museum visitors use digital museum resources in their daily lives," Paul Marty notes, "is critical for the success of the museums in the information age."[23] Since the evolution of the World Wide Web, and with the diverse modes of technology at users' fingertips, visitors to such websites now have expectations, and at times demands, about the quality, content, and nature of their digital experiences. The desire for greater website sophistication is undoubtedly upon us. Even NZOC's site has additional links for users to download iPhone applications, purchase merchandise, or link the site to their personal Facebook and Twitter accounts. This is, Marty reminds us, all part and parcel of the contemporary museological (e-)trend. "Developers of museum websites," he adds, "should take advantage of the online environment to offer unique experiences that cannot be duplicated in physical museums, including customization and personalization technologies."[24] In support, Ross Parry reminds us that a key agenda of the museum/heritage sector is to employ a wide breadth of digital strategies to facilitate better interactive relationships between users and institutions.[25] The best of such interactions/experiences are not unidirectional, or tantamount to passive consumption, but rather necessitate users' agency in a narrative process. The experiences of museums and heritage institutions mentioned here are useful for understanding some of the issues for sport organizations attempting to create effective, and affective, online profiles.

NZOC's work in developing a website that invariably employs a multitude of e-based tools and virtual engagement strategies indicates that they are at least in sync with current, progressive, museological, and digital practices. Not unlike the websites of galleries, museums, and heritage locales, the current content of www.olympic.org.nz, and in particular the history-focused *imuseum* section, is a constantly evolving entity. The *imuseum* is a virtual space where visitors can access selected stories, images, and facts about the country's Olympians and find historical information about the Olympic Games and New Zealand's involvement in the Olympic movement. Visual elements are added, deleted, shifted, integrated, hyperlinked, and updated, all in an attempt to better appeal to a broader audience, and to engage that audience with the New Zealand Olympic movement, its components, and its history. Perpetual website alteration is, however, more than merely a cosmetic practice to refresh the organization's digital façade. Rather, the site is an important interface between the organization and its visitors (which include affiliated members, stakeholders, and the general public). As the needs and interests of these visitors to the site change, NZOC must reconsider the structure and content of its Internet presence. As Jerome de Groot suggests, organizations, museums, and similar popular/public cultural entities wishing to capitalize on their online presence need to carefully attend to their virtual architecture(s).[26] Online visitors are not physically within the institutional space, for example, and thus necessitate different considerations about representation and engagement. Online visitors, Laurajane Smith adds, navigate their experience in nonlinear and quite abstract ways.[27] Consequently, institutions need to ensure that they create freely negotiable e-spaces able to be traveled and constructed at will and by whim.

While historians and museologists may be left contemplating the (f)utility of e-spaces, many sport organizations have forged a path along the digital superhighway. The allure of the net to sport bodies is perhaps unsurprising. Indeed, some sport organizations like the IOC (see www.olympic.org) and NZOC appear to have considered matters of engagement, relevance, adaptation, and interaction within their own website development. The IOC, for example, has been particularly innovative in using YouTube and Twitter to make the organization appeal to younger generations. As laudable as tailoring the website to the youth ethos may be, NZOC and the IOC are still market-orientated organizations. As such, their sites are important tools for maintaining their public image and brand profile. In the case of NZOC, which has a comparatively small administrative and executive team, the Internet enables the organization to have a substantial national and international reach that belies its size.

As Paul Christ explains, "as a communication channel, the internet allows even small organizations to quickly establish a global presence and, by doing so, expand their potential target audience to many times its current size."[28] Hye Min Yeon, Choi Youjin, and Spiro Kiousis, too, add that for nonprofit organizations (such as NZOC), websites are an important element to their public relations strategies.[29] "Websites," Yeon and colleagues note, "are particularly effective and efficient communication tools for nonprofit organizations to promote their philanthropic causes and attract potential donors and volunteers."[30] This is evident with NZOC's site, which incorporates sections devoted to the idealistic and philosophical basis of the Olympic movement, and its related Solidarity work supporting youth athletes and smaller NOCs abroad. Yeon and colleagues warn, however, that there is no clear, or sustained, evidence to suggest that the quality and content of the website, and efforts to fortify stakeholder relations through the site, will invariably lead to increased revenue. Nonetheless, developing an effective web presence is an instrumental part of the arsenal that nonprofit organizations can employ in their economic pursuits.

NZOC and its Digital Drive

The NZOC website, which I have followed for nearly a decade, provides a good example of the innovation shown by some sport organizations to embrace digital technology. More so than this, the extensive nature of the site, and its merging of historical and contemporary elements, provokes thought about how sport historians might best use such spaces and what work they might produce as a result. Notwithstanding the academic utility of NZOC's website, it is necessary to approach an examination of the site with critical concern; namely (though not limited to), an acknowledgement of the inherent political agendas of the organization the space represents, the interests and values projected (and/or those amiss or suppressed) in the site, and the production qualities that explicitly or implicitly craft the narrative and its potential interpretation.

Over the last decade, NZOC, like other members of the Olympic family, has taken a role in reinvigorating the Olympic movement. Part of this project has involved using new media forms to showcase the history and work of NOCs to broader audiences. Concomitantly, this reinvigoration has also been an attempt to fortify relationships with key stakeholders, such as sponsors, former Olympians, national sport bodies, athletes, and the general public. One of NZOC's measures in this regard was developing *Zeus* Technology, an extranet network that effectively revolutionized the ways NZOC could communicate with national federations and their constituents, particularly during and around Olympic Games time. One other initiative, initially led by Paul Ryan (marketing director) and Gordon Irving (communications manager), and welcomed by NZOC executives, has been the careful and continued development of its public website, www.olympic.org.nz. For NZOC, the perpetual development of its online presence has been instrumental in ensuring that the organization maintains an attractive public profile and recognized status as the country's premier sports authority.

As mentioned earlier, the site serves several purposes. For example, it has been a key tool for advertising the work of the organization, providing information on the structure of the administration, highlighting the stories and experiences of Olympic athletes, and offering insight into the history of the Olympic movement and the country's lengthy participation in the Olympic Games. Prior to the London 2012 Olympic Games, NZOC specifically used the site to encourage fans to contribute to the national sporting fervor via Facebook, Twitter, and YouTube. Moreover, and in addition to other projects, the site operates as an outlet to showcase New Zealand's Olympic Museum and its role in anchoring the present to the past.

For sport historians or scholars interested in the Olympic movement in New Zealand, the site is a valuable resource. The site would certainly be a first stop for researchers, educators, and students unfamiliar with NZOC or the country's Olympic history. As the brief description below indicates, the site contains multifarious sections that detail the organizational infrastructure, athlete narratives, seminal historical moments, outreach work in education and athlete support, public announcements, and notes on the country's contemporary sporting action. Yet, the site is a constantly evolving entity. Indeed, in the duration of time taken to write this chapter, the site has undergone considerable changes. The issue of temporality, specifically capturing and recovering the site, I will return to shortly. For now, a brief description of the site is perhaps necessary.

Logging On to www.olympic.org.nz

Greeting all first-time users is the home page, predominately colored black (New Zealand's iconic sporting hue) (see Figure 3.1). Here we are treated to a seemingly endless spread of information: advertisements about Kiwi House in London, a countdown to the Games, historical stories retrieved from newspaper archives, details about athletes' Olympic preparations, notes on the progress of the Olympic torch relay in the United Kingdom, and announcements about the ever-increasing number of Internet fans.[31] We can jump from the Māori blessing of New Zealand's Olympic accommodation, to Embassy warnings about security, and back to tales of the country's epic historic moments. We can also see how athletes interact with their fans and the media. In mere moments, and seemingly all at once, we can travel across the ether from our distant desktops to the bowels of New Zealand's Olympic organization. We can furrow in its histories, understand its present

ORGANIZATIONAL WEBSITES AND E-SPACES · 87

Figure 3.1: www.olympic.org.nz, one of NZOC's ever-changing home pages. Courtesy of www.olympic.org.nz.

administration, interact with elite athletes, and network our private online existence(s) with an increasingly popular and populated social sporting space.

Yet, the site draws us in deeper still. Historians, for example, might be keen to segue to the page composed by established Games journalist and historian Joseph Romanos. Here Romanos reminds us about New Zealand's first gold medalist, Malcolm Champion, who competed with Australians in the 4x200 meters swimming relay at the 1912 Stockholm Olympic Games. Unlike 2008 champion Michael Phelps, Romanos reminds us, Champion "competed in a long-forgotten era. The motor car was in its infancy when he was at his peak. No-one had heard of aerodynamic swimsuits then, never mind jet engines, computers and other marvels of the modern world." From here, we could then take the links to the *imuseum* pages—the space dedicated to athletes' individual profiles. Search here for the country's first female gold medalist, long jumper Yvette Corlett (née Williams). Upload her profile page, complete with basic biographical statistics, a short commentary on achievements, a list of her athletic successes (across various athletic disciplines), and a small selection of black-and-white photographic images (see Figure 3.2). Although now 83 years old, Corlett smiles back at us as a vibrant 22-year-old, remembered, immortalized, memorialized, and digitized.

A few further clicks and key taps take us to the page of iconic 1960s middle-distance runner Peter Snell. Voted New Zealand Athlete of the Century in

Figure 3.2: The athlete page of Yvette Corlett (née Williams), found (for now) at http://www.olympic.org.nz/nzolympic/athlete/yvette-corlett. Courtesy of www.olympic.org.nz.

2000, Snell remains at the pinnacle of New Zealand sport. Despite his accolades, the layout mirrors that of his fellow Olympians: synopsis, biography, statistics, and images. Tantalized by the tidbits on this page, historians might be keen to transpose Snell's achievements into an analysis of the evolution of middle-distance running or follow the biographical threads further to reveal Snell's sporting genealogies and contemporary trajectories into medicine and exercise science. Change the search parameters to more recent athletes and up pops renowned equestrian rider Mark Todd. Because he has now competed at seven Olympic Games, Todd's page is one of the most extensive on the site. His list of equine achievements in dressage, cross country, eventing, and jumping begs to be cut and pasted into historical debates about performance and success. The photographic images, too, may tell historians something about sport and class, discipline, and the costuming of athletic bodies.

Hit the back button, back, back, back. We can momentarily return to the home page. It seems to look the same. But wait. Refresh. It has changed. In minutes new sections have been added (see Figure 3.3). The site now has 20,000 fans. There are 292 likes about the upcoming team flag-bearer announcement. There are a further 45 comments about the building of the Kiwi House in London. Fresh tweets have been added in support of the women's football team. Archival images have been also added about the country's sailing history. You are tempted to continue scrolling, to keep clicking, and to constantly renew the searching. Maybe you upload all this to your iPhone (you think, do I know how to do this?). You maybe ponder, is there an app?

ORGANIZATIONAL WEBSITES AND E-SPACES · 89

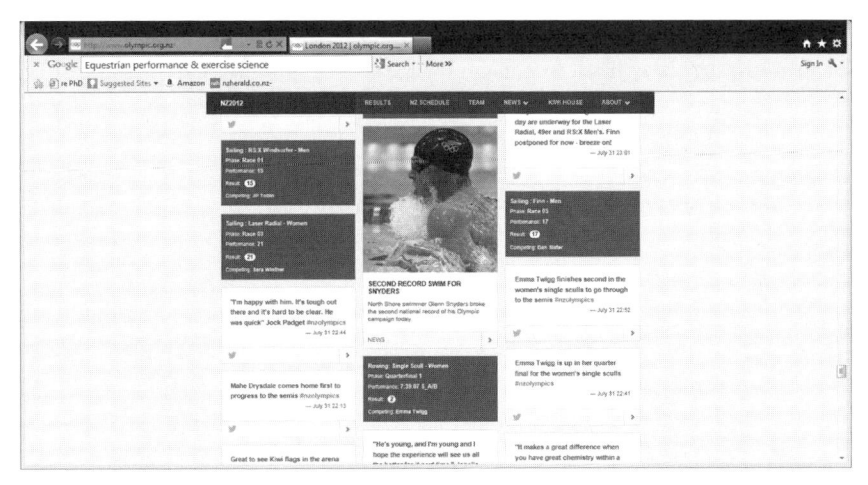

Figure 3.3: NZOC's home page, captured during metamorphosis. Courtesy of www.olympic.org.nz.

Do you print this material? No, you will find it again, for you assume it will all still be here, accessible, waiting for you tomorrow.

If you have, while reading this, logged on to the site you will (hopefully) find many parts of the site I have described above. You may have clicked on various links and been transported through cyberspace portals to other areas of the site. Maybe you arrived at the education section and read all about the innovative work of the country's Olympic academy. Or, maybe, like me, you navigated to the athletes' section and were able to search for your favorite Kiwi Olympian, board sailor Barbara Kendall. Perhaps you liked sailor Blair Tuke's birthday message. Or, maybe you clicked on the journalistic coverage of Joseph Romanos to get his take on the country's past performances on the track. You might have followed anonymous posts being tweeted on the Olympic team's progress to London 2012, or you may have followed the hyperlink to the Facebook site to leave a message of inspiration for the New Zealand team. As scholars, in particular as historians, maybe you found useful archival material on the site that you were able to turn to affective means in your narratives about the country's sporting past.

The site is effectively the live electronic repository of the country's paramount sporting body. As such, there is plenty of material on the site for researchers to use in their work. The most innovative among us may also examine the site, and others like it, as archives/histories in and of themselves. That is, Internet sites, as others in this book attest, exist as a particular type of historical narrative in their own right. Composed, at times by various authors (often adopting the guise of site administrators), www.olympic.org.nz has become a mixture of explicit historical segments about New Zealand's enduring Olympic participation sutured to contemporary stories about the endeavors of current athletes. Add to this the administrative updates that evidence the managerial prowess of the organization. Furthermore, there are the occasional mentions of NZOC's key sponsors that demonstrate the committee's marketing responsibilities. Then there are the important strands reaching out through cyberspace that tie NZOC and its website to other times and spaces. These include links to the IOC, NOCs, sport federation sites, the conglomeration of e-spaces associated with the London 2012 Olympic Games, government websites, athletes' blog sites, sponsor links, and a plethora of social network spaces (see Figure 3.4). All of these connect users (wherever they happen to be, and whenever they happen to be online) to NZOC, but also to its history, its athletes, and information about the country and the values and ideals associated with the notion of a collective history and national (sporting) identity.

Yet, the spatial and temporal parameters of websites are unlike those of other sorts of paper-based history forms, such as books, articles, and journals. Differing from histories that largely have a permanent physical presence, web-based histories are peculiar entities. Once they are written and have gone online, their existence is not really fixed. Websites such as the NZOC's are constantly evolving in response to real-time events and interactions. As evidenced by the NZOC's site, adaptation is a defining feature. In order to

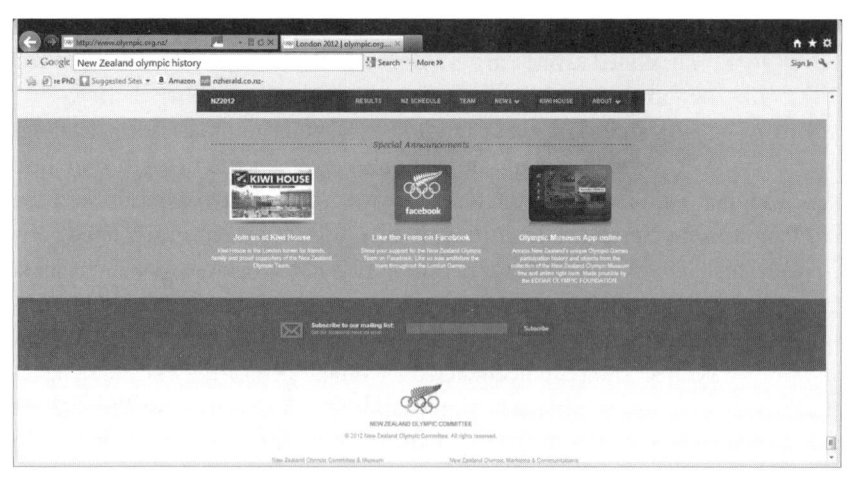

Figure 3.4: Links to others sites and spaces make it possible for visitors to www.olympic.org to continue their journey in a perpetual loop of digital discovery. Courtesy of www.olympic.org.nz.

maintain a captive audience, the home page, for example, is frequently updated. Indeed, over the last five years the site has also undergone a series of makeovers to improve its aesthetic appeal and user accessibility.

More recently, in the lead-up to the London 2012 Olympic Games, substantial emphasis was placed on improving the quality and quantity of information posted to the site. Previously, the site focused on a smaller selection of newsfeeds about specific highly successful athletes, and remained unchanged, often for weeks and months. As the home page has demonstrated, prior to and beyond the London 2012 Olympic Games, there is continuous change, typically in the form of more frequent updates about the organization generally and a greater number of stories about, and from, former and current athletes. There are also more images and clips being posted, and more noticeable efforts made to integrate the site with popular social media forums. Consequently, and unlike past visits to the invariably less-engaging site, users are confronted with a range of potential navigational pathways, each of which may tell users something about the organization, its histories, and its contemporary characteristics. For instance, users may read about the current composition of the administration; from there they may uncover how the early NZOC helped prepare athlete competitors for Games abroad, and a click or two away they may then see how the country's Olympic history is being used in tandem with elements of Māori culture to engender a team spirit in the lead-up to the London 2012 Olympic Games. In this sense, the site can be conceived of as an evolving historical project. Every user's navigation may be considered a unique historical composition and, not unlike a constantly edited series of drafts, changing and changeable.

Thoughts on Websites, Narrative Making, and Considerations for Future Sport Historians

The growth of the Internet, and evolution of digital technologies writ large, has been paralleled by, and influenced, innovations in museum practice and sport history scholarship. This triumvirate of fields (digital, museological, sporting) holds exciting possibilities for researchers in the pursuit of new analytical and theoretical terrain. Future historians, born of a visual culture, will do well to embrace, express, and consume histories, and the production thereof, through visual media, computers, and the Internet (and its derivatives). "While there is every reason to believe that historians will continue to value words, and use digital technology solely as a means of storing textual culture," Staley reminds us, "there is also reason to believe that future historians will value digital visualizations as tools of scholarly inquiry and narrative."[32] In this regard, the websites of sport organizations—NZOC's is just one particular example—provide ideal sites to examine historical issues, discuss matters of representation, and contest historiographical conventions. By suturing aspects of their past with the present, NZOC's website has become a key site for promoting its contemporary image and memory making. However, although digital sources, like NZOC's website, may excite sport historians, they also raise questions about history making and archival use.

As enticing as the digital world might be, there are still considerable unknowns about how historians might best work with these new spaces. The fragility of e-spaces, for example, is worrisome. As some of the chapters in this book have raised, issues of temporality are particularly important, and raise questions about how (sport) historians might best go about their work. The web, Barnet notes, "is by nature a transient, evanescent medium. Software and mark-up language are updated every three months. Links are outdated, information daily replaced or removed."[33] Accordingly, we should appropriately ask how might, or will, websites like NZOC's, and other sorts of e-spaces for that matter, survive without becoming obsolete or being constantly changed? As I alluded earlier, in the time it has taken to research and write this chapter, NZOC's website has changed dramatically. The site bears little resemblance to the one I first accessed years ago, and in some cases material I wanted to find has simply disappeared, either buried deep in cyberspace, moved elsewhere, or deleted altogether.

These frustrations, which other scholars may share, raise further questions that the discipline may need to consider. For example, what archaeological tools might be required of future sport historians to retrieve Internet narratives and sources? Will completing a qualification in computer forensics be helpful? What fragments of contemporary sport Internet spaces will remain for us to work with in the coming decades? Will the frequently changing, and sometimes fleeting, nature of e-spaces and Internet sources bother historians? Moreover, what might our reconfigurations of these spaces look like? How will sport historians use digital sources to analyze future social, political, and economic issues? What new strategies might we need to employ to deal with the Internet of tomorrow? Will sport historians become digital butterfly chasers, using our net skills to capture each page, URL, or hyperlink as best we can for fear it will disappear? In what ways might historians use these many versions of the site once they are captured? And, how might they evaluate the continuities and discontinuities found between each electronic iteration?

What sorts of new histories will emerge in this visual world? What roles will digital media have in the creation of historical narratives? What will be the consequences and effects? What will they look like? How will they be known?

In order to understand how sport historians might begin to work with websites like NZOC's, and engender creativity and innovation in our practice, it is useful to return to Staley's work. One mechanism that Staley suggests that digitally minded historians should investigate is the use of hypertext/hyperlink. Hypertext is essentially a digital connection of words within a web passage to another web passage. In a section on the history of NZOC, for example, users may click on the name of an administrator, country, athlete, or event and be transported to another section of the website, or another website altogether, in a seemingly endless process. When considered in a historiographical sense, this type of navigation offers an alternative approach to the linearity of historical writing. That is, it affords readers and creators some power over the direction and flow of the historical narrative. "In theory," Staley suggests, "a history written in hypertextual fashion would permit the reader to choose the path of events."[34] The beauty in this approach is that "while an historian might assemble blocks of texts, the reader would choose the connections between those blocks. Thus, the final narrative would be as much the reader's decision as the historian's."[35] Staley's suggestion may be considered playful. Yet, it grates against the majority of historical research that privileges at the very least a coherent approach to narrative making. But, perhaps playful innovation, concomitant with some of the postmodern turns mentioned at the outset of this chapter, is what the discipline needs.

In addition to aiding archival research, the Internet provides fertile spaces for narrative making and historical critique. "The Internet," asserts Landsberg, "has made available texts and archives that once were accessible only to the privileged few. Many critics, for example, overlook the great strides that have been taken to make the Internet a legitimate tool in both the dissemination and archiving of history, and the work of some historians has shown the Internet to be educational as well as commercial."[36] As scholars such as de Groot, Kaley, Staley, and others have variously contended, new digital technologies are prompting historians to reconsider the ways they go about their research and teaching practice.[37] Sport history scholars, including those represented in this book, are well placed to use the Internet to advance epistemological and disciplinary change. The concern is not necessarily encouraging historians to embrace the digital turn, but rather for historians to keep pace with rapid technological advancements that have given rise to, and mobilized, new forms of archival material. This is particularly the case if we are to collectively better prepare future researchers for sport history in the digital era.

Notes

1. For example, Mike Huggins, in "The Sporting Gaze," encourages scholars to better appreciate the breadth and depth of theoretical and historiographical possibilities that can be found within visual sports material. Huggins suggests that sources such as art, sculpture, design, and architecture may provide an important, and alternate, means to connect with human (sporting) experiences. Similarly, in "The Culture of Boxing," Kath Woodward draws historians' attention to the affective qualities of sporting practices. In particular, Woodward calls for historians to move beyond conventional, deterministic narratives of athletic performance and to work innovatively to reconceptualize sporting terrains as sites of embodied meaning, corporeal power, and emotive creation.

2. McLachlan, "'You Can't Take a Picture of This"; Thorpe, "The Politics of Remembering"; Osmond and Phillips, "Enveloping the Past"; Booth, "Bondi Park."

3. McLachlan, "You Can't Take a Picture of This."

4. Thorpe, "The Politics of Remembering."

5. Osmond and Phillips, "Enveloping the Past."

6. Booth, "Bondi Park."

7. Barnet, "Pack-Rat or Amnesiac?"; Brown, "Forum"; Landsberg, *Prosthetic Memory*; Wilson, "Digital Heritage"; Staley, *Computers, Visualization, and History*.

8. Barnet, "Pack-Rat or Amnesiac?" 217.

9. Ibid., 218.

10. Staley, *Computers, Visualization, and History*.

11. Ibid., 4.

12. Landsberg, *Prosthetic Memory* .

13. Ibid., 9.

14. Kohe, "The *Un*exceptional"; Kohe, *At the Heart of Sport*.

15. Landsberg, *Prosthetic Memory*, 11.

16. de Groot, "Perpetually Dividing and Suturing the Past and the Present," 271.

17. Wilson, "Digital Heritage," 373.

18. Kalay, "Preserving Cultural Heritage through Digital Media."

19. Etzioni and Etzioni, "Face-to-Face and Computer-Mediated Communities."

20. Peacock, "Making Ways for Change."

21. Ibid., 334 (emphasis in the original).

22. Bandelli, "Virtual Spaces and Museums."

23. Marty, "Museum Websites and Museum Visitors," 81.

24. Ibid., 96.

25. Parry, *Museums in a Digital Age*.

26. de Groot, "Historiography and Virtuality."

27. Smith, *Uses of Heritage*.
28. Christ, "Internet Technologies and Trends Transforming Public Relations," 7.
29. Yeon, Youjin, and Kiousis, "Interactive Communication Features."
30. Ibid., 67.
31. The research for this chapter was primarily conducted during the eighteen months leading up to the London 2012 Olympic Games. As is usual in the immediate year or so before any Olympic Games, the period saw an increase in Internet activity by NZOC in an effort to build support for the organization and enthusiasm for the impending sporting spectacle.
32. Staley, *Computers, Visualization, and History*, 5.
33. Barnet, "Pack-Rat or Amnesiac," 218.
34. Staley, *Computers, Visualization, and History*, 31.
35. Ibid., 31.
36. Landsberg, *Prosthetic Memory*, 154.
37. de Groot, "Historiography and Virtuality"; de Groot, "Perpetually Dividing and Suturing the Past and Present"; Kalay, "Preserving Cultural Heritage through Digital Media"; Staley, *Computers, Visualization, and History*.

References

Bandelli, Andrea. 2010. "Virtual Spaces and Museums." In *Museums in a Digital Age*, edited by Ross Parry, 148–52. London: Routledge.

Barnet, Belinda. 2001. "Pack-Rat or Amnesiac? Memory, the Archive and the Birth of the Internet." *Continuum: Journal of Media and Cultural Studies* 15, no. 2: 217–31.

Booth, Douglas. 2012. "Bondi Park: Making, Practicing and Performing a Museum." In *Representing the Sporting Past in Museums and Halls of Fame*, edited by Murray G. Phillips, 204–30. London: Routledge.

Brown, Joshua. 2004. "Forum: History and the Web: From the Illustrated Newspaper to Cyberspace: Visual Technologies and Interaction in the Nineteenth and Twenty-First Centuries." *Rethinking History* 8, no. 2: 253–75.

Christ, Paul. 2005. "Internet Technologies and Trends Transforming Public Relations." *Journal of Website Promotion: Innovations in Internet Business Research, Theory, and Practice* 1, no. 4: 3–14.

de Groot, Jerome. 2010. "Historiography and Virtuality." In *Culture, Heritage and Representation: Perspectives on Visuality and The Past*, edited by Emma Waterton and Steve Watson, 91–103. Surrey, UK: Ashgate.

———. 2011. "'Perpetually Dividing and Suturing the Past and the Present': *Mad Men* and the Illusions of History." *Rethinking History* 15, no. 2: 269–85.

Etzioni, Amitai, and Oren Etzioni. 1999. "Face-to-Face and Computer-Mediated Communities, a Comparative Analysis." *The Information Society* 15: 241–48.

Huggins, Mike. 2008. "The Sporting Gaze: Towards a Visual Turn in Sports History—Documenting Art and Sport." *Journal of Sport History* 35, no. 2: 311–29.

Kalay, Yehuda E. 2008. "Preserving Cultural Heritage through Digital Media." In *New Heritage: New Media and Cultural Heritage,* edited by Yehuda E. Kalay, Thomas Kvan, and Janice Affleck, 1–10. London: Routledge.

Kohe, Geoffery. 2010. "The *Un*exceptional: New Zealand's Very Ordinary Olympic History." *Sport History Review* 14, no. 2: 146–63.

———. 2011. *At the Heart of Sport: The New Zealand Olympic Committee and the History of the Olympic Movement in New Zealand, 1911–2011.* Wellington: New Zealand Olympic Committee.

Landsberg, Alison. 2004. *Prosthetic Memory: The Transformation of American Remembrance in the Age of Mass Culture.* New York: Columbia University Press.

Marty, Paul F. 2008. "Museum Websites and Museum Visitors: Digital Museum Resources and their Use." *Museum Management and Curatorship* 23, no. 1: 81–99.

McLachlan, Fiona. 2012. "'You Can't Take a Picture of This—It's Already Gone': Erased Evidence, Political Parody, Postmodern Histories." *Sporting Traditions* 27, no. 2: 91–99.

Osmond, Gary, and Murray G. Phillips. 2011. "Enveloping the Past: Sport Stamps, Visuality and Museums." *The International Journal of the History of Sport* 18, no. 8–9: 1138–55.

Parry, Ross (ed.). 2010. *Museums in a Digital Age.* London: Routledge.

Peacock, Darren. 2008. "Making Ways for Change: Museums, Disruptive Technologies and Organizational Change." *Museum Management and Curatorship* 23, no.4: 333–51.

Smith, Laurajane. *2006. Uses of Heritage.* London: Routledge.

Staley, David J. 2002. *Computers, Visualization, and History: How New Technology Will Transform Our Understanding of The Past.* London: M.E. Sharpe.

Thorpe, Holly. 2012. "The Politics of Remembering: An Interdisciplinary Approach to Physical Cultural Memory." *Sporting Traditions* 27, no. 2: 113–25.

Wilson, Ross J. 2011. "Digital Heritage: Behind the Scenes of the Museum Website." *Museum Management and Curatorship* 26, no. 4: 373–89.

Woodward, Kath. 2011. "The Culture of Boxing: Sensation and Affect." *Sport in History* 31, no. 4: 487–503.

Yeon, Hye Min, Choi Youjin, and Spiro Kiousis. 2005. "Interactive Communication Features on Non-profit Organizations' Webpages for the Practice of Excellence in Public Relations." *Journal of Website Promotion: Innovations in Internet Business Research, Theory, and Practice* 1, no. 4: 61–83.

4

"Dear Collective Brain..."
Social Media as a Research Tool in Sport History

MIKE CRONIN

I want to begin far away from sport history, but right at the heart of the issues surrounding social media. It is November 2011, and the presidential election campaign is entering its last week in Ireland. The position is one that is largely ceremonial, rather than political, but that in 2011 had attracted the biggest field of candidates ever to seek the office. With a few days to go before polling, an independent candidate, who had made his name as one of the dragons on the Irish version of the television show *Dragon's Den*, Seán Gallagher, was holding a ten-point lead in the opinion polls and was the odds-on favorite to win with the bookmakers.

The final television debate, to be held three days before polls opened, was expected to be a sedate affair, and certainly never envisaged as a game changer. However, the Sinn Féin candidate, Martin McGuinness, pressed Gallagher on his former connections with the Fianna Fáil party and suggested he was not as independent as he made himself out to be. Crucially, McGuinness charged that Gallagher had collected a €5,000 check from a businessman and convicted fuel smuggler for a Fianna Fáil fundraiser in County Louth in 2008. Gallagher denied the charge against him, and the debate seemed to move on. However, because this was a major, live, televised debate, the production team was also receiving questions and comments for the panel, from the public, via Twitter. A tweet arrived that was fed to the presenter, Pat Kenny, which he chose to read aloud. He stated: "[There is] a development which I want to put to Seán Gallagher. On the @MartinMcGuinness4President Twitter account, Sinn Féin say they will produce the man who gave you a cheque for €5,000."[1] At this point Gallagher imploded, accepted that he may have taken the money, and his support dwindled. By the end of the program, the Irish bookmaker Paddy Power had dropped his odds back to 9/2, and on election day he lost to the Labour candidate, Michael D. Higgins, by an 11% margin.

So why I am telling you this story, and how does it help illuminate the discussion here? It is important because, as various investigations and inquiries have discovered since, the tweet that brought Gallagher down was unattributed, and no one on the production team had made the necessary phone calls to check the validity of the statement.[2] The tweet was an untruth, a bombshell that altered the course of the democratic process. The question, then, in this case for a news broadcaster, but more generally for all of us involved in research, is how do we, indeed should we, engage with Twitter and other social media? Are we at risk of engaging with a series of potentially exciting social media tools that are vast in their scale and reach but that do not conform to any of the normal rules that scholars have established for checking the truth and provenance of research materials?

And by way of moving toward a consideration of sport, what issues do the 2012 case of Liam Stacey raise, one of the many sport-related examples of the dangers of social media? Stacey, a Swansea University student, was watching an English Premier League soccer match on television between Bolton and Spurs. During the game, a Bolton player, Patrice Muamba, collapsed due to a heart attack. The game was stopped, and eventually postponed, while medics and doctors tried to revive the player (he eventually made a good recovery), and from his seat in the pub, Stacey tweeted, "LOL!! Fuck Muamba, he's dead." Many people on Twitter criticized Stacey for his comments, but he responded further, replying, "I ain't your friend you black cunt . . . go pick some cotton."[3] Although he subsequently tried to backtrack on his comments, complaints were made to the police about Stacey's tweets, and he was subsequently arrested and charged with inciting race hatred. At a speed that is unusual for the British court system, Stacey went on trial ten days after committing his offense, was found guilty, and was sentenced to 56 days in prison. The tabloid press delighted in the sentence, with the *Sun* leading with the headline, "Tweet Justice. Lol—HaHa!"[4]

OK, so what do we actually have here? A drunken student tweeting inexcusable racist diatribes, at a moment when, on live television, a 24-year-old footballer is fighting for his life, who is then fast-tracked through the judicial system and sent to prison. However, Stacey would not be alone in expressing such views among the soccer-watching pub-goers of Britain. Racist statements are not unusual on Twitter, Facebook, or YouTube (no matter how those companies try and police themselves) and are endemic across the wider reaches of the Internet where all kinds of right-wing and racist extremism find a home and an audience. Stacey's problem, if you like, was that he was commenting, in real time, on a near-tragic event that was being played out in front of a large television audience. The sight of a young athlete seemingly dying (Muamba's heart stopped beating for 78 minutes and was defibrillated fifteen times) live on television captured the public's imagination, and in the context of that horror, the racism of Stacey was deemed unacceptable. It was the immediacy of the tweet to a large number of people (the very power of the medium, as well as its danger) that led Stacey to the courthouse.

I would suggest that if he had racially abused a player via Twitter in the course of a normal, incident-free, ninety-minute game, then Stacey would have never been visited by the police. He was, I would argue, arrested not because of his racism but because his unpalatable statements were made about a man who was seemingly dying live on television, which he placed, instantaneously, into the most public of domains. While the majority of the media celebrated the prison sentence handed down to Stacey, other voices, such as the *Observer*'s Victoria Coren, questioned the knee-jerk reaction to the case. She argued that many commentators had failed to understand either the process by which comments on Twitter enter the public domain, the complexity of framing exactly what harassment is, or the rapid process of trial and imprisonment in the case. She concluded, in relation to Stacey and his actions, that, "it isn't illegal to be a stupid bastard."[5]

So, faced with such a large but potentially volatile research tool, how should we, as sport historians, respond to the challenges of new social media? I will begin by explaining about how I have used such tools in a recently completed research project I undertook, and then widen the discussion to see what lessons I learned, as well as what can be learned, by such an interaction.

Between 2008 and 2012, I was the lead researcher in two, major, Irish-based projects. The first was an oral history of Ireland's largest sporting and cultural organization, the Gaelic Athletic Association (GAA), and the second was an investigation into the range and extent of Ireland's built sporting heritage.[6] While the outputs of these two projects were traditional, that is, a series of books and articles (with the digital archive of the GAA oral history project being housed in their own museum), it was in the design of the two projects that the decision was made to embrace social media.[7] In practice, this meant that both projects were supported by a website and a digital database, and that these would be enhanced by interacting with the public through the use of social media platforms, in particular Facebook.

Both of these projects were underpinned by the ideas of public history, and in both cases, the project funders expected us to engage with the public at large. Facebook pages were established for both projects, outlining the extent of the research, and asking the public to friend and like us. The idea was that the Facebook pages would become platforms through which the projects would become widely publicized and therefore generate a mass of research material for us. In the case of the GAA project, this would result in people offering themselves for interview as part of our oral history remit, and with the sporting heritage project we hoped that people around the country would post material about heritage sites in their localities.

The principle at the start of this engagement was quite simple. By launching our sport history projects into the world of social media through Facebook, we would multiply our potential research audience, our research subjects and materials if you like, and the project would benefit from tapping into the local knowledge of people across Ireland.

But it didn't work like that.

To explain, I first want to deal with some practical issues, and then move onto what I feel is the most fundamental issue facing historians as they grapple with social media.

From my own experience with these specific projects, I would suggest that the use of social media, while an interesting aside, did not move us on greatly and certainly had no impact on the shape of the research projects at their end. I would argue that the biggest problem for any such use of social media is simply getting the message out there. While I never expected the contents of the Irish Sporting Heritage Facebook page to go viral, I was disappointed with its reach. The page was mentioned in the many traditional media reports on the project, and details of it were contained in all publicity material relating to the project, but it garnered only a small number of followers, and most of the likes were from people that we already knew. There was, or so it appeared, a disconnect between people listening to news stories about the projects on the radio and then actively seeking us out on Facebook. Without a large number of engagements with the projects on Facebook, the attempt to fish for a wider pool of research participants had clearly failed. Indeed, this is part of a wider problem that has been identified, particularly with Facebook, in understanding how the engagement of the individual with their own social network can be broadened so that they become engaged with people and products beyond their own, self-selected group of friends.

For Facebook, this failure to widen people's engagement was most clearly illustrated by its initial collapsing share price after the company was floated in 2012. While investors initially rushed to buy the stock, the rapid realization that the company has difficulties in converting its site members into consumers of its advertisers and their products has meant that hard questions have been asked about Facebook's future profitability. In essence, the economic survival of Facebook relies on the company convincing its members to move beyond their own friends and begin befriending corporations selling everything from cornflakes to car insurance. However, it appears that individuals, for whatever reason, do not wish to move, en masse, beyond their own circle of friends. In this, I would argue, Facebook's problem in monetizing its membership is the same as the one researchers face in convincing strangers to engage with their work through social networking. Put simply, individuals have their friends, and they don't see the need, through an instrument like Facebook, to make a new friend of an academic researcher and his or her project. They conceive the site as a social tool to connect with those that are known to them, rather than as something that presents them with opportunities to assist the unknown with the advancement of their project or product.

In my own case, one of the problems in making the research work through social media was simply a lack of support from the bodies that were paying for the research. While the GAA and the Irish government, respectively, were happy to pay for the research, neither of them saw it as their job to promote the projects during their lifetime. As such, rather than the social media presence being announced in GAA match programs or by government ministers, it was only pushed (obviously ineffectively) by ourselves. With any research tool or methodology that attempts to engage with the public, the key to success is publicity and awareness. Indeed, it has usually been history programs on television that have garnered the greatest followings and participations of late (but most of these have been around an interaction that asks the public to vote).

In hindsight, I actually think the biggest problem was that while we decided a social media platform was desirable for the projects, we didn't reconfigure our traditional research methodology accordingly. Rather than seeing social media as a specific type of research tool, we saw it as a portal through which we could publicize the project, and that this would bring people to us who would then work within our traditional networks and methodologies. In this we made a fundamental mistake, because people visiting our Facebook page weren't given clear instructions as to what we expected of them: put simply, we didn't tailor our needs for the technology.

What we wanted, for example, on the sporting heritage project, was for people to identify heritage sites in their local area, and to upload pictures, maps, and other details of them onto the page. This is asking a lot for a social networking site where the majority of interaction is between people known to each other. In this I would suggest that of the big two social media forums, Twitter is better suited as a research tool because access is far more open and the style of engagement much more focused. Facebook has become evermore privacy aware and the purpose of it has relied on the personal more so than the reactive. The power of the medium in terms of the Arab Spring will need further analysis. Meanwhile, the 1.3 million members of the Save Darfur Facebook page, which supported a fundraising drive for the war-torn Sudanese town, produced donations of less than 15 cents each.[8] It is here that the gap between liking and joining (passive acts) and taking part (activism) becomes clear, as Gladwell argued in relation to the Save Darfur page: "Facebook activism succeeds not by motivating people to make a real sacrifice but by motivating them to do the things that people do when they are not motivated enough to make a real sacrifice."[9] The challenge then for any use that Facebook may have for the sport historian researcher is understanding how liking can be translated into doing, essentially figuring out how (indeed even if) we can convert the passive observer into the active research participant.

Moving beyond my own experiences, I want to assess more broadly how social media does, and might in the future, affect what we do as sport historians. In our approach to social media I think we have to distinguish between three impulses. The first is when we use social media to gain assistance from our friends, the second is using the medium to gather research material and data, and the third is when we look to use it as a reservoir of already collected material.

In addressing the first issue I look to the title of this chapter, which is taken from a line that I am increasingly seeing among scholars who use Facebook: "Dear Collective Brain . . ." This is the most direct form of research (and teaching) assistance that social media offers. Put simply, and presuming your friends include your fellow scholars, a question can be put out there, and the collective brain of your scholarly friends finds the answer. It is research at its most collective, and one of the most obvious ways in which sport historians (and other scholars) can instantly connect with a global network to access the information or advice that they need to move their work forward.

The two other issues relating to research and social media are more complex and in essence I would argue that the latter (accessing previously collected data) is much simpler than the former (harvesting data). In gathering raw data, the best results have been seen on projects that use simple voting formulas, such as with Facebook's Questions tool, SurveyMonkey, or Zoomerang. In this, social media favors quantitative data collection, and is a useful and cheap way of collecting information. For a more qualitative engagement, such as the one I envisaged and hoped for in my research projects, the difficulty seems to be that there has to be clarity of what is expected by any respondent, and also an allowance that anyone who does respond is, to a degree, self selecting, as they have chosen to dedicate the time necessary to engage with a more qualitative approach.

The best uses of social media in research that I have seen to date are those that use Twitter as a resource, and therefore use previously generated data. The research takes a responsive rather than proactive role, that is, using material from Twitter as data, rather than using Twitter to create data specifically in response to a predefined research question. There are various projects that can serve as examples, but excellent ones include those such as the *Guardian*/London School of Economics' exploration of the 2011 riots in Britain, *Reading the Riots,* that used the 2.6 million tweets that were sent during the days of rioting, and read them as the data to understand how and why the riots took place in the form that they did.[10] Similarly, the Centre of Excellence for Creative Industries and Innovation, at the Queensland University of Technology, used the Twitter feed that emanated during the 2011 Queensland floods, arguing, I think quite rightly, that Twitter was an excellent resource to "harvest civilian sentiment."[11]

What Twitter, Facebook, and other forms of social media allow for is the analysis of large sets of data to understand how events and themes trend, and an understanding of how different individuals (and their followers) react to each other and to what is happening around them. While a relatively new departure, such collection and analysis of trending topics is one that became obvious, and crossed into the mainstream, given the ways the traditional print and broadcast media used the social networking data emerging in response to the debates during the 2012 U.S. presidential election to instantly gauge, and represent, the mood of the nation. In this, while questions of authorship and editorial control may shift, the value of Twitter's archive, in terms of understanding what is trending and the subjects that preoccupy the public mind, serves a similar function to the newspaper archives that would have been the historian's previously favored friend.

A further issue I would comment on is the use of social media to showcase history and the research associated with it, as opposed to its use as a research tool. Again, this is an important but valuable distinction. If I understand our own use of social media as a research tool as largely a failure, I would also argue that when we used an Internet platform to showcase the work we had done, such as excerpts from oral history interviews on the GAA project, then we had a large volume of online traffic (perhaps suggesting that people prefer passive consumption of readymade history rather than active participation).

Again, examples abound of successful social media projects in which history has been pushed out to its audience, such as the recent Twitter recreation of the Titanic's ill-fated voyage. The @TitanicRealTime Twitter feed was seen as very successful, and was based on extensive research and the use of contemporary documents and photographs.[12] In it, various passengers and crew tweeted their experience of the journey for each day of the voyage, and this allowed the receivers of the tweet to understand the recreated journey in real time. In a similar vein is the American National Park Service's ongoing @CivilWarReportr, produced to coincide with the sesquicentennial commemoration of the Civil War.[13] In this, a fictional journalist, Beglan O'Brien, tweets most days about what is happening. Unlike the Titanic experience, which covers a short time span of weeks, the Civil War Reporter is covering events over years and across a large landmass. Some days, during intense battles, there is a lot happening, whereas on others, little is there to be tweeted. To keep people's interest, the Civil War Reporter is used to explore wider historical issues and foster interest beyond the actual fighting. For example, the tweet for November 2, 1862, reads: "All Souls Day, to break the tedium, we go soul-caking tent to tent." Beneath the tweet there is a link to a page on the National Public Radio website, which details the history of various foodstuffs and traditions related to All Souls Day, including the background to the offering and meanings associated with soul-caking. While nothing to do with the Civil War, per se, the tweet is an excellent example of real-time information that brings wider issues relating to social history to the fore.

I believe that these types of real-time, recreation projects will grow in number, and sophistication, in the coming years, especially as we enter a period crammed with significant centenaries, such as those relating to the First World War. The value of these history feeds that are available via social media is that they inform and entertain people, as well as promote digital literacy as part of the educational process. Those that work best, such as those from the Titanic and the American Civil War, are those that provide more than the simple, text-based tweet and offer additional material in the form of photographs and documents, or else are linked to larger reservoirs of information elsewhere on the Internet.

It is also crucial, as with any form of social media, that the information flows on a regular basis. Any Twitter feed or Facebook site that is allowed to remain unchanged for any length of time will quickly lose its followers. The most successful feeds are those that deliver information on a daily (or even hourly) basis and thereby keep its followers fully engaged and interested. This has ramifications for the planning of historical research projects via social media. To provide a constant source of information to a large number of followers requires either the enthusiasm of a dedicated individual who will work for his or her belief in the project (Damian Shiels' project, "The Irish in the American Civil War," is a fine example of high-quality, regular material being provided by a committed individual[14]) or a sizable budget and an employed team of researchers. While social media might be put forward as a democratizing tool that is free and open to all, the production of high-quality historical content, supported by scholarly research with access to archival material and repositories, is not often the work of the lone enthusiast in the bedroom, but rather demands high levels of planning, staffing, and resources. In this there will be a distinction between social media history projects produced by national institutions or media outlets, and those produced by the engaged individual.

This in turn goes back to my earlier point about how such projects are promoted. The British National Archives used Twitter to recreate the events of 1944 by tweeting material from the Cabinet Papers of that year.[15] It not only promoted the newly digitized and online Cabinet Papers, but also collected thousands of followers as it was supported by a major institution and an intense media campaign. The question for sport historians (and sports associations and federations) is how they bring together the information they wish to feed to the public via social media, how the whole exercise is resourced, and, in other forms of media, how it is promoted to gather the widest audience.

For all the benefits of social media as a potential research tool, there are big questions that will have to be tackled by our profession. The comparison I would draw to make sense of what we face is to look at the state of social media now (fluid, exciting, bursting with possibility and new ways of doing) in contrast with the field of oral history in the 1970s. Seen as a new research tool of the time, oral history set out to recover that much-heralded "history from below."

In due course, scholars were dispatched with the tape recorders of the time, a subdiscipline grew, and an extra methodology was added to the tool kit of historians. How quickly the world of oral history changed though: where once there was a sense of freedom and innovation, soon there came regulation. If we take the first bible of oral history, Paul Thompson's *The Voice of the Past: Oral History*, published in 1978, it barely mentions any ethical or legal concerns that might be attached to the collecting or storing of oral history interviews.[16] Move forward and look at Donald Richie's 2003 *Doing Oral History: A Practical Guide,* and there is a whole section on the law, and even more recently John A. Neuenschwander's *A Guide to Oral History and the Law*, which takes the topic into full, book-length coverage.[17] Essentially, what was supposed to be a liberating new tool for historians has become one that is fraught with legal complexities (one that my own institution can attest to, having spent the bulk of 2011 and 2012 in the U.S. courts contesting the ownership and privilege of an oral history project it conducted[18]), and interviews are now begun with a legal preamble, the signing of paperwork, and explanations of the complexities of informed consent.

Oral history, like the sciences, now keeps the human ethics committees of universities across the world very busy. Oral history is no longer something that is simply undertaken by historian and tape recorder, but rather is a methodology that has become institutionalized and regulated. While a vitally important methodology, it no longer offers the sense of a liberating new approach, as it did in the 1970s, and has instead tightly controlled rules and approaches that exist around it so that its correct application is standardized.

Social media currently exists, in terms of how sport historians may use it, as an exciting new frontier, full of (and fraught with) exciting possibilities. It is potentially about innovation and new ways of doing history. But can this actually happen? Can a new technology be applied to history, in this case social media, that will abandon the rules, regulations, and approaches that govern what we do? I would argue not. It is my view that the use of social media as a research tool will undoubtedly go the same way as oral history did: from free spirit to fully regulated methodology. Indeed, it's already happening. In biomedical research, using SurveyMonkey, North York General Hospital, among others, has had to begin every survey with the warning that "No personal identifiers will be collected on the survey but it is possible that the views and opinions you expressed may be accessed and linked to you without your knowledge or consent by the U.S. government under the U.S. Patriot Act."[19]

This warning for U.S.-based users of SurveyMonkey flags one of the concerns of social media research. This is not simply a two-way discussion between researcher and respondent, but rather is a conversation, as it is digital and conducted via our Internet connections, that can be listened into, and used by, in this case, the U.S. government under its laws. The same issue was at the heart of a 2012 legal case between Twitter and the U.S. courts. Prosecutors demanded that Twitter hand over the message and posting archive of an Occupy Wall Street activist, but Twitter argued that it did not have the authority to do so given that its terms and conditions state that users "own" their personal content. The case was highly complex, and went to the heart of who owns social media content, the individual who posted or the company that carried the message. In the Occupy Wall Street case Twitter was defeated and, in September 2012, handed over the relevant archive of material to the authorities.[20] The ruling provokes real questions for historians (and other researchers) using social media as a platform to either collect or share their research. When we decide that any given research project is ripe for using social media, who then will own the material? And who, be it the state, criminals, and others, will be able to listen in, as it were, to the discussions that we have with research subjects?

Quickly, a technology that was imagined as a tool that would allow us to chat freely and exchange information, the much-heralded democratization of information, has become policed (and the legal and scholarly controls will only increase in time). What, for example, do we tell the student who comes to us for advice on his or her dissertation? The student decides that he or she is going to use social media to gauge the mindset of soccer supporters who follow lower league clubs in the north of England. The student is interested in how ideas of loyalty and community function beyond the bright lights of the Premier League. As supervisor, we agree that this is a valid topic, and the student goes ahead and conducts the research project via social media. At the draft stage of the dissertation, the supervisor sees that the student has used quotes of someone identified as #bigladinburnley, and that the person has alluded to minor acts of hooliganism as part of proving his loyalty to his club.

If we apply normal (or perhaps traditional) ethical and legal standards, then (1) at least the researcher should know the real identity of that person, (2) the person quoted should have been told about why his or her opinions were sought, and what the vehicle for them later being used would be, and (3) both researcher and subject should understand whether, and if, the material would be stored/archived in the future (and given the hint of an illegal act, is that archive secure from legal agencies—indeed can such security of the archive and anonymity be guaranteed anyway?). The issue of storage via social media (and the Internet) is an important question because unless a post is taken down, it exists for as long as the technology remains unchanged. So, do we have to adapt to the nature of social media and alter our research and ethical approval processes accordingly, or do we argue instead (and the law may force us to do this anyway) that whatever the value of social media in potentially reaching a large subject base, the traditional standards have to apply? In this scenario is my earlier-mentioned student forced to go back to #bigladinburnley and get the requisite release forms, informed consent forms, and archival copyright forms signed in the good old-fashioned format of hard-copy, paper-and-ink signatures? Has that student embraced a potentially exciting new avenue for sport-related history research, simply to be squeezed back into what we understand as the norm?

Facebook offers one more nightmarish issue that will dominate many of the debates around social media and research in the university environment in the coming years. In the sports heritage project I undertook, we gathered around us a collection of people who liked or friended us. Do I, the researcher, have any responsibilities toward them? After all, they are only helping me with my bona fide research project. Well, no. By engaging with these people I have access, presuming they are not meticulous in their security settings (and most people aren't), to all kinds of data about them, their home, family, work, and so on. This is the complexity of Facebook, in that any given research project in which I invite people in, to befriend me, allows me to access huge sums of data about them (after all, companies want me to friend them not to see my holiday snaps or my inane banter but to access my personal information). So, if someone joins a research project via Facebook, what data protection issues do I have to consider? In a world where access to, and the storage of data, particularly in the university research environment, is highly sensitive, research on Facebook does provoke questions as to how researchers make the access to such personal data secure, especially given that access to that data is an unintended byproduct of the research. This is true not simply for the type of sport history research envisaged here but also applies to researchers across a range of subdisciplines and methodologies across sport studies generally. There is a central ethical issue that all researchers should seek to protect their research subjects, and the advent of social media will have an impact on oral historians, ethnographers, and many others.

This chapter has concentrated on my own experiences in using social media as a research tool, and has suggested a series of questions and issues that will come to face us in the coming years as sport historians interact with and use such technology. My own instinct is that controls and restrictions will be imposed on our use of social media in a research setting, much as they have been with any research that involves human subjects. This is not necessarily a negative, but an acceptance that because social media is primarily driven by individuals, any engagement with their posts puts them into the same ethical location as interviewees or other subjects of historical research.

I began with the story of the Irish Presidential candidate and the problematic, unattributed tweet on a television debate. The TV company was damned in the subsequent enquiries because they had not checked their facts. It is a salient lesson, and one that we need to bear in mind as we use social media in our research and also (though not the topic for this chapter) in our teaching: facts, however harvested during our research, have to be checked and the correct procedures followed in ensuring the validity and source of the material that we use. Likewise, the example of the racist soccer supporter is instructive. For some reason, and the bulk of research backs this up, people consider their online persona as operating under different rules in contrast with their real-life behavior.[21] As researchers we have to understand that someone's personality, their testimony, and the way they may answer questions in a social media setting will often be distinct from their usual values and opinions. This being the case, do we have to treat and understand what we harvest from social media (and more broadly in any online setting) in a different light to traditional archives? Do we need a new mindset to read this material?

Ultimately, I feel that I am arguing that while social media will prove to be an important research tool, I don't feel that it's a game changer. As Michael O'Driscoll noted:

> In recent years, digital technologies have made way for a new range of practices (such as blogs, wikis, crowd-sourced review, open access journals, self-archiving, podcasting, remote conferencing, Twitter, Facebook, YouTube, Academia.edu, LinkedIn, and more localized online research consortiums) that might be seen to have dramatically altered the dynamics of intellectual activity in the humanities. For better or for worse, the social parameters of scholarship have shifted. Or have they?[22]

O'Driscoll argues that the potential for social networking via social media is huge, but that it is a new variant on traditional forms. Social media has not invented networking, it delivers it in a different form. Building on this, I would state that social media will be another addition to our research and teaching arsenal, allowing us new ways to find and transmit our research. For sport historians it offers much. In the same way that the ranks of the popular history are populated by genealogists and war historians (online and in real life), so sports clubs have active, well-defined, and interested online communities. I know from my own experience that we found more suggestions for people who we might interview for the GAA Oral History project through the fansites, the Hogan Stand, and An Fear Rua, than we did through conventional channels. For research projects that seek to capture data and information from those who follow, and who are passionate about sport, social media offers an excellent research opportunity.

It is true that most sporting clubs, whether elite or mass participation, have their own social networking sites. In the case of those who follow professional elite sports, such sites are usually dominated by fans and range from those that are authorized by the club to those that are the work of individuals. These are used for commenting on games and gossip, as well as organizing travel to matches, socializing, and so on, and, as has been shown, such social networks allow for the disparate individuals to bridge barriers and develop new relationships in the context of their shared enthusiasm for a team or sport.[23] For local and amateur clubs, social networking sites are predominantly used to arrange fixtures and keep club members informed about what is happening on a week-to-week basis. Both of these communities are online, so they are more readily available and approachable than they have been before. For sport historians, sociologists, and others, such networks (while they have always existed in some form or other) are now available en masse through one portal. Research design will be a key issue, and the host of complexities discussed in this chapter will be brought to bear on making such a virtual community work for us. It is clear from my own experiences, recounted here, that we must tailor our research to fit the styles and demands of social media and, as with all research involving human subjects, we have to be alert to new ways of thinking about the associated legal and ethical issues. Addressed properly, however, and with research designed specifically for the social media space, this will be a profitable venue for future research.

Notes

1. Ó Caollaí, "Frontline Tweet," 12.
2. *Irish Times* reporters, "RTÉ to conduct review," 3.
3. "Liam Stacey."
4. Coles, "Tweet Justice," 1.
5. Coren, "So what did the Troll actually say," 34.
6. For details on the GAA project, see www.gaahistory.com, and for the Sporting Heritage Project, see www.irishsportingheritage.com.
7. See, for example: Cronin, Duncan, and Rouse, *The GAA: A People's History*; Cronin, Duncan, and Rouse, *The GAA: County by County*; Cronin, Murphy, and Rouse (eds), *The GAA, 1884–2009*; Cronin and Higgins, *Places We Play*.
8. Gladwell, "Small Change."

9. Ibid.
10. *The Guardian,* "Reading the Riots."
11. Bruns et al., *#qldfloods and @QPSMedia.*
12. "TitanicVoyage."
13. "Civil War Reporter."
14. "Irish in the American Civil War."
15. "War Cabinet."
16. Thompson, *The Voice of the Past.*
17. Richie, *Doing Oral History;* Neuenschwander, *A Guide to Oral History.*
18. For background to the case, see PBS Newshour.
19. David M. Kaplan, March 30, 2011, "Using SurveyMonkey in Biomedical and Social Science Research," Healthybits. Accessed October 25, 2012. http://davidkaplanmd.wordpress.com/2011/03/30/using-survey-monkey-in-biomedical-and-social-science-research/.
20. BBC, "Twitter hands over messages at heart of Occupy case."
21. Thompson, "The Intersection of Online Social Networking with Medical Professionalism," 954–57.
22. O'Driscoll, "Face/Book/Net/Work," 1.
23. Phua, "Use of Social Networking," 109–32.

References

BBC. "Twitter hands over messages at heart of Occupy case." Accessed September 17, 2012. http://www.bbc.co.uk/news/technology-19597437.
Bruns, Axel, Jean E. Burgess, Kate Crawford, and Frances Shaw. 2012. *#qldfloods and @QPSMedia: Crisis Communication on Twitter in the 2011 South East Queensland Floods.* Brisbane: ARC Centre of Excellence for Creative Industries and Innovation, Queensland University of Technology.
"Civil War Reporter@CivilWarReportr." Accessed 26 October 2012. https://twitter.com/CivilWarReportr.
Coles, John. 2012. "Tweet Justice. Lol—HaHa!" *Sun,* March 28, 1.
Coren, Victoria. 2012. "So what did the Troll actually say." *Observer,* April 8, 34.
Cronin, Mike, Mark Duncan, and Paul Rouse. 2009. *The GAA: A People's History.* Cork: Collins Press.
———. 2011. *The GAA: County by County.* Cork: Collins Press.
Cronin, Mike, William Murphy, and Paul Rouse (eds). 2009. *The GAA, 1884–2009.* London: Irish Academic Press.
Cronin, Mike, and Roisin Higgins. 2011. *Places We Play: Ireland's Sporting Heritage.* Cork: Collins Press.
Gladwell, Malcolm. 2010. "Small Change: Why the Revolution will not be Tweeted." *New Yorker,* October 4. Accessed April 10, 2013. http://www.newyorker.com/reporting/2010/10/04/101004fa_fact_gladwell?currentPage=all.

The Guardian. "Reading the Riots." Accessed October 12, 2012. http://www.guardian.co.uk/uk/series/reading-the-riots.

"Irish in the American Civil War: Exploring Irish Involvement in the American Civil War." Accessed August 15, 2012. http://irishamericancivilwar.com/.

Irish Times reporters. 2012. "RTÉ to conduct review after Gallagher Tweet controversy." *Irish Times,* March 12, 3.

"Liam Stacey Twitter racism against Fabrice Muamba, don't lose the evidence." You Tube. Accessed October 25, 2012. http://www.youtube.com/watch?v=nA5v2eZ5ZZE.

Neuenschwander, John A. 2009. *A Guide to Oral History and the Law.* New York: Oxford University Press.

Ó Caollaí, Éanna. 2011. "Frontline Tweet Earth Shattering." *Irish Times,* November 14, 12.

O'Driscoll, Michael. 2010. "Face/Book/Net/Work: Social Networking and the Humanities." *ESC: English Studies in Canada* 36, no. 4, 1–3.

PBS Newshour. "US and UK entangled in legal battle to release former IRA militants' stories." Accessed August 24, 2012. http://www.pbs.org/newshour/bb/law/july-dec12/ireland_08-23.html.

Phua, Joe. 2012. "Use of Social Networking by Sports Fans. Implications for the Creation and Maintenance of Social Capital." *Journal of Sports Media* 7, no. 1, 109–32.

Richie, Donald. 2003. *Doing Oral History.* New York: Oxford University Press.

Thompson, Lindsay A., Kara Dawson, Richard Ferdig, Erik W. Black, J. Boyer, Jade Coutts, and Nicole Paradise Black. 2008. "The Intersection of Online Social Networking with Medical Professionalism." *Journal of General Internal Medicine* 23, no. 7 (July), 954–57.

Thompson, Paul. 1978. *The Voice of the Past: Oral History.* Oxford: Oxford University Press.

"TitanicVoyage@TitanicRealTime." Accessed 26 October 2012. https://twitter.com/TitanicRealTime.

"War Cabinet@ukwarcabinet." Accessed 26 October 2012. https://twitter.com/ukwarcabinet.

5

Into the Digital Era

Sport History, Teaching and Learning, and Web 2.0

TARA MAGDALINSKI

With each passing day, there seems to be a new gadget, a new app, or a new functionality that allow users even more opportunities to network or connect with others. Far from the early days of the Internet, when websites provided static information that had to be sought out, the Web 2.0 revolution has created dynamic relationships with content and extensive global interactivity delivered directly to our screens or phones. Increasingly, teachers of sport history are encountering so-called digital natives, who are as comfortable conversing online as they are in person, and whose understanding of the digital superhighways often far surpasses those teaching them. There is some degree of expectation from these millennials that lecture content and support materials be available around the clock, and there is increasing pressure to use different learning technologies to enhance the overall educational experience. Although not everyone who teaches sport history will want to adapt to this new digital landscape, and there are certainly a plethora of pitfalls to be negotiated, there are nevertheless a range of opportunities to move out of the classroom and engage students in an online environment to place them at the center of their own learning.

This chapter examines some technology-based teaching, learning, and assessment strategies appropriate for sport history pedagogy, including wikis, blogs, and social media, and locates these within a constructivist paradigm that foregrounds the learner as participant in the construction of learning experiences. Although sport history may seem a little more dusty than techie, this chapter examines the role of Web 2.0 in contemporary teaching and learning practice and offers practical suggestions for even the most dusty among us to inspire students to take sport history out of the archive and place it online. Finally, it considers some of the challenges for teaching and learning through web-based applications.

What is Web 2.0?

Before discussing the role of Web 2.0 in the teaching and learning of sport history, it is important to understand the radical shift in online technologies that provides for some of the pedagogical interactions discussed in this chapter. The Web 2.0 concept initially referred to the second coming of the Internet following the dotcom crash in 2001, and although it has now been popularly adopted as shorthand for all social and interactive online platforms, the term more accurately describes a set of "principles and practices"[1] rather than reflecting a set of technical specifications. Predicated on a "philosophy"[2] or an "attitude,"[3] Web 2.0 foregrounds the cultural experience of open and democratic interaction. Jim McNamara summarizes these various approaches to assert that Web 2.0 is characterized by

> increasingly widespread connectivity through always-on open networks that allow people formerly confined to "audiences" to become producers as well as consumers (what some call prosumers or produsers) resulting in creativity, diversity and plurality in content, and facilitating interactivity including two-way human-to-human interaction, collaboration with others to pool and share ideas and intellectual property (what Pierre Levy calls collective intelligence) and engage in cocreativity, community building, and communication through conversation and dialogue between people interacting with authenticity.[4]

Despite these initial conceptualizations, in practice Web 2.0 refers most commonly to online interactivity. Significantly, the advent of Web 2.0 applications predates the coined phrase by a number of years, and heralded a move away from static websites where information was simply read toward a dynamic, interactive, and collaborative experience, where consumers could view, comment on, create, share, repurpose, and generally engage with digital content.[5] These web-based platforms allow complex interactions between user and producer and between users themselves to create "produsers,"[6] a term that both acknowledges the dual user/producer roles of Web 2.0 consumers and simultaneously dissolves established borders between passive consumption and active production. As such, Web 2.0 shatters linear communication models, first rendered graphically by Shannon and Weaver in the 1940s, which reduce the transfer of knowledge to a simple unilateral act where the message is disseminated uncritically to a waiting audience. This rudimentary model has instead been replaced by open, flexible, multidirectional information channels where content circulates instantaneously between producers and users, generating responses and feedback from multiple sources.

It is important to note that producers, users, and produsers are plural terms, highlighting that it is not possible to identify single origin points of information, or at least not an always easily discernible one. Attempts to restrict the message to a particular interpretation or audience are ineffective, and an expectation that the material cannot be adjusted or manipulated once available for comment is unrealistic. Once content goes viral, it can be shared, altered, parodied, contextualized, and appropriated for a range of alternative uses unconnected to the author's original intention. While traditional media is certainly subject to the same sorts of revisions, the speed with which content is transmitted and the number of people it might reach has been heretofore unfathomable.

The key features of Web 2.0, such as its interconnectivity; its multidirectional information flow; and the opportunity it provides for both users and producers to discuss, reflect, critique, and collaboratively create content on an online platform, suggest this platform could inspire useful innovation in the classroom or lecture theater. Web 2.0 applications, such as wikis, blogs, social bookmarking, discussion forums, social media, content sharing sites, and a host of other apps that provoke the development of connections and communities and allow for the almost limitless circulation of information, may be effectively employed in teaching and learning strategies. Indeed, the Internet should rightfully be reconceived as not merely a repository of information, but a site where knowledge is actively constructed and refined.[7]

Incorporating Web 2.0 into Teaching and Learning

There is increasing interest and a growing body of literature that deals with the integration of Web 2.0 into higher education, particularly given the ubiquitous nature of social media in the lives of teenagers and young adults. The quest to use these alternative communication forms and embed them within educational practice is underpinned by questions about how this media is used socially and the ways that it might be effectively embraced as a method to create learning experiences that will appeal to and captivate the attention of digital natives for whom online interaction is *de rigeur*. Nevertheless, the rapid shift from a page-based to a screen-based medium of communication[8] over the past decade or so has not always found its parallel in the academy in quite the same way. Whereas administrative communication and document management may have largely shifted to the electronic realm, there has been more resistance to similar innovation within the context of teaching and learning, outside, perhaps, distance learning.[9] The ubiquitous PowerPoint presentation has been perhaps the most successful electronic infiltration of the lecture hall, though these are often little more than heavy, text-based scripts with illustrative images that simply allow learners to read along together with the lecturer, whereas virtual learning environments more often are relegated to the role of document repository or "electronic filing cabinet."[10] This is, however, slowly changing as academics begin to understand the value of Web 2.0 tools in the context of student-centered learning.[11]

There is a wide variety of opportunities to employ Web 2.0 to extend traditional classroom settings or, indeed, to transform on-campus teaching to create more engaging learning experiences for students. Increasingly, Web 2.0 is being incorporated into tertiary education in an effort to access and assess students on and through platforms with which they are familiar, responding, in essence, to Jennifer Brill and Yeongjeong Park's assessment that we are moving from simply an "information age" to an "interaction age."[12] In line with an era of interactivity, education becomes less a process of establishing an authoritative voice that transmits knowledge to recipients, and more an opportunity for students to learn by doing. As such, Web 2.0 applications may be better used as part of a learner's tool kit, whereby they have a number of avenues to seek information (Internet/traditional forms of research/online discussion forums), experiment with their interpretations and forms of presentation (blogs, Twitter, YouTube, wikis), receive and respond to feedback (comments on blogs, Facebook, discussion forums), and defend or revise their positions as a result of discussion (new blog entry).

Embracing learning through digital platforms requires a concomitant revision of basic pedagogical principles and modes of delivery, underpinned by a constructivist or co-constructivist approach that places the learner at the center of the learning experience, not merely as a passive recipient of information, but as an active participant in the construction of knowledge and understanding.[13] This means Web 2.0 applications challenge educators to rethink the teaching structure to move from a focus on predetermined learning outcomes, or the notion that one size fits all, toward an emphasis on the process of learning in which outcomes and assessment are customized, flexible, and negotiated. As such, Betty Collis and Jef Moonen recommend that "both instructors and students must value an educational approach where learner participation and contribution are balanced with acquisition," so that "students create at least some of their own learning resources."[14]

The interconnectedness and collaborative potential of Web 2.0 applications mean that students can interact not only with the lecturer and each other but with related communities, either expert or novice, beyond the academy on topics of mutual interest. At the same time, they can locate, edit, and generate content that can be shared, commented on, and, in turn, edited by other users, either in their class or more broadly. By expanding pedagogical opportunities beyond the classroom, learning, reflection, and application become asynchronous and ideally embedded in students' daily lives. Learning on the go is necessarily flexible, but it also allows students to become "contributing member[s] of a learning community," so that "learning . . . is active" and "driven by process rather than content," thus inspiring students to become "self-directed and independent learners."[15]

Rosemary Luckin et al. suggest that online platforms "support deeper levels of engagement" through, among others, "the development of a sense of audience and shared purpose."[16] Linking with wider communities can be achieved, for example, by making student work, such as blogs, Facebook pages, or wikis, publicly accessible. Making blogs public, for example, can empower students by acknowledging that "their ideas are being heard and taken seriously,"[17] so that research and writing become an exercise in actual communication rather than simply an academic exercise in which the potential for meaningful debate about their ideas, positions, or interpretations is curtailed at submission. Allowing students access to each other's materials helps them to clarify their own thoughts by creating a conversation in which students are prompted to defend or revise their positions based on the quality of the arguments presented in response to their blogs. It means that students need to reflect on their posts, consider how their arguments can be (mis)interpreted, and ensure that their writing is precise and concise enough to communicate effectively with what may be a largely unknown, but authentic, audience. Finally, ideas are collectively shaped and refined in light of alternative perspectives, critiques, or commentary from peers, allowing for a more meaningful learning experience.

Peer or broader community engagement is not exclusive to blogs and can be effected through a number of Web 2.0 applications, and importantly, can be used to foster digital literacy among millennials, who tend to value information sourced from online equally. Cullen Chandler and Alison Gregory outline the effective use of Wikipedia to encourage students to critically reflect upon the production of public knowledge.[18] Previously banning Wikipedia as a poor source for undergraduate research papers, they reconceived it as a learning space where students worked on developing novel entries or editing and revising previously published pages at the same time that they learned the technical, ethical, and procedural aspects of contributing to the online repository. Not only did the students learn to integrate research, synthesis, and online publishing for a public audience, they learned to engage with Wikipedia as an information source. As they watched their entries change and develop across the semester with input from many others around the world, they learned how to interact with other contributors and editors, as well as contend with comments, feedback, and edits on their own work. Significantly, by engaging in the process of writing for Wikipedia, the students started to recognize the varying quality of entries, became concerned about the motives and qualifications of authors, and overall started to doubt their previous reliance on it as an unproblematic source and, in short, became critical consumers of online information, particularly after they learned their work had been plagiarized by a student at another university![19]

In addition to encouraging independent learning, Web 2.0 encourages students to create, share, and critique content on a digital platform, allowing for group work projects that are truly collaborative. Group work is notoriously despised by most students who fear that an inequitable distribution of work will not be reflected in grades[20] and that freeloaders will receive credit for work to which they have not fairly contributed.[21] Such responses are typical for standard group projects that are often not designed with true collaboration in mind. Students receive their assignment, immediately divide it into sections that are assigned to individual members, who dutifully flee in all directions never to be seen again until the individual contributions need to be stitched together. Rather than students individually doing their bit, with a self-appointed leader being responsible for linking individual submissions together, a single document can be worked on by all students via online workspaces, such as Google Drive, a group wiki, or other e-document sharing systems. While the evidence on their efficacy is mixed,[22] it is clear that with all of the technologies outlined in this paper, the use of wikis is not always intuitive and instruction needs to be given in how to use the application, the rationale for their incorporation in the curriculum, as well as expectations for its use.[23] Furthermore, traditional project design may not easily translate to this medium, so it is incumbent on educators to design appropriate collaborative learning activities that are properly aligned with learning outcomes[24] as well as actively encourage and support interaction and collaboration among students.[25]

Given the overwhelming number of students who engage with social media on a daily basis, particularly Facebook and Twitter, it is no surprise that attempts to incorporate these platforms into the learning process have been made,[26] and researchers have noted the potential for Facebook to support student interaction and peer feedback.[27] As a primarily social experience, establishing Facebook as a specific learning tool has not been straightforward, and evidence suggests that while social engagement is high, cognitive engagement is less apparent.[28] Students have particular expectations for social networking sites, which typically do not include formal teaching and learning activities. Meeting people, establishing networks, finding new friends, and keeping in touch with existing friends have been identified as the primary reasons students use Facebook, with the possibility of informal learning acknowledged, but not foregrounded as an initial motivation for using social media.[29] Clare Madge et al. note that students were categorical in their desire to keep Facebook and their studies as separate entities,[30] and while slightly more receptive to administrative announcements or updates appearing in their newsfeed, they nevertheless resisted efforts for their social space to be colonized by lecturing staff.[31] Significantly, a subsequent study determined that students were more open than teaching staff to the use of Facebook for formal learning activities, with most faculty insisting the medium is both private and a social tool.[32]

Rather than using social networking to engage students in discrete learning tasks, Facebook and Twitter may be better used to generate a sense of community, where students can seek informal support from one another.[33] This does not need to be instigated or monitored by teaching staff, and students might be encouraged to set up their own course- or degree-relevant Facebook group, if they have not already done so, where they can solicit feedback or assistance in their learning, as well as bond socially with their peers. Twitter, for example, can be more than the distribution of individual thoughts, and might be used to take notes, share resources, comment on other students' or the lecturer's ideas, ask questions of peers, help one another, and offer suggestions—in short, creating a larger learning community than perhaps a face-to-face study group might allow.[34]

Web 2.0 also offers other benefits, such as providing instant feedback to lecturers on content or to pose questions during the lecture. By encouraging students to use discussion boards, blogs, or wikis, students can indicate—even anonymously—how much they understand. Trena Paulus et al. suggest that blogs offer insight into student learning and help "contextualize instruction" by allowing lectures to identify areas of confusion, misunderstanding, or struggles with course content and providing a space for students to raise questions or highlight areas that need clarification.[35] Feedback can be synchronous or asynchronous. Richard Buckland lectures from a live wiki so that students can add examples and questions in real time as he goes through the lecture material.[36] Similarly, a live Twitter feed can be displayed on a screen as students work together in small groups and post their questions and comments about their discussion for the entire class to see. Similarly, in large lectures where students might be reluctant to ask questions in front of the group, questions could be posted to Facebook or Twitter with the lecturer responding every so often.[37] Some applications, such as Google Moderator, allow students to vote up or down specific comments, thus ranking queries from most to least important.

Despite some of the advantages, there are a number of obstacles to successful integration of Web 2.0 in the higher education classroom. In addition to the resource implications that come with any review of teaching and assessment formats, some lecturers experience significant anxiety at the thought of allowing students to direct the message or create the content that they subsequently learn. Others are concerned that the informal communication methods on social networking sites—txt spk—will spell the end of vowel-infused academic discourse. Yet others might be worried about the authenticity of sources being used in an online environment. The one thing that stitches these concerns together is an overarching fear of displacing the academy as the voice of intellectual authority or, more colloquially, letting the inmates run the asylum. Nevertheless, the way we engage those who have never known a world without the Internet requires creativity and use of the various tools at our disposal. Of course, employing e-learning techniques and principles does not automatically mean a wholesale abrogation of academic integrity and rigor, and it can certainly provide the opportunity to create critical digital consumers who are aware of the restrictions, risks, and implications of online and electronic data gathering and production. It is easy to get swept up in the diverse and ever-changing Web 2.0 applications, so it is important to remember that technology is a "mediator of interaction and a means of representing content," rather than an end in and of itself, and that it is the "thinking processes in which students engage that determines the quality of learning."[38] As such, the selection of digital tools to support student learning depends entirely on the type of experience needed to deliver pedagogical outcomes, and technology cannot be used simply for the sake of using technology.

There are also related anxieties about the need to learn complicated new software when many of us have barely mastered virtual learning environments. Technology does indeed move quickly and often times as fast as e-learning technologies are learned, they are superseded by bright, shiny, new programs. Nevertheless, we have a responsibility to digital natives to engage in and with platforms they understand but more importantly to prepare them for the world in which they will operate. Digital literacy familiarizes students with additional sources of data, expands their critical thinking abilities, and exposes them to innovative ways to disseminate the results of their research, an increasingly important part of the academic imperative. Web 2.0 and other online technologies dismantle the need for linear narratives and prompt students to consider more creative ways of displaying history embodying perhaps a range of media—images, video, and documents—interspliced with their critique and analysis.

Despite their overwhelming familiarity with online communication, research confirms that students may resist using social networking platforms as part of formal learning as well as wonder about the motives of educators who make friend requests of them.[39] Many students do not, for example, want their lecturers as friends, and vice versa, and yet the online presence of the educator has been identified as a positive influence on student engagement with learning via social media.[40] It is critical to bear in mind that despite the apparent saturation of social media, not all students are comfortable with using or indeed have access to technology,[41] and the level of Internet usage skills varies considerably within student cohorts.[42] Melissa Cole notes that most students in her study had read a blog (72.5 percent), but less than 10 percent had written one, and that more students engaged in passive consumption (browsing, watching) than active production (uploading, tagging).[43] Olivia Halic et al. similarly note that although students find that blogging, for example, enhances their learning and encourages them to share knowledge, they were less forthcoming when it came to engaging with each other's material in terms of the number and sophistication of peer commentaries.[44] Finally, access to educational technologies is divided along class, ethnic and racial, and gender lines, further entrenching existing inequalities through a digital divide whereby only some students are able to benefit from the incorporation of Web 2.0 into the classroom.

Including Web 2.0 Applications in Sport History Pedagogy

Although it may appear that Web 2.0 has more of an application for subjects such as digital media studies or popular culture, the incorporation of these platforms to teach history is growing. From the use of Twitter to re-enact historical events or tweet them in real time,[45] to the development of Facebook profiles for long-past figures, history educators are seeking new ways to engage students and expose them to not just facts and figures but to the processes of constructing history. Furthermore, the development of digital literacy is critical for students engaging with historical method as increasingly archives will be stored and accessed online, whereas research into emerging topics of interest, such as the history of Wikipedia, social media, or indeed the Internet itself will necessarily be situated in the electronic realm. As such, incorporating Web 2.0 and other digital resources into a sport history course could draw upon existing strategies to use social media tools in history education, as well as adapt these to suit the peculiarities of studying sport. In this final section, various examples are outlined to provide practical inspiration for sport history educators.

One of the key outcomes in sport history education—indeed history education overall—is to develop students' familiarity with, and appreciation of, the historical method, such that they understand the subjective nature of constructing histories as well as the accepted methods used in this process. A structured approach to allowing students to experience the process of gathering primary materials and generating a historical account can be facilitated via online platforms, such as Curatr, which houses documents, images, podcasts, and other media to create a customized, explorable "museum" (www.curatr.com). Lecturers determine and upload the content, and students access resources in a nonlinear fashion, allowing them to choose and explore discrete items in a guided rather than open context. Each item encourages student participation by introducing a gaming element, so that providing a comment generates points that unlock higher-order content. A museum could be filled with pictures of artifacts, newspaper clippings and other historical documents, older texts, diary entries, first-person accounts, photographs, paintings, or other relevant materials. Students then conduct their primary research from these sources—accessed in whichever way takes their fancy—and evidence of their decisions about which artifacts merit attention or which might be filtered out can be recorded in the comments and then discussed by their peers. Students could then produce an appraisal of the sources or the "history" that they have constructed from the raw materials to provide both the experience of searching for content and an interactive discussion about the quality of the sources or their relevance to the "story." Students would share their histories with one another and be asked to comment on differences and similarities in the final versions to reflect on how their own choices and selections, or even simply the order in which they viewed primary sources, influenced their history. Learning by doing is certainly a more effective way of understanding the subjective nature of historical work, and as the process is facilitated by a digital, interactive platform, students are able to engage at a time that suits them and still benefit from peer engagement. Situating the processes of historical enquiry in broader theoretical paradigms can also be encouraged through social media. YouTube lectures from leading scholars outline the diverse perspectives on the historical method; alternatively, students could be asked to create their own online resource in the form of videos or wikis to shift learning away from simple acquisition toward a more participatory model. For example, the TED-Ed Flip this Lesson video-editing tool allows online videos from TED or YouTube to be annotated and customized with questions, quizzes, and links,[46] and while the lecturer could produce such a resource, individual or small groups of students could also be asked to find, or even make, relevant videos and convert these into lessons to share with their peers. Annotating the video, devising relevant questions, and finding appropriate supplementary resources requires additional research and engagement with the content, and the final product facilitates peer-to-peer teaching, which is recognized as a successful learning strategy.[47]

Institutions and museums are increasingly engaging with the public through online platforms. For example, the Smithsonian Museum of American History has a blog; Facebook, Flickr, and Twitter accounts; online podcasts; and a YouTube channel, which contain material relevant to the teaching of sport history. The Museum of American History's "O Say Can You See" blog has recent entries on topics as diverse as the history of croquet, the development of snowboarding, Civil War baseball, and Olympic artifacts. Written primarily by curators at the museum, these blogs could serve as a starting point for a student's investigation of sport historical collections prior to a field trip or as a way of understanding public history compared with traditional, academic histories of the same topics. A related assessment item may be for students to write and publish their own blogs identifying the relationship between these different types of sport history, or providing an alternative narrative based on the primary materials that they discover across these different applications or across a series of museums internationally.

An exciting way to encourage students to become "active producers of historical narratives" is by asking them to "interpret and create primary sources outside traditional media."[48] A class group, or small groups within a larger class, could document their own sporting experiences (personal, collegiate, state, and/or national) to archive for future historians. A digital hub could be set up for blogs, video, podcasts, images, reflections, and comments, which could be preserved. So not only do students learn how to gather materials, but they can learn the basics of online archiving, which will increasingly be the type of repository that they will access as historians. At the same time, they can reflect on the value and limitations of technology in the production of history generally and sport history specifically.

Similarly, students can create wikis of information relevant to sport history focusing on their local community, an issue of national or global importance, or other topics to facilitate collaborative documentation. Wikis can be used on a more rudimentary level to create collaborative class notes for a course, where small groups are responsible for summarizing the key points and finding relevant resources to create a useful multimedia site that enables the rest of the class to understand the lecture content. Students are particularly motivated to create comprehensive records of the classes if a take-home exam means that they are able to consult these resources when constructing their responses. These hubs or wikis can be opened to the public to provide the authentic audience that motivates students to take these exercises seriously. The authentic audience can also be readily found among the authors and readers of Wikipedia, so following Chandler and Gregory's suggestion,[49] students could be asked to work together in pairs or groups to develop new or edit existing Wikipedia pages dealing with aspects of sport history.

Concerted efforts can be made to connect groups of students across institutions or internationally to create broader learning communities where information, ideas, and perspectives are shared, assessed, critiqued, and used to facilitate cross-cultural perspectives. This might alleviate some of the isolation experienced by students engaging with sport history within larger kinesiology or exercise science departments, and allow them to share and consolidate their interests with other scholars of the sporting past. In this context, students could be given similar tasks to work on before coming together to share and comment on each other's blogs, wikis, or other materials, or could be asked to work together across institutional or national boundaries. Using the Abraham Lincoln Presidential Museum's "The Civil War in Four Minutes" as inspiration,[50] one idea might be to produce collaborative digital maps.[51] The changing location of sports, stadia, and teams can be traced over time to identify the influence of social, political, economic, and other factors on the emergence, practice, and dissemination of modern sport within a nation or internationally. The resulting interactive or animated online map could be expanded by subsequent classes and annotated with documents, artifacts, photographs, links, and other relevant sources.

Web 2.0 technologies can be used to bring historical figures and events into the present. For example, profiles for key figures in the emergence of the Olympic Games could be created on Facebook, where the characters could then interact with each other in real time, posting to each other's pages or leaving comments. Twitter has been used with notable success to recreate specific events or periods of time.[52] To create accurate Facebook pages or to tweet a historical event, students need to conduct significant research into the events or people they are portraying. Furthermore, these exercises can provoke discussion about how a complex life is reduced to a few lines, perhaps inspiring students to reflect on how accurately their own online personas represent the complexity of their lives.

The production of sport history websites as capstone assessment pieces could provide a multimedia and interactive experience for users, and free both student and lecturer from linear narratives and unidirectional analyses. Sound, image, video, podcasts, written narratives, and links to additional material all provide a rich context in which to present interpretations, perspectives, and analyses. It can be confronting for academics to regard websites as useful as a mechanism to communicate history as the standard essay or paper, and many fear that the integrity of the historical process may be lost. But it need not be this way. Regardless of the types of data sources or even the mode of presentation, the basic methods of creating histories are common across a number of paradigms, and uploading histories onto social networks or using collaborative tools to work more effectively as a team does not mean that the standard is lower or less sophisticated than a traditional written paper. Indeed, knowing that their thoughts and perspectives will find an audience beyond simply the person grading their paper may inspire students to produce better quality work.

Conclusion

Although in many cases the transfer of Web 2.0 to the classroom has been gradual, there are endless possibilities for incorporating interactive, collaborative, learning technologies into sport history pedagogy. Nevertheless, the revision of traditional pedagogical approaches and the development of appropriate assessments that align with student-centered learning outcomes may be confronting for, or seem beyond the ability of, many academics in this field for a variety of personal, institutional, financial, or organizational reasons. Accordingly, this chapter has briefly outlined the use of such tools and provided some concrete examples of how they might serve sport history education and be used alongside or instead of traditional assignments to provide alternative and flexible learning opportunities that use what are essentially everyday technologies. We cannot escape the fact that digital natives are increasingly familiar with an online environment, and that sport historians of the future will need to be competent and critical users of these technologies. It is the responsibility of educators to ensure that students have the skills to successfully navigate the online world and to apply the same level of rigorous analysis to digital sources as they would to archival materials. Embracing Web 2.0 applications within a teaching and learning context allows students to develop critical competencies as they participate in a collaborative and interactive learning environment.

Notes

1. Tim O'Reilly, September 30, 2005, "What is Web 2.0: Design Patterns and Business Models for the Next Generation of Software," *O'Reilly Media*. Accessed February 4, 2013. http://oreilly.com/web2/archive/what-is-web-20.html.

2. Peter Merholz, August 10, 2005, "It's Not About the Technology," *Peterme.com*. Accessed February 4, 2013. http://www.peterme.com/archives/000560.html.

3. Richard McManus, September 7, 2005, "What is Web 2.0?" *ZDNet*. Accessed February 4, 2013. http://www.zdnet.com/blog/web2explorer/what-is-web-2-0/5.

4. McNamara, *The 21st Century Media (R)evolution*, 38–39.

5. O'Reilly, "What is Web 2.0."

6. Grinnell, "From Consumer to Prosumer to Produser," 577.

7. Carter, "Blogging as Reflective Practice in the Graduate Classroom."

8. Kress, *Literacy in the New Media Age*.

9. Collis and Moonen, "Web 2.0 Tools and Processes in Higher Education."

10. Fry and Love, "Business Lecturers' Perceptions and Interactions with the Virtual Learning Environment," 53.

11. Brown, "Seeing Web 2.0 in Context."

12. Brill and Park, "Facilitating Engaged Learning in the Interaction Age," 70.

13. Collis and Moonen, "Web 2.0 Tools and Processes in Higher Education."

14. Ibid., 100.

15. Melville et al., "Higher Education in a Web 2.0 World," 8.

16. Luckin et al., "Do Web 2.0 Tools Really Open the Door to Learning?," 101.

17. Sisson and King, "Using Technology in the History Classroom," 243.

18. Chandler and Gregory, "Sleeping with the Enemy."

19. Ibid.

20. Payne and Monk-Turner, "Students' Perceptions of Group Projects"; Pfaff and Huddleston, "Does it Matter if I Hate Teamwork?"

21. Burdett, "Making Groups Work."

22. Witney and Smallbone, "Wiki Work"; Su and Beaumont, "Evaluating the Use of a Wiki for Collaborative Learning"; Judd et al., "Using Wikis for Collaborative Learning"; Minocha and Thomas, "Collaborative Learning in a Wiki Environment."

23. Collis and Moonen, "Web 2.0 Tools and Processes in Higher Education."

24. Judd et al., "Using Wikis for Collaborative Learning."

25. den Exter et al., "Using Web 2.0 Technologies for Collaborative Learning in Distance Education."

26. Selwyn, "Faceworking."

27. Mason, "Learning Technologies for Adult Continuing Education."

28. Lu and Churchill, "The Effect of Social Interaction on Learning Engagement."

29. Madge et al., "Facebook, Social Integration and Informal Learning at University."

30. Ibid.

31. Cole, "Using Wiki Technology to Support Student Engagement."

32. Roblyer et al., "Findings on Facebook in Higher Education."

33. Selwyn, "Faceworking."

34. Derek Bruff, January 21, 2010, "Backchannel in Education: Nine Uses," *Agile Learning*. Accessed February 4, 2013. http://derekbruff.org/?p=472; Elvasky, Mislan and Elvasky, "When Talking Less is More."

35. Paulus, Payne, and Jahns, "Am I Making Sense Here?," 13.

36. Buckland, "Wikis in University Teaching and Learning."

37. Bruff, "Backchannel in Education."

38. Bower, Hedberg, and Kuswara, "A Framework for Web 2.0 Learning Design," 196, 181.

39. Cole, "Using Wiki Technology to Support Student Engagement"; Madge et al., "Facebook, Social Integration and Informal Learning at University"; Karl and Peluchette, "'Friending' Professors, Parents and Bosses."

40. Callaghan and Bower, "Learning Through Social Networking Sites."

41. Huang, Hood, and Yoo, "Gender Divide and Acceptance of Collaborative Web 2.0 Applications."

42. Hargittai, "Digital Na(t)ives?"

43. Cole, "Using Wiki Technology to Support Student Engagement."

44. Halic et al., "To Blog or Not To Blog."

45. Jensen et al., "TwHistory"; Lee et al., "ReTweeting History."

46. Emily McManus, April 25, 2012, "Flip this lesson! A new way to teach with video from TED-Ed," *TED Blog*. Accessed February 22, 2013. http://blog.ted.com/2012/04/25/flip-it-a-new-way-to-teach-with-video-from-ted-ed/.

47. Magolda and Platt, "Untangling Web 2.0's Influences on Student Learning"; Boud, Cohen, and Sampson, *Peer Learning in Higher Education*.

48. Bonamici et al., "Rebooting the Past."

49. Chandler and Gregory, "Sleeping with the Enemy."
50. Abraham Lincoln Presidential Library and Museum, "The Civil War in Four Minutes."
51. Mitchell and Elwood, "Engaging Students through Mapping Local History."
52. Lee et al., "ReTweeting History."

References

Abraham Lincoln Presidential Library and Museum. "The Civil War in Four Minutes." Accessed 15 January 2013. http://www.lincolnlibraryandmuseum.com/m5.htm.

Berg, Susan. 2010. "Web 2.0 Technologies in Higher Education Teaching: A Practical Introduction." *Kentucky Journal of Excellence in College Teaching and Learning* 8, no. 1: 19–27. Accessed April 2, 2013. http://encompass.eku.edu/kjectl/vol8/iss1/2.

Bonamici, Andrew, Heather Briston, Kevin Hatfield, and Matt Villeneuve. 2010. "Rebooting the Past; Uploading the Future. Web 2.0 and the Study of History Through a Living Learning Community." The University of Oregon. Accessed April 30, 2012. http://www.educause.edu/sites/default/files/library/presentations/ELI10/SESS07/RebootingPast_ELI2010.pdf.

Boud, David, Ruth Cohen, and Jane Sampson (eds). 2001. *Peer Learning in Higher Education: Learning From and With Each Other*. London: Kogan Page.

Bower, Matt, John G. Hedberg, and Andreas Kuswara. 2010. "A Framework for Web 2.0 Learning Design." *Educational Media International* 47, no. 3: 177–98.

Brill, Jennifer M., and Yeongjeong Park. 2008. "Facilitating Engaged Learning in the Interaction Age: Taking a Pedagogically Disciplined Approach to Innovation with Emergent Technologies." *International Journal of Teaching and Learning in Higher Education* 20, no. 1: 70–78. http://www.isetl.org/ijtlhe/.

Brown, Susan A. 2012. "Seeing Web 2.0 in Context: A Study of Academic Perceptions." *The Internet and Higher Education* 15, no. 1: 50–57.

Buckland, Richard. 2009. "Wikis in University Teaching and Learning." *UNSWelearning*. Accessed April 13, 2012. http://www.youtube.com/watch?v=m1-8OOrBi00.

Burdett, Jane. 2003. "Making Groups Work: University Students' Perceptions." *International Education Journal* 4, no. 3: 177–91.

Callaghan, Noelene, and Matt Bower. 2012. "Learning Through Social Networking Sites—The Critical Role of the Teacher." *Educational Media International* 49, no. 1: 1–17.

Carter, Teresa J. 2011. "Blogging as Reflective Practice in the Graduate Classroom." In *The Professor's Guide to Taming Technology: Leveraging Digital Media, Web 2.0 and More for Learning*, edited by Kathleen P. King and Thomas D. Cox, 89–104. Charlotte, NC: IAP.

Chandler, Cullen J., and Alison S. Gregory. 2010. "Sleeping with the Enemy: Wikipedia in the College Classroom." *History Teacher* 43, no. 2: 247–57.

Cole, Melissa. 2009. "Using Wiki Technology to Support Student Engagement: Lessons from the Trenches." *Computers & Education* 52, no. 1: 141–46.

Collis, Betty, and Jef Moonen. 2008. "Web 2.0 Tools and Processes in Higher Education: Quality Perspectives." *Educational Media International* 45, no. 2: 93–106.

den Exter, Kristin, Stephen Rowe, William Boyd, and David Lloyd. 2012. "Using Web 2.0 Technologies for Collaborative Learning in Distance Education—Case Studies from an Australian University. *Future Internet* 4, no. 1: 216–37.

Elvasky, C. Michael, Cristina Mislan, and Steriani Elvasky. 2011. "When Talking Less is More: Exploring Outcomes of Twitter Usage in the Large-Lecture Hall." *Learning, Media and Technology* 36, no. 3: 215–33.

Fry, Nadine, and Nia Love. 2009. "Business Lecturers' Perceptions and Interactions with the Virtual Learning Environment." *International Journal of Management Education* 9, no. 4: 51–56.

Grinnell, Claudia K. 2009. "From Consumer to Prosumer to Produser: Who Keeps Shifting My Paradigm? (We Do!)." *Public Culture* 21, no. 3: 577–98.

Halic, Olivia, Debra Lee, Trena Paulus, and Marsha Spence. 2010. "To Blog or Not to Blog: Student Perceptions of Blog Effectiveness for Learning in a College-Level Course." *The Internet and Higher Education* 13, no. 4: 206–13.

Hargittai, Eszter. 2010. "Digital Na(t)ives? Variation in Internet Skills and Uses Among Members of the 'Net Generation.'" *Sociological Inquiry* 80, no. 1: 92–113.

Huang, Wen-Hao D., Denice W. Hood, and Sun J. Yoo. 2013. "Gender Divide and Acceptance of Collaborative Web 2.0 Applications for Learning in Higher Education." *The Internet and Higher Education* 16: 57–65.

Jensen, Marion, Tom Caswell, Justin Ball, Joel Duffin, and Rob Barton. 2010. "TwHistory: Sharing History Using Twitter." In *Open ED 2010 Proceedings*. Barcelona: UOC, OU, BYU. Accessed February 5, 2013. http://hdl.handle.net/10609/4942.

Judd, Terry, Gregor Kennedy, and Cropper, Simon. 2010. "Using Wikis for Collaborative Learning: Assessing Collaboration through Contribution." *Australasian Journal of Educational Technology* 26, no. 3: 341–54.

Karl, Katherine A., and Joy V. Peluchette. 2011. "'Friending' Professors, Parents and Bosses: A Facebook Connection Conundrum." *Journal of Education for Business* 86, no. 4: 214–22.

King, Kathleen P., and Thomas D. Cox (eds). 2011. *The Professor's Guide to Taming Technology: Leveraging Digital Media, Web 2.0, and More for Learning*. Charlotte, NC: IAP.

Kress, Gunther. 2003. *Literacy in the New Media Age*. London: Routledge.

Lee, Victor R., Brett E. Shelton, Andrew Walker, Tom Caswell, and Marion Jensen. 2012. "ReTweeting History: Exploring the Intersection of Microblogging and Problem-Based Learning for Historical Reenactments." In *Designing Problem-driven Instruction with Online Social Media*, edited by Kay K.J. Seo, Debra A. Pellegrino and Chalee Engelhard, 23–40. Charlotte, NC: IAP.

Lu, Jie, and Daniel Churchill. 2012. "The Effect of Social Interaction on Learning Engagement in a Social Networking Environment." In *Interactive Learning Environments*. doi: 10.1080/10494820.2012.680966 (Published online: 29 May).

Luckin, Rosemary, Wilma Clark, Rebecca Graber, Kit Logan, Adrian Mee, and Martin Oliver. 2009. "Do Web 2.0 Tools Really Open the Door to Learning? Practices, Perceptions and Profiles of 11–16-year-old Students." *Learning, Media and Technology* 34, no. 2: 87–104.

Madge, Clare, Julia Meek, Jane Wellens, and Tristram Hooley. 2009. "Facebook, Social Integration and Informal Learning at University: 'It is More for Socialising and Talking to Friends About Work than for Actually Doing Work.'" *Learning, Media and Technology* 34, no. 2: 141–55.

Magolda, Peter M., and Glenn J Platt. 2009. "Untangling Web 2.0's Influences on Student Learning." *About Campus* 14, no. 3: 10–16.

Mason, Robin. 2006. "Learning Technologies for Adult Continuing Education." *Studies in Continuing Education* 28, no. 2: 121–33.

McNamara, Jim. 2010. *The 21st Century Media (R)evolution: Emergent Communication Practices*. New York: Peter Lang.

Melville, David, Cliff Allan, Julian Crampton, John Fothergill, Adrian Godfrey, Michael Harloe, et al. 2009. *Higher Education in a Web 2.0 World: Report of an Independent Committee of Inquiry into the Impact on Higher Education of Students' Widespread Use of Web 2.0 Technologies*. Accessed April 30, 2012. http://www.jisc.ac.uk/publications/generalpublications/2009/heweb2.aspx.

Minocha, Shailey, and Peter G. Thomas. 2007. "Collaborative Learning in a Wiki Environment: Experiences From a Software Engineering Course." *New Review of Hypermedia and Multimedia* 13, no. 2: 187–209.

Mitchell, Katharyne, and Sarah Elwood. 2012. "Engaging Students through Mapping Local History." *Journal of Geography* 111, no. 4: 148–57.

Paulus, Trena M., Rebecca L. Payne, and Lisa Jahns. 2009. "'Am I Making Sense Here?' What Blogging Reveals About Undergraduate Student Understanding." *Journal of Interactive Online Learning* 8, no. 1: 1–22.

Payne, Brian K., and Elizabeth Monk-Turner. 2006. "Students' Perceptions of Group Projects: The Role of Race, Age, and Slacking." *College Student Journal* 40, no. 1: 132–39.

Pfaff, Elizabeth, and Patricia Huddleston. 2003. "Does it Matter if I Hate Teamwork? What Impacts Student Attitudes toward Teamwork." *Journal of Marketing Education* 25, no. 1: 37–45.

Roblyer, Margaret D., Michelle McDaniel, Marsena Webb, James Herman, and James V. Witty. 2010. "Findings on Facebook in Higher Education: A Comparison of College Faculty and Student Uses and Perceptions of Social Networking Sites." *The Internet and Higher Education* 13, no. 3: 134–40.

Selwyn, Neil. 2009. "Faceworking: Exploring Students' Education-Related Use of Facebook." *Learning, Media and Technology* 34, no. 2: 157–74.

Sisson, Keith, and Kathleen P. King. 2011. "Using Technology in the History Classroom." In *The Professor's Guide to Taming Technology: Leveraging Digital Media, Web 2.0 and More for Learning*, edited by Kathleen P. King and Thomas D. Cox, 239–58. Charlotte, NC: IAP.

Su, Feng, and Chris Beaumont. 2010. "Evaluating the Use of a Wiki for Collaborative Learning." *Innovations in Education and Teaching International* 47, no. 4: 417–31.

Weaver, Warren, and Claude E. Shannon. 1963. *The Mathematical Theory of Communication*. Urbana: University of Illinois Press. First published 1949.

Witney, Debbie, and Teresa Smallbone. 2011. "Wiki Work: Can Using Wikis Enhance Student Collaboration for Group Assignment Tasks?" *Innovations in Education and Teaching International* 48, no. 1: 101–10.

6

"Get excited, people!"
Online Fansites and the Circulation of the Past in the Preseason Hopes of Sports Followers

MATTHEW KLUGMAN

I want to start this chapter with a provocative quote from the American sociologist Gary Alan Fine: "The essence of sport," claimed Fine in 1985, "is not exercise, but memory."[1] Fine made this glorious rhetorical assertion at the end of an abstract detailing his pioneering ethnographic study of the significance of the *seasonal* nature of team sports—in this case Little League Baseball. The history of the season, he argued, becomes the lens through which meaning is given to specific sporting actions, and thus frames the memories and tales that come to be told. As is often the case, it seems obvious once we start to think about it. Yet while the best popular accounts of spectator sports *tend* to be structured around a season or several seasons (Nick Hornby's *Fever Pitch* notwithstanding), few scholars have followed Fine in critically examining the importance of sporting seasons.[2] Those who have explored the religious-like aspects of modern sporting cultures are a key exception.[3] But these scholars tend to be more interested in the functioning of sports as a so-called civic religion than in questions of seasonal memories and histories. Joseph Price, for instance, notes that "sports seasons cultivate the growth of hope," but his interest lies not in the specific dynamics of hope as a seasonal emotion but in the similarities of sport seasons to religious and/or liturgical calendars, which also produce moments of "hope and promise."[4]

The relevance of sporting seasons to the current collection is that online sporting fansites—in particular those built around blogs and discussion forums—provide a wonderfully rich resource for sport historians to study the seasonal emotions of spectator sports, and to explore questions of sporting memory and popular history more generally. Each week hundreds of thousands, if not millions, of sport fans gather together online to read, chat, and blog about their favorite teams. Indeed, many supporters now log onto team-specific fansites on an almost daily basis to dissect the results of games just past, preview forthcoming games, and respond to games in progress, sometimes even posting their thoughts as they sit in the stands at a game itself. Fan traffic to these sites remains significant, even in the offseason, and at times increases, as fans digest the year that has passed and then build up once more to the fresh start that the new season will bring. While many fan posts on the Internet are characterized by their immediacy—as if they were purely a spur of the moment response—they are still a valuable source for sport historians. For what these posts almost invariably show is how readings of the past infuse the present and shape (and arguably also facilitate) the very passions that modern spectator sports are so renowned for. They are thus an ideal source to study how, in Linda Borish and Murray Phillips' evocative phrase, the "sporting past circulates in the present."[5]

There are many reasons for sport historians to turn their attention to sporting fansites. These sites, for example, can provide insight into the new forms of communities that grow around sport teams, they can be analyzed for the way they further the entanglements between following sports and playing fantasy versions of these sports, they can be explored for the place of humor in sport fan cultures, and they are a critical site for engaging with the gendered, racial, and sexualized aspects of spectator sports culture.[6] In this chapter however, I want to build upon Fine's observation to chart the way sporting fansites can help illuminate the way the emotions provoked by spectator sports tend to be grounded in seasonal readings and experiences of the past. In particular, I am interested in the way sporting passions, desires, and beliefs intersect with memories and histories, and how this might further our understanding of the complicated role the past plays in the lives of sports fans. In so doing, I hope to create space for further exchange between studies of religion, passions, memory, and the history of sport.

Questions of memory and the associated acts of remembering and forgetting have recently gained some much needed currency in the history of sport.[7] Drawing on influential sociologists like Maurice Halbwachs, Pierre Nora, and Chris Healy, sport historians have begun to tease out the way collective and social sporting memories are made, contested, and often intertwined with myths.[8] What is still missing, however, is an engagement with the ways in which the memories fostered by spectator sports might be shaped by the seasonal dynamics and rhythms of these sports. In part this is due to the general paucity of literature on the impact of seasons on experiences of time and its passing. And yet, "every society has its calendar," as David Cressy noted in his pioneering study of national memory and England's protestant calendar: "Whether shaped and paced by the circling of the heavens or the seasons of the soil, or structured and punctuated by anniversaries of religious or secular significance, every human community finds regularity and periodicity in the unbroken passage of time."[9] Calendars, in other words, help structure collective relationships to time, to history, to what is to be remembered (and how), and what is forgotten. Moreover, as Gabrielle Spiegel shows, different calendars can be imbued with contrasting, at times conflicting, versions of time—in her case, arguing for a distinction between liturgical and historical time.[10] This distinction echoes the differentiation that Halbwachs and Nora made between collective memory and history. For Nora, collective memory, and the communities it bound together, has been forever lost, consumed by "the flames of [objective enlightenment] history."[11] What remained are *les lieux de mémoire*, sites of memory torn away from history to be preserved in archives and commemorations, in which we can trace what were once living memories, both "affective and magical," that nourished "recollections," taking "root in the concrete, in spaces, gestures, images and objects."[12] Yet, while modern spectator sports are infused with seemingly objective values and measures—think of the precise systems of points, the reams of statistics, the sports science, and cognitive sports psychology—the fan cultures that have grown around *and* shaped these sports remain to a large degree affective and magical.[13] And at least at times, online fansites appear to be places of living memory, nourishing recollections, full of dynamic and strange gestures, images, and objects, and offering a window, therefore, into different experiences of time and its passing.[14]

The task of mapping out the intricate seasonal rhythms of sporting calendars, and the interplay of memories within these, is too large for one chapter. Instead, I want to focus here on the seasonal emotion that tends to be the most clichéd and taken for granted: the *hope* that supposedly rises with the approach of each new season.[15] For such hope inevitably raises questions about the past—why do supporters whose team probably finished the previous season (and most of the seasons before that) either out of the playoffs/finals or on a losing note come to hope as a new season approaches? How, in other words, does hope arise after the experience of loss? Drawing on several sports fansites in Australia and the United States, this chapter charts expressions of this hope and the other emotions that frequently accompany it. Like other emotions, however, hope is notoriously slippery and so the process followed is one of dipping and delving into particular moments and then teasing out the traces and intimation of hope, memories, and the particular, at times mythical, relationships to the past that these point to.[16] I begin first, though, with the emotion of hope itself.

Hope

Like many emotions, hope seems simple until we begin to focus on it. Is it just the innocent wish for something, or a more insidious, necessarily deluded, expectation? A powerful motivating factor or a lazy resort of the presumptuous? The debates as to the nature and value of hope (or lack thereof) go back at least to the ancient Greek tales of Pandora—the woman fashioned by the Gods in revenge for the theft of fire, whose curiosity unleashed all the ills hence known to humankind. At the heart of this myth, and its continual retellings, is the place of hope.[17] Some, like Friedrich Nietzsche, favor the notion of hope as part of the curse, the thing that makes living with evil tolerable, but in so-doing hope only "prolongs the torment" of human life and is thus actually the worse evil of all.[18] Others, like Graham Little, speak instead of hope as the saving grace, that thing that reassures "humankind not all is lost; every cloud will be made with a silver lining, hope itself will appear on the brink of defeat, in extra-time when we're down to the last man left standing."[19]

The contrasting portrayals of hope in these two versions of Pandora's box bring to mind Allen Davies's point that hope tends to be judged in extremes.[20] Hope, it seems, is generally viewed as a great good, or as a fearsome delusion.[21] Australian sociologist Valerie Braithwaite, for example, has suggested that there are really two forms of group hopes: a positive collective hope "that is genuinely and critically shared by a group" and the more negative "public hope, at its worst a contagious but superficial form of hope peddled by spin doctors and uncritically accepted by expectant beneficiaries."[22] The psychoanalyst Ernest Schachtel was another to argue that the term "concealed two profoundly different kinds of feeling."[23] On the one side lies "magic hope," characterized by the "wishful expectation and anticipation that somehow things will change for the better."[24] On the other side, "realistic hope" is found, a hope grounded not in magical expectations but in an awareness of reality and an assessment of the actions likely to bring about "the hoped-for change."[25]

I am not interested in seeking to define which hopes of sports fans are worthwhile and which are not. Rather, I think that the intensity of the arguments over hope, with the highly polarized positions of its critics and proponents, points to a richer issue: to the difficulty of living with hope, of trying to use it productively without being enchanted by it. What are the consequences of hoping, the risks, the pleasures, the possible intoxications? In seeking to explore these questions, this chapter is concerned with the way sports fans experience and live hope. With what it means to come to hope again as the new season approaches, and with what happens to this hope.

The main theorist of seasonal hopes—Mircea Eliade—was more interested in the why of these hopes than in judging them. He believed that the hopes signified by the new year celebrations of traditional societies represented a response to past losses and suffering. In Eliade's words, such festivities signified "the hope that the abolition of time *is* possible at this mythical moment, in which the world is destroyed and re-created."[26] The hope is that life can be begun afresh, *despite* all that has just been; despite history. Past suffering, misfortune and sin are, it is hoped, erased, for the new year is a return to the original beginning when everything seemed possible.[27] For Eliade then, these hopes have a historical dimension, but it is a dimension that manifests as an attempt to erase the past.

Theologian Joseph Price has suggested that Eliade's theories of cyclical religions and the mythic time they instantiate can illuminate the structure of seasonal sports.[28] Taken together with Price's brief description of the hope that accompanies a new season, the implication is that the hopes for a new season are an attempt to live as if the (likely) suffering of the past season can be erased. And the seasonal structure of most spectator sports does seem to facilitate this. For regardless of who triumphed the previous season, with the new season all teams begin on zero points, as if the results of past seasons do not matter. But if we look more closely at fan postings on the Internet as a new season approaches—at hope in action, as it were—we can see that something a bit more complicated is occurring than the simple elision of the past.

New Players

Observe the online posts of sports fans in the lead-up to a new season, and they often appear to be searching, sometimes even craving, for reasons to hope. One of the main places these hopes coalesce is on the backs of the new players their team has recruited. The intense hunger for fresh recruits is manifest in discussions around recruiting for most major spectator sports. It is especially obvious with regard to the drafts that some sports hold in that liminal time before the new season begins. Indeed, the drafts of competitions such as the National Football League (NFL), National Basketball Association (NBA), and the Australian Football League (AFL), have become dominant features of their liturgical calendars. This is especially true for Internet fansites associated with these sports, many of which receive more traffic (measured in both visits to the website and also comments on their message boards) than they will experience at any other point during the season, despite the fact that no games are being played, no points are on offer, and no pride or identities seem on the line. Yet this is a time of promise like almost no other.

Over on the NFL team blogs associated with SB Nation, anticipation starts building for the draft as soon as the Super Bowl is over, if not before, despite the draft being more than ten weeks away.[29] In the 2011–12 season, the SB Nation San Diego Chargers blog—Bolts from the Blue—went even further, running a weekly post previewing college football games through the lens of promising players the Chargers might target.[30] The AFL modeled itself on the NFL, and so the situation with Australian Rules football, and blogs such as Big Footy,[31] is similar. At the heart of the feverish Internet attention is the *history* of the particular people who might soon be selected by their team. Countless words are written on their strengths, weaknesses, upsides, deeds and misdeeds, and above all the promise that might be gleaned by analyzing their past. "Knightmare's 2012 Mock AFL Draft" garnered more than 270,000 views and received more than 2,500 replies as fans came to read and debate the athleticism of Nathan Hrovat, the meaning to be made from Troy Menzel's past knee troubles, the defensive accountability (or lack thereof) of Jackson Thurlow, and the character of Dayle Garlett.[32] Over in the NFL, the greater number of teams and supporters leads to an even more forensic analysis of the attributes deciphered from the past of possible new draftees. "It's been pretty well documented how much of an athlete the 6'6" 302 pound Quarterback turned Tight End turned Tackle is," began one emblematic if only mini-profile of potential NFL pick Lane Johnson on the Bolts from the Blue website. "We know he can move, legend has it that he could break the 4.7s at his size right now. His short shuttle should be just as impressive, he's very quick in short areas. The thing we need to know is how strong is he?"[33]

"Need to know." These are strong words. As if what is at stake goes beyond wishes, desires, and even demands to that which it is simply necessary to have.[34] Contra Eliade, these fans are feverishly mining the past to find something upon which to base their hopes for the new season. And the search is for *the* player or players that fans crave, the one(s) who will lead their team to glory. Here we have a strong intimation of another religious system, the search for a hero, or maybe even a messiah. Such millennial hopes for a savior are one of the recurring elements of Western culture and religion.[35] The reason for this, according to the psychoanalyst Wilfred Bion, is that millennial hopes are a typical product of groups wishing to displace feelings of hatred, destructiveness, and despair.[36] In a famous passage, Bion cautioned that for millennial hopes to be effective they must stay unrealized: "It is a person or idea that will save the group—in fact from feelings of hatred, destructiveness, and despair, of its own or of another group—but in order to do this, obviously the Messianic hope must never be fulfilled. Only by remaining a hope does hope persist."[37] This can be read as Bion's answer to the enigma of hope. Groups can reap benefits from hopes, he suggests, but only at the cost of not getting what they're hoping for. Yet sports fans desperately want their hopes to be realized. Indeed, the search for a savior suggests the belief that a savior is possible. Here is another possible connection to Eliade's schema. For though only implied by Eliade, faith marches hand in hand with hope in his vision of traditional yearly cycles. Faith that a better life is possible, even destined, despite past mistakes and sin.

But the need to know hints at an anxiety accompanying this faith and the hope that it fuels. For if fans turn to the past for signs of the promised player(s) for whom they so long, they also seek to free themselves from the litany of past failures and disappointments. Approach the past from a statistical perspective and you find out that even those players picked in the first round of drafts for competitions like the NFL and AFL are quite likely (25–33%) to be busts (have negligible impact), and only a few will become stars.[38] But this lesson from history, that success is never ensured, indeed that noteworthy success is often unlikely, tends to be denied in favor of investing in hopes that, while grounded in past deeds, also run counter to past experiences. Yet the fever of this investment suggests a lurking awareness and concern with past failures that spurs fans on to search for every detail concerning the histories of the people their team might recruit. It is as if their tireless search for information will allow them to find the players of true promise, the one(s) who *will* succeed, and thus liberate the fans and their team from past mistakes. There is a particular mix here of work and magic, for the hopes are based on the exhaustive gathering of information but still have a strong wishful element to them—if only the fan works hard enough (and invests enough anxious energy) to find all the necessary facts, then they will know enough to ensure a glorious future.

One factor in this is the element of perceived control. Sports fans give over much of their weekly and seasonal emotions to their team. The acts of recruiters, and the players they recruit, can bring enormous joy but also great devastation.[39] The Internet, with its countless layers of information (and misinformation) and spaces for discussion and debate, provides fans with an unprecedented chance to evaluate the drafting of players. They can act then, as if they are in control of their destiny. But rather than using this information to protect themselves from the dangers of hoping for too much, the information and sense of control tends to instead foster dreams. Similar things occur with periods of free agency and trade.

"The trade winds are whistling through cyberspace, from Melbourne to Perth, London to Dubai," reported the Australian journalist Rod Curtis at the start of October 2004.[40] "Thousands of supporters, aged 10 to 90, are meeting on supporters' websites—Bomberblitz, Saintsational, TheBlueView, Hawk Headquarters—in a fast-growing, modern-day blog phenomenon."[41] Like the liar's month of the intersecting NFL free agency and draft periods, the Internet has become one of the prime places in which AFL fans engage with, and promulgate, the news of which players might be going where, and for what.[42] The result is an intense intertwining of traditional media sources—newspapers, radio, and television—with the new media of blogs and social media.[43] "Half of [the information on BigFooty is] wrong but who cares," noted the Western Bulldogs supporter Daniel, only half-jokingly. "News is news."[44] Others, however, become frustrated by the profusion of hearsay. The Bulldogs fan with the nom de web of "always right" gave this cynical summary during the 2006 trade week: "In trade week the message boards are filled with unsubstantiated rumours from people who are 'in the know' about players with dubious credentials supposedly being sought out by numerous clubs. These are generally players who the same people have bagged for years but are now apparently just players who have been starved of opportunities or have required a change of scenery to have the desired effect on their poor attitude."[45]

"It's one thing to love your club, but why love trade week?" asked Curtis, who was intrigued by the increasing number of barrackers (Australian Rules football fans) involved in this strange process of rumors and make-believe bargaining.[46] "What leads thousands of supporters to post prospective trades in the ether of cyberspace? What turns thousands of supporters into closet coaches two weeks after grand final day?" Part of the answer is that fans are acting out their millennial dreams. The Australian ABC Radio commentator Dan Lonergan put it this way: "When the controversial AFL player trading period takes place each October, hope always springs eternal for supporters of clubs that have suffered through poor years. Fans cling to the hope that perhaps their team can pick up a player or two who could be the difference in lifting their side into finals contention."⁴⁷ These hopes are strongly suggestive of fantasy. Grounded in select aspects of the past, they push toward something that is dearly wanted, something dearly desired.⁴⁸ The feverish return to the past can be read as both an attempt to corral and also guarantee the fantasy, and if so, fails doubly. For, as the psychoanalyst Jacqueline Rose notes, "fantasy's supreme characteristic is that of running ahead of itself. There is something coerced and coercive, but also wild and unpredictable about it."⁴⁹ The intoxicating effects of these fantastic hopes are in turn fueled by the write-ups of draft gurus like Mel Kiper and Mike Mayock with the NFL, and Kevin Sheehan with the AFL. As "always right" noted with regard to the AFL draft: "As for the draft, this is the most exciting part ... Every young player up to about pick number 30 is a budding champion. I love reading the papers listing your draft picks. You've never seen them play but the description of each player is usually so glowing that it's difficult to see how we're going to squeeze them all into our team without dropping [star players like] Westy and Johnno."⁵⁰ Not surprisingly perhaps, top picks are often welcomed by fans as if they *will* lead their club to the promised land. "Get excited people!" wrote "gogriff" after the Western Bulldogs selected Jake Stringer with their first pick in the 2012 AFL draft. "I'm seeing the next Matthew Pavlich ... Both great contested marks, great kicks for goal, capable of playing midfield."⁵¹ "He is now my favourite player," wrote "Happy Days," while "dogtown" simply posted "23 tackles in 3 vfl games," succinctly epitomizing the way the past can ground excitement. The excitement provoked by glowing profiles can be so intense that some fans write of it in sexual terms. "Could someone please pass the tissues. I've got a mess to clean up," noted "Scooter600x" after reading a celebrated analysis of new Bulldogs player Ryan Griffin in 2006.⁵² "This makes me feel ... A CERTAIN TYPE OF WAY," posted "Madcat5"⁵³ after reading an ESPN blog claiming, "Folks, San Diego is killing this draft. It is just slaying it. ... A trio of pass-rusher Melvin Ingram (No. 18), defensive lineman Kendall Reyes (No. 49) and Taylor (No. 73) is a wicked group to bring into one defense. All three players were taken later than projected and could all make immediate impacts. Major kudos to San Diego for having a strong plan."⁵⁴ This excitement is reminiscent of the "magic joy," which for Schachtel follows on from "magic hope." A joy "based on the anticipation of the feeling of fulfillment of a drive, a wish. ... It is the joy of being about to get, or of having gotten, something. During this state of joy, usually short-lived, one feels as though the anticipated or present fulfilment has suddenly changed the whole character of life and the world. Everything seems or promises to be perfect—it is indeed a magic transformation of the world."⁵⁵ At moments such as the recruitment of highly regarded players, the Internet postings of sports fans do seem imbued with a sense that things now are as they should be. They have gotten what they wanted, and now glory is on the way. Yet we have also seen the intense work that many go through to build their seemingly magical hopes. And once a player is recruited, the work only intensifies as fans search out even more profiles, devouring all the information they can find—from video clips; to statistics; to the tales of coaches, family, friends, and rivals. Still, this work cannot protect them from the treacherous joy that positive reports bring.

The reaction of many fans to San Diego's 2012 draft was so triumphant that one of the moderators of Bolts from the Blue wrote a series of blog posts to help supporters manage their "ridiculous expectations."⁵⁶ Other fans employ their own strategies for trying to contain dangerous hopes. In 2002 a supporter of the AFL club Collingwood, calling themselves "knuckles," noted on the Collingwood BigFooty fan forum that "I prefer to focus on negatives."⁵⁷ Among the list of negative comments was the following assessment of the recruit that almost everyone else was celebrating, Shane Woewodin: "Woewodin—don't expect much. He last played with one of the best rucks in the comp. He is about to play with one of the worst. Will give some toe though." But even "knuckles" wrote of "Banking on Lonie, Didak, Rocca, Bucks, O'Bree and Cole (moves well, disposal poor atm [at the moment]) to get us to the next level." And banking is a term redolent of expectation.

Another way of managing expectations is to draw on the mordant humor in which fans of losing teams specialize. In another example, this time from early 2007, "Rocco Jones" started a thread on the Bulldogs BigFooty Internet site that both celebrated and mocked his wish that the latest sizeable Dogs recruit—Andrew McDougall—would be the savior by referring to past disappointments: "Ladies and gentlemen I introduce to you the greatest cult hero following group on this board. Our club has desperately searched for a tall forward to lead them to the promised land. A few of us have been fooled into believing false key-forward prophecies such as those of Tom Davidson, Nathan Saunders, Pat Bowden and Aaron James. Children all is forgiven as long as you see the light and take in Andrew McDougall as our key forward saviour."⁵⁸ Yet when fans are disappointed in the recruitment (or release) of certain players, they tend to react without humor (though their outrage can seem comical to outsiders). In 2012 "John Gennaro," the chief writer at Bolts from the Blue, felt he had to explain his "frustration or anger or bitterness over" the Chargers' first-round pick. "It stems mostly from fear. Fear of having Atari Bigby and Darrell Stuckey as the only two options at Strong Safety this season."[59] Such frustration, anger, or bitterness can be absurdly intense. "I feel like someone in my family has died. Went for an hour walk to clear my head and emotions. How can we pass up on Palmer," wrote "Sanj," a follower of the Essendon AFL team when they passed over the much-hyped Rhys Palmer for the lesser-known David Myers.[60] Trades can also occasion considerable anger. "I'm not ********en happy," wrote "SirBloodyIdiot" after the October 2005 trade period.[61] The Bulldogs had traded away two tall players (Jade Rawlings and Patrick Bowden) for speculative draft picks and, among other things, "SirBloodyIdiot" could "just tell one of these two will play well next year." "A frikin joke," concurred "fred cook."[62]

The fear that these fans have is that their teams have missed their opportunity, consigning their supporters to further suffering. At these times they also remember the past failures they have been trying to forget; hence, the compelling intensity of their anger. Past recruiting failures can even, after a time, undermine the thrill of the recruiting events that precede the new year. Though excited by trade week, Daniel also hates it because he believes the Bulldogs have generally lost more than they have gained. "I've been a big believer that every time we trade we've been dudded," he notes, "so don't trade."[63] Daniel's wariness is shared by other Bulldogs fans. "Trade week normally sends a shiver down the spine of a Doggies fan," wrote Rocco Jones on the BigFooty Bulldogs blog.[64] A "Bit like the time leading to a visit to the dentist as a kid (as an 'adult' I just now cho[o]se not to go). Under Rohde [the previous coach] I sure would have loved a needle to numb the pain."[65] Other aspects of the preseason can also lead to further suffering.

The Worst of Times

"Is it just me or is any press coverage on all AFL clubs during the pre-season either exceedingly positive or overwhelmingly negative?" So asked journalist Michael Tormey in early February, 2007, late in the AFL preseason. "This week, in Melbourne alone, we have seen the sports pages of the local newspapers filled with stories of the latest intra-club match, hamstring injury or new recruit who is amazing everyone with his speed/skill/fitness/all of the above."[66] One of the striking features of the recruitment of players is the way the responses of fans frequently seem exaggerated. New players are commonly designated as superstars or duds. There is a correlation here with evaluations of hope as either a dangerous delusion or a supreme good; there is no middle ground. As Tormey's article suggests, this tendency continues through the preseason in a revealing manner.

After recruitment, preseason training is another place in which considerable hope can be found. And yet it is not the often-clichéd acts that lead to hope—emerging youngsters, established players having their best preseason ever, veterans who seem suddenly fit and hungry again, new coaches, or coaching schemes—that give us the greatest insight into this hope. Instead it is the flipside, the despair when something goes wrong, that can help us understand this hope and the seasonal relationship to the past which structures it.

In late 2005, "Yankee Foxtrot Hotel" created a thread asking for preseason training news. "Living up in Qld [Queensland] I never get the chance to see how the guys are going during pre season training," explained "Yankee Foxtrot Hotel." "I was wondering if anyone lucky enough to have seen the guys train to date, would be able to post their thoughts, impressions to date on what they've seen." The request again was for information, in particular if there were any "surprises to date with any of the player(s)."[67] The following day, "dlanor dog" and "OldSchool" reported back. Their reports noted who did what, who was impressive, but also who was injured. In the words of "dlanor dog," Luke Darcy "went for a mark at full forward and came down heavily on his right knee and had to be helped off holding his right knee cap Morgan went off late with a hammy and Smith went off he was pointing to his thigh but he came back later."[68] "OldSchool" was similarly matter of fact. "Darcy knee injury looked serious. . . . Morgan's hamstring I'd be surprised if it was more than a twinge but you never know. Actually Morgan looked pretty good out there before the injury. Smith was off with a thigh injury for 10mins or so. Brad Murphy got a corked leg but stayed out there."[69] Injuries are part of all spectator sports, and these were simply noted in passing. Shortly after, however, came news that Bulldogs captain Luke Darcy, who had missed most of the previous season with a knee injury, had re-injured the knee and was now going to miss all of the upcoming season. The reaction of many was of horror. "*sigh* if its true, lets just hope its not as serious as first feared. Why Lord . . . WHY??" posted "onslaught."[70] "I'm shattered," wrote "SonOfScray," who also railed against the fates. "Poor Darc, just as things were looking to pick up for him and the club something like this happens to take the wind out of our sails just that little bit."[71] "rule" also drew attention to the effect this news had on Western Bulldogs supporters: "this is very devastating news for any Bulldog supporter. darcy is a great player and this news is very disappointing to hear, especially at this time of the year."[72] It was devastating enough to bring some to tears. "I'm going home to cry," wrote "whythelongface," while "Pugsta" confided that "I'm at work crying (discreetly). I love Luke Darcy—my favourite player. Very upsetting news on so many levels."[73] The pain thus was felt was both for the club and player. "Poor us, and what about him?" asked "dogbowl," summing up the feelings of many.[74]

San Diego Chargers' fans reacted with some similar sentiments when hyped running back Ryan Matthews broke his collarbone on his first touch in the first preseason game, the same injury, albeit on a different side, that had ended his previous season. "This is incredible," wrote "tonoxtono," who could scarcely believe it. "i give up," stated "Rockets7," while "bored@work" felt like "It's almost a bad joke at this point."[75] Further distress was evinced when Vincent Brown, one of the Chargers' most promising players, broke an ankle in the next preseason game. "Sigh . . . Are we watching this show again?" wrote "TioTheo." "Damn it, I HATE preseason," exclaimed "TecateBoltsFan." "That picture of Vincent Brown [being carted off in agony] pretty much sums up the way I felt after hearing this news," explained "Ferguson1015," while "Its Mikey" added, "Throw in the broken collarbone. Reason for my tears."[76]

What is most interesting about these responses are the intimations of shock and trauma.[77] It is as if major injuries are a shock in the preseason, when with contact sports like these, they are quite likely. Yet the reactions of these fans are of those who have been wronged. Such things are not supposed to happen, or so it seems. In other words, although past preseasons are filled with similar occurrences (witness the "Sigh" of "TioTheo" above), the response of these two sets of fans suggests they were acting as if in *this* preseason things were supposed to be different. Here we are closest to Eliade's seasonal annihilation of the past, to the hope that the new season would be begun afresh and things were as they *should* be without the stain of mistakes or sin. A time when serious injuries are a dreadful surprise, an unwanted reminder of a broken world, that the promised time might not be on its way (at least not this season). And there is a small step from here to the belief that for some unknown, horrible reason, the sporting gods have turned against these fans and cursed them. "Why Lord . . . WHY??" asks "onslaught," a call that would be plaintively matched by the San Diego Padres' fan "Ron Mexico" in early 2013 when esteemed prospect Rymer Liriano wrecked his elbow to the extent that he needed Tommy John surgery (ulnar collateral ligament reconstruction): "why can't we have nice things?"[78]

Yet while many of the immediate responses to these injuries were maudlin, desolation quickly turned into a search for new hope. In the face of dashed hopes, supporters like "SonOfScray" looked for promise in other players. "Looks like Streety and Wilbur's induction last year will come in handy as they handle the load all by themselves again in 2006!" "SonOfScray" posted, adding "Bugger, I feel so sorry for Darcy. It must be tough, I can't imagine how low he'd be feeling!"[79] After typing "ARRGGHHHHHH!!!!!!!" "Cyberdoggie" even found two "real positives" for the one "big negative."[80] The first positive was "that it happened now which means that the club and players have time to adjust and work around it rather than in the middle of the season or even during the pre-season (jan-feb). It also gives darcy more time to recover, and not rush back." And the second positive was that "we have a rookie in the wings by the name of tom davidson who has had his problems with knees and is ready and raring to go and could quite possibly fill darcy's spot up forward (with a bit of luck!)."

In the same fashion, over on Bolts from the Blue, fans expressed hope in other players to either step in or raise their performance to a new level. In addition, in an only partially comic send-up of the need to find meaningful hope in such distressing events, "AvengingJM" theorized that Ryan Matthews was going to make himself indestructible through a process of breaking and then calcifying his collarbones.[81] It was such a fun idea that when Vincent Brown broke his ankle, "insanebolt21" noted that Brown, too, must have "decided to go with the 'super-calcification' route previously mentioned by a fellow BFTB'er/genius":

> I must say I wasn't a big fan of this strategy when it was first employed by RM24, but now it is starting to make sense. I'm beginning to see the big picture plan of forming a football team out of indestructible warriors. So what we do from here is get the rest of the team to break a bone or two, place them all on the yet-to-be-approved 6 week IR thing, forfeit the first 6 weeks of the regular season (collateral damage), then bring back a fully healthy team built of invincible superhumans who go on a tear, going undefeated, finishing 10–6, winning the division, destroying their competition throughout the playoffs and bringing home the coveted Lombardi trophy! It all makes so much sense. I can't believe I didn't see this before now! And you all thought this was a bad thing.[82]

Here, in this absurd post, we see hope at its intoxicating best, relishing the comic absurdity of invincibility and yet ending with the usual fantasy that while also absurd, somehow it is also a matter of faith (not humor) for many fans. That hope may be found in such distress indicates both the need of many fans to invest in hope as a new season approaches, and also the way they may choose to focus on that which provides hope as opposed to that which takes it away. A year later, Rocco Jones made a similar point. "Living interstate," he explained, "I'm always desperately awaiting [intra-club] match reports. . . . Instead of looked great on the track, we hear about how they got a truckload of trucks, goals, marks, so on and so forth. If a forward kicks a bag, he is great and everyone should ignore the fact that his opponent also plays for us."[83]

Conclusion

"Why do I feel this way?" asked "MJP" on the eve of the 2007 Australian Football League Season.[84] "Something is definitely wrong," "MJP" wrote, before going on to note eight reasons for optimism and then stating that "Everyone is excited and looking forward to the season. Everyone is predicting success. I cannot feel the excitement—I am just worried that something—something bad—is about to happen and the rug is about to be pulled out from under . . . I have a terrible feeling about the Geelong game, and a worse feeling about the season at large." All the signs were good, in other words, but excitement was being replaced by dread. "firstdogonthemoon" had "a quick look on the Internet" and came up with a list of "likely possibilities," including postpartum depression, bronchial asthma, a food allergy, clinical depression, withdrawal from medication, "watching 'A Simple Life' with Paris Hilton and Nicole Ritchie," or "thinking about the possibility of the coalition being returned at the next federal election."[85] He also suggested, in a more serious vein, that "in my experience Dogs fans are the first to grasp at the tiniest straws of hope, and the first to give way in despair." After responding to "firstdogonthemoon's" Internet diagnoses, "MJP" noted that "Our most enjoyable seasons have come from humble beginnings (think '97) and I cant help but worry anytime we are expected to win!"[86]

What we see in this Internet exchange is how growing hopes might become almost unbearable. To expect is to risk disappointment. While anticipation has its own joys, it comes with the vulnerability of exposing oneself to disillusionment, and maybe even opening the door to Bion's trifecta of hatred, destructiveness, and despair. Although he wishes for a premiership, in the end "MJP" struggles to trust all the positive signs because they do not match his experiences of continually having his expectations disappointed. He is haunted by a past that he hopes to escape, possibly even annihilate, but knows the bitter costs often entailed in hoping for such an escape.

This chapter has explored the posts of sporting fans on a number of Internet sites in Australia and the United States to give a sense of how the seasonal rhythms of spectator sports can shape the circulation of the sporting past in the present. In particular, it shows how, during at least the liminal time in the lead-up to a new season, many fans of teams in the National Football League and Australian Football League take an obsessive interest in a particular aspect of history—the moments that provide them with information about the potential players that their team might recruit. The promise of these prospective recruits fills fans with excitement and hope, but such hopes depend on the willful forgetting of past experiences that indicate that most recruits will not realize the often extreme hopes and subsequent expectations placed upon them. The situation is not quite in line with Eliade's schema, but there is an attempted annihilation of past mistakes and an apparent concomitant (underlying) belief that this time glory should be on its way. Yet the hopes of fans are haunted by intimations of past suffering, and when something goes wrong—the wrong player is recruited or a key player is seriously injured—fans respond with excessive anger and/or bitterness that is amplified by the past distress that they had hoped to leave behind. Even when nothing goes wrong, the past can still haunt burgeoning hopes, as "MJP" discovered in 2007, for hope is not easy to live with, and fans like "MJP" know that while their hopes bring joy, they also create the conditions for further suffering.

This chapter has also shown how the theories and insights of religious studies and psychoanalysis might be productively used (and sometimes challenged) in the history of sport. For the seemingly absurd passions of sport fans frequently intersect with beliefs and fantasies that shape engagement with the past, as well as the present. The rich resource of online sport fansites can be further mined for what responses to events occurring during the season also reveal of the way the sporting past circulates in the present, as well as how present events might reshape readings of the past. But I think if we want to engage with these readings, and with the affective and magical aspects of fan memories, we have to grapple with the seasonal nature of these team sports, and the desires, beliefs, fantasies, and passions at play.

Notes

1. I first came across this quote in Schultz, "'Stuff from which Legends are Made,'" 717.

2. Compelling seasonal accounts of sport include St. John, *Rammer Jammer Yellow Hammer*; Parks, *A Season with Verona*; Pippos, *The Goddess Advantage*; and Kahn, *The Boys of Summer*.

3. For impressive, nuanced takes on spectator sports viewed through the lens of religious studies, see Price, "From Season to Season"; Grimshaw, "'I Can't Believe My Eyes!!!'"; Scholes, "The Bartman Ball and Sacrifice"; and Price, *Rounding the Bases*.

For critiques, see Higgs and Braswell, *An Unholy Alliance*; and Chandler, "Sport is Not a Religion."

4. Price, "From Season to Season," 56. This is not to say that Price is uninterested in questions of seasonal meaning, but that his primary focus lies in how modern spectator sports function as civic-religions.

5. Borish and Phillips, "Sport History as Modes of Expression," 472.

6. Much work remains to be done on all of these topics. For a preliminary analysis of the gender and online sports fan discussion forums, see Svennson, "Online Conversation Threads on Ice-Hockey."

7. Hardy, "Memory, Performance, and History"; Osmond, Phillips, and O'Neill, "Putting Up Your Dukes"; and Schultz, "'Stuff from which Legends are Made.'"

8. On collective memory, see Halbwachs, *The Collective Memory*; Nora, "Between History and Memory"; and the rest of the special "Memory and History" issue of *Representations*, 26, Spring (1989). For social memory, see Healy, *From the Ruins of Colonialism*. And on questions of memory, myth, and sport history, see Osmond and Phillips, "Reading *Salute*"; and Osmond, "Myth-making in Australian Sport History."

9. Cressy, *Bonfires and Bells*.

10. Spiegel, "Memory and History."

11. Nora, "Between History and Memory," 13.

12. Ibid., 12, 8–9.

13. See, for example, Oakley, *Football Delirium*.

14. Nora's argument that history has effectively triumphed over memory is of course contestable, as is the broader assumption that modernity ever took hold in any complete sense; on this, see Latour, *We Have Never Been Modern*. More recent studies of collective memory have often read memory and history as entangled (e.g., Zerubavel, *Recovered Roots*; and Hutton, "Mnemonic Schemes in the New History of Memory.") A fascinating alternative is to follow Joseph Mali in seeing myth as an essential part of living history. See Mali, *Mythistory*.

15. Other analyses of particular emotions within spectator sports include Walsh, "What If?"; Scholes, "Professional Baseball and Fan Disillusionment"; Klugman, "Loves, Suffering and Identification"; and Klugman, "'My Natural Environment has Provided Me with About Fifty Different Ways of Expressing Frustration.'"

16. For a review of how sporting emotions might be approached, see Klugman, "'It's That Feeling Sick in My Guts That I Think I Like the Most.'"

17. For an exploration of the myth of Pandora, see Davies, "Varieties of Hope."

18. Nietzsche, *Human, All Too Human*, 45.

19. Little, *The Public Emotions*, 254.

20. Davies, "Varieties of Hope." For a similar argument, see Averill, Catlin, and Chon, *Rules of Hope*.

21. Judeo-Christian writings are replete with the positive reading of hope, though one does not have to be a theist to ascribe to the notion of hope as a good. An atheist, the historian Ernst Bloch was someone who belonged to this tradition of celebrating hope, developing a positive philosophy of hope, with hope something to be learned

and espoused for its potential to transform the world and our understanding of what is possible. Bloch, *The Principle of Hope*. See also the three essays on Bloch's theories in Fitzgerald, *The Sources of Hope*; Bloch, "Hope and Time"; and the piece by renowned Christian theologian Jürgen Moltmann, "In Gratitude to Ernst Bloch." More recently, some cognitive psychologists have argued that hope is at the core of what it means to be human and can be a good that leads to empowerment. See, for example, Snyder, *Handbook of Hope*; Sanna and Chang, *Judgments over Time*; and Peterson and Seligman, *Character Strengths and Virtues*.

22. Braithwaite, "Collective Hope."

23. Schachtel, *Metamorphosis*, 37.

24. Ibid.

25. Ibid., 38. The clumsiness of this last phrase—"the hoped-for change"—already hints at the bind Schachtel was placing himself in. To write instead of a "wished for change" or "desired change" already starts to blur his too-sharp distinction between hope that develops out of a wish and hope that arises from the objective assessment of "the concrete conditions of reality."

26. Eliade, *The Myth of the Eternal Return*, 62 (emphasis added).

27. Eliade returns to this theme in *The Sacred and the Profane*.

28. Price, "From Season to Season." Price was a former student of Eliade's.

29. The self-described "largest and fastest-growing network of fan-centric online sports communities," SB Nation hosts more than 300 sites, primarily for fans of particular teams. Each site has a degree of independence, being run by its own editors. Since August 2012, SB Nation has even employed a sport historian to provide content. For more, see SB Nation, "About SB Nation"; and Pincus, "Inhistoric."

30. See for example, Wonko, November 25, 2011, "2012 NFL Draft - Scouting for Future Chargers Week 13," *Bolts from the Blue*. Accessed November 26, 2011. http://www.boltsfromtheblue.com/2011/11/25/2585630/2012-nfl-draft-scouting-chargers-week-13. Most people who post on online fan forums use a nom de web which I have designated by use of quotation marks. The original spelling, punctuation, and grammar have been retained in the quotations sourced from these posts.

31. Big Footy started off as a website hosting sites for fans of specific AFL teams but, like SB Nation, it has expanded to host forums for other sport teams and competitions and also includes some nonsport forums. For more, see http://www.bigfooty.com/.

32. Knightmare, June 11, 2012, "Knightmare's 2012 Mock Draft," *Big Footy*. Accessed January 27, 2013. http://www.bigfooty.com/forum/threads/knightmares-2012-mock-draft.956129/. (For readership numbers, see http://www.bigfooty.com/forum/forums/phantom-drafts.284/).

33. Mr_Posey, February 22, 2013, "5 players Charger fans should watch for during the Combine," *Bolts From the Blue*. Accessed February 22, 2013. http://www.boltsfromtheblue.com/2013/2/21/4013902/5-players-charger-fans-should-watch-for-during-the-combine.

34. Psychoanalysts like Melanie Klein and Jacques Lacan were especially interested in the interplay between needs, demands, and desires. See, for example, Klein, *Envy and Gratitude*; and Lacan, *Écrits*.

35. Bloom, *Omens of Millennium*. On the relationship of sports fans with their heroes, see Klugman and Ricatti, "'Roma Non Dimentica I Suoi Figli.'"

36. Bion, "Group Dynamics."

37. Ibid., 151–52.

38. See, for example, Kuharsky, "Good Draft Hit Rates"; and AlfredC, July 17, 2011, "Drafts Versus Trades: What's the Recipe for Success?" *The Roar*. Accessed July 17, 2011. http://www.theroar.com.au/2011/07/17/drafting-vs-trading-for-success/.

39. For more on this, see Klugman, *Passion Play*.

40. Curtis, "Cyber Season."

41. Ibid.

42. April is often termed "Liar's Month" in the lexicon of the NFL due to the tendency of teams to willfully spread misinformation and dissemble more generally in an attempt to keep secret the list of players they are targeting for recruitment.

43. For an example, see the summary of the media rumors on the first day of the 2007 trade week by Roolander, October 7, 2007, "Day 1 trade talk," *Big Footy*. Accessed October 7, 2007. http://www.bigfooty.com/forum/showthread.php?t=384028.

44. Interview with Daniel, September 2006. This interview was conducted as part of a broader study examining the seasonal emotions of Australian Rules football followers.

45. always right, October 8, 2006, "trade week versus draft," *Big Footy*. Accessed October 8, 2006. http://www.bigfooty.com/forum/showthread.php?t=274878.

46. Curtis, "Cyber Season."

47. Lonergan, October 25, 2003, "Trade Intrigue Centres on Uncertain Rawlings," posted on Dan Lonergan's [untitled] ABC Grandstand blog. Accessed June 21, 2006. http://www.abc.net.au/afl/s975099.htm.

48. For more on this understanding of fantasy, see LaPlanche and Pontalis, "Fantasy and the Origins of Sexuality."

49. Rose, *States of Fantasy*, 15.

50. always right, "Trade week versus draft."

51. For this and the following quotes see the posts on "WOOF welcomes Jake Stringer," *Whitten Oval Online Forum*. Accessed November 23, 2012. http://www.woof.net.au/forum/showthread.php?t=11319. The Whitten Oval Online Forum (WOOF) is an independent fansite for supporters of the Western Bulldogs AFL team.

52. Scooter600x, November 25, 2004, "Re: Colin Wisbey's Ryan Griffen Profile," *Big Footy*. Accessed June 16, 2006. http://www.bigfooty.com/forum/showthread.php?t=144084.

53. Madcat5, April 27, 2012, "Re. Folks, San Diego is killing this draft," Fanshot, Accessed March 2, 2013. http://www.boltsfromtheblue.com/2012/4/27/2982948/folks-san-diego-is-killing-this-draft-it-is-just-slaying-it-a-trio-of.

54. Bill Williamson, April 28, 2012, "Wrapping up AFC West's Third Round," ESPN NFL, Accessed March 2, 2103. http://espn.go.com/blog/afcwest/post/_/id/43382/wrapping-up-the-third-round.

55. Schachtel, *Metamorphosis*, 40–41.

56. Richard Wade, May 18, 2012, "San Diego Chargers: Managing Expectations of Melvin Ingram," *Bolts From the Blue*. Accessed May 18, 2012. http://www.boltsfromtheblue.com/2012/5/17/3026581/san-diego-chargers-managing-expectations-of-melvin-ingram.

57. This and the following quotes are from knuckles, November 19, 2002, "Re: Your Line Up," *Big Footy*. Accessed June 20, 2006. http://www.bigfooty.com/forum/showthread.php?t=53080.

58. Rocco Jones, October 4, 2007, "Doogs' Droogs," *Big Footy*. Accessed October 4, 2007. http://www.bigfooty.com/forum/showthread.php?t=290848. In another example of sports fans being willing to acknowledge the absurdity of their expectations with moments of self-mocking humor, supporters of the San Diego Padres on the SN Nation *Gaslamp Ball* blog named Chase Headley "the savior" in 2008 precisely because the team management were worried that he would be burdened with expectations that were too great. For the relevant post and associated comments, see jobx, June 10, 2008, "Chase Headley might be a Padre in a week if there isn't too much pressure," *Gaslamp Ball*. Accessed June 10, 2008. http://www.gaslampball.com/2008/6/9/549220/chase-headley-might-be-a-p.

59. John Gennaro, April 28, 2012, "Open Thread: 2012 NFL Draft, Day Two," *Bolts From the Blue*. Accessed April 28, 2012. http://www.boltsfromtheblue.com/2012/4/27/2981510/open-thread-2012-nfl-draft-day-two.

60. Sanj, November 24, 2007, "Re: Anyone upset with todays draft?" *Big Footy*. Accessed November 24, 2007. http://www.bigfooty.com/forum/threads/anyone-upset-with-todays-draft.398278/page-2.

61. SirBloodyIdiot, October 7, 2005, "Absolutely disgusted," *Big Footy*. Accessed October 7, 2005. http://www.bigfooty.com/forum/showthread.php?t=203788.

62. fred cook, October 7, 2005, "Re: Absolutely disgusted," *Big Footy*. Accessed October 7, 2005. http://www.bigfooty.com/forum/showthread.php?t=203788.

63. Interview with Daniel, September 2005.

64. Rocco Jones, October 5, 2006, "Trading Post," *The Can Bar Blog: The Mighty Bulldogs . . . Blogged*. Accessed October 5, 2006. http://www.bulldogsfootyblog.com.

65. Fremantle fans have also been haunted by past trades. In fact, one Fremantle fan set up a Wikipedia page to defend their trading history: Anonymous, June 20, 2006, "Fremantle Football Club Drafting and Trading History," *Wikipedia*. Accessed June 20, 2006. http://en.wikipedia.org/wiki/Fremantle_Football_Club_drafting_and_trading_history.

66. Tormey, "Pre-season."

67. Yankee Foxtrot Hotel, December 20, 2005, "Pre SeasonTraining—Peoples thoughts to date," *Big Footy*. Accessed December 20, 2005. http://www.bigfooty.com/forum/showthread.php?t=215977.

68. dlanor dog, December 21, 2005, "Re: Pre SeasonTraining—Peoples thoughts to date," *Big Footy*. Accessed December 21, 2005. http://www.bigfooty.com/forum/showthread.php?t=215977.

69. OldSchool, December 21, 2005, "Re: Pre SeasonTraining—Peoples thoughts to date," *Big Footy*. Accessed December 21, 2005. http://www.bigfooty.com/forum/showthread.php?t=215977.

70. onslaught, December 21, 2005, "Re: Darcy Out for Season?" *Big Footy*. Accessed December 21, 2005. http://www.bigfooty.com/forum/showthread.php?t=216211.

71. SonOfScray, December 21, 2005, "Re: Darcy Out for Season?" *Big Footy*. Accessed December 21, 2005. http://www.bigfooty.com/forum/showthread.php?t=216211.

72. rule, December 21, 2005, "Re: Darcy Out for Season?" *Big Footy*. Accessed December 21, 2005. http://www.bigfooty.com/forum/showthread.php?t=216211&page=2.

73. whythelongface, December 21, 2005, "Re: Darcy Out for Season?" *Big Footy*. Accessed December 21, 2005. http://www.bigfooty.com/forum/showthread.php?t=216211&page=2; Pugsta, December 21, 2005, "Re: Darcy Out for Season?" *Big Footy*. Accessed December 21, 2005. http://www.bigfooty.com/forum/showthread.php?t=216211&page=3.

74. dogbowl, December 21, 2005, "Re: Darcy Out for Season?" *Big Footy*. Accessed December 21, 2005. http://www.bigfooty.com/forum/showthread.php?t=216211&page=3.

75. See the comments to the following post by Wonko, August 10, 2012: "Ryan Mathews Breaks Clavicle; Expected to Miss Start of Season," *Bolts from the Blue*. Accessed August 10, 2012. http://www.boltsfromtheblue.com/2012/8/9/3232637/ryan-mathews-breaks-clavicle-expected-to-miss-started-of-season.

76. See the comments to the following post by John Gennaro, August 19, 2012: "San Diego Chargers WR Vincent Brown Breaks Ankle in Preseason Game," *Bolts from the Blue*. Accessed August 19, 2012. http://www.boltsfromtheblue.com/2012/8/18/3253030/san-diego-chargers-wr-vincent-brown-breaks-ankle-in-preseason-game.

77. For further discussion of the way sports fans can react to certain sporting incidents as if they are traumatic, see Klugman, "'Each Time I'm Reminded of It, I feel as Though I Need Therapy.'"

78. Ron Mexico, February 16, 2013, "Prospect Rymer Liriano out for the season due to TJ surgery," *Gaslamp Ball*. Accessed February 16, 2013. http://www.gaslampball.com/2013/2/15/3992470/prospect-rymer-liriano-out-for-the-season-due-to-tj-surgery.

79. SonOfScray, December 21, 2005, "Re: Darcy Out for Season?" *Big Footy*. Accessed December 21, 2005. http://www.bigfooty.com/forum/threads/darcy-out-for-season.216211/#post-4383568.

80. Cyberdoggie, December 21, 2005, "Re: Darcy Out for Season?" *Big Footy*. Accessed December 21, 2005. http://www.bigfooty.com/forum/showthread.php?t=216211&page=2.

81. AvengingJM, August 11, 2012, "The indestructible calcification of Ryan Mathews," *Bolts from the Blue*. Accessed August 11, 2012. http://www.boltsfromtheblue.com/2012/8/10/3233852/the-indestructible-calcification-of-ryan-mathews.

82. insanebolt21, August 19, 2012, "San Diego Chargers WR Vincent Brown Breaks Ankle in Preseason Game," *Bolts from the Blue*. Accessed August 19, 2012. http://www

.boltsfromtheblue.com/2012/8/18/3253030/san-diego-chargers-wr-vincent-brown-breaks-ankle-in-preseason-game.

83. Rocco Jones, February 9, 2007, "Not Footy Season Season," *The Can Bar: The Mighty Bulldogs . . . Blogged*. Accessed February 9, 2007. http://bulldogsfootyblog.com/?p=75.

84. MJP, March 28, 2007, "Why do I feel this way?" *Whitten Oval Online Forum*. Accessed March 28, 2007. http://www.woof.net.au/forum/showthread.php?t=468.

85. firstdogonthemoon, March 28, 2007, "Re: Why do I feel this way?" *Whitten Oval Online Forum*. Accessed March 28, 2007. http://www.woof.net.au/forum/showthread.php?t=468.

86. MJP, March 29, 2007, "Re: Why do I feel this way?" *Whitten Oval Online Forum*. Accessed March 29, 2007. http://www.woof.net.au/forum/showthread.php?t=468.

References

Averill, James R, George Catlin, and Kyum Koo Chon. 1990. *Rules of Hope*. New York: Springer-Verlag.

Bion, Wilfred. 1961. "Group Dynamics: A Review." In *Experiences in Groups: and Other Papers*, 141–91. London: Tavistock Publications.

Bloch, Ernst. 1979. "Hope and Time: Theory Praxis in the Long Run." Translated by Dieter Freundlieb. In *The Sources of Hope*, edited by Ross Fitzgerald, 153–161. Sydney: Pergamon Press.

Bloch, Ernst. 1986. *The Principle of Hope*. Translated by Neville Plaice, Stephen Plaice, and Paul Knight. Oxford: Basil Blackwell.

Bloom, Harold. 1996. *Omens of Millennium: The Gnosis of Angels, Dreams, and Resurrection*. New York: Riverhead Books.

Borish, Linda J., and Murray G. Phillips. 2012. "Sport History as Modes of Expression: Material Culture and Cultural Spaces in Sport and History." *Rethinking History* 16, no. 4: 465–77.

Braithwaite, Valerie. 2004. "Collective Hope: Preface to 'Hope, Power and Governance.'" *The Annals of the American Academy of Political and Social Science* 592, no. 1 (March): 6–15.

Chandler, Joan. 1992. "Sport is Not a Religion." In *Sport and Religion*, edited by Shirl Hoffman, 55–61. Champaign, IL: Human Kinetics.

Cressy, David. 1989. *Bonfires and Bells: National Memory and the Protestant Calendar in Elizabethan and Stuart England*. London: Weidenfeld and Nicholson.

Curtis, Rod. 2004. "Cyber Season." *Age*. October 2. Available on Carlton Supporters Club website. Accessed 3 September, 2013. http://archive.carltonsc.com/modules.php?name=News&file=article&sid=643.

Davies, Allen. 1979. "Varieties of Hope." In *The Sources of Hope*, edited by Ross Fitzgerald, 24–35. Sydney: Pergamon Press.

Eliade, Mircea. 1987. *The Sacred and the Profane: The Nature of Religion*. Translated by Willard R. Trask. San Diego: Harcourt.

———. 2005. *The Myth of the Eternal Return: Cosmos and History*. Translated by Willard R. Trask. Princeton: Princeton University Press.

Fitzgerald, Ross, ed. 1979. *The Sources of Hope*. Sydney: Pergamon Press.

Grimshaw, Mike. 2000. "'I Can't Believe My Eyes!!!' The Religious Aesthetics of Sport as Postmodern Salvific Moments." *Implicit Religion* 3, no.2: 87–99.

Halbwachs, Maurice. 1980. *The Collective Memory*. Translated by Francis J. Ditter and Vida Yazdi Ditter. New York: Harper and Row.

Hardy, Stephen. 1997. "Memory, Performance, and History: The Making of American Ice Hockey at St. Paul's School, 1860–1915." *The International Journal of the History of Sport* 14, no. 1 (April): 97–115.

Healy, Chris. 1997. *From the Ruins of Colonialism: History as Social Memory*. Melbourne: Cambridge University Press.

Higgs, Robert, and Michael Braswell. 2004. *An Unholy Alliance: The Sacred and Modern Sports*. Macon, GA: Mercer University Press.

Hudson, Wayne. 1979. "Introduction: Hope and Time: Theory Praxis in the Long Run." In *The Sources of Hope*, edited by Ross Fitzgerald, 144–53. Sydney: Pergamon Press.

Hutton, Patrick. 1997. "Mnemonic Schemes in the New History of Memory." *History and Theory* 36, no. 3 (October): 378–91.

Kahn, Roger. 1972. *The Boys of Summer*. New York: Harper and Row.

Klein, Melanie. 1957. *Envy and Gratitude*. London: Tavistock.

Klugman, Matthew. 2008–9 "'Each Time I'm Reminded of It, I Feel as Though I Need Therapy': Australian Football, Tragedies and the Question of Catharsis." *Traffic* 10,: 97–122.

———. 2009. "Loves, Suffering and Identification: The Passions of Australian Football League Fans." *International Journal of the History of Sport* 26, no. 1 (January): 21–44.

———. 2009. *Passion Play: Love, Hope and Heartbreak at the Footy*. Melbourne: Hunter Publishers.

———. 2013. "'It's That Feeling Sick in My Guts That I Think I Like the Most': Sport, Pleasure, and Embodied Suffering." In *Examining Sport Histories: Paradigms, Power and the Postmodern Turn*, edited by Richard Pringle and Murray Phillips, 159–91. Morgantown, WV: Fitness Information Technology.

———. 2013. "'My Natural Environment Has Provided Me with About Fifty Different Ways of Expressing Frustration': Mining the Visceral Angst of Australian Rules Football Followers." *Emotion, Space and Society*. http://dx.doi.org/10.1016/j.emospa.2013.08.005.

Klugman, Matthew, and Francesco Ricatti. 2012. "'Roma Non Dimentica I Suoi Figli': Love, Sacrifice and the Emotional Attachment to Football Heroes." *Modern Italy* 17, no. 2 (May): 237–49.

Kuharsky, Paul. 2011. "Good Draft Hit Rates: Lower Than You Think." *ESPN*, July 4. Accessed July 4, 2011. http://espn.go.com/blog/afcsouth/post/_/id/22699/good-draft-hit-rates-lower-than-you-think.

Lacan, Jacques. 1977. *Écrits: A Selection*. Translated by Alan Sheridan. London: Tavistock.

LaPlanche, Jean, and J-B Pontalis. 1973. "Fantasy and the Origins of Sexuality." In *Formations of Fantasy*, edited by Victor Burgin, James Donald, and Cora Kaplan, 5–34. London: Methuen.
Latour, Bruno. 1993. *We Have Never Been Modern*. Translated by Catherine Porter. New York: Harvester Wheatsheaf.
Little, Graham. 1999. *The Public Emotions: From Mourning to Hope*. Sydney: ABC Books.
Mali, Joseph. 2003. *Mythistory: The Making of a Modern Historiography*. Chicago: University of Chicago Press.
Moltmann, Jürgen. 1979. "In Gratitude to Ernst Bloch." Translated by Wayne Hudson. In *The Sources of Hope*, edited by Ross Fitzgerald, 162–6. Sydney: Pergamon Press.
Nietzsche, Friedrich. 1984. *Human, All Too Human: A Book for Free Spirits*. Translated by Marion Faber. Lincoln: University of Nebraska Press.
Nora, Pierre. 1989. "Between History and Memory: *Les Lieux de Mémoire*." *Representations* 26 (Spring): 7–24.
Oakley, Chris. 2007. *Football Delirium*. London: Karnac.
Osmond, Gary. 2011. "Myth-making in Australian Sport History: Re-evaluating Duke Kahanamoku's Contribution to Surfing." *Australian Historical Studies* 42, no. 2 (June), 260–76.
Osmond, Gary, and Murray G. Phillips. 2011. "Reading *Salute*: Filmic Representations of Sports History." *The International Journal of the History of Sport* 28, no.10 (July): 1463–77.
Osmond, Gary, Murray G. Phillips, and Mark O'Neill. 2006. "Putting Up Your Dukes: Statues, Social Memory, and Duke Paoa Kahanamoku." *The International Journal of the History of Sport* 23, no. 1 (February): 82–103.
Parks, Tim. 2002. *A Season with Verona: Travels around Italy in Search of Illusion, National Character and Goals*. London: Secker and Warburg.
Peterson, Christopher, and Martin Seligman, eds. 2004. *Character Strengths and Virtues: A Handbook and Classification*. New York: Oxford University Press.
Pincus, David. "Inhistoric." Accessed January 27, 2013. http://www.sbnation.com/sports-history.
Pippos, Angela. 2006. *The Goddess Advantage: One Year in the Life of a Football Worshipper*. Melbourne: Text Publishing.
Price, Joseph, ed. 2000. "From Season to Season." In *From Season to Season: Sports as American Religion*, edited by Joseph Price, 49–58. Macon, GA: Mercer University Press,.
———. 2006. *Rounding the Bases: Baseball and Religion in America*. Macon, GA: Mercer University Press.
Rose, Jacqueline. 1995. *States of Fantasy*. Oxford: Clarendon Press.
Sanna, Lawrence, and Edward Chang, eds. 2006. *Judgments over Time: The Interplay of Thoughts, Feelings, and Behaviors*. Oxford: Oxford University Press.
SB Nation. "About SB Nation." Accessed January 27, 2013. http://www.sbnation.com/about.

Schachtel, Ernest. 1959. *Metamorphosis: On the Development of Affect, Perception, Attention, and Memory*. New York: Basic Books.

Scholes, Jeffrey. 2004. "Professional Baseball and Fan Disillusionment: A Religious Ritual Analysis." *Journal of Religion and Popular Culture* 7 (Summer). http://www.usask.ca/relst/jrpc/art7-baseballfan.html.

———. 2005. "The Bartman Ball and Sacrifice: Ambiguity in an American Ritual." *Journal of Religion and Society* 7: 1–13.

Schultz, Jaime. 2007. "'Stuff from which Legends are Made': Jack Trice Stadium and the Politics of Memory." *The International Journal of the History of Sport* 24, no. 6: 715–48.

Snyder, Richard C, ed. 2000. *Handbook of Hope: Theory, Measures & Applications*. San Diego, CA: Academic Press.

Spiegel, Gabrielle M. 2002. "Memory and History: Liturgical Time and Historical Time." *History and Theory* 41 (May): 149–62.

St. John, Warren. 2005. *Rammer Jammer Yellow Hammer: A Road Trip into the Heart of Fan Mania*. New York: Crown.

Svensson, Anders. 2010. "Online Conversation Threads on Ice-Hockey: A Comparison of Swedish Male and Female Participants." In *Sexual Sports Rhetoric: Global and Universal Contexts*, edited by Linda Fuller, 107–20. New York: Peter Lang.

Tormey, Michael. 2007. "Pre-season: The Best of Times, the Worst of Times for AFL Fans." *Crikey*, February 1. Accessed June 19, 2007. http://www.crikey.com.au/2007/02/01/pre-season-the-best-of-times-the-worst-of-times-for-afl-fans/.

Walsh, Melissa. 2006. "What If? Australian Rules Football and the Uchronic Imagination—Collingwood, Grand Finals and Memory." In *Football Fever: Moving the Goalposts*, edited by Matthew Nicholson, Bob Stewart, and Rob Hess, 233–42. Melbourne: Maribyrnong Press.

Zerubavel, Yael. 1995. *Recovered Roots: The Making of Israeli National Tradition*. Chicago: University of Chicago Press.

7

Interactivity, Blogs, and the Ethics of Doing Sport History

REBECCA OLIVE

Recent theoretical developments have seen many historians rethink what history is, how it can be done, what it can contribute, and how it has impacts beyond the academy.[1] Such discussions may seem problematic for those professional historians solely interested in reconstructing the sporting past, but for a growing number of historians the process of writing and producing histories is unavoidably riddled with methodological, ethical, and political decisions and impacts.[2] Rather than "avoid[ing] questions about the meaning of their work,"[3] or "remaining indifferent about the precise effects of their writing,"[4] postmodern and cultural historians are interested in expanding their understandings of how histories are developed, and their impacts on broader social and cultural understandings of the past. For Jaime Schultz, historians today "[m]ust have the "deepest respect for reality" while concomitantly granting that the past is unknowable and that history is a representation of that past, one of many versions pieced together from the historian's selection of the vestiges that remain . . . Far from suggesting an anti-referentialist position, or that one cannot or should not study the past, this position highlights the limits of empiricism and affirms the idea that any attempt to represent the past inescapably creates meaning."[5] More than addressing truthfulness in reconstructing the past, contemporary research approaches ask historians to consider that how we do history—how we represent the past—has meaning, impacts, and effects beyond the academy.[6] This, in turn, has effects in terms of how we are able to do historical research. In this context, a shift toward questions of research practice is inevitable. Drawing on Wulf Kansteiner, Holly Thorpe argues that changes in how we understand history require a "critical reflection on method and theory, as well as a systematic evaluation of its problems, approaches and objects of study."[7] In taking a postmodern understanding of history as the ways we represent the past, contemporary sport historians are increasingly faced with the kinds of questions more common for researchers in cultural studies and sociology—questions of subjectivity, reflexivity, methodology, ethics, and meaning, and the effects of these on historical scholarship.[8] What historians do, and how we do it, matters.

These disciplinary questions are not exclusive to history. In my own home of cultural studies, recent discussions have turned to consider why cultural studies matters, and how, as Graeme Turner recently argued, scholarship should be more than descriptive, but also "concerned with its contribution to the public good."[9] Such an approach involves critical reflection on the ethics and politics of scholarly practice, as well as the maintenance of quality and rigor in research itself. Lawrence Grossberg explains that asking challenging disciplinary questions such as these "is not a matter of berating cultural studies or those who practice it, but of challenging us to think beyond the institutional constraints and habits to which we have become accustomed."[10] That is, developing a reflexive approach to historical research is not about questioning the value of empirical work but is about critically engaging with the process and effects of doing history.

With this in mind, this chapter takes seriously Douglas Booth's recent argument: "If historians believe that historical knowledge can influence the future, then, logically, they should consider their ethical responsibilities and thus the politics of 'doing' history."[11] I suggest that historians could make use of the interactive qualities presented by blogs as a possible tool to help them explicitly engage with these issues.

This chapter will discuss the potential that the semi-interactive qualities of blogs offer sport historians, and how, despite the philosophical and methodological challenges online spaces pose, researchers might make productive use of them to engage with contemporary research issues and approaches in doing sport history. In particular, it will consider the methodological and ethical potential of historians participating as producers of blogs and as commenters, by contributing to and interacting in the online development of public and cultural histories and understandings of the past. In advocating for blogging as an approach to doing history, I am invested in the politics and ethics of the e/affects of how we do and write histories, in the meaning of historical research, and in what the political and cultural implications of those histories may have on the future.

Blogs: Interactive and Collaborative Memory-Making

The development of Web 2.0 has seen online spaces become more dynamic and interactive, with website producers and users developing communities; self-publishing knowledge and information; and debating issues, ideas, and understandings in what are essentially public spaces.[12] These developments in how we use the Internet have seen Tim Berners-Lee's vision of the World Wide Web, as "more a social creation more than a technical toy," come to life.[13] While blogs, social-networking sites (such as Facebook, Instagram, and Twitter), and other user-generated digital media are now commonly used for research in cultural studies and sociology, historian Rachel Leow suggests that it is only in the second decade of the twenty-first century that "the historical profession is coming to terms with the ways in which the Internet is irrevocably changing what we do and how we do it."[14] Static websites such as archives, libraries, biographies, and other noninteractive online spaces have opened new options for how we access historical sources and evidence to understand the past, but interactive digital media remain problematic and difficult for historians to negotiate and use.[15]

However, in the introduction to their 2006 book, *Digital History: A Guide to Gathering, Preserving, and Presenting the Past on the Web*, Daniel J. Cohen and Roy Rosenzweig note "seven qualities of digital media and networks that potentially allow (historians) to do things better: capacity, accessibility, flexibility, diversity, manipulability, interactivity, and hypertextuality (or non-linearity)."[16] While historians appear to be making increasing use of the digital qualities of capacity (storage), accessibility (to documents and for the public), flexibility (of how we present histories), diversity (who can be represented and have a voice), manipulability (using technology to work with sources in new ways), and hypertext (disrupting the traditional structure of historical narratives), interactivity has proven to be methodologically and ethically challenging.

In an interactive digital context, sources and "cultural objects have no more fixity than liquid" and our ways of understanding and engaging with sources have changed considerably.[17] Until recently, sources, evidence, and cultural artifacts have functioned to "continuously reproduce the producer and consumer as two distinct subject positions," leaving historians confident in their roles of production and reproduction.[18] But as Cohen and Rosenzweig explain, interactive digital media is "a two-way medium, in which every point of consumption can also be a point of production," thus enabling "multiple forms of historical dialogue—among professionals, between professionals and nonprofessionals, between teachers and students, among students, among people reminiscing about the past—that were possible before but which are not only simpler but potentially richer and more intensive in the digital medium."[19]

In this way, they argue, interactivity offers historians the chance to "transform the traditional, one-way reader/writer, producer/consumer relationships" and offers an "ideal medium" for dialogue and collaboration.[20] In this approach to understanding the past, producers and consumers of histories are blurred through interactive and collaborative processes of remembering, forgetting, and creating collective social and cultural memories.[21]

It is important to note that not all digital media can be defined as entirely interactive. This is significant because while interactive sites like Facebook and Twitter explicitly invite high levels of contribution to content, websites like blogs remain semi-interactive in that the producer of the blog retains complete control over content on the site.[22] The first such example is websites where public contribution to text is invited but there is no personal exchange; for example, Wikipedia. On such sites, overseeing editors control the quality and reliability of content by taking responsibility for what is published, but the content itself is developed in collaboration by a number of contributors. Such sites serve a role in providing public input and access to information. A second form of semi-interactive websites is those where there is no public contribution to the initial content, but where opportunities for public feedback are provided and dialogue is invited. The main text on the site establishes initial context and perspective, while allowing for contributions from interested and potentially invested others who may or may not build upon the conversation. It is here, in this semi-interactive space, that blogs fit.

This differentiation is key in this chapter, which argues that semi-interactive sites are possibly more manageable for historians than fully interactive sites, like Facebook, which Mike Cronin rightly argues can be methodological and ethical minefields.[23] The semi-interactive nature of blogs, where the blog producer retains editorial control over the published text but invites and participates in comment and dialogue in the space beneath each post, is key in allowing bloggers to frame ideas and discussions, and to encourage public contributions, while maintaining limited access to personal information of those interacting.

Different than a website, a blog (short for weblog) is an online, public place of expression, characterized by "frequently updated, reverse chronologically ordered posts on a common webpage."[24] While early blogs were little more than repositories for logging or archiving web pages of interest, blogs today are produced by single authors or collectives to provide information, as self-representation, to tell a story; to work toward a political goal; or to represent a culture, experience, idea, or issue outside of mainstream media.[25] As a digital resource, blogs are publicly available, globally accessible, archival in their capacity to store past posts and comments on the website, instantaneous in the ways posts and comments are published, have options for anonymity both for the blogger and for the people who comment, and are often part of a blogging community that centers on a common interest.[26]

Blog posts can be published using a variety of media including text, images, audio, and video, or a combination of each, allowing the potential for accessibility across language and literacy barriers. The majority of noncommercial blogs are hosted on websites that are free to use and that offer an easy interface that requires low technical competency. The relatively cheap running costs mean that content can remain user-generated, rather than filtering publication through an external editorial process or advertising obligations.[27] In terms of their interactivity, it is common for blogs to include an enabled comments section underneath each post that allows readers to engage with blog posts by providing responses, web links, and feedback instantaneously.[28] While many comments are comical or ironic in tone, they can also provide new information related to the topic of the post, argue a different perspective, or further develop the ideas presented in the post. Additionally, when the blog is located as part of a specific community of interest, interested and related bloggers can hyperlink and republish posts and comments between various sites. This networking of ideas broadens the potential audience and creates a hyperlinked web of resources, knowledge, and understanding in relation to a particular topic or event.[29]

A number of historians have begun drawing on the semi-interactive quality of blogs by examining them as texts to understand the processes through which people construct collective social and cultural memories. Most commonly, this work has examined blogs as a source for accessing understandings of the past in cultural or feminist histories, where engaging with the diversity of the meanings and understandings people make of the past is a key concern for researchers.[30] In such research projects, engaging with both blog posts and the comment sections has been key in revealing how these semi-interactive processes work to help us understand the past in the present. An excellent example of this kind of historical research is Stephanie Ho, who explored how the interactions between blog posts and comments contributed to collective and public memory-making of past, everyday experiences of living in Singapore.[31] In particular, Ho compared the ways that a personal, nonprofessional, single-author blog (*Good Morning Yesterday*) and the multi-authored blog of a state-sponsored heritage website (*Yesterday.sg*) engaged audiences to contribute their memories of Singapore's everyday cultural past. With its focus on sharing memories and experiences, *Good Morning Yesterday* was not attempting to develop an official history, nor establish one history as defining. Instead it was successful in encouraging people to share memories and to paint a collective picture of yesterday by maintaining a dialogic approach that took seriously the contributions of others.

More recently, Gary Osmond and Murray Phillips illustrated the ways that the semi-interactive capacities of blogs can help us understand how we make and remake collective and cultural meanings of the past.[32] Osmond and Phillips analyzed the comments readers left on related websites in response to the 2008 documentary film, *Salute*, about Australian sprinter Peter Norman's role in the "black power salute" at the 1968 Mexico Olympics. Their analysis illustrated that we cannot predict responses to the histories we produce (in this case, a documentary film), and that the interpretations historians make of the past may not be shared by their audience. Commenters engaged in discussions, debates, and dialogue about the filmic representation of the past presented in *Salute* and provided personal responses to watching the film. Similar to the readers of *Good Morning Yesterday*, bloggers and commenters begin with personal interests, experiences, and responses, but often relate these to broader cultural and social contexts, memories, and understandings.[33] Holly Thorpe also illustrated the interactive nature of cultural histories on blogs in her analysis of the agendas, processes, and various media through which a collective understanding of snowboarding history has been developed. Like Osmond and Phillips, Thorpe's multimedia analysis was "less interested in the historical 'facts' or commemorative processes stabilizing particular cultural memories, and more concerned with the ongoing negotiations between producing and consuming various narratives of the history of snowboarding."[34]

As illustrated by Ho, Osmond and Phillips, and Thorpe, the connections and dialogue developed between blogging community members, their memories, their experiences, and sources are not static. Instead, they are memory-making in motion; building, exploring, and creating public and cultural histories that may be accessed and developed by a potentially large audience to whom these histories have significant meaning. Understanding how these semi-interactive spaces operate to both represent and produce historical meanings is important, as the dialogue that blog posts and comments can stimulate presents another possibility: that historians might be able to contribute to and participate in these discussions directly.

Leow argues that the exchanges between posts and comments "can broaden horizons of intellectual enquiry and inspire fresh approaches."[35] However, this may require the researcher to participate more actively in the dialogue within and between blogs. For example, after May Friedman explored mommyblogs to consider blog posts as sources for future historians of motherhood, she reflected on the limitations of researching from the semi-interactive margins: "Yet in all my celebration of this community, I have remained outside of it, a 'lurker' on the margins of the interconnectivity of the mamasphere. In this respect then, I have arguably missed out on one of the blogosphere's defining characteristics—its focus on connection and dialogue."[36] More than simply revealing new sources or adding new information, the interactions that occur on blogs highlight that our subjective understandings can be limited and can have serious impacts for our research and work. Had Friedman taken the step of producing a blog herself and commenting on her own and other blogs in this community of interest, she might have been able to access further "connection and dialogue" to enrich her own research and understanding, as well as to contribute to the collective, public history-making process.

The Ethics and Effects of Blogging

Although there are some historians who have been making use of blogs, Cohen and Rosenzweig argue that overall these blogs are more about the opinions and thoughts of the historians themselves, as opposed to history or historical scholarship.[37] The few historians who have reflected on participating in blogging and/or commenting as a form of doing history have largely come from feminist history, where their theoretical positions explicitly commit them to political and ethical approaches to their work in a broader social and cultural sense.[38] Considering the centrality of ethics, activism, and reflexivity to feminist historians, their use of and reflexive participation in digital spaces is not surprising.[39]

Jennifer Ho started her blog, *Mixed Race America*, as a way of thinking through her work-in-progress about race and popular culture in collaboration with others. As she wrote in her first post, "I'm going to use this space to jot down my miscellaneous musings about race. And I invite you to join the conversation."[40] While Jennifer Ho's initial intention was to think out loud, over time she found that her blog became more than a place to talk with interested others. This conversation became an important way of establishing an ethical approach to doing history, or what Ho terms "being held accountable" for her research process, ethics, and politics: "My initial blog entries were a form of pre-writing for my book chapters. Yet the sense of accountability that the blog inspired quickly grew beyond one of writing accountability to one of community accountability."[41]

This approach to ethics and accountability can play out in two ways, the first of which is accuracy. In her analysis of the blog *Good Morning Yesterday*, Stephanie Ho found instances in which readers "separately pointed out errors . . . These errors were subsequently corrected. In this way, the history of Beauty World [a popular shopping area] is constructed by the initial entries and the exchanges that took place."[42] The errors included amendments to maps and collective memories by commenters, which the blogger, Lam Chun See, was able to change in the initial post to develop a shared understanding that became, through the blog, public history. Accessing such dialogue has possibilities for historians to check the accuracy of their histories with an interested and knowledgeable readership who may have been there, or who may have new information or sources to provide on the particular location, period, event, or individual.

Second, and perhaps more importantly, these interactions can help historians engage with the meaning of their work, and the ethics, politics, and impacts of their research. As illustrated by Stephanie Ho, Osmond and Phillips, and Thorpe, blog posts and comments work with each other to coproduce understandings and meanings of histories and texts and allow multiple voices to participate in otherwise difficult-to-access discussions. Through these dialogic processes, Jennifer Ho found that, over time, her blog held her "accountable to a larger public beyond the ivory towers of academia," allowing her to explore the effects and meaning of her research among an interested readership."[43] Ho's identity as a blogger was established through digital relationships, and she came to expect comments on her posts from a range of people—colleagues, friends, and others—who were invested in issues of race and sport. Blogging is different from the process of peer review and publication Ho experienced by publishing in journals, where engagement with the audience is mediated through often-anonymous peer review and delayed publication times. On blogs, the immediate and interactive nature of community engagement and feedback reminded Ho that the histories we write involve people, whose experiences and understandings might be different from the ways we represent events of the past, and for whom the decisions we make have effects.[44] This was also evident in my own experiences writing a blog as a method in my cultural research about women and surfing culture. Participating in an online community, in which I was a contributing and active member, was productive in checking the interpretations I was making of the experiences of women who surf and for getting feedback from a broad audience.[45] However, what was key in this was the role I played in initiating discussions and in sharing my own experiences, understandings, and ideas with my audience.

Blogger Historians: Interacting In Cultural Histories

The particular qualities of blogs—accessible, instantaneous, community-based, archival, multimedia, moderated, dialogic—make them a potentially productive resource in terms of the ethics and politics of doing sport history and as an addition to established research methods.[46] Posting does not confine any author to one location, and author(/s) can publish as frequently as they wish—as long as you have access to a computer and an Internet connection, you can continue to blog. Indeed, it is now even possible to post from a tablet or mobile phone. In this way bloggers can maintain control over their digital time and presence. Posts are published instantaneously, are open for comments and responses from that point on, and stay available as long as the moderator wishes, creating an ongoing exchange between the post and comments. Most importantly however, they allow a space to check the ways we are interpreting the past in our research and the ways these are being developed as historical knowledge.

The accessibility of blogs is only growing as bloggers connect with social networking sites in savvy ways. Claire Bond Potter explains that today blog posts are increasingly being "pushed to an even larger audience of readers through the smart phones that have become cheap and popular since 2007, and via Twitter, a micro-blogging platform," while Holly Thorpe gives the example of the high use of YouTube, with one video history attracting over 160,000 views.[47] The accessible and semi-interactive nature of such sites and methods of presenting history is increasingly productive and effective. This was clear in the way Stephanie Ho found that the personal blog *Good Morning Yesterday* was successful in connecting with readers and stimulating discussion, while the state-sponsored blog, *Yesterday.sg*, struggled. In this case, the political climate of Singapore was a strong factor in influencing why people did not comment on *Yesterday.sg*, but Ho also suggests that audiences used the blogs for two different purposes. The heritage site, *Yesterday.sg*, was used more as a source of public information, whereas the conversational and personalized nature of *Good Morning Yesterday* allowed for more accessible interactions for reminiscing about the past, serving as a place to share memories and for painting a collective picture of yesterday.

Producing a blog that is connected to a related community of interest, as opposed to being directed at a scholarly community, means that understandings and representations are folded back through a relevant sociocultural context—those for whom that past has meaning.[48] As Stephanie Ho, Osmond and Phillips, and Thorpe found, blog responses and comments tend to be from interested or invested parties, so comments engage with the ways the sources are understood, remembered, or responded to, rather than whether they are primary or secondary sources.[49] Although this has implications—that people who comment are engaged and literate, have a stake in the issues, and have access to the Internet—it also offers a broader audience than relying solely on sources or oral history participants to check and recheck the ways work is being developed. In terms of ethics, blogging may also help ensure that research and interpretations are culturally relevant and meaningful, reveal sources that may have been overlooked, or provide new sources, as well as provide multiple readings of sources that might present new perspectives and understandings. Cohen and Rosenzweig go so far as to suggest "It may be that history blogs will be the basis of a new form of historical writing that challenges existing forms like the journal article. At the very least, the format represents a way to break down long-standing barriers separating academics and the public, text and image, research notes and finished narratives, and past and present."[50]

While this level of change may be yet some way in the future, it remains an understandably risky proposition for historians used to engaging in critical processes of peer review, where published work is expected to be fully developed and where critical engagement is (usually) done within respectful and systematic conventions. As Leow explains, "In blogs, academic thinking seems to be caught in the act of undressing: half-formed ideas whip round and gasp, clutching at awkward sentences to cover their nakedness . . . A blog is an always unfinished, always provisional place . . . unlike journal articles, in the case of blog posts, conversations with that audience is almost inevitable, and one's interlocutors are by no means always academics."[51] When a blogger posts, his or her ideas are open to comment and interpretation in ways that he or she cannot control. Yet it is a willingness to share ideas and experiences that allows oversights and subjective understandings to be revealed both to others and to ourselves.

Furthermore, in sharing work-in-progress with invested communities of interest beyond their colleagues, researchers create opportunities for accessing more and varied interpretations and understandings, while also engaging in the ethical and political responsibilities and issues of doing history. For sport sociologist and blogger Sean Smith, while his posts originate from his research, his willingness to share them in an unpredictable space allows them to develop in unpredictable ways.[52] For Smith and others, the diversity and unpredictability of online readership suggests that their work might be misinterpreted. For example, as Osmond and Phillips found, the misinterpretations of the audience of *Salute* led to a focus on a particular and individualized narrative of the film, while broader contexts of race and civil rights were sidelined.[53] However, for both Melissa Gregg and myself, these misinterpretations have been important in keeping our thinking open and in highlighting where and how we are being overly specific, myopic, or exclusionary.[54] As Gregg found through her blogging experiences, "despite my training in feminism and cultural studies, and hence my heightened *theoretical* understandings of the ways in which my identity influences my perspective on the world, having a blog has made me increasingly aware of the multi-faceted ways these identities play out in apparently banal, everyday encounters."[55]

It is important to note that interacting by sharing ideas and experiences online is not about self-indulgence, nor should it devolve in such a way. Instead, by maintaining a critical and reflexive awareness of their role throughout the various stages of the research process, researchers are able to locate the limitations they face in dealing with empirical information. In doing so, historians may allow for "an open acknowledgment of the impossibility of objectivity, an evident expression of relativism, and a perceptible affirmation that any knowledge of the past is, and can only be, *partial*—in all its meanings."[56]

In sharing our work with a possibly interested and invested audience, we can explore how we understand and interpret historical texts in the present by establishing a dialogue with those to whom it has meaning and implications.[57] To give a semi-interactive cultural example, tourism researchers Emma J. Stewart and Dianne Draper used a blog to publish findings from their research project in northern Canada to seek feedback and comments from local indigenous communities.[58] They used the blog as a tool to increase the number of people who could access the research, rather than relying on a locally based and stationary poster display. Their findings could sit online, giving community members longer to digest and respond to the information in a voluntary way for a lengthier time period. To establish further accessibility to the information, text on the blog was developed in collaboration with community gatekeepers and translated into appropriate local languages. The site included images, but could also have included audio and video to further negotiate issues of literacy and online competency. The experience of these researchers shows how blogging can be limited (for example, by access to computers and the Internet, literacy, and online interest), but can also offer ways both to provide feedback to the community and to gather their responses and comments in more accessible and collaborative ways.

Of course, some voices will always remain louder than others, while less popular and more critical perspectives may be cast aside or left unspoken. Despite claims that blogs allow for easy-to-use, cheap, accessible, and democratic online discussions and representation, Turner suggests that blogging and commenting require a certain level of digital literacy, which may privilege a particular online elite whose voices become the newly influential ones.[59] I would suggest this digital elite includes those who have an understanding of search engine optimization whereby writers use key words to increase their chances of appearing in web search engines (for example, Google, Yahoo, Bing), as well as a willingness to publish satirical or controversial posts that are more likely to generate attention and comment, and to be reposted by other bloggers and media sites. While Turner's suggestion weakens claims of global accessibility in broad sociocultural and socioeconomic terms (practically, politically, and financially, and in terms of both bloggers and their audience), this digital elite remains valuable in providing alternative voices to those that have been the most dominant in the past.[60]

Another point to note is the culture surrounding which blogs become popular and are cross-promoted by other blogs and aggregate sites. It is often the case that the most common voices in online communities reflect the power relations and status quo in the offline community. Thus, while bloggers are often ordinary people rather than established or celebrity writers, their identities frequently reflect the subcultural or community majority. For example, women's voices dominate recipe-sharing and parenting blogs, whereas men's dominate news and surfing culture blogs. Yet although many successful individual bloggers reflect majority opinions, this does not mean that less powerful voices are not making contributions to their blogging community. While many bloggers aspire to high readerships and possible professionalization of their blog, Jennifer Lofgren points out that not all bloggers aim for such influence. Lofgren, commenting in the specific context of food blogs, makes a more broadly applicable point when she argues that while it is commonly assumed that bloggers aspire to professional success, "it is important to note that, many food bloggers are content to remain hobbyists. These food bloggers form the majority of the community, and blog about food because they are interested in food, and enjoy sharing recipes and discussing their interest with like-minded people. In this way, they are contributing to, and engaging with, folk culture within the blogging community. However, this does not mean that they do not have a broader impact on mainstream food-related media."[61] In particular, such bloggers may provide a point of connection through which others find the impetus to contribute to a conversation.

This semi-interactive effect appears to have been the hope of the state-sponsored meta-site *Yesterday.sg*, which encouraged articles from "various contributors who are reviewed by a team of editors," as an effort toward the "democratisation of history making in Singapore as it encourages ordinary people to participate in writing history through sharing personal stories on the blog."[62] However, Stephanie Ho argues that the associations of the site with government, the requirement of registering for use, and the inability to make anonymous contributions, limited the popularity and interactivity of the blog and meant "it has become a showcase of existing voices online but has yet to encourage new voices to emerge.[63] Alternatively, the personal blog *Good Morning Yesterday* allowed anonymous comments and "is more than a site for personal recollection: it functions as a place for discussion and joint reminiscing about the past."[64] The author of *Good Morning Yesterday* contributed his own stories and memories, setting the tone and agenda of the site, while encouraging others to participate in the comments sections and valued their contributions when they did. In her analysis of this process, Ho locates blogging as a "more democratic arena for ordinary people to participate in history making," to "jointly construct public histories more reflective of their lived experiences."[65]

Blogging in Action: Encouraging New Perspectives

The democratic capacity of blogging to invite and reflect personalized experiences was illustrated in my own blogging experiences about women and surfing culture when Karen, a female commenter, reflected under one post on the collective blog *Kurungabaa: A Journal of Literature History and Ideas from the Sea* that it was "the only (website about surfing) where I have always felt that my contribution would be more than tokenism" and that "despite constant encouragement from [my partner], the first post on K'baa that I felt the urge to engage with was Bec writing on women in the surf. It was an entry point for me and, once I had got my toes wet, I kept coming back [to read and comment on the blog]."[66] As a woman, Karen continues to be a minority in Australian surfing culture, both at the beach and in historical representations of surfing.[67] Female voices are notoriously rare and difficult to capture in surfing histories, magazines, films, photographs, and other media.[68] Their ongoing absence is highly problematic, yet my participation in this online community writing blog posts—by a woman writing about women—and participating in comments and dialogue, engaged Karen in conversation on related blogs in an ongoing way. In this case, Karen didn't contribute new information or sources. Rather, her participation itself became evidence that women surf and that they often feel excluded. Karen's comments, then, have become evidence today. The efforts by other contributors to develop an inclusive space were key in creating and maintaining space for my own contributions, as well as Karen's. However, without my contributions as a female surfer writing about female surfers, Karen may never have participated in the discussions that happened over time on *Kurungabaa*. In this way my own contribution to, and participation in, these online discussions was important in encouraging the participation of more female voices in a historically male-dominated cultural space.

Admittedly, the outcomes of participating in the semi-interactive exercise of blogging and commenting are not always positive. Like other forms of public scholarship, in exposing ideas in a public and semi-interactive media, researchers are open to nasty, trite, and personal attacks. This has been one of the myriad experiences that I have encountered in publishing online, and one that I initially struggled to make sense of and to understand.[69] These experiences certainly impacted (somewhat naively on my behalf) where and how I was willing to publish. For a time I was a contributor to two blogs. My own blog, *Making Friends with the Neighbours*, is female-focused and completely within my editorial control in terms of what is published and whether or not comments are moderated. The aim of the site was to build a body of resources about women's surfing and to publish writing that engages with some of the experiences women have in surfing, as well as the issues they face. This site mostly generated support from an interested audience, so while it added perspectives and dialogue, it did not generate combative critical discussion. My involvement with *Kurungabaa* proved to be a different experience. *Kurungabaa* is a collective site that is focused more broadly on the culture of surfing and supports a print journal that publishes more generally about "literature, history and ideas from the sea." The tone of *Kurungabaa* was more controversial, more critical, and often more scholarly, and actively promoted discussion. It has a much bigger audience than my own blog, and drew in a wide range of engaged and critical readers who developed lively debates in the comment sections—an achievement for which the site should be commended.

The difference in audience, and thus interactivity, between *Making Friends with the Neighbours* and *Kurungabaa* is clear on the occasions in which I published the same piece of writing on each site. For example, while my critical review of the lack of women in a particular surf publication inspired support but little critical discussion on my blog, a heated debate ensued when I published the same review on *Kurungabaa*.[70] This debate was not spontaneous. The established interactive readership had an ongoing debate about the nature of commenting on websites, a debate that by that time had developed across a range of blog spaces. As is clear from the comments by a number of the *Kurungabaa* contributors and commenters, facilitating and moderating a conversation like this is time- and energy-consuming, and requires a clear position in terms of what is and what is not acceptable in the discussions. Eventually, Clifton Evers, one of the founding editors of *Kurungabaa* and a cultural studies researcher, developed a commenting policy that established guidelines for commenting and other interactive behaviors, which created a more critical space for discussion by defining the parameters within which such discussions should take place on *Kurungabaa*.[71] In blogging, each blog publisher is responsible for the rules and parameters in relation to commenting and whether they take an explicit stand on the issue. While a number of the commenters at *Kurungabaa* neither liked nor agreed with what they saw as a constraint on their freedom of speech and the culture of blog commenting, Evers explicitly drew on his ethical responsibilities as a scholar to encourage ethical and inclusive behavior online.

In my case, participating in often-challenging discussions in both a semi-interactive space (that is, one in which I and others had access to editorial control) and in a community of interest (in which I had developed an identity and presence) allowed me to engage as a participant to address the social and cultural issues that I was raising in the bigger context of surfing culture and of digital media.[72] While this sometimes included the kinds of language and behavior that I usually avoid, through the blogging community to which I belonged I was lucky to have the support and encouragement of colleagues and friends, both on- and offline. By exposing myself and my ideas online,

I explicitly engaged in the ethical responsibilities and implications of my scholarship in ways that highlighted the complexities to me.[73]

Conclusion

With cultural studies and feminist approaches to research influencing and informing my scholarship, taking responsibility for the ethical responsibilities and politics of my contribution to our ways of knowing is important to me personally and in terms of my research practice. Like Jennifer Ho, through blogging "I began to see that my academic writing and my blog writing enrich and enhance one another; they both speak to the feminist ideals I believe in speaking truth to power and equality for all people . . . I must hold myself accountable to practice in my scholarship what I preach in my blog."[74] Conversely, I must hold myself accountable to practice in my blog what I preach in my scholarship. By engaging with interactive forms of doing history on blogs, the boundaries between the historian's role as producer and consumer of sources and histories become blurred. In doing so, historians are able to engage in discussions about the meaning of their work, pushing through traditional approaches and continuing to grow and expand the potential and possibilities of what doing history can look like. This is most certainly not to suggest that blogging could stand alone as a method or approach to ethics in historical scholarship, or that existing historical methods are not important in producing/consuming history in digital spaces. Rather, I am suggesting that with their training, experience, and capacity for critical thinking about the past, historians are well placed to use semi-interactive online spaces effectively to become "potentially at once producers and curators of these virtual sources."[75] In this way, amateur and professional historians could learn from each other how to produce and consume rigorous, accessible forms of history online.[76]

In arguing this point, I recall Synthia Sydnor's innovative article, "A History of Synchronized Swimming," which continues to influence and inspire new generations of sport historians.[77] Sydnor's history illustrates that new approaches to doing and presenting history can be productive and can extend rather than limit traditional approaches to historical research as we move into the future. Similar to Grossberg, in questioning disciplinary traditions, Sydnor's work challenged us "to think beyond the institutional constraints and habits to which we have become accustomed."[78] In her own words:

> The postmodern concerns of this essay have been directed toward illuminating the ongoing production of disciplinary boundaries, to destroying definitional

attempts to classify "sport," and to provoking conversations about sport, history and the world as they are, and as they are becoming.

In writing my history of synchronized swimming, I was loyal to the canon of historical methodology and theory, I was true to my grounding in classical source use, I was faithful to observing continuity and change, I was conscious of the complex problems concerning truth, relativism, and representation that are entangled in the practices of being an historian.[79]

Two decades later, through the increasing presence of digital media, sport historians are challenged to engage with public histories and how these impact and are impacted by the "ethical responsibilities and thus the politics" of our own roles as professional historians.[80] Rather than being wholly intimidated or concerned, sport historians should consider how they can use, and participate with, these resources and possibilities, taking the chance to define for themselves how they can be useful and productive.

The past is gone, and as Murray Phillips points out, the only way for historians to access that past in the present is as a "text."[81] Yet the present has specific contexts, agendas, and implications, which will have ongoing impacts for the understandings and representations we produce.[82] In the context of postmodern, reflexive, and cultural historical research, these texts take multiple forms beyond the written primary sources to include films, photographs, artifacts, stamps, novels, and, increasingly, digital media.[83] In order to make sense of how these sources are read as texts, and how they impact collective ways of knowing the past, historians can take part in the discussion and contribute a critically engaged role in their ongoing production and development. By including interactive, dialogic approaches to researching and producing sport histories today, sport historians are able to engage with the ethics, effects, and complexities of history as research practices and products into the future.

Notes

1. Booth, *The Field*; Grosz, "Histories of a Feminist Future"; Jenkins, Morgan, and Munslow, *Manifestos for History*; Munslow, *Deconstructing History*; Phillips, *Deconstructing Sport History*; Schultz, "Leaning into the Turn"; Scott, *Gender and the Politics of History*.

2. Kansteiner, "Alternate Worlds and Invented Communities," 133.

3. Phillips, "Deconstructing Sport History," 327. This is apparent both among established scholars such as Douglas Booth, Murray Phillips, Synthia Sydnor, and Patricia Vertinsky, as well as among emerging sport historians such as Carly Adams, Matthew Klugman, Fiona McLachlan, Gary Osmond, Megan Popovic, and Jaime Schultz.

4. Kansteiner, "Alternate Worlds," 133.

5. Schultz, "Leaning into the Turn," 51.
6. Ibid.
7. Thorpe, "The Politics of Remembering," 115; see also, Kansteiner, "Finding Meaning in Memory."
8. Phillips, "Deconstructing Sport History"; Booth, "History, Race, Sport"; Schultz, "Leaning into the Turn."
9. Turner, *What's Become of Cultural Studies*, 6–7.
10. Grossberg, *Cultural Studies in the Future Tense*, 66–67.
11. Booth, "History, Race, Sport," 35.
12. Bruns, *Blogs*.
13. Berners-Lee, *Weaving the Web*.
14. Leow, "Reflections," 235.
15. Cohen and Rosenzweig, *Digital History*.
16. Ibid., 3.
17. Poster, "Manifesto for a History of the Media," 45.
18. Ibid.
19. Cohen and Rosenzweig, *Digital History*, 7.
20. Ibid.
21. Thorpe, "The Politics of Remembering," 116.
22. The discussion in this section about interactivity draws from Osmond, "The Elephant in the Room."
23. Cronin, "Social Networking."
24. Hookway, "Entering the Blogosphere," 92; see also Rettberg, *Blogging*.
25. Bruns, *Blogs;* Cohen and Rosenzweig, *Digital History*; S. Ho, "Blogging as Popular History Making"; Olive, "Making Friends with the Neighbours."
26. Hookway, "Entering the Blogosphere"; James and Busher, *Online Interviewing*; Rettberg, *Blogging*; Stewart and Draper, "Reporting Back Research Findings; Tremayne, *Blogging, Citizenship, and the Future of Media*; Wakeford and Cohen, "Fieldnotes in Public."
27. Bruns, *Blogs;* Papacharissi, "Audiences as Media Producers."
28. Bloggers are able to remove the option for interactivity on their site by disabling the option for people to leave comments under their posts. Alternatively, they can leave the option to comment available, but require the commenter to leave a contact e-mail address, thus removing anonymity.
29. Baym, *Personal Connections in the Digital Age*; Beaulieu, "Sociable Hyperlinks"; Castells, "Informationalism, Networks, and the Network Society."
30. Friedman, "On Mommyblogging"; S. Ho, "Blogging as Popular History Making"; Osmond and Phillips, "Reading *Salute*"; Thorpe, "The Politics of Remembering."
31. Ho, "Blogging as Public History Making."
32. Osmond and Phillips, "Reading *Salute*."
33. Ibid.; Lövheim, "Young Women's Blogs as Ethical Spaces."
34. Thorpe, "The Politics of Remembering," 121.

35. Leow, "Reflections," 236.
36. Friedman, "On Mommyblogging," 197–98.
37. Cohen and Rosenzweig, *Digital History*, 41–42.
38. See Potter, "Roundtable: Women Gone Wild"; Lövheim, "Young Women's Blogs as Ethical Spaces"; S. Ho, "Blogging as Public History Making."
39. Thorpe and Olive, "The Power, Politics and Potential of Feminist Sports History."
40. J. Ho, "Being Held Accountable."
41. Ibid., 190.
42. S. Ho, "Blogging as Popular History Making," 72.
43. J. Ho, "Being Held Accountable," 193.
44. Booth, "History, Race, Sport"; Kansteiner, "Alternate Worlds and Invented Communities"; Munslow, *The Future of History*.
45. Olive, "Making Friends with the Neighbours."
46. Hookway, "Entering the Blogosphere"; Olive, "Making Friends with the Neighbours."
47. Potter, "Virtually a Historian," 84; Thorpe, "The Politics of Remembering," 121.
48. Olive, "Making Friends with the Neighbours."
49. S. Ho, "Blogging as Popular History Making"; Osmond and Phillips, "Reading *Salute*"; Thorpe, "The Politics of Remembering."
50. Cohen and Rosenzweig, *Digital History*, 42.
51. Leow, "Reflections," 235–36.
52. Smith, "Monologic, Dialogic, Severalogic . . . Technologic."
53. Osmond and Phillips, "Reading *Salute*."
54. Gregg, "Feeling Ordinary"; Olive, "Making Friends with the Neighbours."
55. Gregg, "Feeling Ordinary," 156 (emphasis in the original).
56. Schultz, "Leaning into the Turn," 52 (emphasis in the original).
57. Olive and Thorpe, "Negotiating the 'F-Word' in the Field."
58. Stewart and Draper, "Reporting Back Research Findings."
59. Turner, *Ordinary People and the Media*.
60. Papacharissi, "Audiences as Media Producers."
61. Lofgren, "Food Blogging."
62. S. Ho, "Blogging as Popular History Making," 73.
63. Ibid.
64. Ibid., 69.
65. Ibid., 77.
66. Karen, April 1, 2011 (7:46am), comment on Simon O, "Japan Disco Inferno Video With 1991 ASP Surfers . . .," *Kurungabaa: A Journal of Literature, History and Ideas from the Sea*, on March 17, 2011. Accessed May 14, 2012. http://kurungabaa.net/2011/03/17/japan-disco-inferno-video-with-1991-asp-pro-surfers/.
67. Booth, "From Bikinis to Boardshorts"; Ford and Brown, *Surfing and Social Theory*; Henderson, "A Shifting Line Up."

68. Olive and Thorpe, "Post-Structural Feminism and Sport History."
69. Olive and Thorpe, "Negotiating the F-Word"; Olive, "Making Friends with the Neighbours."
70. Rebecca Olive, "The Ninth Wave—No Girls Allowed?" first published March 9, 2011, http://makingfriendswiththeneighbours.blogspot.com.au/2011/03/ninth-wave-no-girls-allowed.html, then March 21, 2011, http://kurungabaa.net/2011/03/21/the-ninth-wave-no-girls-allowed.
71. Kurungabaa Comments Policy. Accessed March 23, 2013. http://kurungabaa.net/comments-policy/.
72. See, for example, the comments beneath a post I wrote about the lack of representation of women in surf publications. "The Ninth Wave—No Girls Allowed?" http://kurungabaa.net/2011/03/21/the-ninth-wave-no-girls-allowed.
73. Olive and Thorpe, "Negotiating the F-Word"; Thorpe and Olive, "The Power, Politics and Potential of Feminist Sports History."
74. J. Ho, "Being Held Accountable," 190–192.
75. Leow, "Reflections," 239.
76. Cohen and Rosenzweig, *Digital History*, 43.
77. Sydnor, "A History of Synchronized Swimming."
78. Grossberg, *Cultural Studies in the Future Tense*, 66–67.
79. Sydnor, "A History of Synchronized Swimming," 260.
80. Booth, "History, Race, Sport," 35.
81. Phillips, "Deconstructing Sport History," 334.
82. Munslow, *The Future of History*; Grosz, "Histories of a Feminist Future."
83. McLachlan, "Swimming History after Deconstruction"; Osmond and Phillips, "Enveloping the Past"; Osmond and Phillips, "Reading *Salute*"; Popovic, "Figures from Her rInk."

References

Baym, Nancy K. 2010. *Personal Connections in the Digital Age: Digital Media and Society Series.* Cambridge: Polity.
Beaulieu, Anne. 2005. "Sociable Hyperlinks: An Ethnographic Approach to Connectivity." *Virtual Methods: Issues in Social Research on the Internet*, edited by Christine Hine, 183–97. Oxford: Berg.
Berners-Lee, Tim. 1999. *Weaving the Web.* London: Orion Business Books.
Booth, Douglas. 2001. "From Bikinis to Boardshorts: *Wahines* and the Paradoxes of Surfing Culture." *Journal of Sport History* 28, no. 1: 3–22.
———. 2005. *The Field: Truth and Fiction in Sport History.* London, Routledge.
———. 2011. "History, Race, Sport: From Objective Knowledge to Socially Responsible Narratives." *Sport, "Race" and Ethnicity: Narratives of Diversity and Difference*, edited by Daryl Adair, 13–39. Morgantown, WV: Fitness Information Technology.
Bruns, Axel. 2008. *Blogs, Wikipedia, Second Life, and Beyond: From Production to Produsage.* New York: Peter Lang.

Castells, Manuel, ed. 2004. "Informationalism, Networks, and the Network Society: A Theoretical Blueprint." *The Network Society: A Cross-cultural Perspective*, edited by Manuel Castells, 3–45. Cheltenham: Edward Elgar.

Cohen, Daniel J., and Roy Rosenzweig. 2006. *Digital History: A Guide to Collecting, Preserving, and Presenting the Past on the Web*. Philadelphia: University of Philadelphia Press.

Cronin, Mike. 2012. "Social Networking in Researching Sport History." Paper presented at the 40th annual conference of the North American Society for Sport History, Berkeley, California, June 1–4.

Ford, Nick, and David Brown. 2006. *Surfing and Social Theory: Experience, Embodiment, and Narrative of the Dream Glide*. London: Routledge.

Friedman, May. 2010. "On Mommyblogging: Notes to a Future Feminist Historian." *Journal of Women's History* 22, no. 4: 197–208.

Gregg, Melissa. 2006. "Feeling Ordinary: Blogging as Conversational Scholarship." *Continuum: Journal of Media and Cultural Studies* 20, no. 2: 147–60.

Grossberg, Lawrence. 2010. *Cultural Studies in the Future Tense*. Durham, NC: Duke University Press.

Grosz, Elizabeth. 2000. "Histories of a Feminist Future." *Signs: Journal of Women in Culture and Society* 25, no. 4: 1017–21.

Henderson, Margaret. 2001. "A Shifting Line Up: Men, Women and *Tracks* Surfing Magazine." *Continuum: Journal of Media and Cultural Studies* 15, no. 3: 319–32.

Ho, Jennifer. 2010. "Being Held Accountable: On the Necessity of Intersectionality." *Journal of Women's History* 22, no. 4: 190–96.

Ho, Stephanie. 2007. "Blogging as Popular History Making, Blogs as Public History: A Singapore Case Study." *Public History Review* 14: 64–79.

Hookway, Nicholas. 2008. "Entering the Blogosphere: Some Strategies for Using Blogs in Social Research." *Qualitative Research* 8, no. 1: 91–113.

James, Nalita, and James Busher. 2009. *Online Interviewing*. London: Sage.

Jenkins, Keith, Sue Morgan, and Alun Munslow, eds. 2007. *Manifestos for History*. New York: Routledge.

Kansteiner, Wulf. 2002. "Finding Meaning in Memory: A Methodological Critique of Collective Memory Studies." *History and Theory* 41: 179–97.

———. 2007. "Alternate Worlds and Invented Communities: History and Historical Consciousness in the Age of Interactive Media." *Manifestos for History*, edited by Keith Jenkins, Sue Morgan, and Alun Munslow, 131–48. New York: Routledge.

Kurungabaa: A Journal of Literature, History and Ideas from the Sea. http://kurungabaa.net.

Leow, Rachel. 2010. "Reflections on Feminism, Blogging, and the Historical Profession." *Journal of Women's History* 22, no. 4: 235.

Lofgren, Jennifer. 2013. "Food Blogging and Food-related Media Convergence." *M/C Journal* 16, no. 3. http://journal.media-culture.org.au/index.php/mcjournal/article/viewArticle/638.

Lövheim, Mia. 2011. "Young Women's Blogs as Ethical Spaces." *Information, Communication and Society* 14, no. 3: 344–55.
McLachlan, Fiona. 2012. "Swimming History after Deconstruction." *Journal of Sport History* 39, no. 3 (Fall): 431–44.
Munslow, Alun. 1997. *Deconstructing History.* London: Routledge.
———. 2010. *The Future of History.* Hampshire: Palgrave Macmillan.
Olive, Rebecca. 2012. "Making Friends with the Neighbours: Blogging as a Research Method." *International Journal of Cultural Studies* 16, no. 1: 71–84, published online April 26. doi: 10.1177/1367877912441438.
Olive, Rebecca, and Holly Thorpe. 2011. "Negotiating the 'F-Word' in the Field: Doing Feminist Ethnography in Action Sport Cultures." *Sociology of Sport Journal* 28, no. 4: 421–40.
———. 2011. "Post-Structural Feminism and Sport History: Revisiting Historical Narratives of Surfing in Australia." Paper presented at *Sporting Traditions* XVIII, bi-annual conference of the Australian Society for Sports History, Kingscliff, Australia, July 7–9.
Osmond, Gary. 2011. "The Elephant in the Room: Sport Historians and Uses of the Internet." Paper presented at the 39th annual conference of the North American Society for Sport History, University of Texas, Austin, Texas, May 27–30.
Osmond, Gary, and Murray G. Phillips. 2011. "Enveloping the Past: Sport Stamps, Visuality and Museums." *The International Journal of the History of Sport* 28, nos: 8–9: 1138–55.
———. 2011. "Reading *Salute*: Filmic Representations of Sports History." *The International Journal of the History of Sport* 28, no. 10: 1463–77.
Papacharissi, Zizi. 2007. "Audiences as Media Producers: Content Analysis of 260 Blogs." *Blogging, Citizenship, and the Future of Media*, edited by Mark Tremayne, 21–38. London: Routledge.
Phillips, Murray G. 2001. "Deconstructing Sport History: The Postmodern Challenge." *Journal of Sport History* 28, no. 3: 327–43.
———. 2005. *Deconstructing Sport History: A Postmodern Analysis.* Albany: State University of New York Press.
Popovic, Megan L. 2012. "Figures from Her rInk." *Journal of Sport History* 39, no. 3 (Fall): 445–61.
Poster, Mark. 2007. "Manifesto for a History of the Media." *Manifestos for History*, edited by Keith Jenkins, Sue Morgan, and Alun Munslow, 39–49. New York: Routledge.
Potter, Claire Bond, ed. 2010. "Roundtable: Women Gone Wild: Reflections on the Feminist Blogosphere." *Journal of Women's History* 22, no. 4: 185–243.
———. 2012. "Virtually a Historian: Blogs and the Recent History of Dispossessed Academic Labor." *Historical Reflections* 38, no. 2: 83–97.
Rettberg, Jill W. 2008. *Blogging.* Cambridge, UK: Polity Press.
Schultz, Jaime. 2010. "Leaning into the Turn: Towards a New Cultural Sport History." *Sporting Traditions* 27, no. 2: 45–59.

Scott, Joan W. 1988. *Gender and the Politics of History.* New York: Columbia University Press.
Smith, Sean. 2009. "Monologic, Dialogic, Severalogic . . . Technologic." *sportsBabel*, June 3. Accessed March 23, 2012. http://www.sportsbabel.net/2009/06/monologic-dialogic-severalogic-technologic.htm.
Stewart, Emma J., and Dianne Draper. 2009. "Reporting Back Research Findings: A Case Study of Community-based Tourism Research in Northern Canada." *Journal of Ecotourism* 8, no. 2: 128–43.
Sydnor, Synthia. 1998. "A History of Synchronized Swimming." *Journal of Sport History* 25, no. 2: 252–67.
Thorpe, Holly. 2010. "The Politics of Remembering: An Interdisciplinary Approach to Physical Cultural Memory." *Sporting Traditions* 27, no. 2: 113–25.
Thorpe, Holly, and Rebecca Olive. 2012. "The Power, Politics and Potential of Feminist Sports History: A Multi-Generational Dialogue." *Journal of Sport History* 39, no. 3 (Fall): 379–94.
Tremayne, Mark, ed. 2007. *Blogging, Citizenship, and the Future of Media.* London: Routledge.
Turner, Graeme. 2010. *Ordinary People and the Media: The Demotic Turn.* Los Angeles: Sage.
———. 2012. *What's Become of Cultural Studies.* London: Sage.
Wakeford, Nina, and Kris Cohen. 2008. "Fieldnotes in Public: Using Blogs for Research." *The SAGE Handbook of Online Research Methods,* edited by Nigel Fielding, Raymond M. Lee, and Grant Blank, 307–26. Los Angeles: Sage.

8

Death, Mourning, and Cultural Memory on the Internet

The Virtual Memorialization of Fallen Sports Heroes

HOLLY THORPE

In his widely cited book, *Theatres of Memory*, Raphael Samuel pointed to the function of memory keeping and presentation as being "increasingly assigned to the electronic media."[1] A few years later, John Urry proposed that the "electronification" of memory might provide another twist in understanding how societies and cultures remember the past within an extraordinarily changing present.[2] More recently, a growing number of historians and cultural studies and media scholars recognize that the processes of remembering (and forgetting) are "transforming under the impact of the digital revolution."[3] Digital culture is, according to José van Dijck, "revamping our very concepts of memory and experience, of individuality and collectivity," and "unsettling the boundaries between private and public culture in the process."[4] In this chapter I build upon and extend the growing body of literature on the digitalization of personal and cultural memory by examining how contemporary action sport cultures are using the Internet to *collectively* remember and memorialize their recently fallen sporting heroes.[5]

The term *action sports*, and other related categorizations including extreme and alternative sports, refers to a wide range of mostly individualized activities such as surfing, skateboarding, and snowboarding. Many action sports gained popularity during the new leisure trends of the 1960s and 1970s; early participants embraced anti-establishment and do-it-yourself philosophies and subcultural styles. Over the past five decades, many action sports have experienced unprecedented growth both in participation and in their increased visibility across public space. With the extensive mediatization of action sports competitions and events (for example, the X Games), the most skillful, successful, and marketable athletes have become celebrities within their respective sports culture and, in some cases, mainstream society. Some well-known examples include Tony Hawk in skateboarding; Shawn White and Torah Bright in snowboarding; and Kelly Slater, Laird Hamilton, and Bethany Hamilton in surfing. The recent deaths of top action sport athletes, however, sent shockwaves of grief through the respective sporting communities. For example, when an avalanche tragically killed four-time World Champion snowboarder Craig Kelly in 2003, one journalist likened the loss to snowboarding to "the passing of a Pope or the untimely death of Princess Diana."[6] Similarly, the deaths of legendary Hawaiian big-wave surfer Eddie Aikau and extreme skier and BASE jumper Shane McConkey evoked deeply affective responses within the global surfing and skiing cultures, respectively.[7] In the past, the action sport industries and media responded to such losses with local memorial events, in-depth editorial features in print magazines, and/or segments in videos. But in the increasingly networked and digital world, journalists, family members, friends, and fans around the world are using the Internet to communicate with others, to share their condolences, and to memorialize deceased athletes in highly creative, interactive, and dynamic ways.

In this chapter I draw upon research in cultural memory, death, mourning, memorialization, ritual, and media studies[8] to examine the practices and politics of virtual mourning and cultural memory production following the deaths of two action sports stars, American surfer Andy Irons and Canadian freestyle skier Sarah Burke. As illustrated via these two case studies, virtual memorialization practices are important because they contribute to the ways "current and future generations remember (or forget) historical figures"[9] in contemporary sports and physical cultures. Of course, as Wulf Kansteiner reminds us, "all media of memory, especially electronic media, neither simply reflect nor determine collective memory but are inextricably involved in its *construction and evolution*."[10] Here I examine the Internet as one of an array of "media of memory" that contributes in new and interesting ways to the "dialectics of remembering and forgetting" in contemporary sporting cultures.[11]

Cultural Memorialization in the Digital Era

Death is a universal experience marked differently by individual cultures around the world. Since the late 1950s, anthropologists, historians, and sociologists have studied the unique mourning rituals in cultures and communities across a wide array of local and foreign contexts.[12] As illustrated in such studies, mourning rituals are often "elaborate, lengthy affairs, where those connected to the deceased commune in celebration, in silences, in viewing, in feast, or in some form of communal gathering."[13] Mourning and memorialization practices are typically processes of memory making in which individuals and/or groups privately or collectively remember the life of the deceased. According to Scott Becker and Roger Knudson, mourning is a responsibility, a "heroic act,"[14] a need to "carry on memories of the life of the person, particularly if that life affected the mourner in a positive or meaningful way."[15] Of course, such memorialization practices are temporary acts; they are cultural performances with a duration defined by both the grieving processes of the mourner(s) and by the broader social group.

Despite the general privatization of death, mourning often involves public practices, social rituals, and cultural performances. As Margaret Gibson explains, this is especially observable in cases of deaths from wars, political assassinations, and natural disasters, which have long been "a means of rallying National unity and collective forms of identification, mourning and memorialisation."[16] Some scholars have explored similar themes in relation to historical sporting events, teams, and personalities.[17] In a new context of global media culture, however, the deaths of famous or newsworthy people have evoked cultural mourning beyond the nation-state.[18] Not all public figures are capable of amassing large-scale, transnational, collective emotive responses, but some certainly are. Consider, for example, the millions around the world who mourned the deaths of John F. Kennedy, John Lennon, Kurt Cobain, Princess Diana, and, more recently, Michael Jackson, Steve Irwin, and Amy Winehouse, almost as if they were a personal loss.[19] According to Gibson, celebrity deaths resonate in the lives of some individuals because they "belie simple distinctions between real and fictional, myth and reality, public and private."[20]

Celebrity deaths are increasingly events through which collective and public forms of mourning are becoming ritualized.[21] Spontaneous shrines are often created at places of significance (either during their life or death) to the public figure. For example, thousands visited Kensington Palace to leave flowers and personal notes following Princess Diana's death;[22] mourners decorated the entrance to the Australia Zoo with floral tributes, cards, and khaki shirts hanging on a makeshift clothesline as a tribute to Australian wildlife personality Steve Irwin;[23] and following the death of race car driver Dale Earnhardt, Sr., hundreds of fans flocked to the auto dealership bearing his name in western North Carolina (many others turned their personal cars, or rooms in their houses, into shrines for their NASCAR hero).[24] Through creating their own memorial objects (for example, art and craft, letters), visiting particular sites, and wearing memorabilia, individual fans identify themselves as belonging to a larger group, a transnational community of mourners. Perhaps not surprisingly, when large groups of people are affected by catastrophic death or tragedy, the media play an integral role in the processes of public mourning and memorialization. While many researchers interested in death and memorialization have emphasized how various forms of media (that is, newspapers, the radio, telephones, television) contribute to rituals and mourning practices, the role of digital technologies in this process is only beginning to garner critical scholarly attention. According to Tim Hutchings, online networks and digital media are increasingly being "integrated into contemporary processes of dying, grieving and memorialization," which is "changing the social context in which dying takes place" and "establishing new electronic spaces for the communication of grief."[25] Indeed, the World Wide Web now hosts a vast archive of virtual cemeteries, grief chat rooms, grief blogs, and condolence messages. Web-based memorials, cyber-shrines, and virtual funerals are gaining popularity,[26] and social media sites such as Facebook have developed an array of options for friends and family members to memorialize lost loved ones and participate in virtual "communities of mourning."[27]

The Diana event triggered renewed academic interest in the role of media in representing and producing public mourning,[28] but it was the passing of Michael Jackson in 2009[29] and fall of the Twin Towers on September 11, 2001[30] that prompted scholars to explore in greater depth the role of digital media for cultural memorialization. According to Hutchings, online media is "actually changing the way death is experienced and shared."[31] In his analysis of the global, public response to Michael Jackson's death, Hutchings identifies Twitter and Facebook as "key to the vortextual storm of feedback loops and mutual references" that contributed to what is now known as the "Michael Jackson effect"—a viral response so wide-reaching and immediate that it significantly slows existing systems.[32] More recently, Scott Radford and Peter Bloch note that Twitter traffic reached near record levels following the death of Steve Jobs.[33] Such digital media work in conjunction with other "media of memory"[34] to contribute to the production and consumption of cultural memories of particular public figures and key events.

Web-based memorials and social media contribute to the formation of cultural memory in new ways. During the late nineteenth and early twentieth centuries, public memorialization for public figures or significant events tended toward "controlled, official, carefully planned forms of expression."[35] As Kirsten Foot and colleagues explain, the architects of such public memorials sought to "frame the significance and meaning of the precipitating event for everyone."[36] Official public memorials continue to be developed to commemorate public figures (for example, Princess Diana) or tragic events (for example, the September 11, 2001, attacks on the United States). While such memorials continue to attract visitors, mourners increasingly visit virtual spaces to connect with the deceased and/or other grievers. Not only do memorial websites offer greater accessibility, they also create space for a wider array of voices and the coproduction of cultural memory.[37] In particular, they describe post-9/11 memorial websites as enabling "government employees, private citizens, and volunteers to contribute to corporate understanding and interpretation of events."[38] For John Bodnar, such "collective expression" made it possible for participants and witnesses to tell the story in terms of "heroism and valor rather than of uncertainty and death."[39]

Such observations have led some to suggest that the Internet offers potentially more democratic and interactive spaces for dynamic, fluid, and creative memory construction and public and private mourning practices.[40] Pamela Roberts concurs, arguing that cyberspace bereavement communities do more than serve as a poor substitute for traditional bereavement activities; "web memorialization is a valuable addition, allowing the bereaved to enhance their relationship with the dead and to increase and deepen their connections with others who have suffered a loss."[41] For grieving individuals, web-based memorials and social media give immediate access to highly interactive, dynamic, affective (and affecting) sites of communities of mourning.

It is important to note, however, that while some participants offer critical perspectives and challenge the selective remembering of others, over time most sites eventually work to produce a dominant narrative of the event via the active policing and regulation among users, and the decisions made by owners of these sites. As a record of the multiple, contested, and changing emotional responses, these sites become valuable archives of the public affective responses to cultural trauma, and the operations of power in the production of particular narratives of grief, mourning, and cultural memory. In the following case studies, I am less interested in the historical facts of Irons's or Burke's sporting achievements, or the details surrounding their deaths, and more concerned with the dynamic cultural politics involved in the collective memorialization of action sport athletes in "an age of high mobility, greater technological access, and virtual social connectivity."[42]

Virtual Memorialization of Action Sport Stars: Andy Irons and Sarah Burke

On November 2, 2010, three-time World Champion surfer Andy Irons was found dead in a hotel room in Dallas, Texas. He was en-route to his pregnant wife in Hawaii after withdrawing from a World Tour surfing competition in Puerto Rico citing ill health. Most initial media reports suggested complications from dengue fever as the primary cause of death. But the details surrounding the illness and subsequent death of 32-year-old Irons were blurry with conflicting reports appearing in the mass and niche media. While the mass media delved into Irons's past, digging up details about his previous battles with bipolarism, alcohol abuse, and drug dependency, the niche surfing media "closed rank, refusing to discuss the circumstances of his death,"[43] preferring instead to focus on his achievements and contribution to the sport of surfing. The family delayed the findings from the autopsy report for many months, citing the need to protect his heavily pregnant wife from further stress. Ultimately, the report revealed that Irons had succumbed to a "combination of a heart attack and drugs in his system."[44] As noted above, it is not my intent to reveal the true cause of Irons's tragic death. Rather, here I am interested in the response from the global surfing community.

Highly photogenic, with a dynamic and charismatic personality and nineteen World Tour victories, Irons had achieved legend status. Following the discovery of his body, the Association of Surfing Professionals issued the following statement: "The world of surfing mourns an incredibly sad loss today with the news that Hawaii's Andy Irons has died. Andy was a beloved husband, and a true champion."[45] Indeed, news of Irons's unexpected death shocked family, friends, and fans around the world. Many of Irons's peers and supporters engaged in highly creative rituals and memorialization practices both in local and virtual spaces in their attempts to pay their respects to the fallen surfing star and reaffirm his significant role in the history of surfing. Further revealing his broader social celebrity, the Governor of Hawaii declared February 13 forever Andy Irons Day.

Twenty-nine-year-old world champion Canadian freestyle skier Sarah Burke died in a Salt Lake City hospital on January 19, 2012, as a result of a vertebral artery tear sustained nine days earlier from a fall while training at Park City Mountain Resort (Utah, USA). Winner of five World Cup championships, and a four-time X Games gold medalist, Burke was the darling of the global freestyle ski culture. Shortly after the accident, Canadian Freestyle

CEO Peter Judge made the following statement: "Sarah is the top female half-pipe athlete in the world. She was instrumental in launching the sport and has continued to be a leader moving towards the sport's Olympic debut in 2014."[46] In June 2012, the late Burke was inducted into the 2012 Canadian Olympic Hall of Fame for her contributions to the sport and her successful efforts to include freestyle skiing in the Winter Olympic program in Sochi, Russia.

Combining physical prowess, a daredevil attitude, humor and humility, and a "flirtatious smile and beach-blond hair,"[47] Burke gained eminence in the broader North American popular culture. In 2006, *FHM* readers voted her one of the 100 sexiest women; the following year she received the ESPN Female Action Sport Athlete of the Year award. Burke's death devastated the global freestyle snow sport community, many of whom responded immediately to calls from her agent to contribute to an online fund to help pay the estimated US$200,000 hospital bill not covered by her insurance policy. Less than a week after Burke's death, the site had raised more than $300,000 with donations coming from twenty-two countries and tributes left in English, French, German, Italian, and Japanese.[48] The donations and tributes posted on the website reveal her broader culture impact, with offerings coming from NBA players, NASCAR drivers, television personalities, snowboarders, skiers, and various other sporting celebrities.

Irons and Burke are not the first (nor last) action sports stars to die unexpectedly, and thus it is worth considering why these individuals evoked such strong responses from the action sport communities and broader popular culture at this particular historical moment. Drawing upon Pierre Nora's work in "Between History and Memory," Nicholas Parsons and Michael Stern explain that "in order for a person, group or event to be remembered, there must be a will (expressed by a select group) to keep the memory of the person, group or event alive."[49] As such, our understanding of "important people or events from the past can vary with power shifts among different social groups or may be disproportionately influenced by individuals or groups with relatively high levels of social power."[50] Irons and Burke had been deeply invested in the surfing and freestyle skiing industries, respectively, for many years; they both had multiple major sponsorships with sport-specific companies, and close relationships with many members of the sport media (for example, journalists, photographers, editors). With stakes in how Irons and Burke would be remembered, some of these individuals and companies became what Gary Alan Fine refers to as "reputational entrepreneurs."[51] Their role in memorializing these athletes was not simply a matter of presenting stories and images, and creating spaces for others to share their own memories of them. Rather, the careful selection and presentation of particular photos, videos, and voices contributes to the creative construction of (some) cultural memories (over others).

Cultural memories are passed on to us in various cultural practices, routines, institutions, artifacts, and media (for example, magazines, videos, books, newspapers, television), and they are always political and often contested. For example, in a highly controversial article titled "Last Drop" published in *Outside* magazine two weeks after Irons's death, surfing journalist Brad Melekian exposed the selective silences in the surfing industry and media regarding the less-than-savory dimensions of Irons's lifestyle that led to his death.[52] As a result, he was "threatened by numerous people within the surf industry and accused of spitting on Irons's grave."[53] In the remainder of this chapter I build upon this discussion by focusing on the production and consumption of virtual memorial websites, as well as the creative uses of Facebook, by family, friends, and action sport participants, seeking to mourn and memorialize Irons and Burke. The virtual memorialization practices discussed in this chapter are, to paraphrase Barbara Misztal, culturally significant because they "enact and give substance" to the "group identity" of surfers or freestyle skiers, their "present conditions," and "vision of the future."[54]

Instant Memorialization on the Internet

Within moments of the news of Irons's and Burke's deaths, friends, peers, and fans of the athletes took to using an array of new social media (for example, Facebook, Skype, text messaging, and Twitter) to confirm, discuss, and debate the news among their social networks. The following comments posted immediately after the news of Irons's death was announced on the *Surfer* magazine message board (at 2:50 p.m.) reveal the initial disbelief and shock within the virtual surf community: "if this is a joke you should be hung by your nutsack" (2:52 p.m.); "man, please tell us this is not true" (2:54 p.m.); "Sh1t. I can't fvcking believe it" (2:56 p.m.); "Is there any source on this other than Surfermag blog? Someone could have hacked an account and put up a bogus story" (3:02 p.m.); "Horrifying news. Just in the middle of his comeback too. I'm devastated" (3:03 p.m.); "poop, it's already on Wiki . . . Andy Irons July 24, 1978 - November 2, 2010" (3:10 p.m.). Analyzing the media response to Michael Jackson's death, Joanne Garde-Hansen observed a similar "lack of coherence and consensus" in the early Twitter and forum discussions; these postings spoke in a "variety of voices, modes, tones, styles and registers before the rules of traditional media have encoded a response."[55] One day after Jackson's death, however, "once the mediated memorials on and offline have formed a collective memory," social networks such as Twitter "produced an extensive iteration and reiteration of grief, trauma, sadness and loss, with few detracting voices."[56] This example points to the ways dominant narratives get formed within and across virtual and print media. Similar temporal patterns and cultural politics can be observed in the narrative constructions of Irons's and Burke's deaths.

The memorialization of Irons and Burke commenced almost as soon as their deaths had been confirmed. Within hours of the news, video montages of Irons's and Burke's sporting achievements had been uploaded on YouTube and Vimeo and were being viewed and commented on by thousands from across the world. For example, a video montage created by a 14-year-old fan of Burke garnered more than 106,000 views within thirteen hours of being posted on the *Powder* magazine website. Others uploaded their own creative memorial offerings, including a rudimentary Andy Irons Dead—RIP—tribute song posted on YouTube by an overzealous fan. Friends and fans wrote emotional eulogies on their personal blogs, and some set up memorial websites featuring photos and videos of Irons and Burke. Others posted their (best) personal memories of Irons and Burke on existing websites, forums, and blogs.[57] Such memories range from deeply personal, extended familial relationships or friendships, to fans' brief encounters with their sporting heroes. The comments posted on such forums vary across the five responses to grief identified by Elisabeth Kübler-Ross—denial, anger, bargaining, depression, and acceptance—with an array of communication styles employed to express these emotions.[58] In so doing, these sites contributed to the development of global communities of grief; they offered a "place to mourn collectively, where there is a potential for dialog and constant evolution of memory."[59]

As well as providing space for friends and fans to express their grief and communicate with other mourners, some forums feature debates among members regarding the politics surrounding the death or memorialization of the athletes, or the appropriate social etiquette for speaking of the recently departed. For example, on the Billabong forum dedicated to the memory of Andy Irons, "Mike" questions the involvement of corporate "reputational entrepreneurs" in the media coverage of Irons's death, asking, "why is a clothing company 'managing' [his] death?"[60] Occasionally, heated discussions take place in these virtual forums. For example, in response to a two-page tribute by eleven-time World Champion surfer and long-time rival Kelly Slater,[61] comments ranged from those waxing lyrical about Slater's "sincerity," "honesty," and surfing prowess, to more critical arguments such as the following by "Frank": "Kelly is the ultimate politician . . . stop blindly bobbing your heads to essentially a bunch of words that said NOTHING." "Frank's" comment gained eight likes from other thread-followers, some of whom supported his arguments: "So true . . . the athletes are nothing more than pawns on the chessboard, and a bunch of self-narcissists to boot" ("honesty"); "In the surf biz, truth is what Billabong says it is" ("ASP_Guru"). Many other posters, however, balked at these comments: "This is a eulogy. Your comments are better served in a proper context . . . Grow up" ("Al Baydough"); "(This is) the wrong context . . . respect for Andy's closest family and friends would be appreciated" ("Dandaman"). Although virtual forums provide space for critical comments and questioning, these disquieting voices tend to be heavily policed and regulated by other posters and, in some cases, the website producers. Thus, as time passes, most of these virtual forums settle on a dominant narrative of Irons and Burke as action sport heroes without fault.

There appear to be at least two dominant forms of cultural memory construction operating on such websites. First, the extensive discussions and debates about what really happened to the athlete, who is accountable, and what lessons must be learned for the culture more broadly (for example, the importance of health insurance for athletes training abroad, the dangers involved in high-level freestyle skiing, the silence in the surfing sport and industry surrounding drug and alcohol usage among some professional athletes) work to create a dominant historical narrative that will likely be repeated across an array of future memory products (for example, books, videos, events).[62] Second, although virtual media offer new space for an array of voices from the surfing and skiing communities, some individuals and organizations have more power to define cultural memories than others. For example, selectively remembering Irons's sporting life and controlling details of his death, Billabong was a key reputational entrepreneur in the production of Irons's mythology.[63] In sum, while the Internet and new social media may be transforming some of the practices of mourning, the web is not free from the politics of cultural memory construction and memorialization.

Facebook Memories

Facebook has become the most popular social networking site for people to connect and share their everyday lived experiences and engage in discussion with online communities.[64] The number of Facebook users exceeds one billion.[65] But what happens when a Facebook member dies? How do Facebook members use this medium for the purposes of grieving and memorialization? The Facebook memorial policy offers bereaved family and friends at least two options. First, when a Facebook member dies, friends and family can apply to have his or her profile page converted into a digital memorial. The privacy settings are readjusted and communication functions reduced, but all existing friends of the member can continue to write on his or her wall. The deceased member's profile remains unchanged—previously uploaded photos, posts, and dialogues remain for all existing friends to see. The Official Sarah Burke Fan Page, established in January 2009 by Burke (or her agent), was converted to a memorial page following her death with the addition of the following statement: "This is a memorial page for Sarah. Please do not use it for your political, social or other beliefs. It is for condolences only. Her loved ones are reading this page for comfort."[66] More than six months after her death, the site had more than 60,000 members, many of whom write personal statements to Sarah, or comment, like, link, or upload new photos, videos, and news clips.

The second option allows family or friends to set up a memorial page that does not require visitors to be Facebook members or previously listed friends of the deceased, and thus operates as a public space for the "articulation of grief and remembrance."[67] Within days of his death, the RIP Andy Irons Facebook memorial page had 114,000 fans, and by July 2012 had more than 218,000 likes. The site includes photos and videos of Irons surfing, as well as photos of his young son, comments and tributes from friends and fans (for example, a photo of a friend's leg featuring a new AI Forever tattoo, and a song written by a well-known musician), links to other media coverage, and other surfing-related posts. Multiple memorial pages were set up as tributes to Irons and Burke, some by family and friends, others by fans or opportunistic groups seeking to capitalize on the traffic to the page. Yet, Facebook pages that are maintained by loved ones, or at least by those with access to their personal archives (for example, agents), have more cultural credibility and thus popularity among friends and fans.

In the remainder of this section I briefly identify five key arguments regarding Facebook memorialization pages: (1) Facebook is a unique space to commune with the dead, (2) Facebook offers individual mourners opportunities to participate in a community of living others, (3) Facebook is a digital archive of affect, (4) the dead remain in dialogical limbo in such virtual spaces, and (5) Facebook memorial communities develop a unique etiquette for speaking of, and representing, the dead.

As is common with most Facebook memorial pages,[68] many of the comments posted on Irons's and Burke's memorial walls are addressed directly to the deceased athletes (for example, "RIP Andy. You were the king in the sport of Kings"; "No matter how the weather is, you will always be our snow-angel Sarah"). According to Rebecca Kern and colleagues, such direct communications with the deceased suggest that, for many posters, "Facebook is a place to commune with the dead in a space where the communication may actually be 'received.' The dead live in a virtual cloud."[69] Drawing upon the work of Judith Butler, Kyle Vealey examines the appeal of writing on Facebook memorial sites, asking "what are the rhetorical and performative implications of [such] discursive practices?"[70] He concludes that Facebook offers a unique "space for articulation," one wherein individuals are not "forced to inscribe," but rather "the openness, the possibility of articulation . . . compels inscription, thus rhetorically constructing a community that articulates these affects publically."[71]

This sense of community is important here. While many come to memorial Facebook pages with the intent to "communicate with the dead," in the process of doing so they "come into community with living others"; their seemingly private posts are in fact "public intimacies."[72] Put simply, posting on such websites is a form of cultural performance; the writer posts his or her comment with the implicit understanding that other group members will observe his or her expression of grief. Similar to gravesites in the offline world, Facebook memorial pages provide "a place to 'visit' with dead loved ones," or in this case fallen sporting heroes, but unlike the former, "these online places of remembrance provide a platform where individual conversations with the dead are permanently recorded and publicly displayed."[73] Facebook memorial pages are thus "digital archives of affect," offering a record of both private and public processes of mourning and memory construction.[74]

Vealey raises pertinent questions about the digital remains once the haptic body has gone—"what kind of electronic life persists? How are we to grieve the absence of a body when a digital form of that body remains?"[75] Within virtual spaces such as Facebook, it seems "the dead never really die" but rather "perpetually remain in a digital state of dialogic limbo."[76] Indeed, Burke's husband, Rory Bushfield, admits to keeping her two iPhones close: "It sounds weird, but it feels comforting to know those old text messages and pictures are still right there. It's like part of her still exists."[77] As Andy Clark, Anna Munster, Kyle Vealey, and other scholars of new media point out, new communication technologies and devices, such as iPhones, are increasingly "cognitive and affective extensions of our own bodies."[78] If, as Clark suggests, the mobile phone is "both something you use (as you use your hands to write) and something that is part of you,"[79] Bushfield's comments above suggest a need to rethink the relationship between death, new media, and the (corporeal and virtual) body.

Facebook memorial pages are said to "aid in the bereavement of the deceased" by offering a "continuing space to engage with the deceased in a mediated, virtual and spiritual space," and the "more in-depth the memorial and the greater its permanence, the more the deceased remain with the living."[80] Certainly, Irons and Burke continue to have a visible virtual presence on Facebook; the managers of these pages regularly update their memorial pages with new photos, news, and links, and visitors continue to post messages (although with less frequency as time passes). It is important to keep in mind that such memorialization processes are temporary. Arguably, as with most memorial objects and artifacts, the lifespan of these websites (and thus the digital life of the deceased) will depend on the mourning processes of the producers (that is, family and friends) and consumers (friends and fans).

As with attending a wake or visiting a tomb, Facebook memorial pages are developing their own unique etiquette that is carefully policed and regulated by family, friends, some fans and, occasionally, Facebook employees. Blurring boundaries between the private and public, mourning and memorial sites on the Internet and social networking sites such as Facebook open up a number of potentially "contentious issues,"[81] including the hacking of personal and highly sensitive materials, or disrespectful comments from indignant others or, in some cases, strangers. For example, the RIP Sarah Burke memorial page has had some questionable visitors such that the page is now closely monitored and features the following warning: "Due to some inappropriate photos that have been added, we will from now on moderate this site. This site is a memorial site for Sarah Burke and should be only used as a memorial site. Rest in peace Sarah!" Just as a gravesite can be vandalized, digital memorials can also be subjected to sacrilegious practices.

Final Thoughts: Death, Mourning, and the Digital Body

In this chapter I have examined the contributions of the Internet and social media to the production of cultural memory in contemporary sport and physical cultures. More specifically, I revealed some uses of virtual media for engaging in cultural mourning and memorialization via two case studies of recently deceased action sport stars—surfer Andy Irons and freestyle skier Sarah Burke. While the Internet and social media offer new spaces for personal and collective mourning and cultural memory construction, I am cautious of recent arguments that the Internet offers "a more open, democratic, free-market space"[82] for "communities of mourning."[83] Through the cases of Irons and Burke, I suggested that certain individuals and groups continue to "have more power than others to create cultural memories" in virtual spaces, which is not dissimilar from more traditional objects and media of memory.[84] In conjunction with print media and other memorial events, commemorative practices in virtual media and online spaces work to stabilize particular cultural memories that reinforce the established cultural order within surfing and freestyle skiing, respectively. Thus, future studies of the use of Internet and social media for cultural mourning and memorialization should also consider the broader context within which these practices and performances cannot be separated, and seek to examine the politics involved in the production and consumption of virtual memory products.

Notes

1. Samuel, *Theatres of Memory*, 25.
2. Urry, "How Societies Remember the Past."
3. Brockmeier, "After the Archive."
4. Dijck, *Mediated Memories*.
5. Memory has both individual and collective dimensions. In this chapter the focus is on collective or cultural memory. Barbara Misztal describes cultural memory as "the representation of the past, both that shared by a group and that which is collectively commemorated, that enacts and gives substance to the group's identity, its present conditions and its vision of the future." Collective memory is passed on to us in various cultural practices, routines, institutions, and artifacts, and is always contested. Misztal, *Theories of Social Remembering*, 7. Also see Thorpe, "The Politics of Remembering."
6. Reed, *The Way of the Snowboarder*, 61.
7. Such deaths violently disrupt the fantasy of the action sport star (as possessing super-human characteristics and thus worthy of cultural adoration) repeated across niche magazines, websites, and films. As with most other elite action sport athletes, the niche media had worked to create mythic status for these individuals—not only did they live the dream of traveling to remote and exotic locations where they conquered enormous waves or mountains, but they also appear to cheat death on numerous occasions.
8. Gibson, "Death and Mourning"; Hallam and Hockey, *Death, Memory and Material Culture*; Hewer and Roberts, "History, Culture and Cognition"; Hutchings, "Wiring Death"; Kern, Forman, and Gil-Egui, "R.I.P: Remain in Perpetuity"; Krapp, *Déjà Vu*; Nathan, *Saying It's So*; Pantti and Sumiala, "Till Death Do Us Join."

9. Parsons and Stern, "There's No Dying in Baseball," 66.
10. Kansteiner, "Finding Meaning in Memory," 195 (emphasis added).
11. Brockmeier, "Remembering and Forgetting"; Klein, "On the Emergence of Memory in Historical Discourse."
12. For example, see Corkill and Moore, "The Island of Blood"; Faron, "Death and Fertility Rites of the Mapuche (Araucanian) Indians of Central Chile"; Kong, "No Place, New Places"; Mandelbaum, "Social Uses of Funeral Rites"; Reilly, "Grief, Loss and Violence in Ancient Mangaia, Aotearoa and Te Waipounamu."
13. Kern, Forman, and Gil-Egui, "R.I.P: Remain in Perpetuity," 2.
14. Becker and Knudson, "Visions of the Dead," 713.
15. Kern, Forman, and Gil-Egui, "R.I.P: Remain in Perpetuity," 2.
16. Gibson, "Death and Mourning," 419.
17. See, for example, Corkill and Moore, "The Island of Blood"; Huggins, "Read the Funeral Rite"; Radford and Bloch, "Grief, Commiseration, and Consumption Following the Death of a Celebrity"; Russell, "We All Agree, Name the Stand after Shankly."
18. Gibson, "Death and Mourning"; Wark, *Celebrities, Culture and Cyberspace*.
19. Bennett, "Michael Jackson"; Gibson, "Death and Mourning"; Gibson, "Some Thoughts on Celebrity Deaths"; Sanderson and Cheong, "Tweeting Prayers and Communicating Grief Over Michael Jackson Online"; Thomas, "From People Power to Mass Hysteria."
20. Gibson, "Death and Mourning," 418.
21. Ibid.
22. Thomas, "From People Power to Mass Hysteria."
23. Gibson, "Some Thoughts on Celebrity Deaths."
24. Radford and Bloch, "Grief, Commiseration, and Consumption."
25. Hutchings, "Wiring Death," 43.
26. Arthur, "Pixelated Memory"; Foot, Warnick, and Schneider, "Web-based Memorializing After September 11"; Grider, "Spontaneous Shrines"; Roberts, "The Living and the Dead"; Roberts, "From My Space to Our Space."
27. Kear and Steinberg, "Ghost Writing," 6; Garde-Hansen, "Measuring Mourning with Online Media"; Garde-Hansen, "MyMemories?"; Kern, Forman, and Gil-Egui, "R.I.P: Remain in Perpetuity"; Vealey, "Making Dead Bodies Legible."
28. Kear and Steinberg, "Ghost Writing"; Pantti and Sumiala, "Till Death Do Us Join"; Re.Public, *Planet Diana*.
29. Hutchings, "Wiring Death."
30. Vealey, "Making Dead Bodies Legible."
31. Hutchings, "Wiring Death," 47.
32. Ibid.
33. Radford and Bloch, "Grief, Commiseration, and Consumption."
34. Kansteiner, "Finding Meaning in Memory."
35. Foot, Warnick, and Schneider, "Web-based Memorializing After September 11," 75.

36. Ibid.
37. Ibid.
38. Ibid., 92.
39. Bodner, *Remaking America*, 247.
40. Foot, Warnick, and Schneider, "Web-based Memorializing After September 11."
41. Roberts, "The Living and the Dead," 57.
42. Kern, Forman, and Gil-Egui, "R.I.P: Remain in Perpetuity," 7.
43. Higgins, "Surfer Irons Died of Heart Attack and Drugs."
44. Ibid., para. 11.
45. *Surfer Magazine,* "Andy Irons Passes Away."
46. FIS Freestyle Ski World Cup.
47. Saslow, "One Light Will Not Go Out."
48. Ibid.
49. Parsons and Stern, "There's No Dying in Baseball," 66.
50. Ibid.
51. Fine, "Reputational Entrepreneurs and the Memory of Incompetence."
52. Melekian, "Last Drop." With a dominant position in the billion-dollar global surfing industry and long-time sponsor of Andy Irons, Billabong invested a lot of "money and clout" into maintaining Irons's legacy, including renaming the prestigious Pipeline Masters Hawaiian surf contest the Billabong Pipe Masters In Memory of Andy Irons, and establishing a line of AI Forever products. The Irons family were also involved in the crafting of his legacy. In a statement she later admits to regretting, Irons's widow, Lyndie, argued for the results of the toxicology report to be delayed because they could "tarnish Andy's brand" for which she and her unborn child were financially dependent.
53. Melekian, "Crashing Down."
54. Misztal, *Theories of Social Remembering*, 7.
55. Garde-Hansen, "Measuring Mourning with Online Media," 234.
56. Ibid.
57. *Freeskier Magazine*; *Surfer Magazine*, "Surfer Remembers Andy Irons."
58. Kübler-Ross, *On Death and Dying*.
59. Kern, Forman, and Gil-Egui, "R.I.P: Remain in Perpetuity," 3.
60. Billabong. "Billabong." Accessed May 23, 2013. http://www.billabong.com. Unfortunately, the original source for this quote has since been deleted from the Billabong website. This is illustrative of one of the difficulties of using online sources for academic research. The sources are dynamic and constantly changing; what is there one day may be gone the next. Furthermore, the removal of this forum from the Billabong website may offer another example of the censorship that occurred on some websites when a few surfers posted critical comments about the recently deceased Irons.
61. Slater, "How I Remember Andy."
62. Thorpe, "The Politics of Remembering."

63. Of course, selective remembering (and forgetting) is not a new phenomenon. As Hutchings observed in his analysis of the public response to Michael Jackson's death: "The passing of Michael Jackson led to a striking reappraisal of his life and work, which suddenly returned to popularity and critical approval, and found new audiences after many years of social unacceptability" (Hutchings, "Wiring Death," 46). The same could also be said for Irons's legacy. In contrast to Burke, who seemed to be adored by the freestyle skiing community prior to her death, the surfing culture had been divided over their opinions on Irons's behavior in and out of the water. Following his death, however, the global surfing culture seemed (almost) united in their grief for this fallen hero.

64. Chayko, *Connection*; Miegel and Olsson, "A Generational Thing?"
65. Lyons, "Facebook to Hit a Billion Users in the Summer."
66. "#Celebrate Sarah."
67. Vealey, "Making Dead Bodies Legible," para. 4.
68. Roberts, "The Living and the Dead"; Vealey, "Making Dead Bodies Legible."
69. Kern, Forman, and Gil-Egui, "R.I.P: Remain in Perpetuity," 8.
70. Vealey, "Making Dead Bodies Legible," para. 16.
71. Ibid., para. 18.
72. Ibid., para. 21.
73. Kern, Forman, and Gil-Egui, "R.I.P: Remain in Perpetuity," 7.
74. Vealey, "Making Dead Bodies Legible."
75. Ibid., para. 2.
76. Kern, Forman, and Gil-Egui, "R.I.P: Remain in Perpetuity," 1.
77. Saslow, "One Light Will Not Go Out," para. 28.
78. Clark, *Natural-Born Cyborgs*; Munster, *Materializing New Media*; Vealey, "Making Dead Bodies Legible," para. 7.
79. Clark, *Natural-Born Cyborgs*, 9.
80. Kern, Forman, and Gil-Egui, "R.I.P: Remain in Perpetuity," 9.
81. Gibson, "Death and Mourning," 423.
82. Ibid.
83. Kear and Steinberg, "Ghost Writing," 6.
84. Parsons and Stern, "There's No Dying in Baseball," 69.

References

Arthur, Paul. 2008. "Pixelated Memory: Online Commemoration of Trauma and Crisis." *Interactive Media* 4: 1–19.

Becker, Scott, and Roger Knudson. 2003. "Visions of the Dead: Imagination and Mourning." *Death Studies* 27: 691–716.

Bennett, James. 2010. "Michael Jackson: Celebrity Death, Mourning and Media Events." *Celebrity Studies* 1: 231–32.

Bodnar, John. 1992. *Remaking America: Public Memory, Commemoration, and Patriotism in the Twentieth Century*. Princeton, NJ: Princeton University Press.

Brockmeier, Jens. 2002. "Remembering and Forgetting: Narrative as Cultural Memory." *Culture and Psychology* 8: 15–43.
———. "2010. After the Archive: Remapping Memory." *Culture and Psychology* 16: 5–35.
"#Celebrate Sarah." Facebook. Accessed February 4, 2014. https://www.facebook.com/pages/Sarah-Burke/50553451173.
Chayko, Mary. 2002. *Connection: How We Form Social Bonds and Communities in the Internet Age*. Albany: State University of New York Press.
Clark, Andy. 2003. *Natural-Born Cyborgs: Minds, Technologies, and the Future of Human Intelligence*. New York: Oxford University Press.
Corkill, Claire, and Ray Moore. 2012. "'The Island of Blood': Death and Commemoration at the Isle of Man TT Races." *World Archaeology* 44, no. 2: 248–62.
Dijck, José van. 2007. *Mediated Memories In the Digital Age*. Stanford, CA: Stanford University Press.
Faron, Lois. 1967. "Death and Fertility Rites of the Mapuche (Araucanian) Indians of Central Chile." In *Gods and Rituals*, edited by J. Middleton, 227–54. Garden City, NY: Natural History Press.
Fine, Gary Alan. 1996. "Reputational Entrepreneurs and the Memory of Incompetence: Melting, Supporters, Partisan Warriors and Images of President Harding." *American Journal of Sociology* 101, no. 5: 1159–93.
FIS Freestyle Ski World Cup. 2012. "Sarah Burke Seriously Injured," January. http://www.fisfreestyle.com/uk/mobile/sarah-burke-seriously-injured,346.html?actu_page_42=2?sectorcode=&sector=.
Foot, Kirsten, Barbara Warnick, and Steven M. Schneider. 2006. "Web-Based Memorializing after September 11: Toward a Conceptual Framework." *Journal of Computer-Mediated Communication* 11: 72–96.
Freeskier Magazine. "Celebrate Sarah Burke, 1982–2012." Accessed August 1, 2012. http://freeskier.com/sarah.
Garde-Hansen, Joanne. 2009. "MyMemories? Personal Digital Archive Fever and Facebook." In *Save As . . . Digital Memories*, edited by J. Garde-Hansen, A. Hoskins, and A. Reading, 135–50. Houndmills, Basingstoke: Palgrave Macmillan.
———. 2010. "Measuring Mourning with Online Media: Michael Jackson and Real-Time Memories." *Celebrity Studies* 1: 233–35.
Garde-Hansen, Joanne, Andrew Hoskins, and Anna Reading, eds. 2009. *Save As . . . Digital Memories*. Houndmills, Basingstoke: Palgrave Macmillan.
Gibson, Margaret. 2007a. "Death and Mourning in Technologically Mediated Culture." *Health Sociology Review* 16: 415–24.
———. 2007b. "Some Thoughts on Celebrity Deaths: Steve Irwin and the Issue of Public Mourning." *Mortality* 12: 1–3.
Grider, Sylvia. 2001. "Spontaneous Shrines: A Modern Response to Tragedy and Disaster." *New Directions in Folklore* 5 (October). http://astro.temple.edu/~camille/shrines.html.

Hallam, Elizabeth, and Jenny Hockey. 2001. *Death, Memory and Material Culture*. Oxford: Berg.

Hewer, Christopher, and Ronald Roberts. 2012. "History, Culture and Cognition: Towards a Dynamic Model of Social Memory." *Culture and Psychology* 18: 167–83.

Higgins, Matt. 2011. "Surfer Irons Died of Heart Attack and Drugs, Autopsy Says." *The New York Times*, June 8. Accessed July 12, 2012. http://www.nytimes.com/2011/06/09/sports/cause-released-in-surfer-andy-irons-death.html.

Huggins, Mike. 2011. "Read the Funeral Rite: A Cultural Analysis of the Funeral Ceremonials and Burial of Selected Leading Sportsmen in Victorian England, 1864–1888." *Journal of Sport History* 38: 407–24.

Hutchings, Tim. 2012. "Wiring Death: Dying, Grieving and Remembering on the Internet." In *Emotion, Identity and Death: Mortality across Disciplines*, edited by D. J. Davies and C.W. Park, 43–58. Burlington, VT: Ashgate.

Kansteiner, Wulf. 2002. "Finding Meaning in Memory: A Methodological Critique of Collective Memory Studies." *History and Theory* 41: 179–97.

Kear, Adrian, and Deborah Lyn Steinberg. 1999. "Ghost Writing." In *Mourning Diana: Nation, Culture and the Performance of Grief*, edited by A. Kear and D. L. Steinberg, 1–14. London and New York: Routledge.

Kern, Rebecca, Abbe E. Forman, and Gisela Gil-Egui. 2013. "R.I.P: Remain in Perpetuity. Facebook Memorial Pages." *Telematics and Informatics* 30, no. 1 (February): 2–10.

Klein, Kerwin Lee. 2000. "On the Emergence of Memory in Historical Discourse." *Representations* 69: 127–50.

Kong, Lily. 2012. "No Place, New Places: Death and its Rituals in Urban Asia." *Urban Studies* 49: 415–33.

Krapp, Peter. 2004. *Déjà Vu: Aberrations of Cultural Memory*. Minneapolis: University of Minnesota Press.

Kübler-Ross, Elisabeth. 1969. *On Death and Dying*. New York: Routledge.

Lyons, Gregory. 2012. "Facebook to Hit a Billion Users in the Summer," January 11. Accessed June 13, 2012. http://connect.icrossing.co.uk/facebook-hit-billion-users-summer_7709.

Mandelbaum, David. 1959. "Social Uses of Funeral Rites." In *The Meaning of Death*, edited by H. Feifel, 189–217. New York: McGraw Hill.

Melekian, Brad. 2010. "Last Drop." *Outside*, November 2. Accessed July 10, 2012. http://www.outsideonline.com/outdoor-adventure/athletes/Last-Drop.html.

———. 2011. "Crashing Down." *Outside*, August 1. Accessed July 10, 2012. http://www.outsideonline.com/outdoor-adventure/athletes/andy-irons/Crashing-Down.html?page=all.

Miegel, Fredrik, and Tobias Olsson. 2012. "A Generational Thing? The Internet and New Forms of Social Intercourse." *Continuum: Journal of Media and Cultural Studies* 26: 487–99.

Misztal, Barbara. 2003. *Theories of Social Remembering*. Philadelphia, PA: Open University.

Munster, Anna. 2006. *Materializing New Media: Embodiment in Information Aesthetics.* Hanover, NH: Dartmouth College Press/University Press of New England.

Nathan, Daniel. 2004. *Saying It's So: A Cultural History of the Black Sox Scandal.* Urbana: University of Illinois Press.

Pantti, Mervi, and Johanna Sumiala. 2009. "Till Death Do Us Join: Media, Mourning Rituals and the Sacred Centre of the Society." *Media, Culture and Society* 31: 119–35.

Parsons, Nicholas L., and Michael Stern. 2012. "'There's No Dying in Baseball': Cultural Valorization, Collective Memory, and Induction into the Baseball Hall of Fame." *Sociology of Sport Journal* 29: 62–88.

Radford, Scott K., and Peter H. Bloch. 2012. "Grief, Commiseration, and Consumption following the Death of a Celebrity." *Journal of Consumer Culture* 12: 137–55.

Reed, R. 2005. *The Way of the Snowboarder.* New York: Harry N. Abrams.

Re.Public, eds. 1997. *Planet Diana: Cultural Studies and Global Mourning.* Kingswood, NSW: University of Western Sydney.

Reilly, Michael P. J. 2012. "Grief, Loss and Violence in Ancient Mangaia, Aotearoa and Te Waipounamu." *The Journal of Pacific History* 47: 145–61.

Roberts, Pamela. 2004. "The Living and the Dead: Community in the Virtual Cemetery." *Omega* 49: 57–76.

———. 2006. "From My Space to Our Space: The Functions of Web Memorials in Bereavement." *The Forum* 32, no. 4: 1, 3–4.

Russell, Dave. 2006. "'We all Agree, Name the Stand after Shankly': Cultures of Commemoration in Late Twentieth Century English Football Cultures." *Journal of Sport History* 26: 1–25.

Samuel, Raphael. 1994. *Theatres of Memory: Past and Present in Contemporary Culture.* London: Verso.

Sanderson, James, and Pauline Hope Cheong. 2010. "Tweeting Prayers and Communicating Grief Over Michael Jackson Online." *Bulletin of Science, Technology and Society* 30: 328–40.

Saslow, Eli. 2012. "One Light Will Not Go Out." *ESPN: The Magazine,* June 1. Accessed July 10, 2012. http://espn.go.com/espnw/more-sports/7984690/freeskier-sarah-burke-leaves-lasting-legacy-women-sports-espn-magazine.

Slater, Kelly. 2011. "How I Remember Andy." *The Inertia,* November 11. Accessed July 16, 2012. http://www.theinertia.com/surf/kelly-slater-remembers-andy-irons/.

Surfer Magazine. 2010. "Andy Irons passes away." November 2. Accessed July 3, 2012. http://www.surfermag.com/features/breaking-news-andy-irons-passes-away/.

———. 2010. "Surfer Remembers Andy Irons." November 3. Accessed July 16, 2012. http://www.surfermag.com/features/surfer-remembers-andy-irons/.

Thomas, James. 2008. "From People Power to Mass Hysteria: Media and Popular Reactions to the Death of Princess Diana." *International Journal of Cultural Studies* 11: 362–76.

Thorpe, Holly. 2010. "The Politics of Remembering: An Interdisciplinary Approach to Physical Cultural Memory." *Sporting Traditions* 27: 113–25.

Urry, John. 1996. "How Societies Remember the Past." In *Theorizing Museums*, edited by S. Macdonald and G. Fyfe, 45–65. Cambridge: Blackwell.

Vealey, Kyle. 2011. "Making Dead Bodies Legible: Facebook's Ghosts, Public Bodies and Networked Grief." *gnovis: Journal of Communication, Culture and Technology* 11, no. 2 (April). http://gnovisjournal.org/2011/04/03/making-dead-bodies-legible/.

Wark, McKenzie. 1999. *Celebrities, Culture and Cyberspace: The Light on the Hill in a Postmodern World*. Sydney: Pluto Press.

PART III

Digital History is History

The third dimension of our tripartite conception of history in contemporary times is *Digital History is History*. We perceive that *Digital History is History* is the most radical dimension of the digital humanities, because it provides viable and engaging alternatives to traditional history. As much as Synthia Sydnor makes a strong case for continuities and synergies between play, sport, and the Internet in her chapter, *Digital History is History* has transformational potential on a larger scale for history making. This potential is inextricably linked to the new economy of knowledge production. This knowledge production has many characteristics: a screen-based culture encompassing nonlinear historical narratives, decentralization of information accompanied by large-scale distribution of knowledge, an open-source culture built around creative commons, public collaboration involving citizen and professional scholars, and publish-then-filter models of circulation often involving multiple versions of materials. Fiona McLachlan and Douglas Booth engage with some of these issues by examining how the Internet facilitates the reconceptualization of historical narratives. Their chapter is a preview into the ways in which the new economy of knowledge production challenges the defining features of scholarly history: a (mostly) solitary enterprise that is (often) expressed in the form of a peer-reviewed, paper book under the imprimatur of a university press, and read (usually) by audiences familiar with the discursive traditions of the field.

9

On the Nature of Sport
A Treatise in Light of Universality and Digital Culture

SYNTHIA SYDNOR

In this chapter I attempt to identify and then show how specific cultural and historical studies help create a theory of sport that is compatible with essentializing of origins; these integrative statements help illuminate the human condition.

In the past century the world[1] has seen all-encompassing alterations in communication and sport (both communication and sport broadly and loosely imagined and defined). It is widely understood that such changes in sport and communication are revolutionary, born of technological, industrial, performative, and material inventions and advances that have transformed, enhanced, democratized, and/or accelerated ways that carry on civic culture. Concurrently, there is also nostalgia for older times *sans* the Internet and criticism of the myths spurned by the promises of the digital age;[2] whatever one's take on digital culture, the phenomenon is for the most part assumed to be new, even futuristic.

Is the Internet/digital culture/cyberspace and all that these have instigated, including concerning sport itself, something original and new? Where do thinkers of sport venture from here if we understand such change *not* as transformative or revolutionary but as socio-evolutionary phenomena of humankind? Accordingly, the following deals not with the digital revolution's critique in terms of sport, but with an understanding of sport and digital culture in a transhistorical holistic way.[3]

I reason that we need to pay attention to the history of sport and digital culture from the perspectives of classic anthropology—at its essence, digital culture is something that humans have made to enhance and accelerate their communication, creativity, war, marketplace, and play—ageless human occupations. Humans in all circumstances and environments play and communicate—for example, Robin Dunbar, an evolutionary anthropologist, believes that early hominid (between 1.8 million and 200,000 years ago) grooming behavior (similar to primate behavior observed today) helped to birth language, gossip, intricate communication, alliances, trade; the rise of digital communication does not replace the original crux of human communication.[4] Claude Lévi Strauss understood that the concept of communication from the primal could be extended to include "communication of information, ideas and entertainment, in words and images by means of speed, writing, music, print, telegraphy and telephone, radio, television and internet."[5] The 2000, *Cluetrain Manifesto* argued that the Internet revives human communication as a core of society and trade/marketing.[6]

It is interesting that early studies on games also made similar conclusions about media. John Roberts, Malcolm Arth, and Robert Bush, in their influential "Games in Culture" article (1959), argued that things that occur in a regular, universal fashion are acculturating or selectively useful for human survival—to individual and cultural wellbeing.[7] Brian Sutton-Smith believed that video games are cultural adaptations that acculturate and socialize societal members[8]—the youngest and the old—as to what is important in the particular historical and cultural context; they teach variation and captivate. This idea reasons that the human species has awareness of changing societal priorities (such as the emphasis on screen reading and imaging systems in most aspects of civilization today, which is found to be pleasurable—especially by the young—and practiced through a variety of platforms such as video gaming).

Jussi Parikka and Jaron Lanier highlight an aspect of Internet-digital-technical-media culture that aids in my particular understanding of the nature of sport: "New media remediates old media . . . New media might be here and slowly changing our user habits, but old media never left us. They are continuously remediated, resurfacing, finding new uses, contexts, adaptations."[9] So too we find this in the specific example of sport.

Take C. L. R. James, who saw sports not only as metaphoric of society with cultural contexts, but also with a transhistorical function/value. James argued for the importance of sport in social history, using the ancient Greeks as a beginning point, recognizing the holistic role that sport played within communities: "We respond to physical action or vivid representation of it, dead or alive, because we are made that way . . . we recognize significant form in elemental physical action is native to us, a part of the process by which we have become and remain human . . . they remain part of our human endowment."[10] Roland Barthes, in *What is Sport*,[11] answers: "Sport is a great modern spectacle cast in the ancestral forms of spectacle."[12] William H. McNeill's study, *Keeping Together in Time: Dance and Human Drill in Human History*, invites us to understand humans keeping "rhythmically together" (dancing, military drill, exercise, song, playground activities, any type of sports competitions, and any ritualized work activity) as powerful "kinesthetic undergirding" that creates, sustains, and communicates the well-being of humans in community.[13]

I take these above concepts about the nature or essence of sport and recast them within the framework of understanding cultural adaptation and the universality of human nature. This is a preliminary effort to forward a treatise on the nature of sport that takes into account the digital era at the same time as it has various theories of play, ritual, and culture—to speak to the topic in a comprehensive manner. At the core of my original recasting are the theories of David Sansone, Brian Boyd, and Adam Seligman et al. David Sansone's theory that understands sport and all of its polyphonic, myriad peripherals, however subtle,[14] to have ties to early humans' ritualization of sport is fundamental to my treatise about the nature of sport.

The upshot of believing that there are integrative statements (such as those of Sansone's about sport, Boyd's on stories, and Seligman's concerning ritual) that illuminate the human condition is that new ways to perceive the world are enabled; theories and ideas that more or less once seemed pieced together about the world now seem to harmonize. Therefore, part of the chapter is devoted to an overview of a few subjects of which sport studies scholars might amend their understandings in light of this treatise.

* * *

A key piece for those interested in play and sport is Brian Boyd's innovative *On the Origin of Stories: Evolution, Cognition and Fiction*. Boyd maintains that fiction (and all play through art in general) can be explained bio-culturally.[15] In other words, play is a universal of human nature that gives life a purpose, organizes and makes life complex, helps humans resist "damage and loss" . . . offers "new ways of evolving variety" . . . "emotions, intelligence, and cooperation, and . . . creativity itself."[16] It is my contention that Boyd's thesis brings to some completion the theories of Johan Huizinga, C. L. R. James, Roland Barthes, Roger Caillois, Bernard Suits, Gregory Bateson, Robert Fagen, Victor Turner, Brian Sutton-Smith, and Richard Schechner in the particular ways that their thought can be used to understand sport.

Acknowledgment of the universal nature of play and sport may be an intellectual basis from which we may approach the issues identified by this anthology; it is also a direction for future interdisciplinary work. Indeed, the consideration of play—an enduring topic of study in pedagogical, new media, Eastern, Western, Africanist area studies (to name some), as well as the paradigm that founds most academic sport studies across the world—is the first step I take to approach my treatise. Play[17] is imperative—it appears to undergird human community[18] as echoed in Huizinga's oft-quoted "play is older than culture . . . in myth and ritual the great instinctive forces of civilized life have their origin: law and order, commerce and profit, craft and art, poetry, wisdom and science. All are rooted in the primeval soil of play."[19]

Human play is associated with improvisation, order, liminality, performativity, pleasure, sacramentality, frame, mimesis, kinesis, agitation, trickery; play's nature can be amoral, dark, evil;[20] sometimes play is rule-bound, sometimes free and spontaneous; play may include fasting and bodily deprivation of other kinds.[21] Robert Fagen, a lifelong scholar of play, concludes his 1981 pioneering work, "Play . . . represents timeless experience . . . play remembered and observed, holds the key to understanding human development in its broadest sense."[22]

Plasticity is crucial to play; it stimulates the birth of interminable variations of play (such as seen in sport), "reconfigures minds," remodels environments;[23] without play, the universe would be stagnant.[24] Boyd points out that "core elements of fiction: character, plot, structure, dramatic irony and theme . . . [arise] naturally out of other human and animal behavior"[25] that have been stimulated by the plasticity of play. In popular and academic circles, we often hear the same of sport—that it is a microcosm of life, that these elements (character, plot, structure, dramatic irony, and theme) are what draw people to sport.

Contemplate fun, thrills, danger, gravity play and the like, all of which participate in human interest in sport, including cyber experiences with sport such as with fantasy league play; social and individual memories of sports performance; video and computer games; the seemingly infinite growth of sport performances and stunts showcased on YouTube; tweets; and the colossal transglobal economy associated with sport. Parikka highlights that the "mass-produced thrill . . . is not restricted only to a particular screen event, but to a complex intermedial phase, which ties in with earlier entertainment practices, the emerging screen media of cinematography, social situations, new modes of the capitalist leisure industry and the affects of the body not reducible to the eye."[26] This point—that mass-produced thrill ties in with much earlier ways of human performance—supports the assertion that new materials, technologies, and modes of communication are tools that enable humans to continue doing what has always been at the core of the human condition: living in community, communicating, consuming, gathering, playing: "The second industrial revolution . . . does not present us with such crushing images as rolling mills and molten steel, but with 'bits' in a flow of information traveling along circuits in the form of electronic impulses."[27]

To summarize so far: my thesis is that there is a universal nature to play, sport, and the Internet; there is a universal nature to what it means to be human. I am fascinated by anthropological questions about humankind—What is it that makes us human? Over large time swaths and geographies, how are people the same, yet also different?

* * *

Sport studies have made great accomplishments exoticizing and critiquing particular cultural and temporal practices associated with sport, and these interpretations most always are supported by assumptions that sport originates in one or all of the Enlightenment, the Western industrial revolution, or in Others' folk traditions.[28] Yet in cultural and historical studies of sport, discussion such as I undertake about sport's nature or essence are a bit taboo.[29] There are several reasons for this—logically, if "radical contextualism," conjuncturalism, and an unearthing of the social, economic, political, and technological matrices of cultural forms are key to the epistemology and ontology of critical cultural and historical studies, then supposedly sport cannot be engaged in as "a foundational, originary or essential category"[30] and "cultural humanism"[31] is dismissed. Most of the large body of sport sociology-cultural-historical scholarship over the past half-century strips or never takes into consideration sports' essential meaning; the uniqueness, fluidity of the sociohistorical moment always matters.

Norman Denzin, a leading scholar of qualitative methodology who has influenced a slew of scholars working in sport studies today, applauds our groundbreaking reading of sport as "a major site for the articulation of issues of agency and capital, race and gender, the media and celebrity."[32] He outlines four paired themes in which social texts can be analyzed: "(a) the 'real' and its representation in the text, (b) the text and the author, (c) lived experience and its textual representations, and (d) the subject and his or her intentional meanings."[33] I add an additional theme—"the text's universal nature or origin"—to his list of the possibilities of our analyses.[34]

The notion of universality may at first raise disapproval—it evokes reductionism, utopianism, the idea of stable tradition, rejection of relativism (arguably a core tenet of humanities and social science), dangerous conformity, a return to harmful ideas about gender, race, and ability. Boyd counters that such an approach is "not reductive but expansive; . . . does not entail genetic determinism," and he points out the irony that we accept human physical evolution as fact but "resist seeing human minds and behavior as shaped in any way by our deep past"; anthropologists' "stress on human diversity . . . led them to overlook human universals"; "a biocultural view of human nature does not exclude or slight the social or the cultural."[35] In this light, Bruno Latour writes that human actions are to be recognized as "polytemporal . . . I may use an electric drill, but I also use a hammer. The former is thirty-five years old, the later hundreds of thousands. . . . my habits range in age from a few days to several thousand years . . . Are we traditional then? Not that either. . . . We have never moved either forward or backward. We have always actively sorted out elements belonging to different times. We can still sort. *It is the sorting that makes the times, not the times that make the sorting* . . . We are not emerging from an obscure past . . . Modernization has never occurred."[36]

Here is another example from Daniel Miller and Alfred Gell,[37] anthropologists of art. Each sought to understand the "nature and significance of the internet."[38] They acknowledged the novelty of the "transformation of temporality involved in such an expansion of space-time" as the Internet, but they ended up saying that their conclusions were "highly recognizable in terms of that most classic of anthropological case studies—the Kula. . . . As aesthetic forms, websites may be considered artworks whose purpose is to entrap or captivate other wills so that they will come into relationship with them exchanging either in economic or social intercourse. . . . persons and companies in cyberspace [capture] the attention and custom of others to come back in that form of social efficacy that may be called Fame, which includes wealth, power and reputation."[39] Humans continue to enact and perform classic human behavior via the Internet, so now we turn to sport, one of those archetypal human behaviors. Technologies, materialities, and the scope and size of human communities may change in terms of how sport—including its tools and technologies—are communicated, spectated, played, and consumed digitally, virtually, but sport perseveres as a universal activity with original meaning.

That sport and its peripherals have some foundational, originary, or essential quality does not in any way preclude the idea that sport also has temporal and cultural contexts: sport in all of its manifestations in modernity does serve the interests of the maintenance and ongoing consent of particular dominant visions of race, state, media, nation, and so on; our theorizing of popular sporting institutions and practices can tell us much about "conjunctural moments."[40] For example, Imani Perry and Kyle Kusz shed light on how particular narratives and sites of culture (for Kusz, sport) "whether knowingly or even unwittingly" are "constituted by, and constitutive of," white normativity and white supremacy.[41]

* * *

What, though, is sport? At its simplest, it is organized play and games, an "exclusively human phenomenon,"[42] a universal institution of human community. Bernard Suits's definition of a game, "to engage in activity directed towards bringing about a specific state of affairs . . . using only means permitted by rules . . . where the rules prohibit more efficient in favor of less efficient means . . . and where such rules are accepted just because they make possible such activity,"[43] fits contemporary classification of organized competitive zero-sum sport, but there are also aspects of sport in which participants, spectators, and consumers engage sport as art, pornography, beauty, destruction, mortification, pretend-play, collecting, religion, gambling, and mourning. David Sansone claims that such examples, as well as dance and drama—non-zero-sum activities—are also linked to sport's prehistoric ritual origins.[44] Sansone postulates: "There is no essential difference between modern sport and the sport of other and earlier societies . . . The ethologist's definition of ritual is of great value in the understanding of sport. Specifically it enables us, as no other approach can, to account for the persistence of specific sports in contexts in which they appear to be inappropriate."[45] Sansone stands in contrast to theorists such as Allen Guttmann (who understand sport today as a unique product of modernity),[46] asserting that there is no difference between modern sport and the sport of other and earlier societies. Since he is trained in classics, and because there is an abundance of evidence from antiquity, Sansone employs evidence from ancient Greece and then contemporary ethnographic evidence to substantiate his thesis—the Greeks are no different from modern people; they are in a "unique mediatory position, capable of experiencing what is at the root of human feeling and consciousness and they communicated it to us in terms that are familiar to us."[47] Especially utilizing Karl Meuli, Walter Burkert, and studies of sacrifice such as by Pierre Vidal-Naquet, Sansone comprehends sport to be "the ritual sacrifice of physical energy,"[48] arguing that the exertion and ritual that originally/formerly went into the Paleolithic hunt (2.6 million to 10,000 years before the present) developed into ritualized sacrifice that took the form of sport: the expenditure of energy, a feature of the hunt, was symbolically ritualized as sport.

What kind of symbolic energy is being ritually sacrificed in sport? Sansone's thesis is that humans hunted for over 95 percent of their history, and that this symbolic surplus energy[49] used by the whole community toward hunting became sport when hunting was no longer necessary to human survival. So the preparation of the hunter's body before the hunt; fabrication and care of hunting tools; the hunt itself; preparation, cooking, eating, and storing of the slain animal; appeasement of the slain animal; observation of hunters' departures for the hunt; and creation of art/music associated with the hunt are examples of ways that all community members were somehow ritually/symbolically involved in some aspect of the hunt, however distant that involvement from the actual slaying of the hunted: "The patterns of behavior that developed over a period of more than one hundred thousand years have tended to persist precisely because those were the patterns of behavior that enabled man to develop successfully. Those patterns could not be eradicated in the relatively brief span of time since man has ceased depending upon hunting. Or, rather, there is no need for them to be abandoned, for they could be turned to a different purpose."[50]

From Julian Huxley and Konrad Lorenz, Sansone borrows the concept of "cultural ritualization": "A behavior pattern by means of which a species [or] a cultured society . . . deals with certain environmental conditions, acquires an entirely new function, that of communication. The primary function may still be performed, but it often recedes more and more into the background and may disappear completely so that a typical change of function is achieved."[51] "Cultural ritualization" functions as a means of communication or display, encourages group cohesion, and "tends toward exaggeration, stylization and repetition."[52] By the time of the ancient Greeks (10,000 BC onward), sport is a kind of exaggerated, communicative, symbolic activity that has replaced the symbols and motifs of Paleolithic hunters.[53]

In an explanation too complicated to condense here, Sansone presents evidence that suggests that Paleolithic hunters understood that they must "kill to live," so they ritualized blood sacrifice, vivification of the carcass, as acts of bereavement for, or reconstitution of, the prey after killing; the victim was honored for giving up life:[54] "The message encoded by this ritual is that one must give up something of oneself in order to live. It is not only that the life of the beast must be 'taken' in order for the hunter to survive; the hunter must give of his own energy in order to get. Once this becomes the message that the ritual is intended to communicate . . . it no longer matters on what the energy is expended."[55] He or she who can run the fastest, throw the farthest, lift the most, and so on, has the greatest amount of energy to sacrifice; the winner of a race or contest is symbolically worthiest of honor because he or she has the greatest amount of energy to sacrifice. Thus the fixation on holding up athletes as role models, leaders, celebrities—the status of athletes every bit communicated or played in digital culture today. Sansone's understanding of athletes as sacrificial victims also comments on the persistence of the competitive aspect of sport: "He who sacrifices most lavishly has the most to sacrifice and is therefore worthy of the greatest honor."[56]

Sansone's theory is that sport is inherent to human communities because it is one of the images of the expenditure of symbolic energy to which the collective emote of much earlier trappings/rituals/ceremonies/practices that prehistoric human community intensely devoted/invested itself. Sansone emphasizes that although the athletic contest "is the means whereby the sacrifice of human energy takes place . . . it makes little difference whether I choose to engage personally in the ritual or . . . observe . . . athletic displays on my behalf."[57] His theory also specifies that sport is primarily a symbolic sacrifice not a competition: "The competitive aspects of sport and of other forms of sacrifice are secondary and are not essential to the message that is communicated, which is, in effect, 'I am in possession of a surplus and I am aware that by giving up part or all of my surplus I will ensure the possession of a surplus in the future' . . . Sport becomes competitive as readily as other forms of sacrifice, but competition is epiphenomenal."[58]

* * *

If sport is the ritual-symbolic sacrifice of human physical energy, then following are some considerations.

First, from Jaron Lanier's far-ranging thought on technology and digital culture (of which it is impossible to fully explicate here except to highly recommend) we have again the assertion that there is a primary text to human experience: to reveal themselves, to create, to communicate meaning through things. Cyberspace, music, sport; present-day Wikipedia, Twitter, and Facebook entries all attest to this collective timeless human endeavor.[59] As well, Lanier's ideas mirror the thesis of Huizinga that play makes the human universe—Lanier calls for changes in digital culture that feature humanism and spirituality. Notably, Lanier also identifies and offers solutions for the "dark sides" of digital culture that have to do with anonymity, nostalgia, cybernetic totalism, juvenilia, hive mentality, digital serfdom, posthuman communication/loss of personhood, gadget fetishism, and myths of empowerment, freedom, free market, and democratization. Lanier's many ideas should be processed and critiqued in terms of sport studies; for example, he points out that a good deal of what is on the web comprises "expression originally created within the sphere of old media . . . TV shows, major movies, commercial music releases, and video games . . . The cumulative result is that online culture is fixated on the world as it was before the web was born."[60]

Lanier called my attention to digital serfdom of which I found overpowering illustrations at amazon.com's Mechanical Turk: "Businesses and developers have access to scalable work force" and workers complete "Human Intelligence Tasks" (HITS) in return for miniscule reward. On August 6, 2012, HITS for "sport" include "write a 400 word article . . . 2 dollars [salary];" "Draw circle around moving human joints in a video for 60 minutes . . . [salary] 10 cents;" "Submit Contact Info for Websites and Blogs Related to Sports in the Summer Olympics . . . 50 cents for 60 minutes."[61]

So as can be seen in the above Mechanical Turk samples, just because something is ritually or symbolically ingrained in the human condition (as is sport) does not mean it is savior. Yet interestingly, both the realms of sport and digital culture are glorified as community-building, as vehicles toward peace and development; it's not uncommon for sport to be comprehended as having the capacity to forge "good citizenship," "morals," and "solidarity," and to keep children away from illicit activities.[62] Sport studies, popular culture, and policies such as those of the International Olympic Committee (IOC) and the United Nations Educational, Scientific and Cultural Organization (UNESCO) concentrate on ideas about sport as a right (for example, of all humans to play, have fun, compete, excel, or test physicality) or sport as a tool (for peace, development, equality, freedom, and deterrence from illicit drug use or HIV/AIDS).[63] To me, all of these point to the fact that the symbolic energy expended on practices of the prehistoric hunt that solidified the community and continued as part of the human condition hundreds of thousands of years later (Sansone's thesis about sport) indeed have continuing resonance in the sport of humans today.

Raymond Williams's idea that "certain experiences, meaning and values which cannot be expressed or substantially verified . . . are nevertheless lived and practiced on the basis of the residue . . . of some previous social and cultural institution or formation"[64] also mirrors this appreciation of the enduring essence of sport. But this essence of sport is not about muscular Christianity, peace, development, abstinence, team spirit, role models, nationalism, and/or the many functions sport supposedly serves in modernity as humans convince themselves in their hegemonic narratives. Sport is popular and important today because its original nature carries on. The cultural sensibilities surrounding sport as an instrument and/or individual or communitarian tool of transformative power succeed marvellously because sport is and has always been from its origin (as Sansone's thesis argues) the ritual-symbolic sacrifice of human physical energy.[65] Sport resonates with humans because it is a cultural formation that has biocultural, neurological association with what it is to be human. That many community members have no interest or involvement in sport does not refute this treatise about the meaning of sport. As Sansone demonstrates, the prehistoric hunt had some community members not ritually invested in the activity, but nonetheless the kinesthetic, bioneurological, symbolic logic of the community ritual symbolically grew and endured.

It is here that Seligman et al.'s thesis complicates and adds to Sansone's and Boyd's; in my opinion, Seligman et al. support Sansone's special understanding of ritual in terms of sport, and I find their distinguished volume valuable for the theory-vocabulary that facilitates my own treatise.

For Sansone and Seligman et al., ritual is not some habit that humans do when they are at a certain stage of community evolutionary development, nor is it a particularly or solely religious phenomenon or event,[66] nor would ritual be limited to define things such as opening ceremonies, players' ritual activities, or calendrical rites tied to sport. Instead, ritual in all of its expressions functions *not* to provide harmony to human community but ritual formally constructs boundaries and repetition (ritual is repetitive, social, temporary, and sometimes has no speakable meaning).[67]

For Seligman et al., the human condition has always been "incomprehensible," "broken," "tragic"; these are not unique conditions of modernity or our present day. The authors contend that utopia cannot be achieved (the world is fundamentally broken) and that it is in the doing of action through ritual that we recognize and learn how to live within and between different boundaries *rather than seeking to dissolve them*.[68] If Seligman is correct, then our innumerable sport for peace and development projects need to take a different view of sports' functions. Concurrently, global sport can be explored in ways other than "indigenous," "other," "non-Western"; instead, "geographical region or tradition can be explicated . . . [sport can be] treated as regional inflections of a global phenomenon."[69]

Seligman et al.'s thesis criticizes modern preoccupation with autonomy and "sincerity" (believed to be crucial to understanding ritual). The authors define sincerity as truth, unity, wholeness, order, autonomy, coherency, authenticity, and individualism, and they observe the tension today between ritual and sincerity—we moderns have erroneously understood sincerity as vital to the organization and workings of human society and there are enormous pressures in modernity to move in sincere directions: "The world we currently inhabit has an overwhelming tendency to understand reality (shared social reality as well as individual reality) in terms taken from the sincere side of the spectrum rather than from the ritual one."[70] One of Seligman et al.'s examples of the "sincere side of the spectrum" is that much music today is judged to be good when it appears to come from depths of the self rather than music that repeats or uses old traditions.[71] And in contemporary Christian church services, there is a move toward sincerity as criticized by Seligman et al. because novelty, stimulation, and entertainment are weighed positively in contrast to repetitive chanting, ancient liturgies, or trance-like states. The authors' various examples show how particular sincere engagements with the world reject the subjunctive "as if" of the world, replacing it with "as is": "a substantive content that can then be manipulated in terms of whatever grand narrative the culture advocates . . . We are often too concerned with exploring different forms of self-expression and individual authenticity to appreciate the rhythmic structure of the shared subjunctive that is the deepest work of ritual."[72] Interpreting sport via Seligman et al. and Sansone, the grand narrative—the *as is* of modernity that alternately suspects and celebrates sport as a form of recreation or entertainment—can be replaced with the subjunctive *as if* that outrightly accepts sport "as part of our serious cultural life."[73]

With Seligman et al., Sansone, and Boyd, we can say that sport is a ritual whose repetition continually makes the past into the present;[74] sport repeats itself in the world, in digital culture, because it is a human ritual that has symbolic imperative in human society.

* * *

Related to the theme of universality and sport is the topic of gender identities. If sport is ingrained in what it is to be human, then what does biological sex have to do with creativity and sport? Many cultural and feminist studies assume women and men to be identical in given nature—that from birth it is cultural relativism that constructs woman to be a deviant binary of man. Yet, although the body's biological sexes, male and female, may not oppress and may not be identical in nature, sport theorists shy away from acknowledging or explaining what seem to be natural biological sex tendencies; for example, in females to have special caring ways, holistic spirituality, "sisterhood," and unique ontological and epistemological comprehensions of sport. In my opinion, queer understandings of the body, efforts such as Luce Irigaray's call for new language,[75] seem to parallel what inquiry might continue in terms of the nature of sport. The promise of using Sansone, Seligman et al., and Boyd to found my understanding of sport is that these theories are queer in the sense that they imagine sport and play in their ritualized context to be void of sexual existence. Sansone's thesis allows the interpretation that women, children, and the disabled were symbolically taken up in the hunt.

Relativistic analyses of the pleasures, emotes, eros, and beauty of sport in academic sport studies also seem to speak to the collective human condition, yet the existence of a shared universal experience is rarely acknowledged in our scholarship. Correspondingly, if we centralize the premise that sport is primarily a symbolic sacrifice—not a competition—then insightful transdisciplinary journeys are ahead.

As we undertake consideration of these above paradigms, it might mean altering definitions of research and data. For example, the "neuroscientific *turn*"[76] holds promise to illuminate my argument about digital culture and the nature of sport. Jenell Johnson and Melissa Littlefield identify new subfields in which the aims of the humanities/social science are pursued by scientists, and in which technologies such as magnetic resonance imaging (MRI) and computed tomography (CT) scanners are used to evaluate beauty, fitness, knowledge, and morals.[77] Victoria Pitts-Taylor asserts: "This manifesto is for those of us who do not consider ourselves as belonging to one of the scientific fields generating official brain knowledge. We need a neurocultural manifesto because the brain has been put forward by others as foundational for knowing about the self and social life, because neuroscientists are being asked to be the philosophers, sociologists and gender theorists of our era—they are being asked to do our jobs—are responding with enthusiasm, and also because brain matter is mattering."[78] Alva Noë, considered a pioneer of the neuro-cultures turn, reiterates: "In this era of expensive and flashy new brain-imaging technologies . . . hardly a day goes by without . . . reports of important breakthrough and new discoveries . . . Our problem is that we have been looking for consciousness where it isn't . . . consciousness is not something that happens inside us . . . Human experience is a dance that unfolds in the world and with others. You are not your brain."[79]

Because research into neuroscience, neural connections, neuro plasticity, and so on has only recently become possible,[80] scholars can study embodiment, perception, consciousness, and environment in relation with thought about the nature of sport.[81] We can take up earlier (1983) lines of thought (from Victor Turner in the year of his death): "Creative processes result from a coadaptation, perhaps in ritual itself, of genetic and cultural information . . . of play and 'ludic recombination.' Intimately related to ritual, play may function in the social construction of reality analogous to mutation and variation in organic evolution . . . My career focus mostly has been on the ritual process, a cultural phenomenon . . . But I am at least half convinced that there can be genuine dialogue between neurology and culturology."[82] And too, Raymond Williams, one of the founders of cultural studies, regarding the brain: "The evolution of the human brain, and then the particular interpretations carried by particular cultures, give us certain 'rules' or 'models,' without which no human being can 'see' in the ordinary sense."[83] Hence, there is a challenge to characterize play and sport further in terms of ideas of neuroscience.

* * *

By linking various stand-alone schools of thought about play, sport, and evolutionary and phenomenological understandings of human nature, I tried to further understanding of the nature of sport, tried to come to terms with an essential quality of sport. A predominant modern mythos embedded in popular and academic perceptions of sport decrees that ping-pong serves as cultural diplomacy, that the Paralympics help to normalize the "Other," that playing on the youth football team builds character, that Palestinians and Israelis who skateboard or surf together are contributing toward world peace, and so on. I straightforwardly argue that these and all such sport-embellished circumstances/settings/conditions are not about sport but are circumstances of any and all activities of public life, including those aspects of public life performed in solitary or secret (such as watching sports on TV, or daydreams about an Olympic medal). What we should find riveting about sport is that it continues to be the cultural vehicle that pools neurological (?), primal (?) (there is absolute need to concentrate expert studies on these aspects of sport) "restored behavior"[84] of survival and human community, and it is to those subconscious essences of sport that the human race is drawn and finds readily accessible to attach all genera of invention and selected tradition.

From Boyd's work on the primacy of play and human stories, and Sansone's grand theory about the origin of sport, I emphasize that sport has an originating nature that is at the core of sports' historical universalism, longevity, and popularity. Confessing an original nature of sport does not mean, however, that people are constrained by their prehistoric consciousness, brains, or destiny; instead, to paraphrase Lanier, "free will allows us to live larger than the world's problems."[85] Sport, then, displays a variety of culturally and temporally contextual manifestations that are relative to specific conjunctural matters. However large sport allows humans to live, though, it is not sport itself that cures or heals societies or fosters development and/or peace. Sport is a formal symbolic ritual born in prehistory; yes, humans creatively embellish this cultural imperative "sport" in infinite ways (as the recent digital revolution confirms), yet in the end (as Seligman et al.'s oeuvre reasons), all sport does is place disparate individuals, communities, and nations next to each other.

Notes

1. The author acknowledges drawbacks in use of the label "the world."
2. Mosco, *The Digital Sublime: Myth, Power and Cyberspace*, 38–39, 53, 85–87, 117.
3. Calvino, *Six Memos for the Next Millennium*, 7, inspires: "I have to change my approach, look at the world from a different perspective, with a different logic and with fresh methods of cognition and verification."
4. Dunbar, *Grooming, Gossip and the Evolution of Language*.
5. Briggs and Burke, *A Social History of the Media: From Gutenberg to the Internet*, 1–14.
6. Levine et al., *The Cluetrain Manifesto: 10th Anniversary Edition*, 81–83.
7. Roberts, Arth, and Bush, "Games in Culture."
8. Sutton-Smith, *Toys as Culture*, 70–72; Sydnor Slowikowski, "The Culture of Nintendo: Another Look," 3–5; 11–12. See also Sutton-Smith, "Games as Models of Power."
9. Parikka, *What is Media Archaeology?*, 3. See also Lanier, *You Are Not A Gadget: A Manifesto*, regarding the thesis that there is nothing new in the world; that much of what humans have created in culture stems from early human community.
10. James, *Beyond a Boundary*, 203–4.
11. Barthes, *What is Sport?*
12. Ibid., 3, 45–47, 57, 59.
13. McNeill, *Keeping Together in Time: Dance and Drill in Human History*, 150, 152.
14. By peripherals I mean anything, anyone, and everything connected to sport in any way—see Rinehart, *Players All: Performances in Contemporary Sport*.
15. Boyd, *On the Origin of Stories: Evolution, Cognition and Fiction*, 11. Boyd does not treat sport in his theory, but mentions it once (p. 87) in his explanation of play and art as similar to non-zero-sum games.
16. Boyd, *On the Origin of Stories: Evolution, Cognition and Fiction*, 414.
17. I use the definition of play attributed to Gregory Bateson by colleagues Robert Fagen and Alan Ingham over the years: "Play is play when you know that you are playing." While Bateson perhaps did not publish those specific words, his argument in "Theory of Play and Fantasy" (in *Steps to an Ecology of the Mind*) encompasses

that idea. See also Guttmann, *Sports: The First Five Millennia*, 4, citing anthropologist Ommo Grupe: "Sport means whatever the participants embedded in their cultures say it means."

18. For example, see Huizinga, *Homo Ludens: A Study of the Play Element in Culture*; Seligman et al., *Ritual and Its Consequences: An Essay on the Limits of Sincerity*; Sansone, *Greek Athletics and the Genesis of Sport*; Bateson, *Steps to an Ecology of the Mind: Collected Essays in Anthropology, Psychiatry, Evolution, and Epistemology*; Suits, *The Grasshopper: Games, Life and Utopia*; Caillois, *Man, Play and Games*; Schechner, *Performance Studies: An Introduction*; Marty, *The Mystery of the Child*; Norbeck, "Man at Play," 48; Grupe, "Sport Pedagogy: Anthropological Foundations," 371: "Play is a fundamental phenomenon of existence."

19. Huizinga, *Homo Ludens: A Study of the Play Element in Culture*, 5.

20. As highlighted by Eisen, "The Game of Death and the Dynamics of Atrocity," 275; Brown and Sutton-Smith, "Concepts of Childhood and Play: An Interview with Brian Sutton-Smith," 40; Schechner, *Performance Studies: An Introduction*; Caillois, *Man, Play and Games*, 28. Turner, "Body, Brain, and Culture," 233, says: "Playfulness is a volatile, sometimes dangerous explosive essence, which cultural institutions seek to bottle or contain in the vials of games of competition, chance, and strength, in modes of simulation such as theater, and in controlled disorientation, from roller coasters to dervish dancing."

21. Blanchard and Cheska, *The Anthropology of Sport: An Introduction*, 42–43.

22. Fagen, *Animal Play Behavior*, 495.

23. Boyd, *On the Origin of Stories: Evolution, Cognition and Fiction*, 94–95. See also 192.

24. See, for example, Karshan, *Vladimir Nabokov and the Art of Play*, 1–54.

25. Karshan, *Vladimir Nabokov and the Art of Play*, 210. See also Fagen, *Animal Play Behavior*, ix–xiv, 467, 471.

26. Parikka, *What is Media Archaeology?*, 25.

27. Calvino, *Six Memos for the Next Millennium*, 8.

28. Brownell, *Beijing's Games: What the Olympics Mean to China*, 19–47.

29. As discussed in Sydnor, "Mourning the Mascot's Demise: On Prehistoric Origins and Modern Aftermath."

30. Andrews, "Coming to Terms with Cultural Studies," 111, 114.

31. Ibid., 112.

32. Cited in King, "Stealing Cultural Studies: Dialogues with Norman K. Denzin," 386.

33. Ibid., 385.

34. Sydnor, "Mourning the Mascot's Demise: On Prehistoric Origins and Modern Aftermath," 27.

35. Boyd, *On the Origin of Stories: Evolution, Cognition and Fiction*, 2, 11, 20, 22, 25.

36. Latour, *We Have Never Been Modern*, 75–76 (emphasis in the original).

37. I include Alfred Gell's name here, as Miller makes it a point in this single-authored work (Miller, "The Fame of Trinis: Websites as Traps") that he builds posthumously upon Gell on the anthropology of art.

38. Miller, "The Fame of Trinis: Websites as Traps," 149.

39. Ibid., 153.

40. King, "Stealing Cultural Studies: Dialogues with Norman K. Denzin," 391. Also Jarvie, *Sport, Culture and Society*; Giulianotti, *Sport: A Critical Sociology*; Hargreaves, *Sport, Power and Culture*; Coakley, *Sport in Society*; Markula-Denison and Pringle, *Foucault, Sport and Exercise: Power, Knowledge and Transforming the Self*; Hughson, Inglis and Free, *The Uses of Sport*.

41. Perry, *More Beautiful and More Terrible: The Embrace and Transcendence of Racial Inequality in the United States*, 6–7, 189; King, Leonard, and Kusz, "White Power and Sport"; Kusz, *Revolt of the White Athlete*, 2, 4–5, 169.

42. Sansone, *Greek Athletics and the Genesis of Sport*, 17.

43. Suits, *The Grasshopper: Games, Life and Utopia*, 34, 41.

44. Sansone, *Greek Athletics and the Genesis of Sport*, 47–48.

45. Ibid., 6, 31. See also book reviews of Sansone by Griffin, "Playing to Win," 3–5; Segal, "The Sweat Offering," 455; Gold, book review of David Sansone, *Greek Athletics and the Genesis of Sport.*, 542; Guttmann, book review of David Sansone, *Greek Athletics and the Genesis of Sport*, 361–362. See also Schechner, *Performance Studies: An Introduction*, 221; Bateson, *Steps to an Ecology of the Mind: Collected Essays in Anthropology, Psychiatry, Evolution, and Epistemology*, 130.

46. See Guttmann, *From Ritual to Record: The Nature of Modern Sports*, 1–55.

47. Sansone, *Greek Athletics and the Genesis of Sport*, 5–6, 10–19. My discussion of Sansone's thesis in this essay is borrowed from other of my writings—see Sydnor, "Mourning the Mascot's Demise: On Prehistoric Origins and Modern Aftermath"; Sydnor, "History and Anthropology of the Penn State Tragedy," 338; Sydnor Slowikowski, "Cultural Performance and Sport Mascots," 23–24.

48. Sansone, *Greek Athletics and the Genesis of Sport*, 37.

49. Ibid., 64–66.

50. Ibid., 47.

51. Lorenz, *On Aggression*, 75, as quoted by Sansone, *Greek Athletics and the Genesis of Sport*, 31.

52. Sansone, *Greek Athletics and the Genesis of Sport*, 31–35.

53. Ibid., 49–51, 68–69, 85. See also Sydnor, "Mourning the Mascot's Demise: On Prehistoric Origins and Modern Aftermath," 23–25; Sydnor Slowikowski, "Cultural Performance and Sport Mascots," 30–31.

54. Sansone, *Greek Athletics and the Genesis of Sport*, 58- 61.

55. Ibid., 63.

56. Ibid., 64.

57. Ibid., 65–66, 80.

58. Ibid., 64.

59. See, for example, Lanier, *You Are Not A Gadget: A Manifesto*, 140, 154, 166–168.
60. Lanier, *You Are Not A Gadget: A Manifesto*, 122–123.
61. Amazon Mechanical Turk.
62. These terms are frequently used by organizations such as UNESCO, UNOSDP, UN Sport for Peace and Development, and the National Drug Abuse Resistance Education. See also Sydnor, "History and Anthropology of the Penn State Tragedy," 337.
63. See, for example, Wolff, "Sports Saves the World."
64. Williams, *Marxism and Literature*, 121–123.
65. Sansone, *Greek Athletics and the Genesis of Sport*, 64–66. See also Sydnor, "Man, Play and Games: A Review Essay," 539.
66. Seligman, et al., *Ritual and Its Consequences: An Essay on the Limits of Sincerity*, 6.
67. Ibid., 11, 15, 130.
68. Ibid., 7. See also Sydnor, "History," 338; Sydnor, "On the Nature of Sport and Play: How a Remarkable Book Inspires Rethinking Our Studies."
69. Smith, "Philosophy's Western Bias." In this quotation, Smith refers to "philosophy"; the word "sport" is my substitution.
70. Seligman, et al., *Ritual and Its Consequences: An Essay on the Limits of Sincerity*, 132.
71. Ibid., 8, 101–6.
72. Ibid., 165, 10.
73. Ibid., 164; Sansone, *Greek Athletics and the Genesis of Sport*, 77.
74. Paraphrased from Seligman, et al., *Ritual and Its Consequences: An Essay on the Limits of Sincerity*, 74; see also 103.
75. See Beattie, *New Catholic Feminism: Theology and Theory*, 7–9, 35. See also Coakley, *Sport in Society*, 276.
76. Johnson and Littlefield, *The Neuroscientific Turn: Transdisciplinarity in the Age of the Brain*; see also Johnson and Littlefield, "Lost and Found in Translation: Popular Neuroscience and the Emergent Neurodisciplines," 279–297; Frazzetto and Anker, "Neuroculture," 815–821; Vidal and Ortego, *Neurocultures: Glimpses into an Expanding Universe*. I thank Melissa Littlefield for first teaching me about and then including me in her neuro-cultures network.
77. See, for example, Johnson and Littlefield, "Lost and Found in Translation: Popular Neuroscience and the Emergent Neurodisciplines," 288–290; Johnson and Littlefield, *The Neuroscientific Turn: Transdisciplinarity in the Age of the Brain*, 1–25; 233–240.
78. Pitts-Taylor, "Neurocultures Manifesto."
79. Noë, *Out of Our Heads, Why You Are Not Your Brain, and Other Lessons from the Biology of Consciousness*, xi-xiv. See also Noë and Thompson, *Vision and Mind: Selected Readings in the Philosophy of Perception*; Noë, *Action in Perception*, 231; Frazzetto, "Teaching How to Bridge Neuroscience, Society and Culture."
80. Boyd, *On the Origin of Stories: Evolution, Cognition and Fiction*, 94, 192.

81. See, for example, Anderson and Dietrich, *The Educated Eye: Visual Culture and Pedagogy in the Life Sciences.*

82. Turner, "Body, Brain, and Culture," 221, 243. See also Lanier, *You Are Not A Gadget: A Manifesto*, 186–191; Rolls, *Neuroculture: On the Implications of Brain Science*; Noë, *Action in Perception.*

83. Williams, *The Long Revolution, An Analysis of the Democratic, Industrial, and Cultural Changes Transforming Our Society*, 18.

84. Schechner, *Performance Studies: An Introduction*, 29.

85. Lanier, *You Are Not A Gadget: A Manifesto*, 72.

References

Amazon Mechanical Turk. "Sport" entry in "HITS." August 6, 2012. Accessed August 6, 2012. https://www.mturk.com/mturk/searchbar?selectedSearchType=hitgroups&searchWords=sport&minReward=0.00&x=0&y=0; https://www.mturk.com/mturk/searchbar?selectedSearchType=hitgroups&requesterId=A1B694CLUYMYE1; https://www.mturk.com/mturk/searchbar?selectedSearchType=hitgroups&searchWords=history&minReward=0.00&x=0&y=0.

Anderson, Nancy, and Michael R. Dietrich. 2012. *The Educated Eye: Visual Culture and Pedagogy in the Life Sciences* (Interfaces: Studies in Visual Culture). Lebanon, NH: Dartmouth Press.

Andrews, David L. 2002. "Coming to Terms with Cultural Studies." *Journal of Sport and Social Issues* 26, no. 1 (February): 110–17.

Barthes, Roland. 2007. *What is Sport?* Translated by Richard Howard. New Haven, CT, and London: Yale University Press.

Bateson, Gregory. 1972. *Steps to an Ecology of the Mind: Collected Essays in Anthropology, Psychiatry, Evolution, and Epistemology.* Chicago: University of Chicago Press.

Beattie, Tina. 2006. *New Catholic Feminism: Theology and Theory.* New York: Routledge.

Blanchard, Kendall, and Alyce Taylor Cheska. 1984. *The Anthropology of Sport: An Introduction.* Westport, CN: Bergin and Garvey.

Boyd, Brian. 2009. *On the Origin of Stories: Evolution, Cognition and Fiction.* Cambridge, MA: The Belknap Press of Harvard University Press.

Briggs, Asa, and Peter Burke. 2009. *A Social History of the Media: From Gutenberg to the Internet.* 3rd ed. Malden, MA: Polity Press.

Brown, Stuart L., and Brian Sutton-Smith. 1995. "Concepts of Childhood and Play: An Interview with Brian Sutton-Smith." *ReVision* 17, no. 4: 35–42.

Brownell, Susan. 2008. *Beijing's Games: What the Olympics Mean to China.* New York: Rowman & Littlefield.

Caillois, Roger. 2001. *Man, Play and Games.* Translated by Meyer Barash. Urbana, IL: University of Illinois Press. Originally published as *Les Jeux et les Hommes* (Paris: Librairie Gallimard, 1958).

Calvino, Italo. 1988. *Six Memos for the Next Millennium*. New York: Vintage International.
Coakley, Jay. 2009. *Sport in Society* (10th ed.). New York: McGraw-Hill.
Cox, Richard H. 2012. *Sport Psychology: Concepts and Applications*. New York: McGraw Hill.
Denzin, Norman K. 1997. *Interpretive Ethnography: Ethnographic Practices for the 21st Century*. London: Sage.
Dunbar, Robin. 1997. *Grooming, Gossip and the Evolution of Language*. Cambridge: Harvard University Press.
Edmundson, Mark. 2012. "Do Sports Build Character or Damage It?" *The Chronicle Review* (January 15). Accessed January 17, 2012. http://chronicle.com/article/Do-Sports-Build-Character-or/130286/?sid=.
Eisen, George. 1997. "The Game of Death and the Dynamics of Atrocity." In *The Games of Gods and Man: Essays in Play and Performance*, edited by Peter Klaus and K. Köpping, 272–290. Hamburg: Lit Verlag.
Fagen, Robert. 1981. *Animal Play Behavior*. New York and Oxford: Oxford University Press.
———. 1984. "The Perilous Magic of Animal Play." In *The Masks of Play*, edited by Brian Sutton-Smith and Diana Kelly-Byrne, 147–153. New York: Leisure Press.
Fagen, Robert, and Synthia Sydnor. 2012. "Plotlessness, Ethnography, Ethology: Play." *Cultural Studies ↔ Critical Methodologies* 12, no. 1: 72–81.
Frazzetto, Giovanni. 2001. "Teaching How to Bridge Neuroscience, Society and Culture." *PLOS Biology* 9, no. 10. Accessed January 15, 2012. doi 10.1371/journal.pbio.1001178.
Frazzetto, Giovanni, and Suzanne Anker, 2009. "Neuroculture." *Nature Reviews Neuroscience* 10: 815–21.
Gee, James Paul. 2008. "Video Games and Embodiment." *Games and Culture* 3, no. 3–4 (July): 253–63. Accessed January 15, 2012. doi: 10.1177/1555412008317309.
Gold, Barbara K. 1990. Book review of David Sansone, *Greek Athletics and the Genesis of Sport*. *Classical World* 83, no. 6: 542.
Girard, René. 1979. *Violence and the Sacred*. Translated by Patrick Gregory. Baltimore: Johns Hopkins University Press.
Giulianotti, Richard. 2005. *Sport: A Critical Sociology*. London: Polity.
Graves, Benjamin. 1998. "Beyond a Boundary: The Aesthetics of Resistance." *Political Discourse—Theories of Colonialism and Postcolonialism*. Accessed on 20 April 2005. http://www.thecore.nus.edu.sg/post/poldiscourse/james/james2.html.
Griffin, Jasper. 1988. "Playing to Win." *New York Review of Books* (September 29): 3–5.
Grupe, Ommo. 1992. "Sport Pedagogy: Anthropological Foundations." In *Sport Science in Germany: An Interdisciplinary Anthology*, edited by Herbert Haag, Ommo Grupe, and August Kirsch, 362–378. Translated by Gerald G. Haag. Berlin: Springer-Verlag.

Guttmann, Allen. 1978. *From Ritual to Record: The Nature of Modern Sports*. New York: Columbia University Press.

———. 1988. Book review of David Sansone, *Greek Athletics and the Genesis of Sport*. *Journal of Sport History* 5: 361–62.

———. 2003. "Ideal Types and Historical Variation." In *The Essence of Sport*, edited by Verner Møller and John Naughright, 129–136. Odense: University Press of Southern Denmark.

———. 2004. *Sports: The First Five Millennia*. Amherst, MA: University of Massachusetts Press.

Handelman, Don. 1998. *Models and Mirrors: Toward an Anthropology of Public Events*. Oxford and New York: Berghan Books.

Hargreaves, John. 1986. *Sport, Power and Culture*. New York: Palgrave Macmillan.

Henderson, Robert. 1947. *Ball, Bat and Bishop: The Origin of Ball Games*. Minneapolis, MN: Rockport Press.

Hughson, John, David Inglis, and Marcus Free. 2005. *The Uses of Sport*. London: Routledge.

Huizinga, Johann. 1955. *Homo Ludens: A Study of the Play Element in Culture*. New York: Beacon Press.

James, C. L. R. 1963. *Beyond a Boundary*. New York: Pantheon Books.

Jarvie, Grant. 2006. *Sport, Culture and Society*. London: Taylor and Francis.

Johnson, Jenell, and Melissa M. Littlefield. 2011. "Lost and Found in Translation: Popular Neuroscience and the Emergent Neurodisciplines." *Sociological Reflections on Neuroscience* 13: 279–297.

Karshan, Thomas. 2011. *Vladimir Nabokov and the Art of Play*. Oxford: Oxford University Press.

King, C. Richard. 2006. "Stealing Cultural Studies: Dialogues with Norman K. Denzin." *Journal of Sport and Social Issues* 30, no. 4 (November): 383–94.

King, C. Richard, David J. Leonard, and Kyle W. Kusz. 2007. "White Power and Sport." *Journal of Sport and Social Issues* 31, no. 3.

Kusz, Kyle. 2007. *Revolt of the White Athlete*. New York: Peter Lang Publishing.

Lanier, Jaron. 2010. *You are Not a Gadget: A Manifesto*. New York: Vintage Books.

Latour, Bruno. 1993. *We Have Never Been Modern*. Cambridge, MA: Harvard University Press.

Levine, Rick, Christopher Locke, Doc Searles, and David Weinberger. 2011. *The Cluetrain Manifesto: 10th Anniversary Edition*. New York: Basic Books. First published 2000.

Littlefield, Melissa M., and Jenell M. Johnson, eds. 2012. *The Neuroscientific Turn: Transdisciplinarity in the Age of the Brain*. Ann Arbor, MI: University of Michigan Press.

Lorenz, Konrad. 1966. *On Aggression*. New York: Harcourt Brace.

Markula-Denison, Pirkko, and Richard Pringle. 2006. *Foucault, Sport and Exercise: Power, Knowledge and Transforming the Self*. New York: Routledge.

Marty, Martin E. 2007. *The Mystery of the Child*. Grand Rapids, MI: Wm. B. Eerdmans.

McNeill, William H. 1995. *Keeping Together in Time: Dance and Drill in Human History*. Cambridge, MA: Harvard University Press.

Miller, Daniel. 2001. "The Fame of Trinis: Websites as Traps." In *Beyond Aesthetics: Art and the Technologies of Enchantment*, edited by Christopher Pinney and Nicholas Thomas, 137–55. Oxford and New York: Berg.

Mosco, Vincent. 2004. *The Digital Sublime: Myth, Power and Cyberspace*. Cambridge, MA, and London: The MIT Press.

National Drug Abuse Resistance Education. "The Official Drug Abuse Resistance Education Site (D.A.R.E.). Research/resources/evaluations." Accessed October 11, 2011. http://www.dare.com/home/Resources/Default5647.asp?N=Resources&M=16&S=0.

Noë, Alva. 2006. *Action in Perception*. Cambridge, MA: MIT Press.

———. 2011. *Out of Our Heads, Why You Are Not Your Brain, and Other Lessons from the Biology of Consciousness*. New York: Hill and Wang.

Noë, Alva, and Evan Thompson. 2002. *Vision and Mind: Selected Readings in the Philosophy of Perception*. Cambridge, MA: MIT Press.

Norbeck, Edward. 1971. "Man at Play." *Natural History* 80, no. 10 (December): 48–53.

Parikka, Jussi. 2012. *What is Media Archaeology?* Cambridge and Malden, MA: Polity Press.

Perry, Imani. 2011. *More Beautiful and More Terrible: The Embrace and Transcendence of Racial Inequality in the United States*. New York: NYU Press.

Phillips, Murray G. 2008. "An Athletic Clio: Sport History and Television History." *Rethinking History* 12, no. 3 (September): 399–416.

Pitts-Taylor, Victoria. 2012. "Neurocultures Manifesto." *Social Text* (April 6). Accessed May 29, 2012. http://www.socialtextjournal.org/periscope/2012/04/neurocultures-manifesto.php).

Rinehart, Robert. 1998. *Players All: Performances in Contemporary Sport*. Bloomington, IN: Indiana University Press.

Roberts, John M., Malcolm J. Arth, and Robert R. Bush. 1959. "Games in Culture." *American Anthropologist* 61, no. 4 (August): 597–605.

Rolls, Edmund. 2012. *Neuroculture: On the Implications of Brain Science*. Oxford: Oxford University Press.

Rushdie, Salman. 2003. *Step Across This Line: Collected Nonfiction 1992–2002*. Toronto: Vintage Canada.

Sansone, David. 1988. *Greek Athletics and the Genesis of Sport*. Berkeley, CA: University of California Press.

Sartre, Jean Paul. 1956. "Play and Sport." In *Being and Nothingness*. Translated by Hazel E. Barnes. New York: Philosophical Library. Reprinted in *Philosophic Inquiry in Sport*, edited by William J. Morgan and Klaus V. Meier, 110–13. Champaign, IL: Human Kinetics, 1988.

Scanlon, T. F. 2002. *Eros and Greek Athletics.* Oxford: Oxford University Press.
Schechner, Richard. 1993. *The Future of Ritual: Writings on Culture and Performance.* London: Routledge.
———. 2006. *Performance Studies: An Introduction* (2nd ed.). New York: Routledge.
Segal, Eric. 1988. "The Sweat Offering." *Times Literary Supplement* 4: 455.
Seligman, Adam B., Robert P. Weller, Michael J. Puett, and Bennett Simon. 2008. *Ritual and Its Consequences: An Essay on the Limits of Sincerity.* Oxford: Oxford University Press.
Silk, Michael L., and David L. Andrews. 2011. "Toward a Physical Cultural Studies." *Sociology Of Sport Journal* 28, no. 1 (March): 4–35.
Slowikowski Sydnor, Synthia. 1993. "The Culture of Nintendo: Another Look." *Journal of Play Theory and Research* 1: 1–17.
Smith, Justin E.H. 2012. "Philosophy's Western Bias." *NYTimes.com.* June 3. Accessed June 4, 2012. http://opinionator.blogs.nytimes.com/2012/06/03/philosophys-western-bias/?emc=eta1.
Suits, Bernard. 1978. *The Grasshopper: Games, Life and Utopia.* New York: David R. Godine.
Sutton-Smith, Brian. 1986. *Toys as Culture.* New York: Gardner Press.
———. 1989. "Games as Models of Power." *The Content of Culture: Constraints and Variants. Studies in Honor of John M. Roberts,* edited by Ralph Bolton, 5–18. New Haven CT: Human Relations Area Files Press.
———. 2001. *The Ambiguity of Play.* Cambridge, MA: Harvard University Press.
Sydnor, Synthia. 2001. "New Times, Physical Education and Cyberspace." *Journal of Sport and Social Issues* 25, no. 4: 430–36.
———. 2005. "Man, Play and Games: A Review Essay." *Sport in History* 25, no. 3 (December): 536–44.
———. 2009. "On the Nature of Sport and Play: How A Remarkable Book Inspires Rethinking Our Studies." Unpublished paper presented at the annual meeting of the North American Society for Sport Sociology, Ottawa, Canada, November 4–7.
———. 2010. "Mourning the Mascot's Demise: On Prehistoric Origins and Modern Aftermath." In *Studies in Symbolic Interaction* 34, edited by Norman Denzin and C. Richard King, 15–31. Amsterdam: Elsevier.
———. 2012. "History and Anthropology of the Penn State Tragedy." *Cultural Studies ↔ Critical Methodologies* 12/4 (2012): 333–341. doi: 10.1177/1532708612446434.
Turner, Victor. 1982. *From Ritual to Theatre: The Human Seriousness of Play.* New York: PAJ Publications.
———. 1983. "Body, Brain, and Culture." *Zygon* 18, no. 3 (September 1): 221–45.
Turner, Victor, and Edward Bruner. 1986. *The Anthropology of Experience.* Urbana, IL: University of Illinois Press, 1986.
Vidal, Fernando, and Francisco Ortego. 2011. *Neurocultures: Glimpses into an Expanding Universe.* New York: Peter Lang GmbH.

Williams, Raymond. 1961. *The Long Revolution, An Analysis of the Democratic, Industrial, and Cultural Changes Transforming Our Society*. New York: Columbia University Press.

———. 1977. *Marxism and Literature*. Oxford: Oxford University Press.

Wolff, Alexander. 2011. "Sports Saves the World." *SI.com,* September 26. Accessed September 28, 2011. http://sportsillustrated.cnn.com/vault/article/magazine/MAG1190627/index/index.htm.

10

Who's Afraid of the Internet?

Swimming in an Infinite Archive

FIONA MCLACHLAN AND DOUGLAS BOOTH

> One of the most vexing and interesting features of the digital era is the way that it unsettles traditional arguments and forces us to ask basic questions that have been there all along. If the web page is the unit of analysis for the digital librarian and the link the unit of analysis for the computer scientists, what is the appropriate unit of analysis for historians?
> —Roy Rosenzweig[1]

The Internet is altering fundamental practices of history, including how historians gather, interpret, and present the remnants of the past.[2] In this chapter we analyze the ways that historians of sport have engaged and might engage with the Internet, which we conceptualize as both an infinitely expanding archive (with multiple viewpoints and formats such as audio and video) and a potential host for different forms of history/histories.[3] Like their colleagues working in other subdisciplines of history, historians of sport approach their subject matter through various ontological and epistemological lenses,[4] and to grasp the full extent of their engagement with the Internet, we base our analysis on three historical genres—reconstructionism, constructionism, and deconstructionism.[5]

While all historians regard the remnants of the past as the building blocks of the discipline,[6] they vary widely in the ways they conceptualize these remnants. Reconstructionists afford greatest credibility to those remnants—which they call sources—that they "discover" in official archives, and cast a jaundiced eye over sources pulled from the Internet. Constructionists interrogate remnants of the past as well as the repositories of those remnants such as archives, museums, and the Internet through the lens of social theory, and especially theories of power, which frame their assessment. However, constructionists are not united in their conceptualization of the Internet. Some view it as a site for the democratization of history, others as a threat to disciplinary values and standards, and others as contested terrain.[7] Rather than trying to access the past through its remnants, deconstructionists focus their attention on the production of historical narratives and are as much interested in the form of historical narratives (for example, structural characteristics such as tropes, emplotment, voice) as with the content (that is, the selection of remnants—which deconstructionists call fragments or traces—and their interpretation). The wide range of narrative forms hosted by sites like YouTube makes the Internet particularly interesting to deconstructionists, especially those wishing to produce reflexive forms of historical narrative.[8]

In elucidating these three conceptualizations of, and approaches to, the Internet, we employ a case study of swimming pools. Cultural sites with a long past, multiple histories, and a plethora of interpretations, swimming pools have a considerable presence on the Internet. In this chapter we propose how historians working in different genres of the discipline might engage with the remnants of the past and narratives related to swimming pools that they find on the Internet and how they might use the Internet to present different forms of historical narrative.

Reconstructionism

Given historians' penchant for "stable, authentic, persistent and legible" sources,[9] it is hardly surprising that some "view ... the internet with skepticism."[10] Computer scientist Jeff Rothenberg articulated popular concerns regarding the instability of Internet sources when he observed that "digital documents last forever—or five years, whatever comes first,"[11] while Gertrude Himmelfarb, a leading American historian and well-known critic of alternative historical approaches (for example, quantitative history, Marxist history, psychoanalytical history, social history, postmodern history), alluded to the problem of authenticity when she complained that the Internet "does not distinguish between true and false, the important and the trivial, the enduring and the ephemeral." Internet search engines, Himmelfarb continued, "produce a comic strip or advertising slogan as readily as a quotation from the Bible or Shakespeare."[12] Daniel Cohen similarly identifies a list of problems with the Internet including "lack of stability and persistence" and unfriendly and poor "formats for text, especially for ... long-form narratives."[13] Of course, as Michael Hancher noted in a response to Himmelfarb, new technology invariably produces such laments. As an example, Hancher cited the emergence of the tabloid press a century earlier that provoked warnings of "threats to the dignity of serious publications."[14]

Historians of sport in fact adapted to the Internet quite quickly. Today, they regularly cite historical statistics, anecdotes, and discussions gathered from the Internet. In so doing, historians of sport demonstrate their ability to assess the credibility of Internet sources (for example, whether they derive from a site sponsored by a scientific society, a nameless comment on an unmoderated Usenet newsgroup, a homemade YouTube clip, a remark or photograph on Twitter, or correspondence on Facebook), just as they have always assessed remnants of the past irrespective of origins or form.[15] Increasingly the Internet, and more specifically a Google search and the accompanying Wikipedia hit, is the first port of call for historians broaching a new topic.[16] Indeed, entering "swimming pool history" into a Google search produces a Wikipedia entry that begins with a definition of a swimming pool as "a container filled with water intended for swimming or water-based recreation."[17] Social historians of swimming readily identify with this conceptualization given that most proceed from the assumption that swimming predated public swimming pools, and that most advance the view that public pools emerged as official responses to fears of aimless narcissism in uncontained waters.[18] In this sense, swimming pools represent socially imposed limits and controls over water spaces used for recreational bathing and swimming. Internet sources also typically support the findings from the social history of swimming literature. For example, in a YouTube trailer for their DVD *A History of Swimming*, Ralf Breier and Claudia Kuhland note the long history of swimming and refer to 8,000 year-old cave paintings of swimmers.[19]

The Internet is a convenient repository of various remnants of the past and has removed many of the constraints on access to collections in traditional archives such as "time," "expense," and "entrance requirements."[20] In the case of swimming pools, the Internet hosts sites (for example, San Francisco's Sutro Baths, Australia's ocean baths, watering holes and swimming pools in Texas, Beijing's Water Cube, Rotorua's Blue Baths, and Sydney's Andrew "Boy" Charlton Pool[21]) provide access to artifacts (for example, the International Swimming Hall of Fame virtual museum[22]) and official documents pertaining to the provision of aquatic facilities and services, and the relationship between provision, maintenance, governance, and management of public swimming pools (for example, New Zealand's *Local Government Act* 2002, the New Zealand Ministry of Education's *Handbook Supporting*

Documents and Policies: Section 7 Operational Policies, and Auckland City Council's *Council Swimming Pool Strategy*). Internet tools such as Google Alerts facilitate the collection of news items. For example, a Google alert for articles containing the key words "swimming pool" and "swimming baths" produced nearly 4,000 articles over 18 months between January 2010 and July 2011. These articles included the serious (for example, pool closures in Britain, the provision of public pools in the United States) and the bizarre (a cow swimming in a pool, a wedding ceremony in a pool).[23]

Yet, notwithstanding their adaption to the Internet, reconstructionist historians of sport still gravitate to official websites and digital archives that, like official documents and physical archives, carefully control content and present an aura of stability. Among some historians, the advance of the Internet as an ever expanding, uncontrolled, repository of materials is a concern. "Who will decide," asked Stephen Hardy in 1999, "what 'real' sources should be scanned into a virtual archive?" Continuing, Hardy argued that:

> This is not quite the same as creating bound, hardcopy compilations of primary sources. Most of those are transcribed; many are annotated. Even the lay reader recognises they are processed by intermediaries. Virtual archives are different. They appear to offer everything but smell and touch. This is no small issue; it is one of the *major* questions that professional archivists are now addressing. Their concerns were shared with me by David Kelly, the Library of Congress's reference expert on sport (among other topics): "I think a lot of people are going to use what's convenient. They might have used only their local library or university library and not gone the extra mile or two to use a larger library, so now they can just sit at home and surf." The question is: *which* experts will decide *what* the public researchers surf?[24]

Of course, control over the remnants of the past is not peculiar to the Internet. The issue surfaced long ago in discussions about traditional archival collections.

In his aptly named *Silencing the Past*, Michel-Rolph Trouillot reminds us that archiving, the process of assembling remnants of the past, is by no means a "passive act." On the contrary, archiving is "an active act of production" that "involves a number of selective operations: selection of producers, selection of evidence, selection of themes, selection of procedures which means, at best, the differential ranking and, at worst, the exclusion of some producers, some evidence, some themes, some procedures."[25] The "racialized" colonial archives of the Illawarra region of New South Wales, which Christine Metusela and Gordon Waitt argue "blatantly disregard" Aboriginal cultural attachments to both the beach and swimming, is a good example of active exclusion.[26]

Such discussions further highlight the misleading nature of Himmelfarb's criticisms above regarding the inability of the Internet to discern between relevant and irrelevant, and authentic and inauthentic sources. The remnants of the past do not choose themselves or arrange themselves into narratives; active historians choose which remnants of the past they gather and how they arrange them into a narrative. In our view, it is preferable that historians clearly identify to their readers the criteria they use to guide their choices rather than to persist with the reconstructionist fallacies that official archives are objective repositories of remnants from the past, and that these remnants are transparent reflections of the past and tell a story without any intervention on the part of the historian.

Similarly, concerns about the stability of digital sources and their apparent fleeting and blurred nature apply to many nondigital forms. Ironically, computer technology offers the historian tools to preserve digital sources (and in a sense become their own archivists). Microsoft's snipping tool, for example, enables users to capture pages, texts, images, and pieces of weblogs (or blogs) in the same way that historians have traditionally cut articles, letters to the editor, opinion pieces, and photographs from newspapers. The snipping tool preserves remnants as they looked at the moment of discovery and with such accuracy that it is often difficult to distinguish between some original images and copies.[27] Admittedly, the perfect digital copy does not translate into an eternally preserved copy, as Rothenberg explains:

> The physical lifetimes of digital storage media are often surprisingly short, requiring information to be "refreshed" by copying it onto new media with disturbing frequency. Moreover, most digital documents and artifacts exist only in encoded form, requiring specific software to bring their bit streams to life and make them truly usable; as these programs (or the hardware/software environments in which they run) become obsolete, the digital documents that depend on them become unreadable—held hostage to their own encoding.[28]

But words on documents also fade, manuscripts tear, and fire can destroy archives.[29]

While unofficial websites might raise ontological and epistemological concerns among some reconstructionists, there is nothing inherently different between digital and nondigital data. Both are remnants of human activity and, as such, both constitute the primary building blocks of historical endeavor. In short, the notion of a web-based category of sources is analytically specious. Nonetheless, we propose that diving into the Internet has the potential to afford reconstructionists rich rewards without compromising their practice.

At this point, however, we discuss constructionist and deconstructionist conceptualizations of the Internet.

Constructionism

Recontructionists deem history an objective discipline in which historians verify their sources as transparent reflections of the past and present them in narratives; mediation, whether of the sources or the narrative, is antithetical to reconstructionist practice.[30] By contrast, constructionists insist that *a priori* knowledge in the form of concepts, contexts, and theories always precedes the sources and mediates their gathering, interrogation, and presentation.[31] The Internet throws these opposing genres into sharp relief by expanding the volume of sources requiring mediation (that is, the sources from which historians must choose when determining their interpretations and composing their narratives) and the range of interactivity between authors and their audiences and between different audiences.[32]

Among constructionists, theory is integral to the mediation of sources. "The writer of history who desires to be more than a mere antiquarian must have a thorough *theoretical* training in those fields of inquiry with which his work is concerned," wrote Werner Sombart.[33] While not denying that historians require an intimate and technical knowledge of their sources, Sombart insisted that the "true historian" embraced theory. Constructionists place theory at the center of history for at least three reasons. First, as already noted, the range and volume of evidence bearing on many historical questions is large; the Internet compounds this issue. Historians cannot avoid selection, and theory is a critical tool that provides frameworks and principles for selecting evidence and orienting practitioners toward coherent and consistent explanations. Second, theory brings to the fore interrelations between the components of human experiences at given times and in so doing enriches historical accounts. Third, identifying historical patterns invariably involves some form of abstract thinking and connections to theoretical explanations and interpretations. Responding to the reconstructionist charge that theory predetermines history, constructionists counter that theories enhance understanding and that no one can "approach their evidence innocent of presupposition."[34]

These questions and debates emerge in discussions around the history of swimming, which is also theoretically mediated. For example, evidence for the function of swimming and for the emergence of swimming pools supports different perspectives: swimming appears as both a natural practice and a cultural practice. In the case of the former, swimming supposedly meets physiological,[35] psychological,[36] and spiritual[37] needs. As a cultural practice, swimming has been codified and institutionalized as a social benefit.[38] Might the Internet facilitate further theorization of human swimming and its development?

All histories are selected stories that reflect prevailing material and theoretical conditions, as well as the historian's political position including his or her orientation toward time—past, present, or future—as the repository of the ideal social structure.[39] Jeff Wiltse's *Contested Waters* (2007) is an archetypal example of an emancipatory, social history approach to public swimming pools in the United States that passes judgment on human values and propriety, offers critiques of structures and relations of power, and advocates for social and political change.[40] According to Wiltse, human-made swimming structures are hallmarks of equal opportunities that contribute to the democratization of national culture by facilitating the participation of "ordinary and even marginalized members of society . . . in the production of public culture."[41] The Internet will not eliminate the theoretical and political commitments that historians bring to their narratives and which configure their representations.[42] Nonetheless, the Internet facilitates different types of analyses, not least by enabling searches of the dominant, and dominating, cultural logic that privileges the construction of particular narratives over others. Referring to these new analyses, Cohen notes that historians initially searched the Internet for exhibits, artifacts, and secondary sources; in so doing, they focused on "*nouns* such as webpages and Web sites." More recently, they have switched to "*verbs* such as searching, sorting, gathering and communicating" with a view to "mining" the Internet for patterns and trends, that is, to exploit the Internet's matchless ability to store, scan, and interrelate documents.[43]

The *New York Times* illustrated the potential of mining during the 2012 olympic games in London. The newspaper collected data from 140 olympians with a verifiable Twitter handle (that is, username and URL) and used a streamgraph to visualize discussions and mentions of each athlete on Twitter over the course of the games. (The streamgraph only represented those olympians who received 1,000 or more mentions.) For example, American swimmer Michael Phelps received a relatively modest and stable 150 to 200 mentions per 1,000 followers during the course of his olympic campaign between July 30 and August 5, in contrast to South African swimmer Chad Le Clos, who received over 300 mentions on July 31, and British diver Thomas Daley, who received over 300 mentions on July 30. Graphs, of course, are generalizations and require interpretation and close analysis. The *New York Times* added text boxes to its Twitter streamgraph to explain that Le Clos delivered Phelps a surprise defeat, beating the American by 0.05 seconds in the 200-meter butterfly, and that Daley was "caught in a firestorm" when a youth tweeted that the diver had "disappointed his late father" by failing to win a medal in the 10-meter synchronized event. However, the paper made no mention that Phelps' campaign included winning his twenty-second olympic medal (eighteen gold) to become the holder of the most olympic medals (surpassing Soviet gymnast Larisa Latynina).[44]

Cohen identifies other approaches to mining the Internet that could potentially benefit historians of swimming. Just as "classicists and literary scholars . . . count the frequency of certain words, or compare the various uses of those words, in a text or set of texts,"[45] so historians of swimming could search digitalized collections and manuscripts on the Internet for the frequency of words such as *bathing* and *swimming*. They could investigate the variety of themes associated with these terms (for example, leisure, recreation, sport, survival, therapy, tragedy) and the way such themes change over time. "Future inquiries," Cohen adds, may employ the "extremely powerful computer science method called 'regular expression,'" which enables scholars to "search documents for all kinds of text patterns, not just key words or phrase matches."[46] Historians could collect regular expressions associated with swimming across time and space with a view to assessing various tones and affects such as fear, ridicule, derision, admiration, and celebration.

In a similar vein, the Internet is more likely than official archives to facilitate certain types of narrative. Archive-based histories of swimming, for example, have said little about pleasure and eroticism in water.[47] By contrast, this subject is prominent in the three-part "Naked Swimming in Schools," produced and uploaded by "PublicAccessVideos" on YouTube.[48] Employing standard sources such as photographs, oral testimony, and School Board regulations to configure a history of swimming classes for American children, the author reveals that boys practiced swimming in the nude in many states. As well as recounting this past, the author postulates why contemporaries quickly forgot this practice after it ceased in the 1970s and in so doing raises interrelated questions about source material and access to the past. By inviting comments, the "Naked Swimming in Schools" website also added to the stock of remnants regarding swimming and swimming pools with "francistorchio" and "gwenhafferty" recounting their own experiences. Interestingly, "phourthefunovit" also recommended that the producer "download these videos on other public media, such as

Dailymotion."[49] Increasing the repository of remnants of the past and improving access to that material can only facilitate more history and more diverse narratives of the past.

In keeping with the philosophical and political commitments of constructionism, we thus see the Internet as an opportunity for marginalized groups, such as indigenous, disabled, female, transgender, and gay swimmers, for example, to tell their stories and to give voice to various "other" accounts of the past. Internet activist Brewster Kahle says the medium belongs to "people: the good, the bad and the ugly. The interesting, the picayune and the profane. It's all there."[50] Thus, constructionists may view the accessibility and ease of uploading new content to the Internet as a significant advancement with regard to the types of narratives they are able to tell. In short, they, like reconstructionists, can benefit from the Internet as a source for material and from new processes and tools to search that material.

The third approach to history we discuss is deconstructionism. Deconstructionists focus on representations of history and historical production. They tend to be more flexible in their understandings and commitments to truth, and, perhaps unsurprisingly, have embraced the Internet. Among deconstructionists the Internet has broadened the scope of what counts as historical evidence and narratives and, correspondingly, has liberated the notion of history and historical practice.

Deconstructionism

Deconstructionism is a term that has been interpreted from, and applied to, the work of Jacques Derrida, who argued at length about the implicit political structures present in texts.[51] One of Derrida's key arguments rests on the idea that there are inherent contradictions in the claims that authors make in the process of forming a text—deconstructionists refer to all things as texts.[52] Applying a method of deconstruction to a text can reveal or expose oft-hidden encoded strategies. However, Derrida claimed that deconstruction is not something that is necessarily applied from the outside but rather is already there; deconstruction is at play by virtue of the inherent instability in the process of signification (that is, in the process of establishing relationships between a signifier and the signified).[53] In the words of Terry Eagleton, "meaning is not immediately *present* in a sign. Since the meaning of a sign is a matter of what the sign is *not*, its meaning is always in some sense absent from it too. Meaning, if you like, is scattered or dispersed along the whole chain of signifiers: it cannot be easily nailed down."[54]

In this section we approach deconstruction as both an internal and external process. On the one hand, deconstructionism is the potential to deconstruct the subject of a text that, by its very signification, is already deconstructing. On the other hand, we also employ a form of deconstructionism to question authors' claims to certainty and definitive truth. Here we focus on the fragments of matter that invariably comprise truth and argue that authors can potentially assemble or configure these fragments in a plethora of alternative ways. While the latter does not reflect Derrida's pure philosophical deconstructionism, it is a useful process to explore the assumptions underpinning historical productions.

Deconstructionists focus their attention on the form of history, that is, its production, in contradistinction to its content. Form refers to the ways that historians formally construct narrative explanations by use of language, trope, voice, plot, and argument, and these forms involve ethical, political, and ideological choices.[55] A deconstructionist might comment on other histories and make reference to sources or fragments that have been omitted due to subjective choices, epistemic allegiances, and politics. In the context of digitization, deconstructionists variously challenge the omnipresence of histories or embrace the multiplicities of fragments that they find in the ever-expanding archive. Whereas reconstructionism privileges professionals in the processes of collecting, validating, and presenting the remnants of the past (which other professionals variously accept or reject), deconstructionism begets an entirely different process. Deconstructionism expands the possibilities of cultural production into areas normally associated with consumption, enabling anyone to produce history from the infinite supply of raw materials. The Internet encourages "once passive consumers" to "seek out new information," to "make connections among dispersed [material]," and to "actively produce knowledge."[56]

The Extreme Winter Swimming website, with its slogan "exhilarating, exciting, extreme," is a good example.[57] A dynamic site with links to Twitter and Facebook, Extreme Winter Swimming features news items (relating to the latest swims), a description of the activity ("swimming in temperatures as low as zero"), a discussion of the science of swimming in low-temperature waters ("thermoregulation, conduction, convection, evaporation, radiation"), links to other swimming, partner, and equipment sites, and details about a DVD titled *Winter Swimming*. The latter documents "members of 1.PKO, a swimming club based on the banks of the Vltava River" in the Czech Republic, who swim "outside through the winter in near freezing water temperatures. It isn't just a few crazy people but an organised sport with frequent races through the winter season. In fact . . . the Czech Republic . . . [has] some of the most extreme winter swimming in the world . . . [thanks to] excellent organisation."[58] A trailer titillates viewers, flashing images that highlight the key themes of *Winter Swimming*: "sport," "lifestyle," "challenge," "love," and "health." The trailer also links to seventeen other YouTube clips of extreme winter swimming.[59] Referring to the deployment of trailers on such websites, Gary Osmond and Murray Phillips note that they serve as "substitute experiences" for some audiences who "may never view the entire film" but rely on edited splices to inform their opinions.[60] They also point out that websites can recontextualize subjects for audiences and thus shift readings and interpretations.[61]

The critical point for deconstructionists is not that the Internet offers historians new sources (reconstructionism); or new theories and contexts (constructionism); or, indeed, new values, mores, ideologies, and tropes. The latter, David Leonard reminds us, "emanate from shared political, cultural, and social locations" and are not unique to "traditional media texts" or "new media outlets."[62] However, the Internet is changing the way historians understand historical narratives and the representation of those narratives. Critically, the virtual and fragmentary content and form of the Internet allows historians of swimming to rearrange their subject matter. A search of the term *swimming pool* on the Internet is illustrative. Such a search shattered our preconceived notion of the swimming pool as a comprehensible material and ideological structure. There are no definable limits to swimming pool, which oscillates between the (perceived) real and the imaginary, the material and metaphoric: the swimming pool is simultaneously everything and nothing. In this process the swimming pool dissolved into its original watery form.

This (re)conceptualization negates the rational foundations of the pool and interferes with the rationalist assumptions that underpin reconstructionist and constructionist histories of the pool. Starting with water not only disrupts the notion of the object labeled *pool*, but also leads the historian to realize that accounting for the totality of (the history of) pools is impossible; totality is neither intelligible nor knowable. But rather than a constraint, the impenetrable and enigmatic swimming pool allows the historian to see things in new ways and to reconceptualize their subject matter; it opens infinite possibilities as to what they might draw on as evidence. This is particularly pertinent in light of the fact that historians of swimming concede that they will never know who the first swimmers were or how swimming originated. Origins are beyond knowledge, says Christopher Love, because swimmers leave no physical traces and, unlike other aquatic pursuits such as surfing, body boarding, sea kayaking, and sailing, swimming produces few artifacts.[63] As well as highlighting the classic problem for the historian author, where they should begin their narrative, a question which lies in their judgment rather than the facts *per se*,[64] an absence of definitive sources as evidence for the past, turns attention to the concept of the trace.

Historians have long been shackled to notions of perfect referentialism and verification. Traces free historians from these forms of absolutism. Robert Eaglestone argues that traces "eschew the construction of a 'truth' which claims to be from the past." A trace is not "a traditional piece of historical evidence," it "does not signify a reconstructable past, but the presence of [something or someone] as an irrecuperable absence and otherness," which interrupts totalizing systems such as grand narratives. A "trace imprints itself above and beyond the material evidence" and points to "the aura of the past which is neither the past nor the truth about the past."[65] A trace, what Jacques Derrida subsequently called a cinder (that is, 'visible but scarcely readable' ... that particular fire and that particular burnt 'thing' can never be recreated, brought back, brought to life"),[66] may be remembered and recalled but is never recoverable. In other words, traces do not necessarily illuminate a whole, but they are nonetheless constitutive of the potential of the whole. The concept of trace offers a vehicle through which historians can creatively mediate their subliminal conscious, nonrational images, and representations. Here we seek to show how the Internet might facilitate the use of traces in configuring historical narratives.

While the mediations of constructionists point to a wealth of sources dealing with swimming, they also highlight—particularly in the age of the Internet, which facilitates searching for, collecting, reading, viewing, listening to, and engaging with a wide range of texts—the myriads of traces associated with the subject.[67] For the historian of swimming, the concept of a trace eviscerates the idea of a grand, or totalizing, meta-narrative of the swimming pool. Traces expose a plethora of ways that individuals imagine swimming pools and the diversity of experiences that swimming pools offer; traces reveal an overabundance of affects that manifest in swimmers' bodies, and they bare the potential fates of swimming pools.[68]

Searching for the traces of a thing that cannot be known as a totality requires imagination, desire, dreaming, and an inclination to the sublime. Here the Internet comes into its own. An "absence of linearity, finality, and literality" is a defining characteristic of the Internet[69] that opens the door to a superabundance of traces and corresponding boundless possibilities for conceptualizing and narrating swimming. Traces allow us to think about swimming outside and beyond notions of fixed, or static, evidence and without distinguishing between the real and the imaginary. The remnants available on the Internet include a passing line in an e-book, a picture in an online health magazine, a scene in an uploaded film, a scanned photograph of a swimming costume, or an online news article.

The Internet opens opportunities and possibilities for an approach to history that we believe is highly liberating. It alerts us to the many different forms that histories can take. Indeed, in answering Roy Rosenzweig's question in the quote at the beginning of this chapter, we propose the fragment as the "appropriate unit of analysis" for historians and the arrangement of fragments as constituting a history. Like all histories, our arrangement is purposeful. But in putting together this arrangement we adopt the label "reconfigurationism," a post-deconstructionist reflexive form of history. Here we apply "post" in the sense of extending, rather than exterminating, deconstructionist thought and as an approach which fosters rearranging remnants of the past.[70]

Reconfigurationism

The historian, according to Robert Rosenstone, "digs for the past and comes up with disconnected fragments that do not fit together into a complete and meaningful story."[71] Historical representation involves assembling disconnected fragments into a narrative. Reconfigurationism describes the process of re-presenting fragments from the past as a form of montage to create what Rosenstone calls "new combinations of meaning."[72] Reconfigurationism acknowledges, and indeed in some ways privileges, the aesthetics (or at least the political potential of the aesthetics) of knowledge making. For example, in her reconfigured narratives of swimming, Fiona McLachlan demonstrates an aesthetic attitude that disrupts, parodies, and challenges the logic of conventional signifying practices and representations.[73] This (postmodern) aesthetic attitude embraces fragmentation, ambiguity, parody, pastiche, and assemblage.[74] Paradoxically, reconfigurationism follows the same basic approach as reconstructionism, that is, arranging fragments of the past in a form of narrative. Unlike reconstructionists, however, reconfigurationalists acknowledge their authorship (and history as an ironically self-conscious project) and identify their politics and aesthetics in their narratives, which they recognize as inevitably incomplete.[75]

The postmodern aesthetic of the reconfigurationalist narrative (that is, its fragmentation, ambiguity, parody, pastiche, and assemblage) coincides with the waning of traditional boundaries in the digital era between, for example, public and private, day and night, work and leisure and, of course, past and present time.[76] Capturing the implications for "ever more varied, dispersed and eclectic" historical representations in the digital era, historian David Harlan tacitly points to the role of the Internet when he urges his colleagues "to become adept at finding their way between competing but equally valid truth claims."[77] "It is not so much a commitment to the dead that they [historians] need, or even to the truth," says Harlan, rather they "need . . . the skills of the *bricoleur*": "They must become sophisticated multimedia ragpickers, quick, shrewd, witty readers of all the forms in which their culture represents the past, shuttling back and forth, to and fro, cutting and pasting, weaving and reweaving interpretive webs of their own devising. For only thus can they hope to develop a historical imagination that is morally coherent and politically effective."[78] Among historians who conceptualize the past as the foundation for understanding the social forces and relationships that shape our present, *bricolage* is a recipe for an "eternal present" without the "depth" of the past or the "possibility of [an] utopian future."[79] However, we seize reconfigurationism as an opportunity to reground the present in the past and to open new political possibilities for the future.

By way of illustration we offer the following simple reconfiguration of wild swimming as a cultural and social practice. While the aesthetic of our arrangement is somewhat limited,[80] arguably it evokes a sense of the complex ways in which swimmers, medical practitioners, and those who vicariously swim through swimming websites might experience winter, outdoor, and wild swimming.

WILD SWIMMING

Wild swimming is about beauty and strangeness and transformation[81]

In Europe, they are doing competitive swimming and in the United States it is just about a good feeling, with people celebrating together in the water[82]

Winter swimmers are not crazy, in fact their bodies are tempered or hardened somewhat against cold water by training and they know their limits as well as the power of mother nature[83]

Many winter swimmers swim with standard swimming costumes rather than with wetsuits or other thermal protection[84]

All the "protective gear" needed is actually built into your body[85]

In a time when U.S. prevention in health care is something we should be focusing on more—anything that prevents common illnesses isn't something to be scoffed at[86]

> Cold water submersion can induce a high incidence of cardiac arrhythmias in healthy volunteers. Submersion and the release of breath holding can activate two powerful and antagonistic responses: the "cold shock response" and the "diving response"[87]

> To enter wild water is to cross a border. You pass the lake's edge, the sea's shore, the river's brink—and you break the surface of the water itself. In doing so, you move from one realm into another: a realm of freedom, adventure, magic, and occasionally of danger[88]

Wild Swimming comprises a (reconfigurationalist) arrangement of fragments in contradistinction to a (reconstructionist) layering of narrative over the sources. In the process of arrangement, reconfigurationism makes explicit the role of the author in ordering and making sense of the past. Stripped bare from traditional narrative structures, reconfigurationism requires the reader to "work to achieve" historical meaning.[89]

Reconfigurationism is by no means an overly radical position. It requires historians to do no more than they have traditionally done, that is, to mediate the past after examining its remnants.[90] The Internet facilitates this process by immersing historians in an expanded, and expanding, collection of fragments. As they swim from hyperlink to hyperlink, and potentially lose themselves in the realm of the virtual, historians cannot but come to see their subject matter as both more complex and messy. It is a process that has the potential to open the door to rearranging the remnants of the past in different ways.

Conclusion

Sport history is now firmly enmeshed in an Internet era, which, as Roy Rosenzweig notes at the beginning of this chapter, is forcing historians to ask new questions about their discipline and its practices. The Internet poses any number of fundamental questions about the relationship between historical and archival practices, and the nature and preservation of remnants from the past. These questions are consistent with a broader shift in sport history over the last decade and a half away from its embrace of a social history paradigm to wider ranging cultural and historiographical interests including the literary structure of historical narratives and different forms of historical presentation (for example, films, monuments, museums).[91] The logical conclusion of this development, according to Alun Munslow, is the replacement of "epistemologically assured historical knowledge—based on . . . methodological practices exemplifying objectivity, even-handedness, [and] truth at the end of enquiry"—with "the past-as-history," a "figuratively constructed site of contested meanings (multiple possible truths and competing (hi)stories)."[92]

Yet, in our view, this remains a longer-term project. We do not believe that the Internet will entice historians to abandon their traditional practices in the near future. The Internet will not replace traditional archives or lead to the wholesale adoption of new practices of production, consumption, or representation. Regardless of whether historians believe in the sanctity of sources, or the centrality of context, or the fickleness of form, the Internet is unlikely to destabilize their commitment to a particular genre or paradigm of practice. We suggest that historians will probably continue to assess the Internet based on the longstanding assumptions that underpin their work, and in doing so will most likely find that it variously holds up as a place to find sources and evidence (reconstructionism), a context through which to theorize multiple histories (constructionism), or a form of and for historical representation and reconfigurationism (deconstructionism/postdeconstructionism). In this sense the Internet will remain a site of contested meaning among the spectrum of genres that comprise historical practice. Nonetheless, as the lessons from other debates in sport history (for example, social vs. cultural, material vs. discursive, present vs. past), we anticipate an increasing accommodation of the Internet[93] and recognition of its impact on constantly developing practice with respect to the conceptualization, gathering, interpretation, and presentation of the remnants of the past.

Notes

1. Rosenzweig, "Scarcity or Abundance?" 25.

2. The term *Internet* refers to the global system of computer networks, interconnecting private, public, academic, business, and government networks through a broad array of electronic, wireless, and optical technologies and a suite of protocols (e.g., addresses, routing of information, domain names) to serve billions of users. While the term *Internet* is often treated as synonymous with the web, the latter describes one Internet service or one Internet application, namely the web browsers (e.g., Firefox, Google Chrome, Internet Explorer) and servers that provide access to documents through hyperlinks and uniform resource locators (URLs). Web technology popularized the Internet. See *The Internet*. See also Cox and Salter, "The IT Revolution."

3. On the infinitely expanding archive, see Cohen, "History and the Second Decade of the Web," 296–97. On the Internet as a site for presenting different types of history, see Rosenzweig and Brier, "Historians and Hypertext," and Rosenzweig, "The Riches of Hypertext."

4. The renowned social historian E. P. Thompson recognized the lack of disciplinary coherence when he described history as a field characterized by "diverse" modes of historical writing, "various" techniques, "disparate" themes of enquiry, and "controversial and sharply contested" conclusions. Thompson, *The Poverty of Theory*, 51.

5. For details on these historical genres see Munslow, *Deconstructing History*. For their application in sport history, see Booth, *The Field*.

6. Fulbrook, *Historical Theory*, 100.

7. Leonard, "New Media and Global Sporting Cultures"; Rosenzweig, "Scarcity or Abundance?" 21–22.

8. McLachlan, "Poolspace."

9. Cohen, "History and the Second Decade of the Web," 295.

10. Rosenzweig, "Sport History on the Web," 371.

11. Rothenberg, *Avoiding Technological Quicksand*.

12. Himmelfarb, "A Neo-Luddite Reflects on the Internet." See also Rosenzweig and Cohen, "Web of Lies?" 29.

13. Cohen, "History and the Second Decade of the Web," 295.

14. Hancher, "The Risks and Rewards of the Internet."

15. Polley, *Sports History*, 52 and 64–65. See also Rocklin, "The Risks and Rewards of the Internet."

16. Rosenzweig, "*Wikipedia*," 70–71.

17. Wikipedia, "Swimming Pool."

18. See, for example, Wiltse, *Contested Waters*; Van Leeuwen, *The Springboard in the Pond*; and Metusela and Waitt, *Tourism and Australian Beach Cultures*.

19. Ralf Breier and Claudia Kuhland, "History of Swimming—Excerpt (2004)." Accessed October 11, 2013. http://www.youtube.com/watch?v=Pu9WdqnarRs. Scott Cleary reports swimming being "practiced by civilisations going back to the Egyptians": Cleary, "The Ethos Aquatic," 51. In *The Handbook of Swimming*, Wilkie and Juba note that Egyptian hieroglyphs describe humans propelling themselves through water with "alternating movements" (p. 1). After citing numerous studies comparing the accuracy of *Wikipedia* with more traditional and "seemingly authoritative" sources such as *Encyclopedia Britannica*, Rosenzweig concludes that the former "offers a formidable challenge": Rosenzweig, "*Wikipedia*," 63, 71.

20. Rosenzweig, "Digital Archives."

21. See the following websites: www.sutrobaths.com; http://australia.gov.au/about-australia/australian-story/australias-modern-swimmers; http://www.texasoutside.com/texasswimmingholes/texasswimmingholes.html; www.water-cube.com/en/; http://www.cnngo.com/explorations/play/beijings-watercube-water-park-now-open-040746; http://www.historic-venues.co.nz/Museum/index.html; http://www.abcpool.org/abcj00/.

22. International Swimming Hall of Fame, "Virtual Museum."

23. McLachlan, "Poolspace."

24. Hardy, "Where Did You Go, Jackie Robinson?" 92–93 (emphasis added). See also Rosenzweig, "Scarcity or Abundance?" 19–20, 22–23.

25. Trouillot, *Silencing the Past*, 52–53.

26. Metusela and Waitt, *Tourism and Australian Beach Cultures*, xxviii.

27. Rosenzweig, "Scarcity or Abundance?" 10–11.

28. Rothenberg, *Avoiding Technological Quicksand*. See also Barnet, "Pack-rat or Amnesiac?" 217–18; Rosenzweig, "Scarcity or Abundance?" 9, 13. Rosenzweig also warns against "exaggerating" the loss of digitalized information; see "Scarcity or Abundance?" 8–9.

29. Rosenzweig, "Scarcity or Abundance?" 8.

30. Munslow, *Deconstructing History*, 36–44.

31. Ibid., 44–51.

32. Whannel, "Caught in the Spotlight," 248.

33. Sombart, "Economic Theory and Economic History," 3 (emphasis added).

34. Munslow, *Deconstructing History*, 23, 40.

35. Strang, *The Meaning of Water*.

36. Parker, "Improving the 'Condition' of the People."

37. Strang, *The Meaning of Water*.

38. Winterton and Parker, "A Utilitarian Pursuit."

39. See, for example, White, "The Burden of History," and Alexander, "Modern, Anti, Post and Neo."

40. Berkhofer, *Beyond The Great Story*; Jenkins, *Why History?*

41. Wiltse, *Contested Waters*, 208.

42. As Rosenzweig and Cohen note, purely factual searches on the Internet merely confirm "impoverished" atheoretical and apolitical "views of the past." Rosenzweig and Cohen, "Web of Lies?" 43. See also Rosenzweig, "*Wikipedia*," 64–65.

43. Cohen, "History and the Web," 295 and 298–99. See also Rosenzweig and Cohen, "Web of Lies?"

44. White and Fairfield, "The New Olympic Stars." A streamgraph is a visualization of stacked area graphs with a free baseline. Shifting the baseline enables a viewer to perceive the thickness of any given layer within the data. On the Daley issue, see Harris, Preece, and Parsons, "Youth Detained Over Abusive Twitter Messages."

45. Cohen, "History and the Web," 298.

46. Ibid., 299. Rosenzweig argues that the algorithms used by search engines are becoming increasingly better at "sorting out good information from bad information mathematically": Rosenzweig, "Digital Archives." See also Rosenzweig, "Scarcity or Abundance?" 23.

47. Charles Sprawson writes about these aspects in the *Haunts of the Black Masseur*.

48. PublicAccessVideos, "Naked Swimming in Schools."

49. Ibid., Part 1.

50. Rosenzweig, "Scarcity or Abundance?" 21. See also, Kahle.

51. Derrida, "Structure, Sign and Play," and Derrida, *Of Grammatology*.

52. Rorty, "Philosophy as a Kind of Writing."

53. Caputo, *Deconstruction in a Nutshell*.
54. Eagleton, *Literary Theory*, 128 (emphasis in the original).
55. White, *Metahistory*; Munslow, *Narrative and History*.
56. Leonard, "New Media and Global Sporting Cultures," 3.
57. Extreme Winter Swimming.
58. Winter Swimming—The Film.
59. Winter Swimming—The Film (trailer).
60. Osmond and Phillips, "Reading *Salute*," 1465.
61. Ibid., 1465, 1467. Another relevant site in this context is the New Books Network, a consortium of podcasts in which authors discuss their latest books. The "New Books in Sports" page, for example, includes an interview with Gavin Mortimer, author of *The Great Swim*, which tells the story of Gertrude Ederle, Lillian Cannon, Amelia Gade, and Clarabelle Barrett who, in 1926, attempted to become the first women to swim the English Channel.
62. Leonard, "New Media and Global Sporting Cultures," 4.
63. Love, "Splashing in the Serpentine."
64. "The beginning is never an origin," says Marcus Doel; "one begins where one finds oneself." "Dialectics Revisited."
65. Cited in Eaglestone, *The Holocaust and the Postmodern*.
66. Eaglestone, *The Holocaust and the Postmodern*, 288–89.
67. Polley also observes the power of the Internet to enhance serendipitous findings. Polley, *Sports History*, 72.
68. Eaglestone, "The 'Fine Risk' of History," 318–19.
69. Cited in Leonard, "New Media and Global Sporting Cultures," 6.
70. McLachlan, "Poolspace," 82–89.
71. Rosenstone, *Visions of the Past*, 191.
72. Ibid., 192.
73. See, McLachlan, "Poolspace," and "Swimming History after Deconstruction." McLachlan's work follows in the footsteps of Synthia Sydnor's "A History of Synchronized Swimming." Sydnor captures the epistemic assumptions that underpin reconfigurationism; her work inspired aspects of McLachlan's montages.
74. Hutcheon's *The Politics of Postmodernism* is a useful starting point to understanding these terms and their application to historical representation and especially reconfigurationism.
75. Munslow, *The Future of History*.
76. Ben Agger discusses this process under the concept of "iTime." See Agger, "iTime: Labor and Life in a Smartphone Era." We thank Holly Thorpe for alerting us to this article.
77. Harlan, "'The Burden of History' Forty Years Later," 182.
78. Ibid., 182–83.
79. Agger, "iTime," 127.
80. Ideally, reconfigurationism should retain the aesthetics of the remnants or fragments rather than reproducing or retyping text. For example, McLachlan's

montages in "Poolspace" consist of digitally scanned or captured textual fragments (90–96).
  81. Mcfarlane, "Patron Statement."
  82. Rocchio, "Borough Polar Bears."
  83. Extreme Winter Swimming.
  84. Wikipedia, "Winter swimming."
  85. Wildswimmer, "Cold Water Swimming."
  86. Brian, "Winter Swimming."
  87. Shattock and Tipton, "Autonomic Conflict."
  88. Mcfarlane, "Patron Statement."
  89. Rosenstone, *Visions of the Past*, 192.
  90. Munslow, *Future of History*, 19.
  91. Phillips, *Deconstructing Sport History*; Phillips, "An Athletic Clio;" Osmond, "Reflecting Materiality;" Phillips, *Representing the Sporting Past*.
  92. Munslow, *Future of History*, viii, 82.
  93. Mike Cronin's paper, "Social Networking in Researching Sport History," and Murray Phillips' keynote address, "Storying the Sporting Past in the Digital Age: Multiple Histories of the Paralympic Movement," which were presented at the North American Society for Sport History Annual Convention, Berkeley, 2012, are good examples. For an overview and comment, see Holly Thorpe, "The Internet and the Future of Sport History."

References

Agger, Ben. 2011. "iTime: Labor and Life in a Smartphone Era." *Time and Society* 20, no. 1: 119–36.
Alexander, Jeffrey. 1995. "Modern, Anti, Post and Neo." *New Left Review* 210: 63–101.
Barnet, Belinda. 2010. "Pack-rat or Amnesiac? Memory, the Archive and the Birth of the Internet." *Continuum* 15, no. 2: 217–31.
Berkhofer, Robert. 1995. *Beyond The Great Story: History as Text and Discourse*. Cambridge, MA: Harvard University Press.
Booth, Douglas. 2005. *The Field: Truth and Fiction in Sport History*. London: Routledge.
Breier, Ralf, and Claudia Kuhland. 2004. "History of Swimming—Excerpt." Accessed October 11, 2013. http://www.youtube.com/watch?v=Pu9WdqnarRs.
Brian, Greg. "Winter Swimming: The Often Overlooked Health Benefits." Accessed December 20, 2007. http://voices.yahoo.com/winter-swimming-often-overlooked-health-benefits-729317.html.
Caputo, John. 1997. *Deconstruction in a Nutshell: A Conversation with Jacques Derrida*. New York: Fordham University Press.
Cleary, Scott. 2011. "The Ethos Aquatic: Benjamin Franklin and the Art of Swimming." *Early American Literature* 46, no. 1: 51–67.
Cohen, Daniel. 2004. "History and the Second Decade of the Web." *Rethinking History* 8, no. 2: 293–301.

Cox, Richard, and Michael Salter. 1998. "The IT Revolution and the Practice of Sport History: An Overview and Reflection on Internet Research and Teaching Resources." *Journal of Sport History* 25, no. 2: 283–302.

Derrida, Jacques. 1976. *Of Grammatology*. Translated by Gayatri Spivak. Baltimore, MD: Johns Hopkins University Press.

———. 1978. "Structure, Sign and Play in the Discourse of Human Sciences." In Derrida, *Writing and Difference*, 351–70. Translated by Alan Bass. London: Routledge.

Doel, Marcus. 2008. "Dialectics Revisited. Reality Discharged." *Environment and Planning* 40, no. 11: 2631–40.

Eaglestone, Robert. 1998. "The 'Fine Risk' of History: Post-structuralism, the Past and the Work of Emmanuel Levinas." *Rethinking History* 2, no. 3: 313–20.

———. 2004. *The Holocaust and the Postmodern*. Oxford: Oxford University Press.

Eagleton, Terry. 1983. *Literary Theory: An Introduction*. Oxford: Basil Blackwell.

Fulbrook, Mary. 2002. *Historical Theory*. London: Routledge.

Hancher, Michael. 1997. "The Risks and Rewards of the Internet as a Research Tool." Letters to the Editor, *Chronicle of Higher Education*, January 10. Accessed July 20, 2012. http://chronicle.com/article/The-RisksRewards-of-the/75315/.

Hardy, Stephen. 1999. "Where Did You Go, Jackie Robinson? Or, the End of History and the Age of Sport Infrastructure." *Sporting Traditions* 16, no. 1: 85–100.

Harlan, David. 2009. "'The Burden of History' Forty Years Later." In *Re-Figuring Hayden White*, edited by Frank Ankersmit, Ewa Domańska, and Hans Kellner, 169–189. Stanford, CA: Stanford University Press.

Harris, Paul, Rob Preece, and Chris Parsons. 2012. "Youth Detained Over Abusive Twitter Messages Received by Tom Daley When He Failed to Win a Medal Issued With Harassment Warning." *Mail Online*, August 19. Accessed October 20, 2012. http://www.dailymail.co.uk/news/article-2181068/Tom-Daley-Twitter-troll-detained-abusive-messages-issued-harassment-warning.html.

Himmelfarb, Gertrude. 1996. "A Neo-Luddite Reflects on the Internet." *Chronicle of Higher Education*, November 1. Accessed July 20, 2012. http://chronicle.com/article/A-Neo-Luddite-Reflects-on-the/74797/.

Hutcheon, Linda. 1989. *The Politics of Postmodernism*. London & New York: Routledge.

International Swimming Hall of Fame. "Virtual Museum." Accessed 30 July, 2013. http://www.ishof.org/museum/virtual_museum.htm.

"The Internet." Accessed August 20, 2012. http://www.livinginternet.com/.

Jenkins, Keith. 1999. *Why History? Ethics and Postmodernity*. London: Routledge.

Kahle, Brewster. *Wikipedia*. Accessed, August 5, 2012. http://en.wikipedia.org/wiki/Brewster_Kahle.

Leonard, David. 2009. "New Media and Global Sporting Cultures: Moving Beyond the Clichés and Binaries." *Sociology of Sport Journal* 26, no. 1: 1–16.

Love, Christopher. 2007. "Splashing in the Serpentine: A Social History of Swimming in England, 1800–1918." Special edition of *The International Journal of the History of Sport* 24, no. 5: 563–712.

Mcfarlane, Robert. 2008. "Patron Statement." May. Accessed April 5, 2010. http://www.outdoorswimmingsociety.com/index.php?p=about&s=.

McLachlan, Fiona. 2012. "Poolspace: A Deconstruction and Reconfiguration of Public Swimming Pools." PhD dissertation, University of Otago.

———. 2012. "Swimming History after Deconstruction: A Queer Engagement." *Journal of Sport History* 39, no. 3: 431–44.

Metusela, Christine, and Gordon Waitt. 2012. *Tourism and Australian Beach Cultures: Revealing Bodies*. Tonawanda, NY: Channel View Publications.

Mortimer, Gavin. 2008. *The Great Swim*. New York: Walker Books.

Munslow, Alun. 1997. *Deconstructing History*. London: Routledge.

———. 2007. *Narrative and History*. Houndmills: Palgrave Macmillan.

———. 2010. *The Future of History*. Houndmills: Palgrave Macmillan.

"Naked Swimming in Schools." PublicAccessVideos. Accessed August 16, 2012. Part 1 http://www.youtube.com/watch?v=D5mO6sZVufo; Part 2 http://www.youtube.com/watch?v=ARtKG9H85rA; Part 3 http://www.youtube.com/watch?v=Wtl8m1732YQ.

New Books Network. Accessed September 5, 2012. http://newbooksnetwork.com/.

Osmond, Gary. 2008. "Reflecting Materiality: Reading Sport History Through the Lens." *Rethinking History* 12, no. 3: 339–60.

Osmond, Gary, and Murray Phillips. 2011. "Reading *Salute*: Filmic Representations of Sports History." *The International Journal of the History of Sport* 28, no. 10: 1463–77.

Parker, Claire. 2000. "Improving the 'Condition' of the People: The Health of Britain and the Provision of Public Baths 1840–1870." *The Sports Historian* 20, no. 2: 24–42.

Phillips, Murray G. 2005. *Deconstructing Sport History: A Postmodern Analysis*. Albany, NY: State University of New York Press.

———. 2008. "An Athletic Clio: Sport History and Television History." *Rethinking History* 12, no. 3: 399–416.

———. 2012. *Representing the Sporting Past in Museums and Halls of Fame*. London: Routledge.

Polley, Martin. 2007. *Sports History: A Practical Guide*. Houndmills: Palgrave Macmillan.

Rocchio, Patrick. "Borough Polar Bears Compete in Icy Swim in Latvia." Accessed March 7, 2012. http://www.bxtimes.com/stories/2012/9/09_swim_2012_03_01_bx.html.

Rocklin, Tom. 1997. "The Risks and Rewards of the Internet." Letters to the Editor, *Chronicle of Higher Education*, January 10. Accessed July 20, 2012. http://chronicle.com/article/The-RisksRewards-of-the/75315/.

Rorty, Richard. 1978. "Philosophy as a Kind of Writing: An Essay on Derrida." *New Literary Journal* 10, no. 1: 141–60.

Rosenstone, Robert. 1995. *Visions of the Past: The Challenge of Film to Our Idea of History*. Cambridge, MA: Harvard University Press.

Rosenzweig, Roy. 2004. "Sport History on the Web: Towards a Critical Assessment." *Journal of Sport History* 31, no. 3: 371–76.

———. 2005. "Digital Archives Are a Gift of Wisdom to Be Used Wisely." *The Chronicle of Higher Education*, June 24. Accessed July 19, 2012. http://chronicle.com/article/Digital-Archives-Are-a-Gift-of/27488.

———. 2011. "Scarcity or Abundance? Preserving the Past." In *Clio Wired: The Future of the Past in the Digital Age*, 3–27. New York: Columbia University Press.

———. 2011. "*Wikipedia*: Can History Be Open Source?" In *Clio Wired: The Future of the Past in the Digital Age*, 51–82. New York: Columbia University Press.

———. 2011. "The Riches of Hypertext for Scholarly Journals." In *Clio Wired: The Future of the Past in the Digital Age*, 110–116. New York: Columbia University Press.

Rosenzweig, Roy, and Steve Brier. 2011. "Historians and Hypertext: Is it More Than Hype?" In *Clio Wired: The Future of the Past in the Digital Age*, 85–91. New York: Columbia University Press.

Rosenzweig, Roy, and Daniel Cohen. 2011. "Web of Lies? Historical Knowledge on the Internet." In *Clio Wired: The Future of the Past in the Digital Age*, 28–50. New York: Columbia University Press.

Rothenberg, Jeff. *1998. Avoiding Technological Quicksand: Finding a Viable Technical Foundation for Digital Preservation*. Washington: Council on Library and Information Resources. Accessed July 18, 2012. www.clir.org/pubs/reports/rothenberg/contents.html.

Shattock, Michael, and Michael Tipton. 2012. "Autonomic Conflict: A Different Way to Die During Cold Water Immersion?" *Journal of Physiology* 590, no. 14: 3219–30.

Sombart, Werner. 1929. "Economic Theory and Economic History." *The Economic History Review* 2, no. 1: 1–19.

Sprawson, Charles. 1992. *Haunts of the Black Masseur: The Swimmer as Hero*. London: Jonathan Cape.

Strang, Veronica. 2004. *The Meaning of Water*. Oxford: Berg.

"Swimming Pool." Wikipedia. Accessed July 22, 2013. http://en.wikipedia.org/wiki/Swimming_pool.

Sydnor, Synthia. 1998. "A History of Synchronized Swimming." *Journal of Sport History* 25, no. 2: 252–67.

Thompson, E. P. 1995. *The Poverty of Theory: Or an Orrery of Errors*. 2nd ed. London: Merlin.

Thorpe, Holly. 2013. "The Internet and the Future of Sport History: A Brief Commentary." *Journal of Sport History* 40, no. 1: 127–35.

Trouillot, Michel-Rolph. 1995. *Silencing the Past: Power and the Production of History*. Boston, MA: Beacon Press.

Van Leeuwen, Thomas. 1998. *The Springboard in the Pond: An Intimate History of the Swimming Pool*. Cambridge, MA: MIT Press.

Whannel, Garry. 2008. "Caught in the Spotlight: Media Themes in the Build-up to the Beijing Olympic Games." In *Pathways: Critiques and Discourse in Olympic Research, Ninth International Symposium for Olympic Research*, edited by Robert Barney, Michael Heine, Kevin Wamsley, and Gordon MacDonald, 247–255. International Center for Olympic Studies, University of Western Ontario.

White, Hayden. 1966. "The Burden of History." *History and Theory* 5, no. 2: 111–34.
———. 1973. *Metahistory: The Historical Imagination in Nineteenth-Century Europe*. Baltimore, MD: Johns Hopkins University Press.
White, Jeremy, and Hannah Fairfield. 2012. "The New Olympic Stars (of Twitter)." *The New York Times*, August 13, B14.
Wildswimmer. "Cold Water Swimming—Reducing Shock and Hypothermia Risks." Accessed August 18, 2011. http://www.swimclub.co.uk/forum/showthread.php?t=15153.
Wilkie, David, and Kelvin Juba. 1996. *The Handbook of Swimming*. London: Pelham.
Wiltse, Jeff. 2007. *Contested Waters: A Social History of Swimming Pools in America*. Chapel Hill, NC: University of North Carolina Press.
"Winter Swimming." Wikipedia. Accessed July 21, 2013. http://en.wikipedia.org/wiki/Winter_swimming.
Winter Swimming—The Film. Accessed 14 March, 2013. http://www.indiegogo.com/Winter-swimming-The-film.
Winter Swimming—The Film (trailer). Accessed 15 March, 2013. http://www.youtube.com/watch?v=bjNiJoRvoFU.
Winterton, Rachel, and Claire Parker. 2009. "A Utilitarian Pursuit: Swimming Education in Nineteenth-Century Australia and England." *The International Journal of the History of Sport* 26, no. 13: 2106–25.

CONCLUSION

Digital History Flexes its Muscle

MURRAY G. PHILLIPS AND GARY OSMOND

In the Introduction to this book, we created a tripartite conceptualization of the relationship between history making and the digital era. It provided a hermeneutic device to position contributions from sport historians, to group their ideas based on similarities or allegiances as much as to separate their perspectives around conceptual differences, and as a way of acknowledging the complexity of representing the past in this particular historical moment. In creating this conceptualization, the limitations are obvious. There is the slippage between the categories of digital history as approaches cross the porous membranes that we have created, and the impermanence of digital tools, devices, and social media will probably render these categories redundant very quickly as the digital world continually evolves. Nevertheless, in this Conclusion, we extend the discussion about our tripartite conceptualization—*Digital History and the Archive*, *Digital History as Archive*, and *Digital History is History*—by adding muscles to the skeleton created in the Introduction and see what happens to history making when the muscles of digital history are flexed.

Digital History and the Archive

> [H]aving access to vastly greater quantities of data, markedly different kinds of datasets, and a variety of complex tools and methodologies for exploring it means that "using" signifies a much broader range of activities than it has previously.[1]

As indicated above, and detailed in Wayne Wilson's chapter, the digitization of the archive provides incredible opportunities for historians. We now have unprecedented access to unprecedented amounts of historical materials: newspapers, magazines, manuscripts, photographs, other images, maps, and material culture, many of which are available online. This "new infinite archive" created during the digital era, however, has challenged some of the intellectual traditions of the humanities.[2] In particular, the practice of close reading, where meaning is derived from microscopic analysis of a limited number of texts, has to contend with distant reading, where the focus is on evaluating larger units and aggregating massive amounts of data.[3] It is now possible for computers to conduct large-scale, textual analyses to reveal trends, correlations, and relationships of digitized material, and to quickly and easily create visualizations in the form of charts, graphs, maps, tables, and timelines. To focus on larger units to reveal patterns, however, historians need to acquire skills associated with data-driven scholarship and visualizations. Data mining, aggregation, and quantitative text analysis are some of the techniques historians have to grapple with to employ distant reading.[4]

In this book, Martin Johnes and Bob Nicholson use a data-driven technique—culturomics—in relation to newspapers, Google Books, and court records to reveal patterns of British sport in the nineteenth and twentieth centuries. What their work highlights is that the insights gleaned from distant reading in the digital era can be particularly revealing, but are most powerful when combined with the close reading traditions of the humanities. The benefits of combining general surface analysis of distant reading with deep hermeneutic inquiry of close reading, to be able to unite a general view from above with a local view on the ground, are considerable. Distant reading and close reading are most beneficial when they are used in tandem, when they complement each other, rather than compete for methodological privilege.[5] Frederick Gibbs and Trevor Owens encapsulate this dynamic: "As historical data becomes more ubiquitous, humanists will find it useful to pivot between distant and close readings."[6]

Employing data mining, aggregation, and quantitative text analysis—also conceptualized and understood as a "computational turn"[7]—generates philosophical angst in the humanities, which have been steeped in the traditions of qualitative inquiry. Fields like literary studies, art history, and film studies, and the qualitative schools of sociology, anthropology, and ethnography have traditionally employed hermeneutics, thick description, and close reading.[8] By engaging with and implementing quantitative techniques, distant reading, and visualizations, digital history adopts some of the features that have shaped the quantitative schools of economics, sociology, and political science and, for some historians, is reminiscent of the early days of the Annales School and Cliometrics.[9] While proponents of quantitative analysis of historical data point out significant differences to practices in the Annales School and Cliometrics, this shift will understandably induce "epistemological jitters" for many historians.[10]

The philosophical tension associated with this shift toward quantitative analysis is very acute in history, and sport history in particular, because the last couple of decades have witnessed a critical examination of the qualitative dimensions of history, particularly explorations of history as a narrative-making exercise. Following on from the work of Hayden White, a number of historians have led the vanguard in conceptualizing the literary qualities of history—aesthetics, authorship, ethics, form and content, narrative, and reflexivity—which essentially provides a new platform to understand history as a qualitative field of inquiry.[11] As a consequence, the rhetorical attitude to history has gained increased credibility.[12] Similarly in sport history, there is a body of scholarship, building on the insights of Keith Jenkins and Alun Munslow in particular, that applies postmodernism and deconstruction to history in ways that are explicitly rhetorical and qualitative with little or no desire to engage quantitative analysis.[13] In this sense, just as history, and sport history, beat their rhetorical chests, digital history stamps its quantitative feet.

This philosophical conflict has not gone unnoticed. As Johanna Drucker asks: can new tools which are often mechanistic, reductive, and literal be "absorbed from disciplines whose epistemological foundations and fundamental values are at odds, even hostile to, the humanities?"[14] The response to this valid question is to acknowledge that historians have never been without data: "To some extent, historians have always collected, analyzed, and written about data."[15] And historians should apply the same rigor to data and visualizations as has been the case with texts.[16] The rhetorical dimensions of data should not undermine the hermeneutic process any more than the long-standing skepticism about texts has. Part of this process will involve historians explicating the research process by foregrounding data collection, analysis, interpretation, and presentation.[17] Another dimension will comprise developing an intellectual infrastructure that embeds core humanities concepts such as subjectivity, ambiguity, and contingency into new ways of knowledge production in the digital era.[18] There is an imperative to analyze and theorize quantitative methods and computing practice,[19] to develop a humanistic approach to computer code and software[20] and, as Katherine Hayles argues, there is a need to develop a theoretical approach that combines "political, rhetorical and cultural critique with the indigenous practices of digital media."[21]

Digital History as Archive

> For the first time, we can follow imaginations, opinions, ideas, and feelings of hundreds of millions of people. We can see the images and the videos they create and comment on, monitor the conversations they are engaged in, read their blog posts and tweets, navigate their maps, listen to their track lists, and follow their trajectories in physical space.[22]

Despite all of the potential opportunities described above, historians have been particularly reticent to engage with this new environment. This reluctance is particularly obvious in relation to social media where, for some historians, "disciplined and critical inquiry seems to be at odds with the majority of social practices occurring in that space."[23] The hesitancy to engage social media is related to a number of factors, as discussed in the Introduction: benefits, validity, and trust. Accordingly, historians are asking pertinent questions. What information of historical importance can be determined from Facebook, Flickr, Instagram, Twitter, or YouTube? What is the validity and trustworthiness of the material available from social media? Is it worth the time and effort to develop competencies in understanding and analyzing social media?[24] These are all valid questions, but it is hard to deny the emerging relationship between social media and history. As Corey Slumkoski recently reflected about a report on digital humanities that he co-authored in 2008: "I was shocked by our complete lack of discussion of social media and their impact on the practice of history."[25] As the opening citation to this section amplifies, and Slumkoski reinforces, social media is a contemporary phenomenon that intersects with historical practice.

Social media play two major roles in regard to history making. First, and its most popular representation in this book, social media provide material for analysis for historical research. Matthew Klugman, Geoffery Kohe, Rebecca Olive, and Holly Thorpe use fansites, websites, blogs, and Facebook to highlight a number of themes: an understanding of the emotional relationship between fans and their teams, the historical narratives embedded in official sport organization websites, the collective construction of cultural memories, and memorialization of sporting heroes. While each author effectively shows the insights gleaned from their specific case studies, they also address caveats about using social media. Social media is user-driven and mostly unregulated, characterized by brevity either by choice or by regulation, and often created by amateur commentators with an investment in, or affiliation to, the topic, issue, or event.[26] To this can be added that social media does not provide a "transparent window into peoples' imagination, intentions, motifs, opinions, and ideas" as contributors construct themselves in particular ways to exhibit control over their image online.[27] Furthermore, there is the digital divide: inequities related to social media based on technical literacy and access to appropriate devices and Internet connections. Digitization does not guarantee democratization.[28] Finally, it is important to acknowledge that while researchers have access to an incredible range of opinions, feelings, and reactions to analyze in their research, the media companies who control Facebook, Flickr, Instagram, Twitter, and YouTube have access to even larger data sets created by social media.[29]

The second way that social media is embedded in historical practice is as a communication tool that engages communities. That engagement embraces students, scholarly communities, and the general public. Tara Magdalinski in her chapter details the opportunities that social media provide for students of sport history, particularly focusing on the platforms for collaborative learning about the sporting past. Similarly, scholarly communities are increasingly engaging with social media to publicize projects and present new ideas; communicate, debate, and collaborate with colleagues; quickly and efficiently disseminate findings; and extend scholarly exchanges beyond presentations and panels at historical meetings through conference "backchannelling" where social media (Twitter in particular) provide a forum to extend discussions of thought-provoking topics.[30]

In relation to the general public, a number of digital humanities projects including *Ancient Lives*, *Transcribe Bentham*, and *Field Expedition* have received major contributions from volunteer community contributors.[31] As outlined in this book, Mike Cronin's project employed Facebook and Twitter to engage the Irish community, and collect data, about the country's sporting past. Like other historical projects that employ social media, Cronin's approach sought to engage "citizen scholars" and share the authority for history making between cultural institutions and the public.[32] There are, however, methodological, legal, and ethical issues with social media, as Cronin highlights, and the *Field of Dreams* scenario—build it and they will come—is exaggerated.[33] Nevertheless, Cronin's work points toward the incredible potential of social media: the ability to encourage citizen scholars and community engagement.[34]

With this rationale in mind, the project about the history of the Australian Paralympic Movement, which was featured in the Introduction to this book, decided to present a major component of its digital history on Wikipedia. The Australian Paralympic Committee formed a partnership with Wikimedia Australia because Wikipedia harnesses the "wisdom of the crowd" through crowdsourcing, enabling the cocreation of knowledge and the generation of a community of practice.[35] Wikipedia promotes historical knowledge through the "wisdom of the crowd" as contributors cumulatively work to create and edit pages on people, events, and issues about the Paralympic Movement. In these ways, Wikipedia, through its reliance on crowdsourcing as a means of knowledge production, is a form of social media that "shifts the role of authority from being vested solely in a historical cultural domain, such as the museum or the university history department, to being shared with a community or user-generated body of information that is critiqued within the community."[36] Equally importantly for a movement that has always been overshadowed by the Olympic Games, Wikipedia helps create a profile for the Paralympic Games and generates a community of practice of Wikipedians—comprising amateur historians, athletes, administrators, coaches, and sport historians—who, through their editing of pages, embrace the trials, tribulations, and achievements of athletes with disabilities, presenting their stories to a potentially global audience.

Several key issues arise from the discussion about the archival and social media dimensions of digital history. Does data mining, aggregation, quantitative text analysis, visualization, distant reading, and using social media as a source for historical research and a communication tool fundamentally change history making? How do *Digital History and the Archive* and *Digital History as Archive* alter historical practice? Do *Digital History and the Archive* and *Digital History as Archive* represent a paradigm shift in history? Answering these questions in the humanities has created considerable debate. As Matthew K. Gold summarizes: "Fault lines have emerged within the DH [digital humanities] community between those who use new digital tools to aid relatively traditional scholarly projects and those who believe that DH is most powerful as a disruptive force that has the potential to reshape fundamental aspects of academic practice."[37] While we certainly acknowledge Synthia Sydnor's anthropological analysis in this book of play, ritual, and culture, and her argument that there are particular synergies and continuities between sport and the Internet, we are also keenly aware of the potential discontinuities to historical practice posed by the digital era. The dimension of digital history that we see as having the greatest capacity to disrupt and reshape historical practice is our third category: *Digital History is History.*

Digital History is History

> [A]rtifacts created by digital technologies that "live" in digital environments are comparatively different—in terms of material composition, authorship, meaning making, circulation, reading, viewing, navigation, embodiment, interactivity, and expressivity—from artifacts created by the world of print.[38]

As indicated above, *Digital History is History* asks questions about traditional history because digital history has the capacity to challenge, unsettle, and reinvent the fundamental principles of history making. Digital history disrupts traditional historical practice in a multitude of ways: it provides viable alternatives to the culture of individually driven scholarship, to the ability to work from a single-discipline perspective, and to the practice of producing linear narratives. This may well explain why there are so few contributions in this book that fall into the category of *Digital History is History*. One exception is Fiona McLachlan and Douglas Booth's chapter, "Who's Afraid of the Internet? Swimming in an Infinitive Archive," in which they explore how the digital era provides opportunities to reconceptualize historical narratives. For sport historians, McLachlan and Booth's chapter opens a window that reveals the potential of digital history. At its most expansive, digital history is a collaborative venture, multidisciplinary at its core, not wedded to linear narratives, created with community involvement in mind, and employs the multimedia capacities of digital technology to create histories whose shape, form, and function are different from professionally sanctioned historical products: monographs, journal articles, and theses.

One entry point to investigate many of these issues is to examine the relationship between the digital era and the most prestigious artifact of the historical profession, the monograph. Anne Burdick and her co-authors capture the centrality of the monograph to humanities scholarship: "Modern concepts of humanistic knowledge were built on authoring, narrative, and textual models specific to the medium of print, with the monograph gradually supplanting commentaries and critical editions as the inviolable touchstone of scholarly knowledge and achievement."[39] Monographs, along with theses and journal articles, are written in a single media form—written texts on paper—usually by individual scholars for a readership who are familiar with the discursive traditions in the field. The monograph, in particular, remains the "gold standard by which scholarly and intellectual achievement" are measured, and it overwhelmingly influences tenure and promotion decisions.[40]

The monograph, as well as journal articles and theses, are the products of the *mentalities* of print literacy.[41] These mentalities value individuality, originality, authority, ownership, and authorship[42] and are the direct outcomes of the economy of knowledge production that developed in the industrial era. During this period, knowledge production was shaped by a scarcity of material and sources; centralized control of knowledge in institutions such archives, libraries, and universities; hierarchical structures in publishing and scholarly publications; a clear division of labor by authors, editors, and publishers; filter-then-publish models of knowledge circulation; and established systems of property and propriety epitomized by laws about copyright and ownership.[43]

The contemporary globalized economy, however, has generated a new economy of knowledge production. The last half-century has witnessed a transformation of culture, society, and knowledge. Social structures, modes of production, and cultural formations have altered the economy of knowledge production in the digital era. Scarcity, gatekeeping, centralized control, hierarchy, division of labor, and property and propriety systems have been gradually and partially supplanted by an economy of knowledge characterized by an abundance of information, decentralization of control beyond traditional institutions, peer creation of knowledge, creative commons, and an open-source culture. This decentralized and open-information economy promotes large-scale community access to knowledge, collaborative authoring, publish-then-filter knowledge circulation, flexible attitudes to intellectual property, multiple versioning of material, and distributed knowledge production. Not surprisingly, this economy of knowledge production is challenged and resisted by some community groups, business interests, governments, and institutions including universities, all of which seek to protect their vested interests.[44]

The new economy of knowledge production is placing pressure on the "gold standard" of the humanities, the monograph. The monograph is under pressure because there are viable alternatives to the text-based world of the linear narrative found in paper books in the form of histories produced through the multidimensional world of the web. By focusing on the monograph, it is possible to expose, highlight, and comprehend other aspects of traditional humanities scholarship that are challenged by the world of digital humanities.

Some historians recognize the fiscal pressure existing in publishing academic monographs and the need for other models: "We need more experiments to better understand which models might work, which ones will fail, and why. Accepting the status quo is not a fiscally sustainable option."[45] Other historians have already lamented the death of the paper book as a consequence of the digital era. They argue that opportunities for publishing books are diminishing, print runs by publishers are small with first prints of 500 or fewer, and publication is excessively expensive, with many books never gracing the shelves of book stores. As John Lukacs contends: "We have already entered an age where the influence (and consequently the importance) of books has been decreasing." He mourns the devolution of the book because "history, as *we* know it, is hardly separable from the written word. What will happen to history when books will disappear?"[46]

Reports of the death of the paper book, in reality, are premature. Its demise has been predicted many times as a consequence of the advent of mass circulation of newspapers, the development of radio, and the emergence of television in the households of the world. As Leah Price writes, "Every generation rewrites the book's epitaph; all that changes is the whodunit."[47] The book, in fact, has proved to be resilient and, for advocates, remains one of the "primary tools that people use to transmit ideas, record memories, create narratives, exercise power and distribute wealth."[48] Furthermore, holding books and turning the pages provide tactile sensory experiences, the portability of books enmeshes spatial and geographical aspects to reading experiences, and books remain a familiar and reliable mode of knowledge transmission.[49] These endearing features of the traditional book might help explain the recent analogue backlash in the form of artistic and cultural resistance to digital reading experiences.[50]

The future of the monograph as the centerpiece of scholarly history depends on factors internal and external to publishing books. Internally, virtually all universities have engaged with the new economy of knowledge production and have changed as a consequence of the digital era. Teaching, learning, and research are shaped in complex and interrelated ways by online technologies. From the perspective of humanities research, the most active, challenging, and innovative are those scholars working in the digital humanities. From the late 1990s, scholars in this field have engaged with digital technology, initially focusing on text analysis, as Johnes and Nicholson have done in this book, and more recently they have examined "entirely new disciplinary paradigms, convergent fields, hybrid methodologies, and even new publication models that are often not derived from or limited to print culture."[51] At the present moment, historians have the option to engage or not engage with the forms of knowledge production exemplified in the digital humanities.[52] Monographs and journal articles are still the accepted professional artifacts. It is not surprising, then, that many historians, and most sport historians, do not engage with the digital humanities.

Adding to changes occurring at universities and in the humanities, there are also external pressures to re-evaluate the status of the monograph. Economic downturns, changes in library purchasing patterns, and the dominance of contemporary screen culture have created a crisis in scholarly publishing and forced reconsideration of the business model based on the print medium. Kathleen Fitzpatrick sums up the contemporary situation: "The scholarly monograph isn't dead; it is *undead*."[53] What she is referring to is that the monograph is not financially viable, but is still required in the world of academia in terms of reputation, promotion, and tenure.[54] Some book publishers, as a consequence of the fiscal situation and altered reading preferences, are publishing paper books and online versions in the form of complete e-books or print-on-demand individualized options. In these ways, the binary distinction between print and electronic publications is "a misleading fiction."[55]

E-books are certainly popular. Amazon.com realized this when they sold more e-books than paper books in 2011.[56] Two years later, the first sport history e-book, Michael Oriard's *The Head in Football: The History of Concussions and the Future of the Sport*, was published.[57] Predictions are that 40 percent of research monographs in the United Kingdom will be exclusively available in a digital format by 2020; another 50 percent will be available both electronically and in hard-copy, while the remaining 10 percent will be in hard copy only.[58] If e-books take the form of a traditional book published in the same format electronically, essentially a facsimile, as is common practice with dual paper and electronic academic journals, historians have little to do to adjust their work for a potentially larger and more diverse audience.

If, however, historians are asked to bridge print and digital platforms, which is increasingly evident in electronic journals where articles and volumes may be linked to podcasts, Facebook, and Twitter,[59] or hyperlinked to primary sources and databases such as the collaboration between the online journal *Women and Social Movements* and the Alexander Street Press,[60] then producing history will be altered. Consider, for instance, the project about the history of the Australian Paralympic Movement. In addition to the Wikipedia pages, the Australian Paralympic Committee plans an e-history for their readership and audiences. Rather than a facsimile of a traditional paper book, however, they desire an e-history that is flexible through the ability to modify content, as new material emerges about the past and as Australia continues to compete at the Paralympic Games. Equally importantly, the Australian Paralympic Committee wants the written word in the e-history to act as a gateway to other representations of the past found in films, monuments, museums, oral histories, newspaper clippings, photographs, and personal records found in their extensive archive. To create an e-history that combines the written word with other representations of the past requires an understanding of these various "story spaces,"[61] each with their own particular attributes. This type of e-history takes historians beyond their expertise with the written word and requires them to comprehend not only the unique representational features, capacities, and limitations of films, monuments, museums, oral histories, and photographs, but also how these sources can best be used to create multifaceted, sensorial, and immersive historical experiences of disability sport in Australia. This is a different type of history than is created by words on the pages of a book.

In reality, though, the anticipated e-history of the Paralympic Movement is at the conservative end, or minimalistic end, of digital humanities. It certainly embraces the digital environment with its capacity to provide an expanded suite of expressive forms—films, monuments, museums, oral histories, and photographs—and integrate words with oral and visual cultures for a potentially global audience. Nevertheless, the e-history of the Paralympic Movement will be a linear story, created in long-form literary tradition, written by two authors, with limited interactivity for readers. A different type of history, yes; a radical revision of representing the sporting past, no.

At the maximalist end of the digital humanities are projects that fully embrace digital technologies. Digital humanities integrate words and images, drawing on the expertise of communication and media design to create pathways for understanding, often employing grids and templates from computer studies to produce multi-linear stories. Projects may involve animated archives, thick mapping, historical simulations, database documentaries, and even forms of humanities gaming. Authorship is collaborative, and users are empowered and encouraged to contribute, with the end product far removed from the linear narrative of traditional monograph or journal article.

These types of projects provide many challenges for historians. Consider two of these challenges relating to authorship and publishing of monographs. In term of authorship, monographs are traditionally written by a single historian. Munslow explains why: "Historians by nature are not herd animals. Most of the time we are loners only persuaded by the data in the archive."[62] Historians do collaborate as consultants to public exhibitions; assist on museum boards; advise on historical films; and teach in well-established, academic, public history, graduate programs,[63] but researching, analyzing, and writing history monographs is, as we argued in the Introduction, a highly personalized endeavor. In contrast to the solitary historian meticulously crafting his or her monograph, "it is not uncommon for dozens of people to work on a digital humanities project, each contributing domain-specific expertise that enables a research question to be conceptualized, answered, and then re-conceptualized and re-answered."[64] In this sense, the collaborative dimension of the digital humanities cuts against the grain of the work culture of historians.

In relation to publishing, the digital world offers alternatives to the *mentalities* of print culture. Print culture has fostered the filter-then-publish model. A typical historical book requires knowledge, expertise, and literary skills of an author, approval from expert reviewers who are conversant with discursive traditions of the field, editing from a skilled copy editor, and publication from a university press. This system is overwhelmingly based on a one-way communication model from the author to the readership. The digital world turns this process on its head by advocating a publish-then-filter process that involves many people in the discursive production and two-way communication between authors and readers.[65] *Writing History in the Digital Age* is a recent example of the publish-then-filter system.[66] Editors Jack Dougherty and Kristen Nawrotzki initially placed a "call for ideas" on the web and through social media, and they received sixty contributions, which were freely available online for comment and debate. Taking on board comments and their critical assessments, twenty-eight fully-drafted essays and the introduction to the book were made available for open peer review, and finally twenty essays along with the introduction and conclusion were submitted to the University of Michigan Press. At every stage of this process there were two-way communications—comments from reviewers followed by responses and modifications from authors—facilitated by online access. The publish-then-filter process fulfilled the editors' desire to construct "an edited volume of essays on the open web (that) would make our writing meaningful to others, more responsive to online commentary, and as a whole, more intellectually coherent."[67] The final products are a paper book, e-book, and open-access web editions.

As these two aspects—authorship and publishing models—suggest, writing history in the digital era has the potential to be radically different. History that fully embraces the digital humanities comprises far larger and more diverse spheres of influence than traditional humanities scholarship. In order to create digital history projects, a wide range of expertise is required from designers, coders, information architects, server administrators, and scholars.

Each of these areas of expertise is complex. Design, for instance, includes user interface design, graphic and typographic design, metadata design, interactivity design, and project design.[68] Furthermore, digital humanities projects, at their best, connect institutions—archives, libraries, museums, and universities—all of which uniquely relate to the digital era, and their collaborations combine to create vastly larger and more diverse communities, allowing for a revisioning of their missions. The digital humanities also encourage unlimited contributions from citizen scholars including amateurs, archivists, librarians, public historians, and academics, and actively solicit contributions in the form of crowdsourcing to generate content and edit material. It is hard to overstate the potentially transformative dimensions of digital humanities to create "a fundamental rethinking of *how* knowledge gets designed and created, but also a fundamental rethinking of *what* knowledge looks and sounds like, *who* gets to create and interact with knowledge, *when* it is made and recognized, *how* it gets authorized and evaluated, and *how* it is made accessible to a significantly broader (and potentially global) audience."[69]

Concluding Thoughts

We are very wary of predicting the consequences of the digital era. Will historians simply adjust their approaches by merging quantitative and qualitative methods and experimenting with social media, or is this a defining moment as we witness a radical transformation in history making? While the intersection between history and the digital era will be interesting to observe, debate, and engage in, the impact is potentially far-reaching. It contributes to a larger methodological, epistemological, and ontological discussion about history over the last couple of decades.[70] An important consequence of this discussion is the encouragement of experimentation in history making, exemplified by the creation of the journal *Rethinking History* in 1997. Digital history, at its maximalist end, engages with the practice of experimentation by denaturalizing every dimension of traditional history: the dominance of qualitative research, traditional source materials, the practice of sole authoring, one-way scholarly communication, peer review, filter-then-publish models, linear narratives, intellectual property, and, as we have stressed here, the viability of the monograph as the gold-standard, professionally approved, artifact. In these ways, as Stefan Tanaka argues, "the digital does provide us with an important opportunity to explore the possibilities of reconsidering and reformulating the practice and value of history to contemporary society."[71]

Notes

1. Gibbs and Owens, "The Hermeneutics of Data and Historical Writing."
2. Berry, "Introduction," 2.
3. Wilkens, "Canons, Close Reading, and the Evolution of Method," 249–58.
4. For a classic example of this approach, see Moretti, *Distant Reading*.
5. Burdick et al., *Digital_Humanities*, 39.
6. Gibbs and Owens, "The Hermeneutics of Data and Historical Writing."
7. See the contributions to Berry, *Understanding Digital Humanities*, for a sophisticated debate about the "computational turn."
8. Manovich, "Trending," 460–475.
9. Theibault, "Visualizations and Historical Arguments."
10. Gibbs and Owens, "The Hermeneutics of Data and Historical Writing."
11. White, *Metahistory*; Jenkins, *Re-thinking History*; Munslow, *Narrative and History*.
12. For a synopsis of the rhetorical dimensions of history, see Fay, "Introduction," 1–12.
13. See Booth, *The Field*; M. Phillips, *Deconstructing Sport History*; Pringle and Phillips, *Examining Sport Histories*.
14. Drucker, "Humanistic Theory and Digital Scholarship," 86.
15. Gibbs and Owens, "The Hermeneutics of Data and Historical Writing."
16. See Sinclair, Ruecker, and Radzikowska, "Information Visualization for Humanities Scholars" and Clement, "Text Analysis, Data Mining, and Visualizations in Literary Scholarship."
17. Gibbs and Owens, "The Hermeneutics of Data and Historical Writing."
18. Burdick et al., *Digital_Humanities*, 103–106.
19. Liu, "Where is Cultural Criticism in the Digital Humanities," 490–509.
20. Berry, "Introduction."
21. Hayles, "How We Think," 49.
22. Manovich, "Trending," 461.
23. Goulding, "Historical Thinking and Social Media," 19.
24. Ross, "Social Media for Digital Humanities and Community Engagement," 26.
25. Slumkoski, "History on the Internet 2.0," 153.
26. Goulding, "Historical Thinking and Social Media," 11–19.
27. Manovich, "Trending," 466.
28. Graham, Massie, and Feuerherm, "The HeritageCrowd Project."
29. Manovich, "Trending," 465–66.
30. Ross, "Social Media for Digital Humanities and Community Engagement," 23–45.
31. Graham, Massie, and Feuerherm, "The HeritageCrowd Project."
32. Sikarskie, "Citizen Scholars."
33. Robertson, "Putting Harlem on the Map."
34. Graham, Massie, and Feuerherm, "The HeritageCrowd Project."
35. Reagle, *Good Faith Collaboration*; O'Sullivan, *Wikipedia*.

36. Sikarskie, "Citizen Scholars."
37. Gold, "Introduction," x.
38. Burdick et al., *Digital_Humanities*, 29.
39. Ibid., 7.
40. Greetham, "The Resistance to Digital Humanities," 438, 443.
41. Alvarado, "The Digital Humanities Situation," 54.
42. Spiro, "'This is Why We Fight,'" 23.
43. Burdick et al., *Digital_Humanities*, 76–79.
44. For a discussion of many of these issues, see Cohen and Scheinfeldt, *Hacking the Academy*.
45. Dougherty et al., "Conclusions."
46. Lukacs, *The Future of History*, 165 (emphasis in the original).
47. Price, "Dead Again."
48. Eliot and Rose, "Introduction," 1.
49. Nawrotzki and Dougherty, "Introduction."
50. Jones, *The Emergence of Digital Humanities*, 154.
51. Presner, 2010, p. 6, cited in Berry, "Introduction," 3.
52. Fitzpatrick, *Planned Obsolescence*, 1–14.
53. Ibid., 4 (emphasis in the original).
54. Ibid., 1–5.
55. Jones, *The Emergence of Digital Humanities*, 174.
56. Ibid., 158.
57. Oriard, *The Head in Football*.
58. A. Phillips, "Does the Book have a Future?," 549.
59. Slumkoski, "History on the Internet 2.0," 155.
60. Sklar and Dublin, "Creating Meaning in a Sea of Information."
61. Munslow, *Narrative and History*, 16–28.
62. Munslow, *The New History*, 93.
63. Banner, *Being a Historian*, 138–158.
64. Burdick et al., *Digital_Humanities*, 49.
65. Parry, "Burn the Boats/Books."
66. Dougherty and Nawrotzki, *Writing History in the Digital Age*.
67. Dougherty et al., "Conclusions."
68. Burdick et al., *Digital_Humanities*, 118.
69. Ibid., 90 (emphasis in the original).
70. Munslow, *The Future of History*.
71. Tanaka, "Pasts in a Digital Age."

References

Alvarado, Rafael C. 2012. "The Digital Humanities Situation." In *Debates in the Digital Humanities*, edited by Matthew K. Gold, 50–55. Minneapolis: University of Minnesota Press.

Banner, James M. 2012. *Being a Historian: An Introduction to the Professional World of History*. New York: Cambridge University Press.
Berry, David M. 2012. "Introduction: Understanding Digital Humanities." In *Understanding Digital Humanities*, edited by David M. Berry, 1–20. Houndmills: Palgrave Macmillan.
———, ed. 2012. *Understanding Digital Humanities*. Houndmills: Palgrave Macmillan.
Booth, Douglas. 2005. *The Field: Truth and Fiction in Sport History*. London: Routledge.
Burdick, Anne, Johanna Drucker, Peter Lunenfeld, Todd Presner, and Jeffrey Schnapp. 2012. *Digital_Humanities*. Cambridge, MA: The MIT Press.
Clement, Tanya. 2013. "Text Analysis, Data Mining, and Visualizations in Literary Scholarship (2013 version)." In *Literary Studies in the Digital Age: An Evolving Anthology*, edited by Kenneth M. Price and Ray Siemens. New York: MLA Online. Accessed January 20, 2014. http://dlsanthology.commons.mla.org/.
Cohen, Daniel J., and Tom Scheinfeldt, eds. 2013. *Hacking the Academy: New Approaches to Scholarship and Teaching from Digital Humanities*. Ann Arbor: University of Michigan Press.
Dougherty, Jack, and Kristen Nawrotzki, eds. 2013. *Writing History in the Digital Age*. Ann Arbor: University of Michigan Press. Trinity College (CT) web-book edition, Spring 2012. http://WritingHistory.trincoll.edu.
Dougherty, Jack, Kristen Nawrotzki, Charlotte Rochez, and Timothy Burke. 2013. "Conclusions: What we learned from *Writing History in the Digital Age* (Spring 2012)." In *Writing History in the Digital Age*, edited by Jack Dougherty and Kristen Nawrotzki. Ann Arbor: University of Michigan Press. Trinity College (CT) web-book edition, Spring 2012. Accessed July 20, 2013. http://WritingHistory.trincoll.edu.
Drucker, Johanna. 2012. "Humanistic Theory and Digital Scholarship." In *Debates in the Digital Humanities*, edited by Matthew K. Gold, 85–95. Minneapolis: University of Minnesota Press.
Eliot, Simon, and Jonathan Rose, eds. 2007. *A Companion to the History of the Book*. Melbourne: Blackwell Publishing.
Eliot, Simon, and Jonathan Rose, eds. 2007. "Introduction." In *A Companion to the History of the Book*, edited by Simon Eliot and Jonathan Rose, 1–5. Melbourne: Blackwell Publishing,.
Fay, Brian. 1998. "Introduction: The Linguistic Turn and Beyond in Contemporary Theory of History." In *History and Theory: Contemporary Readings*, edited by Brian Fay, Philip Pomper, and Richard T. Vann, 1–12. Oxford: Blackwell.
Fitzpatrick, Kathleen. 2011. *Planned Obsolesence: Publishing, Technology, and the Future of the Academy*. New York: New York University Press.
Gibbs, Frederick W., and Trevor J. Owens. 2013. "The Hermeneutics of Data and Historical Writing (Spring 2012 version)." In *Writing History in the Digital Age*, edited by Jack Dougherty and Kristen Nawrotzki. Ann Arbor: University of Michigan

Press. Trinity College (CT) web-book edition, Spring 2012. Accessed July 14, 2013. http://WritingHistory.trincoll.edu.

Gold, Matthew K. 2012. "Introduction: The Digital Humanities Moment." In *Debates in the Digital Humanities*, edited by Matthew K. Gold, ix-xvi. Minneapolis: University of Minnesota Press.

Goulding, James. 2011. "Historical Thinking and Social Media." *Agora* 46, no. 3 (July): 11–19.

Graham, Shawn, Guy Massie, and Nadine Feuerherm. 2013. "The HeritageCrowd Project: A Case Study in Crowdsourcing Public History (Spring 2012 version)." In *Writing History in the Digital Age*, edited by Jack Dougherty and Kristen Nawrotzki. Ann Arbor: University of Michigan Press. Trinity College (CT) web-book edition, Spring 2012. Accessed July 16, 2013. http://WritingHistory.trincoll.edu.

Greetham, David. 2012. "The Resistance to Digital Humanities." In *Debates in the Digital Humanities*, edited by Matthew K. Gold, 438–51. Minneapolis: University of Minnesota Press.

Hayles, Katherine N. 2012. "How We Think: Transforming Power and Digital Technologies." In *Understanding Digital Humanities*, edited by David M. Berry, 42–66. Houndmills: Palgrave Macmillan.

Jenkins, Keith. 1991. *Re-Thinking History*. London: Routledge.

Jones, Steven E. 2014. *The Emergence of Digital Humanities*. New York: Routledge.

Liu, Alan. 2012. "Where Is Cultural Criticism in the Digital Humanities?" In *Debates in the Digital Humanities*, edited by Matthew K. Gold, 490–509. Minneapolis: University of Minnesota Press.

Lukacs, John. 2011. *The Future of History*. New Haven, CT: Yale University Press.

Manovich, Lev. 2012. "Trending: The Promises and the Challenges of Big Social Data." In *Debates in the Digitlal Humanities*, edited by Matthew K. Gold, 460–75. Minneapolis: University of Minnesota Press.

Moretti, Franco. 2013. *Distant Reading*. Brooklyn, NY: Verso.

Munslow, Alun. 2003. *The New History*. Harlow: Pearson.

———. 2007. *Narrative and History*. Houndmills: Palgrave Macmillan.

———. 2010. *The Future of History*. Houndmills: Palgrave Macmillan.

Nawrotzki, Kristen, and Jack Dougherty, 2013. "Introduction (Spring 2012 version)." In *Writing History in the Digital Age*, edited by Jack Dougherty and Kristen Nawrotzki. Ann Arbor: University of Michigan Press. Trinity College (CT) web-book edition, Spring 2012. Accessed July 20, 2013. http://WritingHistory.trincoll.edu.

Oriard, Michael. 2013. *The Head in Football: The History of Concussions and the Future of the Sport*. Now and Then Reader LLC. Accessed January 20, 2014. http://www.nowandthenreader.com/the-head-in-football-the-history-of-concussions-and-the-future-of-the-sport/.

O'Sullivan, Dan. 2009. *Wikipedia: A New Community of Practice*. Burlington, VT: Ashgate Publishing.

Parry, David. 2013. "Burn the Boats/Books." In *Hacking the Academy*, edited by Daniel J. Cohen and Tom Scheinfeldt, 15–18. Ann Arbor: University of Michigan Press.

Phillips, Angus. 2007. "Does the Book Have a Future?" In *A Companion to the History of the Book*, edited by Simon Eliot and Jonathan Rose, 547–59. Melbourne: Blackwell Publishing.

Phillips, Murray G., ed. 2006. *Deconstructing Sport History: A Postmodern Analysis*. New York: SUNY.

Price, Leah. 2012. "Dead Again." Sunday Book Review. *New York Times*, August 10. Accessed January 27, 2014. http://www.nytimes.com/2012/08/12/books/review/the-death-of-the-book-through-the-ages.html?partner=rss&emc=rss&_r=0.

Pringle, Richard, and Murray G. Phillips, eds. 2013. *Examining Sport Histories: Power, Paradigms, and Reflexivity*. Morgantown, WV: FIT.

Presner, Todd. 2012. "Digital Humanities 2.0: A Report on Knowledge," cited in Berry, David M. "Introduction: Understanding Digital Humanities." In *Understanding Digital Humanities*, edited by David M. Berry, 3. Houndmills: Palgrave Macmillan.

Reagle, Joseph Michael. 2011. *Good Faith Collaboration*. Cambridge, MA: MIT Press.

Robertson, Stephen. 2013. "Putting Harlem on the Map (Spring 2012 version)." In *Writing History in the Digital Age*, edited by Jack Dougherty and Kristen Nawrotzki. Ann Arbor: University of Michigan Press. Trinity College (CT) web-book edition, Spring 2012. Accessed July 20, 2013. http://WritingHistory.trincoll.edu.

Ross, Claire. 2012. "Social Media for Digital Humanities and Community Engagement." In *Digital Humanities in Practice*, edited by Claire Warwick, Melissa M. Terras, and Julianne Nyhan, 23–45. London: Facet Publishing.

Scheinfeldt, Tom. 2012. "Sunset for Ideology, Sunrise for Methodology?" In *Debates in the Digital Humanities*, edited by Matthew K. Gold, 124–36. Minneapolis: University of Minnesota Press.

Sikarskie, Amanda Grace. 2013. "Citizen Scholars: Facebook and the Co-Creation of Knowledge (Spring 2012 version)." In *Writing History in the Digital Age*, edited by Jack Dougherty and Kristen Nawrotzki. Ann Arbor: University of Michigan Press. Trinity College (CT) web-book edition, Spring 2012. Accessed June 30, 2013. http://WritingHistory.trincoll.edu.

Sinclair, Stéfan, Stan Ruecker, and Milena Radzikowska. 2013. "Information Visualization for Humanities Scholars (2013 edition)." In *Literary Studies in the Digital Age: An Evolving Anthology*, edited by Kenneth M. Price and Ray Siemens. New York: MLA Online. Accessed December 15, 2013. http://dlsanthology.commons.mla.org/.

Sklar, Kathryn Kish, and Thomas Dublin. 2013. "Creating Meaning in a Sea of Information: The Women and Social Movement Sites (Spring 2012 version)." In *Writing History in the Digital Age*, edited by Jack Dougherty and Kristen Nawrotzki. Ann Arbor: University of Michigan Press. Trinity College (CT) web-book edition, Spring 2012. Accessed July 21, 2013. http://WritingHistory.trincoll.edu.

Slumkoski, Corey. 2012. "History on the Internet 2.0: The Rise of Social Media." *Acadiensis* 41, no. 2: 153–62.

Spiro, Lisa. 2012. "'This Is Why We Fight': Defining the Values of the Digital Humanities." In *Debates in the Digitlal Humanities*, edited by Matthew K. Gold, 16–35. Minneapolis: University of Minnesota Press.

Tanaka, Stefan. 2013. "Pasts in a Digital Age (Spring 2012 version)." In *Writing History in the Digital Age*, edited by Jack Dougherty and Kristen Nawrotzki. Ann Arbor: University of Michigan Press. Trinity College (CT) web-book edition, Spring 2012. Accessed July 27, 2013. http://WritingHistory.trincoll.edu.

Theibault, John. 2013. "Visualizations and Historical Arguments (Spring 2012 version)." In *Writing History in the Digital Age*, edited by Jack Dougherty and Kristen Nawrotzki. Ann Arbor: University of Michigan Press. Trinity College (CT) web-book edition, Spring 2012. Accessed August 2, 2013. http://WritingHistory.trincoll.edu.

White, Hayden V. 1973. *Metahistory: The Historical Imagination in Nineteenth-Century Europe*. Baltimore: Johns Hopkins University Press.

Wilkens, Mathew. 2012. "Canons, Close Reading, and the Evolution of Method." In *Debates in the Digitlal Humanities*, edited by Matthew K. Gold, 249–58. Minneapolis: University of Minnesota Press.

Contributors

DOUGLAS BOOTH is Dean of the School of Physical Education at the University of Otago and Professor of Sport Studies. His books include *The Race Game* (1998), *Australian Beach Cultures* (2001), and *The Field* (2005). Douglas serves on the editorial boards of *Journal of Sport History*, *Rethinking History*, and *Sport History Review*, and is an executive member of the Australian Society for Sports History.

MIKE CRONIN is the Academic Director of Boston College in Ireland. He has worked extensively in the area of sport history, especially in relation to questions of national identity. He is the author of *Sport and Nationalism in Ireland* (1999).

MARTIN JOHNES is Head of History and Classics at Swansea University where he teaches and researches modern Wales and sport history. He has published various books and articles that look at popular sports, obscure sports, national identity, historiography, disasters, and local government. His most recent book is *Wales since 1939* (2012), which is the first major survey of Wales in this period and has a particular emphasis on ordinary people and what makes Wales, Wales. Martin is currently working on projects on the history of British boxing and the role of history in Welsh culture. He also co-edits the journal *Sport in History*, is a past chairman of the British Society of Sports History, and is a current executive member of Llafur: The Welsh People's History Society. He is a regular contributor on history, sport, and politics to the Welsh print and broadcast media.

MATTHEW KLUGMAN is Senior Lecturer in the College of Sport and Exercise Science at Victoria University, and an Associate of the Institute for Sport, Exercise, and Active Living. He is the author of the books *Passion Play: Love, Hope and Heartbreak at the Footy* (2009), and *Black and Proud: The Story of an Iconic AFL Photo* (with Gary Osmond, 2013), and his research interests include sport fandom and images of sport and race.

GEOFFERY Z. KOHE is Lecturer in Sport Studies and Sociology in the Institute of Sport and Exercise Science at the University of Worcester, UK. His research interests include the socio-cultural, historical, and political aspects of the Olympic movement, moral pedagogy, politicizations of the body, sport tourism, and historiography. He has also taught across a variety of undergraduate sport studies modules including history, sociology, and body cultures. His recent projects include the centennial history of the New Zealand Olympic Committee, research on apologies and public history, and Olympic legacies and education.

TARA MAGDALINSKI is the Associate Dean for Teaching and Learning in the School of Public Health, Physiotherapy and Population Science at the University College Dublin. She has published widely in the area of sports studies, focusing most recently on the cultural construction of performance enhancement. She co-edited (with Timothy Chandler) *With God on their Side: Sport in the Service of Religion* (2002), and has published a well-reviewed monograph, *Sport, Technology and the Body: The Nature of Performance* (2009), and a textbook, *Study Skills for Sports Studies* (2013).

FIONA MCLACHLAN is Lecturer in the College of Sport and Exercise Science at Victoria University in Melbourne. Her research interests lie in historiography and experimenting with historical methods to explore contemporary culture.

BOB NICHOLSON is a Cultural Historian of nineteenth century Britain and America who lectures in the Department of English and History at Edge Hill University in the UK. His doctoral thesis was awarded the Gale Dissertation Research Fellowship in 19th-Century Media (2009) in recognition of his innovative use of digital archives. His research interests include digital repositories, nineteenth-century Britain, digital humanities, Victorian studies, American history, periodicals, digital history, nineteenth-century (history), newspaper history, journalism history, print culture, and cultural history.

REBECCA OLIVE is a Post-Doctoral Research Fellow in the Department of Sport and Leisure Studies, University of Waikato, New Zealand. Her research interests include culture, gender, bodies, cultural theory, physical activity, and blogging. She has published widely, including in the journals *Journal of Sport History*, *Sport, Education and Society*, *Sport in Society*, *Sociology of Sport Journal*, and *International Journal of Cultural Studies*.

GARY OSMOND is Senior Lecturer in sport history in the School of Human Movement Studies, The University of Queensland. His research interests include digital history, race and sport, and non-written representations of the sporting past. He is the co-author, with Matthew Klugman, of the book *Black and Proud: The Story of an Iconic AFL Photo* (2013). He is currently a chief investigator, with Murray Phillips, on a research project on the Australian Paralympic movement that includes a digital history dimension.

MURRAY G. PHILLIPS is Associate Professor in the School of Human Movement Studies at The University of Queensland. He has published books on the histories of swimming and sport coaching, and edited books on the philosophy of history, sport museums, and digital history. He is currently collaborating with Gary Osmond on a digital history of the Australian Paralympic Movement. He is President of the Australian Society for Sports History, Editor of the *Journal of Sport History*, and serves on several other editorial boards.

STEPHEN ROBERTSON is a Cultural and Social Historian of the twentieth-century United States, and Director of the Roy Rosenzweig Center for History and New Media, and Professor in the Department of History and Art History at George Mason University. Digital history has occupied a central place in his research since 2003, and his website, *Digital Harlem*, which he created with his collaborators in the Black Metropolis project at the University of Sydney, won the American Historical Association's inaugural Rosenzweig Prize for Innovation in Digital History and the American Library Association's ABC-CLIO Digital History Prize in 2010.

SYNTHIA SYDNOR is Associate Professor at University of Illinois at Urbana-Champaign, where she has appointments in Kinesiology and Community Health; Recreation, Sport and Tourism; and Cultural Studies and Interpretive Research. She earned her doctorate at Pennsylvania State University. She is the co-author of *To the Extreme: Alternative Sports, Inside and Out* (2003), and her work has appeared in journals such as *Quest*; *Journal of Sport & Social Issues*; *Studies in Symbolic Interaction*; and *Interface: A Forum for Theology in the World*.

HOLLY THORPE is Senior Lecturer with the Department of Sport and Leisure Studies, University of Waikato, New Zealand. Her research interests include social theory, physical youth culture, gender, and action sports, and she has published widely on these topics. She is the co-editor of the *Berkshire Encyclopedia of Extreme Sports* (2007) and author of *Snowboarding Bodies in Theory and Practice* (2011) and *Transnational Mobilities in Action Sport Cultures* (2014).

WAYNE WILSON is a Vice President of the LA84 Foundation, where he supervises the sports library, digital resources, and research projects. He earned his doctorate in Sports Studies at the University of Massachusetts, Amherst, and an MLS. at Syracuse University. His publications include articles on sport history, sport media, and information studies. Wayne is the co-editor of the anthology *Doping in Elite Sport: The Politics of Drugs in the Olympic Movement* (2000) and the forthcoming *Oxford Handbook of Sport History*.

Index

ABC-CLIO Online History Award, 2, 26n3, 273
Abraham Lincoln Presidential Museum 124
Academia.edu, 109
ACRL. *See* Association of College and Research Libraries
Allsport Photography, 41
Amateur Athletic Foundation of Los Angeles, 42. *See also* LA84 Foundation
amazon.com, 212, 260
American Historical Association, ix, 2, 6, 26n3, 29, 273
Annales School, 252–53
Association of College and Research Libraries (ACRL), 44, 48–49, 51n19, 51n23
Association of Surfing Professionals, 185
Australian Football League (AFL), 21, 137, 146–47
Australian Institute of Sport, 50
Australian National Sports Information Centre, 1, 14
Australian Society for Sports History (ASSH), 43, 178, 271, 273
Australian Sports Commission, 41
Ayers, Edward, xi

Berners-Lee, Tim, 159, 174n13, 176
Bing, 168
Big Footy (blog), 137
blogger historians, 165–69
blogosphere, 163

blogs: and collaborative memory-making, 159–63, 254; as digital archive, 9; ethics of blogging 22, 163–65; fans use of, 21, 47, 132–33, 254, 137, 139–42; 'grief' blogs, 183, 188, 254; historians use of, 6, 10–11, 22, 25, 78–79, 165–69, 254; interactive qualities, 75, 158, 169–72; New Zealand Olympic Committee's use of blogs, 18–19, 90; politics of blogging 22; as research source, 22–23, 231; use in teaching, 20–21, 113–30 passim. *See also under individual blogs*
Bolts from the Blue (blog), 137, 141, 145
born-digital (documents), 14–15, 18, 21, 28n51, 46, 50
bricolage, 240
British Library, 18, 49, 56; Newspaper Archive, 69; *19th Century British Library Newspapers*, 55–56, 58–59, 70; *17th and 18th Century Burney Collection*, 55–56
British National Archives, 105
British Newspaper Archive, 55–56
British Periodicals. See ProQuest
BRS (online database system), 37
Burdick, Anne, 11, 257

Centre of Excellence for Creative Industries and Innovation, Queensland University of Technology, 103
chat rooms, 2, 21, 133, 183
Chronicling America, 55
citizen scholars, 33, 255, 263

Cliometrics, 253
close reading, xi, 33, 57, 62, 252
Cohen, Daniel J., ix, 17, 28n51, 62, 159, 163, 166, 228, 233–34, 242n3, 244n42
collective memory, 22, 78–81, 133–34, 148n8, 148n14, 160–62, 164, 180–93 passim, 254
computational turn, 252, 264n7
constructionism, 11, 25, 113, 116, 227, 232–35, 237, 242
court records 17, 61, 72n24, 252. *See also* legal records
cultural memory: definition, 193n5; digitalization of, 180; forms of construction, 189; politics of, 23, 189; social media and production of, 23, 181, 183–84, 192–93
cultural ritualization, 210
culturomics, 17, 62–64, 66, 69–70, 73, 252
Curatr, 20, 122
cyberspace, 4, 8, 37, 41, 89, 90, 92, 139, 184, 203, 208, 211

Dailymotion (video-sharing website), 235
Dana, John Cotton, 36
data: analysis, xi, 103, 253; big, xi; collection, 19–21, 102–3, 108, 120, 253; digital and non-digital, 231, 253; digital literacy and, 121; qualitative, x; quantitative, 7, 103, 253; rhetorical dimensions, 215, 253; social media generation, 19–21, 25, 102–3, 110, 255; storage and protection issues, 108; volume of digital, xi, 33, 251–52. *See also* data mining; data aggregation
data aggregation, 33, 252, 256
Database of Mid-Victorian Illustration, 55
databases: early examples, 37; emergence of multi-title databases, 55–6, 58; historians' use of, x, 4, 6, 17, 61–62, 99, 260–61; storage of digitized records, 15. *See also under individual databases*
data mining, 6, 33, 71, 233–34, 252, 256. *See also* culturomics; distant reading; text mining software
deconstructionism, 11, 25–6, 227, 235–39, 242, 253
DIALOG (online database system), 237
digital archives, 9, 16–17, 53–71 passim, 191, 230, 272
digital culture, 24, 77, 180, 203, 211–12, 214–15
digital elite, 168
Digital Harlem, ix–x, 1, 5, 10, 27n18, 31, 264n33, 268, 273. *See also* digital history projects

digital history: definition, 4–6; ethical issues 2, 15, 20, 22, 47, 75, 106–8, 110, 118, 157–60, 163–67, 171–73, 255; legal issues, 20, 47, 75, 107, 110, 255; methodological issues x–xi, 2, 7, 9, 11, 15, 20, 24–25, 33, 54, 73n35, 75, 80, 101, 106, 157–60, 251–52, 255, 259; resistance to, 6–11, 254
digital history and the archive, vii, 3, 13–17, 26, 33, 251–53, 256
digital history as archive, vii, 3, 13, 17–23, 26, 75, 251, 254–56
digital history is history, viii, 3, 13, 23–26, 201, 251, 256–63
digital history projects: Australian Paralympics, xi, 1–2, 5, 11, 26n2, 255–56, 260–61; @CivilWarReportr, 104, 111; *Europe, Interrupted*, 5; *Quilt Index*, 5; *Slave Revolt in Jamaica: A Cartographic Narrative*, xi; *The Civil War in Four Minutes*, 124, 128n50; *The Irish in the American Civil War*, 105, 111n14, 112; *The Roaring Twenties*, xi; *The Valley of the Shadow*, 5; @TitanicRealTime, 5, 31, 104, 112; *Who Built America*, 5. *See also Digital Harlem*
digital humanities: ix–xi, 3, 75, 201, 254–63, 272; projects, 27n13, 255
digital literacy, 104, 117, 121–22, 168
digital media: 77, 93, 121, 253; definition of, 24; historians' engagement with, 6; memorialization, 183; qualities of, 159–60; recent past, 2, 9; stability/instability of, 19, 21, 92, 120–21, 228, 231; texts, 173; types, 2, 159; typologies, 13
digital methodology, x–xi
digital museums, 21, 82–83, 229
digital natives, 20, 38, 113, 115, 121, 126
Digital Public Library of America, 44
digital revolution, 24, 35, 71, 180, 203, 217
digital tools, x–xi, 2–6, 8–10, 13, 18–21, 24, 71n3, 98–99, 116, 120, 122, 231, 235, 251, 256. *See also under individual tools*
digital turn, 71, 77, 93
digital visualization, x–xi, 19, 33, 63, 67, 92, 252–53, 256
digitization: archival material, 9, 13, 38, 53–54, 57, 77, 236; copyright issues, 16, 55; cost issues, 53; debates on, 16; materiality of sources, 54; methodological opportunities, 54, 57, 59–61, 251; photographs, 28n60; quality issues, 16; research outputs, x; social media, 9, 255; sport collections, 14, 39, 48–49

distant reading, 33, 252, 256
Dougherty, Jack, 262

e-books, 260
economy of knowledge production, 201, 258–59
Eighteenth-Century Collections Online, 55
electronification of memory, 180
e-mail, 4, 17, 48, 71n1
ESPN (Entertainment and Sports Programming Network), 41, 140, 186
Extreme Winter Swimming (website), 236–37, 247
e-zines, 19, 78–79

Facebook, 4, 17–19, 75, 83, 86, 89, 116, 211, 260; activism, 102; as digital archive, 9, 23; control of data, 255; criticism of, 7, 98; as historical representation, 25, 78, 236; history-related sites, 5, 10; memorialization, 23, 183, 187, 189–92; Questions tool, 103; research tool, 6, 19, 21, 25, 78–79, 99–103, 108–9, 160, 229, 254–55; teaching tool, 20, 117–25 passim
fan sites, 2, 4, 10, 17, 21–23, 25, 75, 78–79, 109, 132–47 passim, 254
fantasy league play, 24, 206
FIFA (Fédération Internationale de Football Association), 41
Fine, Gary Alan, 44, 132, 186
Firefox, 242n2
Flickr, 123, 254–55
fragments (traces), 25–26, 228, 236, 239, 241, 245n80

Gaelic Athletic Association (GAA) oral history project, 19–20, 99–101, 104, 109, 110n6, 271
Gale (Digital Collections), 55–56, 58–59, 70; *Nineteenth-Century Collections Online*, 55, 57; *19th Century UK Periodicals*, 55; *19th Century U.S. Newspapers*, 55
geospatial visualization, x. *See also* digital visualization
Getty Images, 41
Gold, Matthew K., 256
Good Morning Yesterday (blog), 161–62, 164–66, 169
Google, 38, 168, 229
Google Alerts, 230
Google Books, 17, 46, 55, 66–68, 252
Google Chrome, 242n2

Google Drive, 118
Google Maps, x
Google Moderator, 120

HathiTrust, 44–46
Himmelfarb, Gertrude, 228–29, 231
Historical Newspapers. *See* ProQuest
History web, 17, 20
Hitchcock, Tim, xi
hyperlink, x, 5, 18, 83, 89, 92–93, 161, 241, 242n2
hypertext, xi, 4, 36, 38, 93, 159

infinite archive, 13, 25, 33, 227, 242n3, 252
information turn, 15
Instagram, 4, 17, 75, 159, 254–55
interaction age, 116
International Association for the History of Physical Education and Sport, 35
International Association of Athletic Federations (IAAF), 41
International Committee for the History of Physical Education and Sport, 35
International Olympic Committee (IOC), 14, 18, 41, 43, 49, 56, 78, 212; technological innovation 41–42
International Society for Comparative Physical Education and Sport, 43
International Society of Olympic Historians, 43
International Sports Heritage Association, 44
Internet: critical reflection, 7, 19, 23, 105, 114, 168–69, 184, 193, 228, 255; growth, 41; site of contested meaning, 242n2. *See also* Web 1.0; Web 2.0
Internet Archive, 46, 55
Internet Explorer, 242n2
intranet, 47
IOC. *See* International Olympic Committee
iPhone, 83, 88, 191
Irish Sporting Heritage Facebook page, 100

John Johnson Collection, 55
Jones, Steven, 4
JSTOR, 46

Kurungabaa (blog), 169–71

LA84 Foundation, 14, 42–3, 50, 274
legal records, x, 61. *See also* court records
LexisNexis (online database system), 37

libraries: changing role of librarians, 46–47; death of the paper book, 259; end-of-libraries debate, 36–38; hybrid or gateway, 14, 39–40; patron-driven acquisitions (PDA), 46; retrospective (digital) conversion projects, 44–47; specialized sports collections, 44. See also under individual libraries
Library of Congress, 43, 230
LinkedIn, 109
listserves, 4
local networks, 47

Making Friends with the Neighbours (blog), 170–71
Mark H. McCormack Collection (University of Massachusetts, Amherst), 39, 45, 48, 50
Mechanical Turk (amazon.com), 212
Microsoft, 37
Mixed Race America (blog), 163
Moretti (Franco), 264n4

National Basketball Association (NBA), 137, 186
National Football League (NFL), 21, 137, 147
National Library of Australia, 1, 47
Nawrotzki, Kristen, 262
NBA. *See* National Basketball Association
neuroscientific *turn*, 215, 220n76
new millennials, 38, 113, 117
New Zealand Olympic Committee (NZOC), 18–19, 78, 80–92, 95n31, 272
NFL. *See* National Football League
Ngrams: definition, 66–68, 73n36; Ngram Viewer, 66
Nineteenth-Century Serials Edition, 55
North American Society for Sport History (NASSH), xiii, 35, 43, 246n93
North American Sport Library Network, 42

Olympic Studies Centre (Lausanne), 14, 39, 43, 49–50
optical character recognition (OCR), 54, 56–57, 63
oral history, 1, 9, 19, 99–100, 104–9 passim, 166, 234, 261, 271
Organization of American Historians, ix
Oriard, Michael, 260

Papers Past, 55
Podcasts, 109, 122–25, 260

PowerPoint, 4, 116
print literacy, mentalities of, 258
produsers, 114–15
Project Gutenberg, 55
ProQuest: *British Periodicals*, 55; *Historical Newspapers*, 55

quantitative text analysis, 33, 252, 256

Reading the Riots, 103, 111n10
recent history, 2, 8–10, 25, 27n33
reconfigurationism, 20, 26, 239–42, 245n73–74, 245n80
reconstructionism, 11, 25, 227–32, 236–37, 239, 242
Robertson, Stephen, ix–xii, 5
Rosenzweig, (Roy), 12, 17, 159, 163, 166, 227, 239, 241, 242n3, 243n19, 244n28, 244n42, 244n46
Roy Rosenzweig Center for History and New Media (CHNM), 6, 273
Roy Rosenzweig Prize for Innovation in Digital History, 2, 26n3, 273

Salute, 148n8, 162, 167
SB Nation (online community), 137, 149n29
Seagle Electronic Golf Library (USGA), 43
Skype, 4, 187
Smithsonian Museum of American History, 123
snipping tool, 231
social media: criticism of, 7, 9–10, 254; cultural memory production, 23, 183–84, 187, 189, 192–93; digital archives, 9, 21, 25, 75, 256; digital history, 5–6, 9–10, 21, 251; historians' engagement with, 6, 254, 262–63; institutional use of, 13; public engagement in history production, 24–25, 75, 255; relationship with traditional media, 139; as research tool, 19–20, 23, 75, 97–116, 254–55; as teaching tool, 113–26, 255. *See also under individual types*
social memory. *See* collective memory
social networking, 20, 22, 78, 101–3, 109–10, 119–21, 159, 165, 189, 192
SPONET, 50
sport and internet: interrelationship, 2, 40–42
Staley, David J., 19, 80, 91, 93
Stark (H. J. Lutcher) Center for Physical Culture and Sports (University of Texas, Austin), 39, 45, 49–50

story space, 12, 261
streamgraph, 233–34, 244
SurveyMonkey, 103, 106

TED-Ed, 20, 123
text mining software, 6. *See also* data mining
Thomas III, William G., 4–5
Trove, 55
Twitter, 4, 17, 19, 49, 75, 83–84, 86, 105, 116, 165, 211, 260; as digital archive, 9; as historical representation, 25, 78, 236; control of data, 106–7, 255; criticism of, 7, 98; history-related sites, 5, 104; memorialization, 23, 183, 187–88; research tool, 6, 19–20, 22, 25, 78–79, 97–99, 102–4, 109, 159–60, 229, 233–34 254–55; teaching tool, 20, 118–25 passim. *See also under individual Twitter projects*

United Nations Educational, Scientific and Cultural Organization (UNESCO), 212, 220n62
United States Golf Association (USGA), 43
United States Golf Museum, 45
United States Olympic Committee, 41
Usenet, 229

video editing tools, 21, 123
Vimeo, 188

virtual archive, 230

Web 1.0, 13. *See also* Internet
Web 2.0, 13, 20, 113–26 passim. *See also* Internet
weblog. *See* blogs
Weller, Toni, 4, 16
Wikimedia Australia, 26n2, 256
Wikipedia, 4–6, 10, 18, 24, 75, 160, 211, 229, 260; debates about, 7, 11, 243n19; narrative making, 10–12, 256; rules, 5, 11–12; teaching, 20, 117–18, 122, 124; wisdom of the crowd, 256
wikis, 6, 20, 109, 113, 115–19, 123–34
World Wide Web, 37, 82–83, 159, 183. *See also* Internet

X Games, 181, 185

Yahoo, 168
Yesterday.sg (blog), 162, 165, 169
YouTube, 10, 17, 19, 24, 75, 79, 84, 86, 98, 109, 116, 123, 165, 188, 206, 228–29, 234, 237, 254–55

Zeus Technology, 85
Zoomerang, 103
Zotero, 4

The University of Illinois Press
is a founding member of the
Association of American University Presses.

Composed in 10.5/13 Adobe Minion Pro
by Lisa Connery
at the University of Illinois Press
Manufactured by Cushing-Malloy, Inc.

University of Illinois Press
1325 South Oak Street
Champaign, IL 61820-6903
www.press.uillinois.edu